John Nichol se... ...ve duty during the first Gulf War in 1991, his Tornado bomber was shot down during a mission over Iraq. Captured, tortured and held as a prisoner-of-war, John was paraded on television, provoking worldwide condemnation and leaving one of the most enduring images of the conflict.

John ... ...author of many highly acclaimed Second World War epics, including *Return of the Dambusters*, *Tail-End Charlies* and the hugely successful *Spitfire*. He has made a number of TV documentaries with Second World War veterans, written for national newspapers and magazines, and is a widely quoted commentator on military affairs.

www.johnnichol.com

## Praise for *Lancaster*

'A wonderful homage to one of the most iconic aircraft ever built: compelling, thrilling and rooted in quite extraordinary human drama.' **James Holland, author of *Normandy 44***

'A completely wonderful book; an emotional roller coaster of a read and a brilliant tribute to the men who flew the Lancaster.' **Clive Rowley, Former Officer Commanding, Royal Air Force Battle of Britain Memorial Flight**

'This remarkable, enlightening book ... The human cost of these raids was enormous ... The great strength of Nichol's book is that it takes us beyond the statistics. Through the words of the airmen themselves, it illuminates individual lives. The Lancaster was, and is, more than just an aircraft. John Nichol's book is a fitting tribute to her and to all those who flew in her.' **Nick Rennison, *Daily Mail***

'His work will appeal to those fresh to this particular branch of Second World War heroism ... Nichol tells a succession of human stories well and clearly. *Lancaster* leaves us marvelling yet again at the bravery, stoicism and sheer level-headedness of our forebears.' **Simon Heffer, *Sunday Telegraph***

'This book excels in the gripping descriptions of the raids over Germany. "I can relate to the fear, exhilaration and desperation of battle," writes Nichol, and this understanding helps him paint a vivid picture of the atmosphere inside the cramped interior of a Lancaster ... With his readable style and impressive credentials, Nichol is certain to have another winner with this book.' **Leo McKinstry, *Spectator***

*Other books by John Nichol*

NON-FICTION

Spitfire
Return of the Dambusters
The Red Line
Arnhem
Medic
Home Run
Tail-End Charlies
The Last Escape

AUTOBIOGRAPHY

Tornado Down
Team Tornado

FICTION

Point of Impact
Vanishing Point
Exclusion Zone
Stinger
Decisive Measures

# LANCASTER

*The Forging of a Very British Legend*

## JOHN NICHOL

SIMON &
SCHUSTER

London · New York · Sydney · Toronto · New Delhi

First published in Great Britain by Simon & Schuster UK Ltd, 2020
This paperback edition published by Simon & Schuster UK Ltd, 2021

Copyright © John Nichol, 2020

The right of John Nichol to be identified as the author of
this work has been asserted in accordance with the
Copyright, Designs and Patents Act, 1988.

1 3 5 7 9 10 8 6 4 2

Simon & Schuster UK Ltd
1st Floor
222 Gray's Inn Road
London WC1X 8HB

www.simonandschuster.co.uk
www.simonandschuster.com.au
www.simonandschuster.co.in

Simon & Schuster Australia, Sydney
Simon & Schuster India, New Delhi

The author and publishers have made all reasonable efforts to contact
copyright-holders for permission, and apologise for any omissions or errors
in the form of credits given. Corrections may be made to future printings.

A CIP catalogue record for this book is
available from the British Library

Paperback ISBN: 978-1-4711-8049-1
eBook ISBN: 978-1-4711-8048-4

Typeset in Sabon by M Rules
Printed in the UK by CPI Group (UK) Ltd, Croydon, CR0 4YY

MIX
Paper from
responsible sources
FSC® C020471
www.fsc.org

In memory of
Grey Atticus Fox Grumbridge
17 November – 8 December 2019

# CONTENTS

*Acknowledgements*       *xi*

*Foreword*       *1*

ONE     'Just Another Day in Bomber Command'     9

TWO     The Coming War     27

THREE     'Keep it Simple': The Birth of a Warhorse     46

FOUR     'A Bad Way to Spend an Afternoon'     59

FIVE     Joining Up Together, Training Together, Dying Together     83

SIX     'Strike and Return'     107

SEVEN     'It Won't Be Long Until I See You Again'     122

EIGHT     Towards the Big City     151

NINE     The War on the Ground     185

TEN     Pilots of the Caribbean     226

ELEVEN 'For Christ's Sake, Do Something,
or We're All Going to Die'          241

TWELVE Face to Face with the Enemy        267

THIRTEEN 'I Needed to Kill Him Before He
Could Kill Me and My Crew'          292

FOURTEEN Saved by the Bell              323

FIFTEEN 'The Best Raid of the War!'      360

SIXTEEN Looking Back                    383


Afterword                                409

Endnotes                                 413

Bibliography                             426

Picture Credits                          429

Index                                    431

*This book is dedicated to all the courageous
men and women involved with the Lancaster
bomber's wartime operations.*

# ACKNOWLEDGEMENTS

Many people willingly offered their valuable time and considerable expertise while I researched and wrote this book. I cannot mention every person individually but I am eternally grateful to you all.

My sincere thanks also go to:

Squadron Leader Dicky James, the IX(B) Squadron Association Historian for his incredible assistance in locating veterans, memoirs and photographs.

Squadron Leader Clive Rowley, a former Commanding Officer of the RAF Battle of Britain Memorial Flight, provided many of his own articles on the Lancaster and offered expert advice on the draft manuscript. Sqn Ldr Mark Discombe, the current OC BBMF and his wonderful assistant Diane Law-Crookes for their help locating veterans and sourcing pictures.

Peter Devitt from the RAF Museum in Hendon and curator of their excellent online display, 'Pilots of the Caribbean: Volunteers of African Heritage in the Royal Air Force', who gave me access to their archive and put me in contact with surviving relatives.

Andrew Panton and Liz Dodds from the Lincolnshire Aviation Heritage Centre at East Kirkby for hosting a number of my visits to view their Lancaster, *Just Jane*. And Andy Marson and Caterina

Scott from the Metheringham Airfield Visitor Centre for showing me around their museum and sourcing photographs from
their archive.

Tim Dunlop, the former 'Bomber Leader' on the RAF Battle of
Britain Memorial Flight, who provided a number of contacts and
proofread the manuscript.

Andy Saunders, editor of *Iron Cross* magazine, who supplied background information, photos and proofread the manuscript.

Graham Cowie, from 'Project Propeller', which organises reunions
for Second World War personnel, provided many valuable introduc-
tions to the veterans.

Nigel Price, John Ash and Stuart Qualtrough from *Britain at War*
magazine, who sourced countless articles for me.

Authors and historians: Ken Ballantyne, Stephen Darlow, Mark
Hillier, Peter Jacobs, Rob Long, Martin Middlebrook, Steve Potter
and Chris Stone for access to their archives, books and photographs.

The team at my publisher Simon & Schuster for their encouragement and expertise, and to Anton Gill for his time and assistance.

I am ever grateful to my friend and agent of twenty-nine years,
Mark Lucas, who has been unstinting in his support and is always
available with his wise counsel and sharp eye for detail, even when
he and his family were experiencing truly troubled times.

My wife Suzannah and daughter Sophie, who are always there with
their love and support.

Finally, I am truly grateful to the countless veterans and their
relatives who told me their Lancaster stories; sadly, time takes its

toll and they are diminishing in number. I was only able to use a fraction of the incredible stories I heard. I hope I have done all of the veterans justice.

\* \* \*

I was assisted by countless other enthusiasts, researchers, authors and historians who offered invaluable information and contacts. It is impossible to name them all, but the following provided important leads, accounts, pictures or advice:

Gerry Abrahams, Angela Addington, Bob and Chris Ankerson, Richard Bailey, John Bell, Julie Blake, Marcus Burton, Peter Burton, Chris Cannon, William Chorley, Stephen Darke, Chris Dean, Ken Delve, Rob Dodd, Chris Downes, Gary Eason, Sue Efthimiou, Dan Ellin, John Elliott, Patrick Eriksson, Ken Fawcett, Keith Fraser, Donald Fraser, Ivan Frost, Beryl Garlick, Norman Gregory, Cherry Greveson, Claire Hartley, Wendy Hawke, Dave Homewood, Mark Howard, Martin Keen, Harold Kirby, Cain Leatham, Philip Leckenby, Allyson MacIntosh, Reuben Massiah, Andrew Millikin, Vernon Morgan, Sami Moxon, Maria Needle, Taff Owen, Nigel Parker, Harry Parkins, Peter Potter, Nigel Price, Dick Raymond, Brian Riley, Harry Rossiter, Rod Sanders, Ron Saul, Jim Sheffield, Philip Skinner, Craig Sluman, Ajay Srivastava, Gordon Stooke, Ian Strong, Alan Tait, Rob Thomas, Steve Thompson, Gordon Thorburn, Frank Tolley, Ryan Tomlinson, Dean and Russell Towlson, Allan Wall, Simon Watkins, Richard Wiltshire, Jim Wright.

# FOREWORD

Ron Needle is relaxing in the neat living room of his sheltered-housing flat near Birmingham, part of a complex owned by the Bournville Village Trust, and founded in 1900 by the world-famous chocolate-making Cadbury family. Sitting in the automated easy chair bought for him by a military charity that cares for veterans who have lost limbs, he can gaze through his windows at well-manicured lawns and flower beds filled with purple petunias. The bright summer sun is streaming in but the ongoing heatwave is 'a bit much' for him. 'Still,' he says, 'there are always worse things that can happen!' He tells me he is the luckiest man alive, grateful for every day of his life.[1]

Ninety-three-year-old Ron is a veteran of Royal Air Force Bomber Command, where he served as a rear gunner on the Lancaster bomber. He is the only Second World War veteran residing in the home, which he loves. He likes to get involved in the many activities on offer; the crafts, coffee mornings and more. A widower, living alone, Ron enjoys the company.

He is surrounded by memorabilia from his time in the RAF; books about Bomber Command and his beloved Lancaster crowd the shelves. A large wooden carving of St Evre church in the small village of Méligny-le-Grand in north-east France has pride of place on the wall behind him. Beneath it, on the floor, sits a framed print entitled *The Eternal Salute*, depicting a wartime Lancaster surging through a turbulent, overcast sky. In the corner of the picture, above the clouds, five aircrew gaze into the distance.

It is not a specific aircraft, or five particular young men, but a simple tribute to the thousands of Lancasters downed during the Second World War and the many members of Bomber Command who gave their lives. A tribute to the many friends and colleagues Ron lost in battle. The print cost him £100 – a significant sum for the war pensioner. But he won't be hanging it here; he is taking it to Méligny-le-Grand in a few weeks. He has some difficulty walking or standing for extended periods these days, but age and weary bones will not prevent him from making this journey. It has a very personal significance for Ron. It harks back to a time when his life hung in the balance.

The other residents and staff in his home regularly ask him what he did in the war. He answers their questions politely but keeps much of the detail to himself. Many of those memories, though seventy-three years old, are still raw and distressing. More importantly, Ron doesn't want to seem to be boasting about his role in the conflict.

I have experienced this reluctance to talk freely with almost every veteran I have interviewed; they have to be pressed, to be cajoled to open up. As part of the military family, albeit a somewhat younger member, I understand their caution. While I could never compare my own experiences as a young RAF Tornado navigator over a mere seven weeks during the first Gulf War in 1991 with Ron's countless sorties in the skies above Germany in the 1940s, I can certainly relate to the fear, exhilaration and desperation of battle, having been shot down over Iraq in January 1991, then captured, tortured and paraded on television screens around the world.

My personal war had been relatively short but deeply unpleasant. In the aftermath, I attended a number of military functions and began to meet some of my forebears who had flown the early bombers into the heart of German-occupied Europe during the darkest days of the Second World War. I noticed immediately that they were more comfortable sharing their experiences of combat over a beer with someone who could really understand its complex and often confusing cocktail of fear and excitement. They were more guarded with those outside the military family, who they worried might think they were 'shooting a line' or exaggerating their involvement in a conflict that defined a generation and changed the shape of the modern world. The refrain I continue to hear most often is, 'I didn't do anything extraordinary. There were no heroics. I just did the same job everyone else was doing.'

On one level, Ron Needle's reluctance to go into detail is entirely understandable; he *was* doing the same as all the other young men and women who stood in the way of the existential threat posed by Nazi Germany. However, both individually and collectively, they *were* a truly exceptional generation.

*Ron Needle during training as a rear gunner*

Excited chatter fills the aviation halls at the RAF Museum in Hendon, north London, as parties of young schoolchildren skip around the iconic exhibits. Ron Needle and I are less vocal, but still delighted to be at the heart of this incredible display. We have come to visit one of the few surviving Lancaster bombers so we can share his memories of the giant aircraft. His legs are weak now, so I push his wheelchair slowly past some of the other items tracking the history of flight from the Wright brothers' first foray in 1903 to the jet-powered air force of today. As the kids dash from hall to hall, we meander, revelling in our shared enjoyment of time spent in the skies.

We pause at the wood and canvas 'string bags' of the First World War and wonder how anyone could have had the courage to take these flimsy machines beyond the runway, let alone into battle. I show Ron the Tornado I spent much of my RAF career flying; he gasps when I tell him it was capable of around 600 miles per hour. Sitting beneath the wing is a WE177 tactical nuclear bomb, the type of weapon I spent so much time preparing to use against our Cold War enemies.

It is sobering for us to reflect that a handful of WE177s could have caused exponentially more devastation than the astonishing thousand-bomber raids Ron's Bomber Command colleagues embarked upon during the Second World War. One display is playing Winston Churchill's famous 'never in the field of human conflict' tribute to the incredible bravery and sacrifice of 'The Few' during the Battle of Britain. Ron remembers listening with his family to those speeches as a schoolboy: 'We were always inspired by Churchill's broadcasts, though I didn't really understand how I would become involved in the war myself.'

Finally, there she is, in a cavernous hangar, dwarfing all other exhibits. *S-Sugar* towers above us, by far the biggest beast in Hendon's jungle. Although now confined to the ground, she is the world's oldest surviving Lancaster bomber, flying her first operation into the heart of Nazi Germany in the summer of 1942. Her final mission[2] in May 1945 was collecting liberated prisoners of war, many of whom had survived being shot down flying her kith and kin into battle.[3] Bomber Command took the fight to the enemy when no one else could, and the statistics are as impressive as the aircraft herself.

The four mighty Merlin engines mounted along the 102ft wingspan gave her a top speed of around 280mph and a range of some 2,500 miles. With a 69ft-long fuselage, the aircraft was essentially built around a 33ft bomb bay designed to carry a 14,500lb payload. In later years some Lancasters would be converted to deliver the massive 22,000lb 'Grand Slam' earthquake bomb; the largest conventional weapon dropped during the Second World War.

At the height of the conflict, over a million men and women were employed producing the aircraft and its myriad parts at hundreds of factories on two continents. More service personnel were involved in flying and maintaining the Lancaster than any other British aircraft in history.[4] Sir Arthur Harris, the no-nonsense chief of Bomber Command, called it his 'shining sword'; 'the greatest single factor in winning the war against Germany'.[5]

The average age of the seven-man crew was a mere twenty-two. Of 7,377 Lancasters built during the war, over half (3,736) were lost to enemy action and in training accidents. S-Sugar and Ron Needle are among the lucky survivors. With 137 ops under her belt, S-Sugar is one of only twenty Lancasters to have completed over one hundred wartime missions.[6] A neat tapestry of falling bombs depicting her incredible tally of ops is painted on the fuselage under the cockpit. Beneath the bombs is inscribed Germany's Reichsmarschall Hermann Göring's arrogant boast, 'No enemy plane will fly over the Reich territory.'

Göring had been very wrong.

The RAF's bomber squadrons carried out offensive operations from the first day of the war until the last, more than five and a half years later. They flew nearly 390,000 sorties and dropped around 1 million tons of explosive on enemy targets. Over 10,000 aircraft were lost.[7]

The human cost is also breathtaking. Of the 125,000 men who served in Bomber Command, 55,573 were killed and another 8,400 wounded.[8] Some 10,000 survived being shot down, only to become prisoners of war. In simple, brutal terms, if you flew in Bomber Command, you had no more than a 40 per cent chance of surviving the war unscathed, at least physically. The mental toll was largely unrecorded and unrecognised.

At the time, of course, young men like Ron Needle had no idea, indeed no information, about these casualty rates or the odds against survival. Sipping tea in a quiet café a few yards from his beloved Lancaster, Ron says, 'When I look back now, of course I had no sense of the risks I would face or the deaths I would see. You just didn't think about those things.' He throws his head back and laughs. 'Good God, if I'd thought about it, I'd never have joined up!'

I suspect that even if he had understood the meagre chances of survival, it would have made no difference. Ron and his young comrades *wanted* to be part of the war; were *desperate* not to miss out on the action. Along with almost every single veteran I have spoken to, Ron felt it was his duty to join up, to be *seen* to be part of the fight for survival. 'The future was unimaginable. I was young and the future simply didn't concern me! I just wanted to be part of the war; to take the fight back to Germany. I suppose I knew people were dying but I didn't think of death or the reality of killing anyone myself. I just knew I had to join up and do my bit.'

One of the groups of visiting schoolchildren gathers beneath the Lancaster a few yards from where we are sitting. These five- and six-year-olds in their neat grey pullovers and pink ties are not as tall as the wheel of the undercarriage. They listen to one of the museum staff explaining what the aircraft did and who flew it. Ron listens quietly too. When the guide points out where the rear gunner sat and how it must have been a lonely job, I gently interrupt to tell them that the old man in the wheelchair is one such veteran. The children, and their teachers, stare at Ron in amazement, perhaps wondering how this diminutive figure could have achieved and experienced so much.

The teachers thank him for their freedom. The children give him a round of applause, which attracts other museum visitors. Asked if he might say a few words, Ron struggles out of his wheelchair.

Leaning heavily on his walking stick, he looks into the eager faces of the children and is suddenly overcome with emotion. Eyes glistening, he finds it impossible to speak.

Feeling somewhat guilty that I have initiated the encounter, I step in to explain a little about what life was like for the men who flew the Lancaster. As I tell our audience how many of Ron's friends and colleagues died, my own voice cracks with emotion. The children's eyes, already wide as saucers, widen further when Ron manages to say a few words about what it was like to sit in the rear turret, how cold it was, how dangerous it could be. Eventually, one of the teachers steps forward to take his hand. Turning to her class, she says, 'Children, what do we say to this gentleman and his friends for what they did for all of us during the war?'

'Thank you!' they yell in unison.

I look over to Ron and tears are running down his face.

It is time to move on, and as we continue our own tour of the Lancaster, Ron murmurs, 'Oh, those innocent children! Thank heavens they can have no concept about what we all really went through back then.'

What he 'really went through' is the story I am eager to hear, and some of his memories surface as I wheel him around the bomber. Staring at the narrow door on the side of the fuselage where he and his friends had clambered aboard all those years before, it is clear Ron feels a real affinity with the aircraft.

'Seeing the Lanc up close again brings back so many memories,' he tells me. 'I have always had a fond feeling for her; she took me to war and looked after me in the worst of times. You can see how strong and powerful she looks. Her strength undoubtedly saved my life. The Lanc is the reason I am still alive today, the reason I have a family; my own children and grandchildren.'

Gazing up at the rear turret, a Perspex bubble the size of an oil drum where he spent so many hours over enemy territory, his tired eyes brighten and he sits up in the wheelchair, reaching forward.

'This was my office; how on earth did I fit in there! I spent so much time in this tiny space, on my own, separated from the rest of the crew, isolated apart from their voices on the intercom. There were so many deaths back then, each one was a father, brother or son to someone. I always try to look on the positives in life. My philosophy has always been simple: whatever will be, will be. But there is also real sadness at the loss of my friends. The camaraderie was so important during the war; we lived together, flew together, drank together and sometimes died together. Being so close to the Lanc again really takes me back to happier times . . . and sad times too.

'You know, John, I really miss my old crewmates; even after all these years. I still say a prayer and raise a glass of whisky to them every night. Every single night without fail.' Ron stares into the distance, pain etched on his face. 'I'm tired of being on my own and I'm looking forward to seeing my mates again.'

His eyes mist over and his head dips. 'It's as though it all happened yesterday. I can still see it unfolding in front of my eyes, as if it were only five minutes ago . . .'

*John Nichol, Hertfordshire*
*Spring 2020*

## CHAPTER ONE

# 'JUST ANOTHER DAY IN BOMBER COMMAND'

Late afternoon, Sunday 7 January 1945. The leaden skies spread from horizon to horizon. Ground crews had been working the snowploughs all day to keep the runways clear.[1] Now at last the snow had abated and the job was on. Dusk was falling fast as the drab green Fordson crew bus took the seven men out to their giant Lancaster bomber – one of sixteen from their base scheduled to be part of this operation, scattered at their dispersal points[2] around RAF Metheringham, 12 miles south-east of Lincoln.

Metheringham was a new, purpose-built affair, which had risen from the flat, windswept Lincolnshire farmlands and become operational a year earlier. It was a nondescript place; bleak Nissen huts and a concrete block of a control tower. There were hundreds of such bases dotted across eastern and southern England, though Lincolnshire – 'bomber county' – had the lion's share, being the best-placed platform for taking the war to the enemy.

The Fordson's engine stuttered in the cold as it reached its destination. Jettisoning their last cigarettes, nerves taut, the aircrew disembarked, the oldest of them twenty-six, the two youngest still only nineteen. Breath pluming in the frigid air, they stamped their feet and rubbed their hands, glancing at one another, waiting for the tensions to settle, focusing on the task ahead. They did their best to echo their driver's cheery smile as she waved goodbye before they walked the short distance to the looming beast that lay in wait for them.

Towering on its undercarriage over 20ft above them was the spearhead of the British assault into the heart of Nazi Germany; their Lancaster's upper surfaces were coated with camouflage greens and browns, matt black on its lower flanks, belly and the undersides of its wings. The ghostly attire of the night bomber.

They each climbed the short ladder through the square door on the starboard side of the Lancaster, just forward of the tailplane: Jim Scott, twenty-three, the pilot and captain; Bob Dunlop, also twenty-three and the bomb aimer who doubled as front gunner; Ken Darke, twenty-one, the navigator; Harry Stunell, the wireless operator, also twenty-one; Les Knapman, the flight engineer and 'old man' of the crew at twenty-six, whose responsibility was to ensure the smooth running of the aircraft as well as covering for the pilot. The mid-upper gunner, Jack Elson, was one of the nineteen-year-olds. The other gunner, and the 'baby' of the crew, was Ron Needle. He held the loneliest position of all, far from the rest of his friends in the rear gun turret at the back end of the aircraft, hence his nickname: 'Tail-end Charlie' or, more colourfully, 'Tail-arse Charlie'.

They boarded in silence and without ceremony. Many crews had long-established rituals from which they dared not deviate – relieving themselves on the rear wheel of the aircraft, perhaps. Their ground crews complained that this rotted the rubber, but toilet facilities were minimal once airborne. Others would give voice to their favoured songs before embarking. On a night like this, voices, some quivering, some firm, could ring out with the resonance of a choral mass.

Many carried mascots or talismans, some personal, some for the entire aircraft, and woe betide them if by chance they left their lucky charm behind. But that wasn't the way things worked on this Lancaster. Ron Needle, in particular, had no time for superstitions. 'I've always accepted life as it is. What will be, will be.'[3] It was a good philosophy for a young man who had to face death on a near-nightly basis. In the job they'd signed up for, boys had to grow up fast.

The down-to-earth Brummie had volunteered for the RAF eighteen months earlier, as soon as he'd reached the age of eighteen. 'I saw my first enemy aircraft one Wednesday afternoon while in the back garden at home,' he recalls. 'The Luftwaffe bombed the Royal Orthopaedic Hospital in Northfield on 23 November 1940. I was around a hundred yards away as it unfolded. I was only fourteen but I was so angry! That was the point I decided to join the RAF and fight back against the Germans.'

Ron was going to get his wish. He exchanged a quick, tight grin with his friend, wireless operator Harry Stunell, 'a gentleman with a great sense of humour', whom he'd got to know well over the months they'd been together. Humour was a great weapon against fear, so long as you always treated fear with respect.

It was a short climb into the Lancaster, a brisk prelude to a long and dangerous journey, from which evasion in a crisis was far from straightforward. For Ron, the Lancaster would always remain an 'elegant and very beautiful aircraft'. For some of his older colleagues, the fact that it wasn't easy to get out of in an emergency counterbalanced its other undoubted virtues. Apart from the main door, the only other exit (other than the two sea-ditching hatches on the top of the fuselage, and not designed for a parachute escape) was the tiny forward hatch, just 22 inches by 26, tucked under the padding where the bomb aimer lay in the nose of the aircraft when dispatching his deadly payload.

At least Ron, as rear gunner, had the possibility of rotating his turret to one side in an emergency and baling out backwards from his Perspex bubble. *If* all went well. *If* he had had time to firstly open the doors behind him and reach into the aircraft for his parachute (it was too bulky to wear in the turret) stowed in a pannier on the side of the fuselage. *If* he could then connect it to his harness in the midst of the chaos and confusion. There were a lot of '*ifs*' for the men flying Lancasters in Bomber Command. This was his crew's eleventh sortie. They'd scraped through their tenth only forty-eight hours earlier. On a night run against a pocket of enemy troops near Bordeaux, all hell had broken loose. They'd been caught in anti-aircraft fire. Their first bombing run had been aborted so they'd had to go round again, their Lancaster shuddering as the flak hammered and burst around it, far too close for comfort, buffeting the men so violently that Ron Needle's only thought had been, *Let's get the hell out of here*.

At last the payload had gone, and, relieved of its weight, the Lancaster had leapt skywards, leaving the airmen's stomachs hollow. The thought of being shot at while carrying fourteen 1,000lb high-explosive bombs – a typical load for such a target – wasn't comfortable for any of them. However often you flew, you knew that every time could be the last. Each sortie was like 'going over the top' for the troops in the trenches in the First World War. You could never take anything for granted, never leave anything to chance – but at the same time you knew that so much was entirely out of your hands. They'd got home safely – no injuries, no damage to the aircraft – but very shaken. They all knew that, in their line of business, survival was never something to be taken for granted. Never far from their minds was the thought that whenever they lifted off from the runway, death was 'the eighth passenger'[4] in their Lancaster.

*Aircrew clearing snow from around their*
*Lancaster in January 1944*

The briefing room that afternoon had been blue with cigarette smoke. Everyone had groaned when the briefing officer drew back the security curtain that covered the map and revealed the red cotton line marking their route.

Munich.

A long run; four hours or so there, another four back.

This was to be the last major aerial assault of the war on the heart of a city already pulverised by over seventy raids during the previous five years. The Western Allies, having achieved near-total dominance in the air, were pushing their point home, softening up the Germans to facilitate the Russians' westward advance. Ken Darke and his fellow navigators made notes on turning points, tracking and heights; pilots paid close attention to the route and the other elements of the attacking formation. They were all familiar with the routine.

'It was a totally normal day,' Ron recalled. 'We'd had breakfast. We had such good food as aircrew; bacon, real eggs – not the pow-dered variety! – tea, toast and jam. We really were well looked after. Then we would just wait to see what the day would hold. It was just another day in Bomber Command.'

The briefing over, the time had hung heavily. There were checks to be run, the ground crews busy about their cherished aircraft, night-flying tests to be completed. However often you did it, your nerves tingled and you longed for the moment of take-off. After checking the guns and ammunition, rear gunner Ron could only wait. 'We would just hang around and chat. But you never really talked about what we were going to do, what we might face. I sup-pose no one wanted to really acknowledge what we might be feeling. Even if you felt it, you could never admit to being afraid.'

Once aboard their Lancaster, Ron turned left – all the others turned right – and clambered aft through the narrowing fuselage, past the Elsan, bucket-like toilet, slotted into its place amidships and fitted with a lid that, in theory at least, stayed clamped down on its contents when not in use. For the duration of the flight, he was now separated from the rest of the crew, firstly by a set of double swing doors on the fuselage, and then by the sliding doors of his capsule. All communication would be by intercom. Squeezing himself into the Perspex turret protruding from the tail, he would face outwards from the aircraft, without the advantage of knowing what he was flying into, until they – hopefully – landed back at base over eight hours later. It was the loneliest spot on earth. And one of the most cramped.

From the outside, the Lancaster was a giant. Less so inside. Barely 6ft across and 6ft high at best, the interior was traversed near the centre by the twin metal spars that attached the wings to the airframe – spars that narrowed the gap between floor and ceiling to just a couple of feet the crew had to clamber through when moving forward or aft. To compound their difficulties, they had to squeeze between the equipment racks and crew stations which narrowed the interior further, taking care that their heads and bodies didn't connect with jutting metalwork. You might be reasonably secure when in your confined position, but moving around was hard enough in normal circumstances. In flight, in darkness – and the Lancaster was a night worker first and foremost – wearing a bulky flying suit, it was much tougher, even when you were as accustomed to it as these young men were. Moving around while under attack or on fire was something else again.

Ron's role was one of the most vital to the safety of the Lancaster. Perched on a padded leather seat, knees bunched, in an area about the size of an oil drum, he was exposed on all sides through his flimsy Perspex turret. Gloved fingers never far from the triggers of his four 0.303-inch Browning machine guns, his job was to scan the night sky ceaselessly for threat. The Lancaster wasn't built for comfort. Temperatures at 20,000ft could be as low as -40°C. Ron's electrically heated flying suit kept the worst of the chill at bay – if it worked. Sometimes one side was burning hot, the other stone-cold. But that was the kind of thing you got used to. Cold was always a problem in a Lancaster.

Ron hadn't felt any sense of foreboding before taking off that day, beyond the usual nerves and adrenaline rush that came no matter how often you flew. That apprehension almost always disappeared, if you were lucky, the minute you set your mind to the task at hand. But his mate, the wireless operator, 21-year-old Harry Stunell, couldn't suppress his concerns. Each Lancaster crew was tight-knit, seldom fraternising seriously with other crews. The ever-present threat of death made men chary of close friendships. But Harry had befriended a fellow wireless operator, and before the flight that afternoon, as they stood by the kit lockers, he'd confided, 'Bill, I've got a strange feeling about this bloody Munich job.'[5]

Bill Winter had already noticed that his buddy, normally so cheerful, had been a bit long in the face that day, and did his best to reassure him. It was Harry's father's birthday, wasn't it? Maybe Harry was just desperate to be celebrating with him in a Brighton pub. Bill, the calm, good-natured son of a policeman, patted his friend on the back. 'We all get these feelings sometimes. You'll be OK.'

'Tonight feels different. I don't feel happy at all,' Harry replied.

But he had to keep his feelings to himself. The unspoken, golden rule was that you never let on any misgivings to your crewmates. And the rest of them, like Ron, seemed to feel this was just another operation; dangerous of course – they all were – but routine. They'd spent the time before boarding chatting idly about what they'd do when it was over, whether to go out for a few pints of weak war-time beer, or have a drink in the mess, or, if there was time, visit friends or family away from the base. There was still a life to be lived away from the skies over Germany. Harry quietly took his place a short way aft of the navigator's station, exchanging a grin with Ken Darke.

Ken was twenty-one years old and a London bank clerk in civvy street. Fair-haired, handsome, bookish and reserved, he was the brainbox of his family, and dearly loved by them.[6] He had settled down in the RAF, found his niche, and made friends quickly with fellow airmen and WAAFs (members of the Women's Auxiliary Air Force). Initially, the RAF had looked to the middle classes and public schools for its ideal recruits. As the war progressed, the backgrounds of air crews had broadened; now everyone mixed in, more or less happily. Harry had been an upholsterer before joining up; Ron a butcher from Birmingham. Nobody cared about class or schooling, least of all the senior echelons of Bomber Command, for as casualties mounted to unprecedented levels, they could no longer pick and choose who would fly their aircraft to war.

Ken drew the curtains round his cubbyhole to shut in the light from his desk lamp and spread out his charts. At 6ft 2in, he was lucky to have the luxury of the navigator's space. There were rear gunners even taller than he was,[7] but their knees must have been jammed under their chin.

Ron waited for his pilot to go through the cockpit checks. Everything had to be in perfect order before take-off. The pilot was the boss, the 'skipper', even if other crewmen outranked him. Ron's pilot, Jim Scott, was a Flying Officer, while Ken Darke was a more senior Flight Lieutenant. None of that mattered now. Ken would take orders from Jim for the duration of the flight. Everyone would watch everyone else's backs. That was the way to survive, unless survival was taken out of your hands by German anti-aircraft guns or by the deadly fire of Messerschmitt or Junkers fighters.

Once all the checks were completed to the skipper's and flight engineer's satisfaction, Ron heard the low growl of the four Merlin engines as they each burst into life, finally giving vent to a deep-throated roar as the huge aircraft lumbered towards the runway. Through his turret, he could see about twenty well-wishers who'd gathered to wave them off. 'The squadron commander was there, the ground crew who all but mothered the aircraft, and a group of WAAFs who worked round the base, as radio operators, parachute packers, drivers and debriefing officers.'

Jim powered up the engines, waiting for the take-off signal as their roar reached a crescendo. Then the green light flashed and he released the brakes. Ron's chest pushed against the controls of his Browning machine guns as the Lancaster thundered down the runway. The crowd gathered around the airfield watched as they departed. 'I always drew comfort from seeing them – there was a sense of us all being in it together. They knew what we were facing;

they'd seen so many eager young crews set out on an op and fail to return. As we sped down the runway, all I could see was the blackness of the concrete, a slight glow from the snow, and all those people waving, disappearing from view.'

He felt the tailwheel lift beneath him first, which always gave him a curious sense of elation, then the main wheels left the ground and the Lancaster lifted into the night sky, soaring with a lightness that belied its size. RAF Metheringham grew tiny beneath them as they set course to join the rest of the 50-mile-long bomber stream, bound for the Bavarian capital.

*Well-wishers gather to wave off a crew on another operation*

It grew colder as they climbed, dropping around 2°C for every thousand feet. As they crossed the French coast at 7.45 p.m. that freezing January night, the temperature at 19,000ft was bitter. The men in front could benefit from the Lancaster's heating system, which was at its most efficient there, but Ron Needle, exposed to the freezing outside air in his Perspex turret, was grateful for his heated flying suit and thick gloves.

Time passed both too slowly and too fast; suddenly it was only forty-five minutes to target. As they drew closer, Jim urged them all to keep a lookout for enemy fighters. Ron kept his eyes

even more strictly peeled for Messerschmitt 110s and Junkers
88s, whose cannon were more powerful and had a longer range
than his machine guns. To his relief, none came. If they had, the
Lancaster's wonderful manoeuvrability might just have kept them
out of trouble, but he was glad they didn't need to put that to the
test right now. Their experience two days previously had been bad
enough. Hopefully tonight would be different. Light sparkled off
the sheen of the upper surface of the wings and their aircraft jolted
and shook in the turbulence of the bomber stream. They were part
of a co-ordinated attack that night comprising nine Mosquitos and
645 Lancaster bombers. The black skies around them were crowded
and dangerous. Stunell recalled that 'tension was at concert pitch,
reaction speeds intensified. Young lads who had not long ago feared
our strict headmasters were now flying into the Third Reich, which
was presided over by one of the biggest bullies of all time.'[8]

Ron could hear the voice of the bomb aimer over the intercom.
'Route markers ahead, Skipper.'

Though he was aware of the glow in the sky, he couldn't see
what Bob Dunlop could: the brightly coloured red, green and
yellow indicator flares dropped by the Pathfinder Force which had
preceded them to mark the route and the target itself. He didn't
look directly at the glowing sky. Gunners never did. 'Bright lights
affect night vision. It takes about ten minutes for eyes to readjust
to the dark.'

The skies above Munich began to glow as the fiery rain of
bombs from the aircraft at the head of the attack force began to
fall. Harry Stunell pushed any forebodings to one side and moved
up to look forward from the cockpit onto 'a bloody great coloured
nightmare of stark proportions. The whole wild scene resembled a
contorted Turner landscape daubed with deft, fiery brushstrokes.
Within it there was a huge sea of boiling red broth, emitting thousands of surface bubbles. Cavorting flashes of the most startling
brilliance waxed and waned in accordance with the savagery
being inflicted from above.' Ahead of him, the Pathfinders were
swooping in to replenish burnt-out target indicator flares in order

to ensure subsequent bombs were concentrated on the heart of the city.

Munich was ablaze.

Pilot Jim Scott kept a watchful eye out for other Lancasters in the stream – jostling for position to commence their attack runs. Collisions happened at moments like this, or, worse, you could be on the receiving end of bombs falling from an aircraft above you. Some would drop their payload out of sequence, some too early. The darkness was bursting into a maelstrom of noise and flame, and, coupled with the roar of the engines and the stabbing brightness of the searchlights, you could never be sure of anything. Stunell decided he didn't want to see the horrors unfolding below and returned to his station.

Their Lancaster was approaching the target. Bob's voice, striving to be calm, talking to Jim, crackled in Ron's intercom too: 'Steady ... steady ... right a bit ... steady ... correct left a tad ... steady ...'

Ron prayed it wouldn't be a dummy run again.

'Keep her there. Right!' A moment's silence, then: 'Bombs gone!'

The Lancaster's load, a massive 4,000lb 'Blockbuster' bomb escorted by 954 4lb incendiaries, hurtled towards the stricken city. The Blockbuster, or 'cookie', as the name suggested, was designed to blast structures apart, leaving them exposed to the incendiaries, which would ignite the exposed and shattered interiors. War from the air was a brutal business.

Released of its burden, the pilot had to control the aircraft as it leapt upwards – another moment of potential risk if someone was flying above you.

Then came the moment they all loathed. 'Hold her for the photo.'

It meant keeping straight and steady for a few seconds while the camera behind the bomb aimer took automatic flash shots of their run through its own small porthole on the floor. How the crewmen hated those few seconds, vulnerable to attack and unable to manoeuvre. The pictures were vital, mandatory. Analysed back home, they served a dual purpose: proof that the Lancaster – and her crew – had done their job; and material to assess the success of the raid. But those brief moments seemed like the longest of the entire flight.

Then, disaster struck.

A bomber stream would normally fly to its target on one course and return home via another. No marker lights showed on any aircraft, and apart from the blazing target and the pale glow of the moon, it was dark – too dark to see fast-moving allies close by. Ron had heard the 'bombs gone' announcement and was thinking, *Good, now we can go home.* Jim Scott, holding the Lancaster steady for the photo-run, had suddenly caught sight of something out of the corner of his eye: a huge dark shape, heading straight for them through the flame-reddened sky.

*Another Lancaster.*

Jim wrenched on the controls to take evasive action, while Harry Stunell watched events unfold.

'The rogue Lancaster seemed to be making a premature exit from the starboard flank of the stream, as if being pursued by a night-fighter, but more likely it was attempting to get away from the target area. It came like a bat out of hell, in a sky bathed in a weird greyish light, its engine nacelles thrust belligerently forward, closing fast. A shit or bust situation. At the last moment, it attempted correction, as did Jim Scott. But it was too late. It appeared to feather-flick[9] our starboard wingtip.'[10]

Harry Stunell's foreboding hadn't been misplaced.

Somehow they managed to sweep past each other, but the slipstream of the other Lancaster, perhaps the slight brushing of wingtips, was enough. With a roar, their aircraft was flipped out of control. Engines screaming, it plummeted towards the burning city they had just bombed. Ron's single, frantic thought was: *What the hell is going on?*

Engines howling as they continued to fall, Jim yelled, 'Prepare to abandon aircraft!' while he and his flight engineer fought to regain control. Wireless operator Harry Stunell immediately reached for his parachute, which should have been stowed on the fuselage wall opposite his seat – but it wasn't there. He felt his stomach hollow with panic.

The Lancaster was being stretched to breaking point. A violent wind ripped through its fuselage; presumably someone had jettisoned an escape hatch in preparation to abandon the aircraft. Biceps bursting as he wrestled with the wildly bucking Lancaster, Jim finally managed to bring it under some kind of control. But they were far from out of danger, and the 'abandon aircraft' order stood.

As the Lancaster gradually levelled out, Harry was able to leave his seat and search for his missing parachute. Panic mounted again as he moved fruitlessly through the fuselage, barking his shins on jutting metalwork. His earlier fears returned as he made his way forward again, to where Ken Darke was still anchored to his navigator's table, his own parachute strapped to his chest. The howling wind made communication all but impossible, but he managed to shout, in desperation, 'I've lost my chute! I'll have to come with you. I'll hang onto your harness straps!'

Ken looked at him. In that awful moment Harry had to accept the message he read in Ken's eyes. They both knew the notion was impossible. Heart lurching, Harry turned and retraced his steps, trying to prepare himself for the worst, when he stumbled over something. He knelt down and felt a rush of relief. His parachute must have been dislodged after the near-collision, and by sheer good fortune hadn't been bundled out of reach in the following dive, or out of the aircraft entirely. His hands shook as he struggled to strap it on.

Ron didn't have time to think. Instinct took over. He hadn't needed to hear the pilot's order to bale out. He knew this was a very bad one, and he had to get going. Fighting down panic, he'd managed to get hold of his parachute – there was no room to wear it inside his turret, so he had to recover it from outside the sliding doors that enclosed him – and clip it onto his chest as the Lancaster had fallen out of the sky. The speed of its near-vertical descent had created a gravitational force that prevented Ron from turning his gun turret 90 degrees to the fuselage and baling out backwards, reversing into the relative safety of the night sky.

Somehow the aircraft righted itself, but not without cost. A glacial wind now cut through the fuselage. Perhaps they had lost their bomb-bay doors, or the forward escape hatch – maybe both. The interior of the aircraft was in chaos. But it wasn't all bad. They were still alive. And they were still airborne. Having regained some semblance of control, Jim Scott rescinded the bale-out order and they began to take stock of their dire predicament.

Ken Darke shook off his confusion and got busy plotting a new course for home, but his hands were numb in the biting cold, so Scott told Ron to come forward and lend the navigator his gloves. Ron unplugged his intercom and oxygen supply and fought his way forward. Clambering over the wing spars, banging his head on the Lancaster's metal ribs, he was relieved that, at this much lower altitude, he didn't need to use one of the portable emergency oxygen bottles clipped to the inside of the fuselage, which would have restricted his movement further. Ken took the gloves gratefully, and Ron couldn't fail to notice the grimness of the pilot's and flight engineer's expressions as he did so. The cabin was strewn with charts, maps and, more dangerously, cartridges for the 'Very' flare pistol, ripped from their storage rack.

It was time to take stock. They'd lost a lot of height, the altimeter read 10,000ft, and heaven only knew what damage the airframe had suffered, but for the moment the Lancaster seemed to be bearing up. Cautiously, the pilot began to gain altitude. The flight engineer continued to carry out damage assessment as best he could.

There was some hope of salvation. Ken Darke had plotted a revised course home, heading north and east for Juvincourt, about 20 miles north of Reims. Liberated by the Americans four months earlier, it had been the largest Luftwaffe base in France, and boasted emergency landing facilities. Ron returned to the rear of the bomber, forward of his turret, near the main door. They weren't out of the woods yet. He couldn't forget the set faces of his skipper and the flight engineer. Now, to make matters worse, a blizzard had begun to pelt the aircraft's aluminium alloy shell. Everyone was frozen. Ron's heated flying suit was no longer plugged in, the interior was frosting, and visibility both inside and out was almost zero.

The chances of making it to Juvincourt were slim, but at least they knew that they'd passed out of Germany and into France – Allied territory. Jim Scott brought the aircraft down to a lower altitude to try to get his crew a little warmer, and to shift the ice he feared was building up on the wings, but in doing so he noticed that the altimeter didn't seem to be responding correctly.

Shortly afterwards, over the mercifully still-functioning inter-com, Ron heard his anxious voice ask if anyone could see any sign of the ground. Ron didn't like that note of anxiety. The skipper was a cheerful, indomitable Scot whose lively blue eyes had melted the heart of more than one aircraft-woman back at Metheringham. It was unlike him to worry without very good reason. Enclosed in the rear fuselage, Ron was unable to see out, but he heard Jack Elson, the mid-upper gunner, answer: 'I can, Skipper – it's right below. I can see some trees.'

'Can't be!' came the taut reply. 'Altimeter's at 4,000 feet, safety height.'

Everyone's stomach tightened.

*Christ, was this it? What was happening?*

They hit the treetops seconds later. The Lancaster bucked and jolted, ripping itself apart as it plummeted through the forest. Fuel burst from its shattered wing tanks and the engines burst into flames as they careered onwards and downwards, 30 tons of mortally wounded dragon cutting its way through the forest until the irresist-ible force of the trees brought it to a gradual halt. Fuel rushed into the interior and flooded the floor. Harry Stunell saw flames shooting up between his legs and realised that it had been ignited by sparks from the generators under his desk. Fire danced around him.

'God, get me out!' he shouted.

He could see no one else, hear no one else, could think of nothing but how to douse the fire that was already licking at his flesh. When he tried to steady himself against the sides of the fuselage, his hands stuck to the red-hot metal, tearing the skin as he pulled them away.

Machine-gun ammunition was popping in the heat, and the stench of burning Perspex caught in the back of his throat. Molten plastic dripped on him from the edge of the astrodome, the observation bubble just aft of the cockpit. Biting his lip against the pain, shielding his eyes, he looked up. The dome had gone now, and here, if he could only make it, was a possible way out. Burning to death was every airman's deepest fear; driven by a survival instinct that forced him to ignore further pain, Harry hauled himself up towards the hole where the astrodome had been.

'I managed to place my buttocks on the outside surface. My backside was burning. I was in terrible pain. I drew up my knees, dragged my feet through the hole. I was now free to jump down on the port wing. Unfortunately, the wing had gone.'[11]

He fell the 20ft from the top of the aircraft heavily, jarring his ankles as he landed on the frozen ground. Pain seared through his legs. He almost passed out, but knew that simply wasn't an option. He shook his head to clear it. The port wing lay burning several yards to the rear.

Dimly aware of the trail of destruction the dying aircraft had left in its wake, he staggered, still on fire, away from the inferno, ripping through brambles, half falling, trying to stamp out the burning embers in his flying boots, finally reaching the deep snow that nestled under undamaged trees. He rolled in it, gasping in agony and shock, but also with relief. The snow had put out the fire that had threatened to engulf his body. When he was finally able to take stock, he could see that the front of his Lancaster had been destroyed by the force of the onrushing trees. The main section of the fuselage was melting, and exploding ammunition still peppered its remains.

Harry wondered if anyone else had survived. He wondered if he would do so himself.

Alone at the back of the aircraft, Ron Needle heard 'no noise, felt no sensation of a crash'. He was suddenly thrown forward and, smashing heavily into the fuselage, immediately passed out. When he came to, he found himself hanging upright from his parachute harness, hooked onto the fuselage. He knew the jutting metal that had trapped his harness had undoubtedly saved him. Without it, he would have been hurled into the inferno.

Mercifully, the fire hadn't reached his position, and the flames he could see ahead of him looked as if they were losing their force; but they could draw fresh energy at any moment from a hitherto untouched puddle of fuel, the smell of which was everywhere, coupled with the acrid smell of burning Perspex and now, he realised, of burning flesh. Machine-gun bullets[12] popped and ricocheted around him. Ron hadn't a second to waste. He pressed his harness release button, dropped to the floor and winced as he felt a stabbing pain from his right ankle and lower leg. He thought he'd dislocated his right shoulder, and his chest burned when he breathed. But somehow he had to get out.

It didn't look as if anyone else had. Ron could see Jack Elson's legs, shattered and burned, hanging from his hammock seat, still suspended in his upper gun turret. 'He was a terrible mess and I knew immediately he was dead. To see my dear friend hanging lifelessly like that was horrendous, but survival now became paramount.'

Ron could only imagine what lay further forward, ahead of the mid-upper gunner's position, but he knew that the nose of the aircraft must be smashed to pieces. He was exhausted, the pain in his leg was excruciating, and all he wanted to do was lie down and sleep. Instead, he forced himself on, dragging his way back down the fuselage to the main door on the starboard side. With a superhuman effort he manipulated the lever that opened it – not the easiest of tasks at the best of times, as every Lancaster flyer knew. It was a miracle it hadn't buckled and jammed in the crash. At last it swung open. 'I simply fell out of the door and pain shot through my body. I was surrounded by towering trees. I crawled towards them through the freezing snow and found myself in the blackness of the forest.'

He managed to get about 10ft under the canopy and prop himself against a trunk. He was done in but, at nineteen, the will to live was strong in him. Though God only knew what would happen next.

There was no other sign of life. Apart from the soughing of the wind in the branches and the last, broken crackles of the furnace, there was only the silence of the snow. He was alone; as far as Ron knew, the crash had claimed all his other crewmates. He didn't think of his family, or the girl he'd met and whom he hoped one day to marry. His only thought was of survival.

From where he lay, Ron could see the silhouette of the ruined Lancaster. 'It was no longer a beautiful machine; it was dying before my eyes, blackened and charred; it was a wreck in the forest. I felt a personal loss as I gazed at her, but I thanked her for my survival – if it hadn't been for the strength and determination of this Lanc, I had no doubt I would not be alive. She saved my life.'

He lay back, in a state of utter collapse. Even the pain from his wounds had numbed for now. All he could feel as his thoughts raced was the biting cold. He knew he was in France, and in an area already liberated from the Germans. He listened in the darkness, hoping against hope that the noise of the crash would have alerted someone, someone who would even now be coming to investigate, to help . . .

Too exhausted to call out, he cocked his ears.

There was nothing.

He longed to live, but he knew that, unaided, he would die.

# CHAPTER TWO

# THE COMING WAR

Though he never spoke of it much, Ron Needle's father, Edward, had seen service with the Royal Warwickshire Regiment during the First World War – he'd been gassed at the Battle of the Somme. The resulting bronchitis would kill him at the age of sixty-five, but his motto was always, 'Life is sweet, and whatever it holds for you, make the most of it.'

The family lived in the inner-city Birmingham district of Ladywood, where Ron, born on 17 March 1925, was the fourth of eleven children. It was quite a squeeze in their small, back-to-back terraced house – the only windows faced the street, so it was poorly lit, poorly ventilated and without the luxury of any back garden, or yard. Ron was proud of his dad. He was kind and loving, a well-respected trades union official who'd 'fight tooth and nail if he believed that a colleague had been wronged'.[1] Good grounding for a son who would later fly Lancasters, fighting to right one of the greatest wrongs of the twentieth century.

Ron's introduction to flight came at an early age. On a family outing late in 1929, Edward told him to look skywards. There the young Ron saw the majestic, recently completed R-101 civil airship soaring high over the city. The sight left a vivid and lasting impression on him. 'Seeing the airship was an amazing experience. It was the first flying machine I had ever seen and it looked like some sort of creation from a science-fiction comic. To see a flying machine like this was mystical, almost magical. I was a child of four, so the thought that I could ever be flying through the skies myself never entered my head! How could that ever happen?'

Fourteen years later, Ron had his answer.

Almost all the men who flew Lancasters were born, give or take a year or two, in the first half-decade of the 1920s. Many of their parents and grandparents remembered the Zeppelin raids of the First World War – indeed, Ron Needle's mum, Ellen, had mistakenly told him that the airship he'd seen as a four-year-old was actually a German Zeppelin.

These massive, lighter-than-air craft brought terror to British towns and cities. Early in 1915 the Germans bombed Great Yarmouth, Sheringham and King's Lynn, causing slight damage and a handful of fatalities. Though Kaiser Wilhelm II had for a short time forbidden attacks on London, raids on the docks took place from February that year and, at the end of May, Zeppelins dropped 120 bombs in a line stretching from Stoke Newington to Stepney and then out again to Leytonstone. Damage and fatalities were still relatively slight – seven killed, thirty-five injured, and seven buildings destroyed – but over forty fires were started and the fear instilled was as effective as the damage inflicted.

Waging war from the skies was a reality.

\* \* \*

Maurice Garlick was a toddler when he experienced the First World War raids that made his mother 'very nervous'. The family had constructed a self-made 'shelter' in their home in Hatfield, to the north of London, consisting of 'the stout dining table piled high with heavy tomes, like the *Encyclopaedia Britannica*, family Bibles and Mrs Beeton's cookbook'.[2]

Maurice was the same age as Ron Needle when he saw his first airship – but that was in 1918, and in this instance the airship really was a Zeppelin. 'One moonlit night, my dad popped his head under the shelter and said, in an urgent voice, "Come on, lads. Come and see something you will probably never see again." So my brother, eight years old, and I crawled out sleepily, still in our pyjamas, and from the front garden in Hatfield stared towards London.' Trapped in a cone of about six brilliant-white searchlight beams 'was this slim, long, white cigar. Suddenly a tiny silver fly appeared, and seemed to be spitting fire at it. "That's a German Zeppelin, that big thing, probably been bombing London," Dad explained, "and that little one is ours. It's called an aeroplane, and it's shooting bullets at it."

'We stood in awe. All of a sudden that long, sleek pencil burst into flames, which rapidly spread from end to end. It seemed to bend in the middle, and then it fell to earth, lighting up the sky for miles around. We stood open-mouthed. Afterwards, I often thought about those poor crewmen trapped inside, although they had just come back from bombing the capital, probably killing many inno-cent Londoners. I believe it was the first time a Zeppelin had been shot down at night. It was my introduction to aerial combat, at a very tender age.'

Though the four-year-old Maurice could never have imagined it at the time, he too was destined to be at the forefront of aerial warfare in the years to come.

In reality, Zeppelins weren't that efficient. They could fly at 10,000ft, out of the range of British fighters, but they had to come lower for bombing runs. Even then, the conventional ammunition the British fighters' guns could fire hardly had any effect, and the Germans, who retained a great faith in the power of the Zeppelin, were continually developing and improving its design. All that changed at the beginning of September 1916, when a new prototype was shot down by 21-year-old William Leefe Robinson in a BE2c night-fighter equipped with a new kind of explosive bullet. The airship went down in flames over Hertfordshire, Robinson was awarded the Victoria Cross – the nation's highest honour for valour in the face of the enemy – and the writing was on the wall. By 1917 it was Gotha bombers that took over the main thrust of attacks on London, and they were far more effective. Though development continued well into the 1930s, the fate of the airship was sealed.

Few at that point had seen an aircraft soar over them, let alone travelled in one. But progress was swift. When the Lancaster was delivered to its first base on Christmas Eve 1941, it was only thirty-eight years since Wilbur and Orville Wright had made aviation history in the fragile *Wright Flyer* with the world's first powered flight – getting airborne for a mere twelve seconds and covering just 120 feet – at Kill Devil Hills, North Carolina. On 25 July 1909, Louis Blériot's Type XI monoplane took thirty-six and a half minutes to fly from Calais to Dover, winning him £1,000 from the *Daily Mail*. Young minds were fired by such exploits.

In 1932, Alan Cobham, a former First World War fighter pilot, a test pilot for the de Havilland Corporation and a pioneer of long-distance flight, introduced a series of 'National Aviation Day' displays up and down the country. His 'flying circus' visited hundreds of sites across Britain over the next three years, using cleared fields as well as established aerodromes, and showcased a variety of machines, from single-seaters, which gave aeronautical displays, to small passenger craft such as the de Havilland Fox Moth, which gave thousands of people their first experience of flight – if they could afford it. Ten minutes in the air cost half a crown (12.5 pence) – a lot of money at the time – but Cobham's aircraft were only able to carry three or four passengers at a time for their short hops into the sky.

Maurice Garlick got airborne with Cobham's Flying Circus for the first time at the age of twenty-one. 'My introduction to flying was a white-knuckle experience. I volunteered for a daredevil publicity trip round the area in an open, rickety two-seater biplane. We did some diving and looping and I hung on and enjoyed it. I vowed to do my own piloting one day.'

\* \* \*

Ted Watson, who hailed from Cockfield, 8 miles south-west of Bishop Auckland in County Durham, had marvelled as a little boy at the R-101 airship when it flew along the east coast in 1930. Then, in the summer of 1935, aged ten and a half and out haymaking, he heard a new engine noise – much louder than those of the motorbikes that occasionally passed along the nearby country road. He realised it was coming from the sky.

'I looked up to see some sort of dart flashing across the sky. It was an aeroplane! I'd heard about them but never seen one before; what a sight it was!'[3] Excitedly, Ted called out to his friends and pointed to where a biplane, not 300ft above, seemed to be making a beeline for them. Ted waved to the pilot, who waggled his wings in acknowledgement.

'I had glimpsed the future. I knew that, whatever else I did, at some point in my life I wanted to do that. I wanted to be up there, looking down at the myriad scenes which would unfold as I passed over the countryside.' Because Ted could see the pilot, he could *identify* with him, and his youthful imagination was profoundly stirred. 'I imagined what it must be like to be a bird, to soar and glide over the land.'

He knew then that he'd had an experience that would affect his entire life.

'I had no idea that one day I could be up there myself doing a far less peaceful job. Eight years later that memory was still imprinted on my mind when it came to volunteering for the RAF. It was my chance both to get into the skies and to be part of the war effort – there was a general notion among my friends that we "really should be doing our bit".'

Ted was destined to 'do his bit' as a flight engineer on Lancaster bombers.

\* \* \*

In August 1939 the Germans signed a non-aggression pact with the USSR. Britain responded by signing an Agreement of Mutual Assistance with Poland. On Friday 1 September, the Luftwaffe bombed the city of Wieluń in the south-west of Poland. The first significant military action of the Second World War claimed 127 lives.[4] Without television, with little newsreel, people could only imagine what was going on in the world outside. Few travelled beyond their own shores. Few knew what 'foreigners' were really like. Now people were going to be thrown together, and at each other, in a manner for which the First World War of only twenty years earlier was only a taster.

On 3 September, two days after the bombing of Wieluń, Britain was enjoying the warm, early autumn weather. Churches were unusually crowded as Sunday morning prayers were said in the hope that a peaceful solution would be found to the developing situation. Few actually believed peace was a possibility, however, and they didn't have long to wait for their fears to be confirmed. The Prime Minister was to make a broadcast to the nation.

While Ted Watson's family waited for the announcement, his mother calmly made tea, then they gathered around the kitchen table, listening to the light orchestral music on their wireless. At 11.15 a.m. Neville Chamberlain's voice came into parlours, kitchens and drawing rooms throughout Britain. He spoke carefully and deliberately:

'I am speaking to you from the Cabinet room at 10 Downing Street. This morning the British ambassador in Berlin handed the German government a final note stating that unless we heard from them by eleven o'clock that they were prepared at once to withdraw their troops from Poland, a state of war would exist between us. I have to tell you now that no such undertaking has been received, and that consequently this country is at war with Germany.'

The speech was followed by the national anthem, and much of the country stood to attention in their homes until the final notes rang out.[5]

Ron Needle, six months into his job in a pork butcher's shop on Bristol Road South and very happy in his work, listened to the announcement with his family. 'I didn't really comprehend what war was, but I was soon to learn. I had no comprehension of what the future would hold; I didn't dream I would ever be involved. There was no sense of how the war would touch the country, or me as an individual. The future was unimaginable. I was fourteen, and the future didn't concern me!'

A sense of unreality took over as church bells rang out, followed by public announcements, sudden and dramatic, regarding the immediate closure of cinemas and theatres, the cancellation of all sporting events and any activities involving large crowds. Further information followed about air-raid warnings and the wearing of gas masks. 'Listening to this unfold as a young boy,' Ted Watson remembered, 'I had no idea what it meant or how the war would affect me personally. I had no concept about the toll it would take, the deaths I would witness. It all sounded rather exciting, to be honest.'

Within moments of the broadcast finishing, a wailing air-raid siren was heard in London. It proved to be a false alarm, but it made many realise what might be in store.[6]

At one minute past noon that same day, a Blenheim light bomber adapted for reconnaissance became the first RAF aircraft of the war to fly over German territory, taking seventy-five photographs of enemy warships in the port of Wilhelmshaven, west of Hamburg. The crew and aircraft returned home safely. Many of those who followed in their wake would not be so lucky.

*Stan and Elsie Shaw on their wedding day*

That September in 1939, Stanley Shaw, the son of a Nottinghamshire miner, had been married to Elsie Stendall for nearly four years, and their little girl, Elaine, was approaching her third birthday. Since 1936, Stan had worked for a local family firm, the hosiery manufacturers Johnson and Barnes, in Kibworth, having served an apprenticeship as a hosiery knitter with his older brother, Victor. He'd moved to Stapleford near Nottingham that same year with his family, and the last three years had been, if not luxurious, then at least contented. But, as with so many other families, that contentment was soon to be violently disrupted. One of Elaine's earliest memories was of the family listening to Chamberlain's broadcast: 'We were living in Birley Street. It was a little three-bedroomed detached house with an open coal fire in the sitting room. We didn't have much money at all – I remember we seemed to live on onions! Boiled, fried, stewed – anything at all. But it was a very happy and settled life.

'I remember that the family sat around the radio listening to the Prime Minister and the King[7] when war was announced. I remember my mother saying, "Oh my God." It didn't make much sense to me, really. I didn't know what it all meant, or have any conception of how the news, and the war, would come to affect the rest of my life.' Her father's immediate response was to join the local Home Guard. 'I remember him coming home when he first got his rifle. He put the bayonet on and started to go through the rifle drill in the parlour – and thrust his bayonet through the ceiling. My mother was not very impressed!'[8]

The march to war was slow. The period from September 1939 to May 1940 was marked by that strange period known as the 'Phoney War'. The French invaded the Saarland, and there was a plan to invade Norway in order to cut off Germany's supply of iron ore. This came to nothing except the triggering of the German invasion of Denmark and Norway in April 1940. The RAF increased its strength to 135 squadrons, including seventy-four bomber squadrons.

The war burst into life when the German *Blitzkrieg* offensive saw General Heinz Guderian's Panzer tanks sweep through the

Netherlands, Belgium and into France, and the subsequent defeat of
the British Expeditionary Force and its evacuation from Dunkirk.
The war in the air was soon to follow, with devastating consequences on both sides. The German bombers that had flown over
Spain and Poland now menaced France and Britain. The Battle of
Britain, when the Germans paid a high price for underestimating
the stamina and integrity of the RAF's fighter squadrons, over-
lapped with major German bombing assaults on Bristol, Coventry,
Glasgow, Liverpool and London.

The area around Elaine Shaw's home became a target too; it was
close to Chetwynd Barracks, the Stanton Ironworks, and a number
of railway sidings.

'One night a bomb dropped in the Arches Farm at the end of our
street – it blew all the glass out of the houses on the opposite side,
but, strangely, only blew over a bureau in our house! The noise was
incredible, but I don't remember being scared – I didn't really understand what it all meant. Next morning, my mother said, "You're off
to your grandma's – you can't stop here!"' Her father, Stan, joined
the Royal Air Force Volunteer Reserve in summer 1940 – the first
step on the road that would lead to him becoming a rear gunner
on Lancaster bombers, and meting out similar treatment to the
German population.

'My dad said he didn't want the Germans setting foot in England
and he felt he needed to protect me and my mother so he decided
to join the RAF – so many others were doing just the same. It just
felt the right thing to do at the time. I loved him to bits – he was my
favourite person in the world. My mother was really upset when he
joined. She didn't really talk about it, but even as a child I sensed
he was heading into danger. It was the way adults whispered, the
sense of dread in the air sometimes, the looks they gave each other.'

\* \* \*

Smarting after their defeat in the Battle of Britain, the Luftwaffe's
bombers had taken to launching many of their assaults at night.

The distinctive drone of their engines would soon become familiar, striking terror into every heart.[9] Older men met the assaults head-on. Maurice Garlick, like Stan Shaw, was already a grown man when the war started. He'd been academically bright at school, and by 1935 he was working in advertising. It wasn't to be a long career. By 1938 'it was obvious war was coming, and if you had any bottle you joined the Territorials, the Police or the RAF'. Maurice hadn't forgotten his white-knuckle flight with Cobham's Flying Circus, and put his name down for the RAF, only to be told it'd be over a year before training for new volunteers would begin. Nothing daunted, he joined the Auxiliary Fire Service.

'It was one of the most enjoyable times of my life. How we enjoyed the slippery pole! We learned first aid, knot-tying, ladder work, firefighting, how to rescue people from burning buildings. Up to then I'd been a bit scared of heights, but soon I was training by going up after people on cinema roofs, with a hook ladder over my shoulder.' He ended up in charge of a fire station. During the London Blitz, Maurice took part in what he calls the second Great Fire of London, on 29 December 1940, when firefighters from all over the capital raced to save St Paul's Cathedral from destruction. It was the first time he had diced directly with death. As he fought the flames, his thoughts were simple: *Nemesis! Revenge!*

'It seemed as if all London was alight that night. It was around this time that I saw a Spitfire shoot down a German Dornier bomber in flames over Enfield and cheered with the rest of the onlookers.'[10] Maurice would never forget the 44,000 civilians killed during the fifty-seven nights of continuous bombing of London: 'I had some scores to settle, from my time in the London Fire Service.'

At the forefront of his mind was the terrible occasion when German bombs fell on a local dance hall when a party was in full swing; the bombs brought it to an end amid shattered bodies and rubble. Such experiences, fighting the death and destruction that came from the air, seeing the effects at first hand as a firefighter, reinforced Maurice's desire to join the RAF and fight back. But he always retained a sense of humanity. A little less than four years later, with his own Lancaster under attack from German night-fighters, his thoughts would return to the stricken Dornier he had seen come down over London, realising in his own moment of ulti-mate danger how its crew must have felt then.

\* \* \*

Ken Trent, a serious-minded east Londoner and future Lancaster pilot, was only three years older than Ron Needle when the Second World War broke out, but those three years equipped him far better to understand what was going on. Ken was working for a soap manufacturer in the Port of London. He saw the effect of the Blitz on Londoners, and of the swift annexing of the Channel Islands by Germany (Guernsey would become a favoured rest-and-recuperation location for the German military) soon after. Britain, unwilling to accept the inevitability of another world war so hard on the heels of the last, had dragged its military feet a little in the twenty years or so that separated 1918 from 1939, but reluctant preparations had been in train since the mid-1930s, and as people braced themselves for the German fist, the country was now pulling out all the stops to counter the threat to its freedom.

Ken remembered the early daylight assaults: 'The Germans didn't wait long before beginning their dreadful attacks on our country. You would see the trails of condensation high up in the blue sky, as the British fighters and the German bombers and escorts duelled to the death, and sometimes a parachute would float lazily down. You never knew whether it was one of theirs or one of our own.

'Winston Churchill, who became prime minister in May 1940, quickly had enough of us being attacked without retaliation though, and in a daring raid on 25 August 1940, about one hundred bombers flew all the way to Berlin and let them have it. We were delighted that at last we were striking back at the hated Hun, but inevitably there were serious consequences. Even though he was gaining ground by smashing up RAF airfields and radar stations, Hitler decided he would rather go after London. It meant that I, in my little world of work and cycle racing, and my parents with their little shop, became a target.'[11]

Ken would never forget his first experience of a German daylight raid – the disquieting throb of the enemy bombers as they approached London, and the lighter note of their fighter escort. When the RAF engaged them, and one fighter was shot down, he was out on his bike. Seeing a parachute open and an airman drift earthwards, he pedalled furiously to where he thought the man would land, not knowing whether the downed airman was German or British. He was overtaken by an open-topped car, rushing in the same direction. In it was a young man brandishing a rifle, clearly convinced that the airman was German. 'His determination to get to grips with the Hun really summed up the mood of the time for me; everyone wanted to get their own back on the men who had bombed our homes.'

For propaganda purposes, and to encourage morale, cinema newsreels and reports on the radio overstated the losses the Germans sustained, but the losses were great enough, and the RAF's response robust enough, for daytime raids to cease. Night-time raids, however, were stepped up. Some of Ken's father's customers were killed; other people didn't turn up for work and their workmates knew that they must either have been killed or bombed out.

'When I close my eyes and think of those times, I always hear the *brrrmmm brrrmmm* of the engines, the wail of the sirens, the all-pervading smell of the dust and dirt which was thrown up by the bombs, and people coming out of their shelters in the mornings in wonderment that they were still alive.'

As in Maurice Garlick's house twenty-two years earlier, there was no air-raid shelter for the Trent family, but a stout table (government-issue this time) designed to hide under during an air raid. Ken and his sister Janet usually slept under it, while their parents took refuge under the stairs. 'The first time the windows were blown in we were all under that table in a flash!'

Ken's father had been wounded in 1914–18. 'I remember him saying, "We're not going to move for that bastard Hitler!" He would have fought them to the last bullet if he'd had to, and then chased them down the road with a stick.'

The Blitz had a profound effect on Ken Trent. He, his family and his neighbours in the East End, which bore the brunt of the air raids, somehow had to come to terms with the fear and the sense of desperation that attended it, the stress of never being able to relax; but the effect was never forgotten. Some of those early memories marked Ken deeply. For example, when an evacuee centre in Silvertown, filled with children awaiting transport to the safety of the countryside, fell victim to a direct hit. It was destroyed. All the children sheltering there were killed.

'It only fuelled the anger we felt towards the Germans. As far as I was concerned, the only good German was a dead German. I hated them, and wanted to get back at them in any way I could. Later in the war, when I was dropping bombs on German cities, I felt no remorse at all.'

Ken was keen to get into the RAF as soon as he could, and he'd joined the Air Defence Cadet Corps soon after leaving school. But it wasn't just the thought of getting back at the Germans that motivated him. At High Beech in Epping Forest there was a beautiful old pub that had a great view to the west and the setting sun, and this was where all the fighter pilots used to take their girlfriends. They would turn up in their sports cars, revving the engines and showing off their impossibly glamorous companions. They wore immaculate uniforms. Ken burned to join them – 'as did virtually every other young man of my age'.

Soon, he would.

\* \* \*

It wasn't just England that felt the fury of the German air attacks. In early spring 1941, as Ken Trent was fulfilling his ambition and joining the RAF, Don MacIntosh, a young working-class Glaswegian the same age as Ken, and also destined to become a Lancaster pilot, was working as a police cadet telephone operator for Clydebank Police. Don was a tough cookie, handsome and self-confident; he'd left school four years earlier, aged fourteen, and was accustomed to Glasgow's mean streets. Things had been quiet recently, but everyone knew that they lived in what was then Britain's chief industrial shipbuilding base. It was only a matter of time before they heard from the Germans.

Don was nearing the end of his shift at the police station and was looking forward to two days off. It'd been a quiet night so far, but at about 9.10 p.m. a call came through from his control centre: 'Air-raid warning RED. This is not, repeat NOT, a practice alert.' At the same time, the sirens started howling in the street outside, and all Don's switchboard lights started springing up in quick succession. Then there was more noise from outside – the drone of approaching aircraft engines high above, and the thudding of anti-aircraft guns. Swallowing hard, Don started to answer the calls that were cramming his switchboard. The first was from a woman who'd lost her cat. *Didn't she know what was going on?* Don reassured her as politely as he could and plugged in the next socket. Six people injured and two dead opposite a pub in Dalmuir, on west Clydebank.

Don hardly had time to respond to this when all hell broke loose. A warship in the nearby shipyard opened fire, and this was quickly followed by the sound of an aircraft's engines, low and close, then a massive explosion. Don rang the fire station and a tense voice told him the library had sustained a direct hit. Don's own building shook as more bombs screamed down. Instinctively, he grabbed his steel helmet.

'I don't remember any real fear as the bombs were falling; they were on the way, so there wasn't much to be done! I had a deep belief that I would survive – I never feared death as I didn't expect it to happen. There was no desire for revenge on the bombers; I had no hate for the Germans or a desire to get back at them. There was no point in worrying about any of it; whatever would happen was going to happen and my thoughts or worries wouldn't affect the outcome! This was the reality of war and I wasn't particularly concerned by it all.'[12]

All he could do as death thundered down from the sky was wait for further explosions – this time on his doorstep, perhaps bringing the end with them. After a moment of eerie silence, the desk sergeant rushed outside, returning quickly: 'Incendiaries. They haven't gone off. I'm going to cover them in sand.' Don's mind was racing, but he carried on taking the calls that streamed into his switchboard. Nothing seemed real. It was as if his mind were shielding him. There wasn't time to think or react, even when he saw four men come in from the street carrying a body covered in a white sheet on a smashed-off door. Another body soon followed the first. The two corpses were those of a couple who'd been sheltering under a walkway near the library. The blast had blown them into the street, ripping their clothes off as it killed them. This wasn't the dashing, heroic war that had stirred Don's youthful imagination as he'd read about it in the newspapers.

He worked on for six solid hours. At last the firing and bombing seemed to ease up, though the calls kept coming in thick and fast. Finally, at six the next morning, the sirens sounded the all-clear. But now the police station had filled with officials from the navy and the fire service. A 500lb bomb had fallen just beyond its walls but had failed to explode. They needed to disarm it. Was it simply a dud? Or was it one with a delayed-action mechanism? Don couldn't afford to worry; there were others who'd deal with it.

His relief cadet – due at ten the previous night – finally made it to the station at 8 a.m. They spent the day trying to check that the jumble of emergency calls had all been dealt with – an almost impossible task, but if there was a repeat raid on the coming night, everything had to be made ready; they had to be on top of things. Finally, at 5 p.m., the duty sergeant told Don he should go home for a few hours' rest; after all, he was due back on duty again at ten that night. There was no question of days off now.

He walked home through a city transformed – no one in the devastated streets; a bus on its side in a crater, its roof gone, empty, no clue about the fate of its passengers; buildings ripped open, leaving rooms exposed, the wallpaper bright in the open air, furniture bizarrely intact on remaining floors. Although he was angry, Don had no concept that he would be meting out similar treatment from a Lancaster bomber in the years to come.

Once home, he tried to persuade his widowed mother to take refuge with friends in Paisley, 10 miles to the east of Glasgow, away from the shipyards, but she refused to leave their home, telling him she'd be fine in their corrugated-iron Anderson bomb shelter[13] in the garden, and he had to make do with that. There was another raid that night, however, and it started early enough to catch him on his way back to work. He'd thrown himself to the ground, but the force of the explosion 100 yards ahead off him lifted him a foot in the air. Two houses had just disappeared, utterly obliterated. Don hurried back to make sure his mother and those others in the shelter were safe. They were, but he later heard that a bomb had hit another local air-raid shelter and killed everyone in it – several families. Others had left town and taken to the countryside. The RSPCA had to deal with a pack of dogs that had formed and were running wild. In the wake of the bombing, looters set to work, and they, too, had to be rounded up.

One thing above all had a profound influence on Don, and affected the decision he was soon to come to. When the lists of the dead were drawn up, over five hundred of them, containing whole families, he came across one name in particular: Julia. He'd never met her; he didn't even know her surname, but she was a fellow telephone operator, working at the post office, and they'd frequently had long, friendly chats over the phone during quiet periods.

'This was my first real experience of death. It was war, and death was to be expected, but Julia's really affected me. One minute she was alive and chatting, the next minute she'd gone. I barely knew her, but the suddenness was an insight into how the war would be. Anonymous death from the skies in seconds. Of course, I had no idea that, in the not-too-distant future, I'd be doing the same thing myself.'

Don was in a reserved occupation; he could be exempted from joining up. Two months after the Glasgow raids in which Julia had died, however, on his nineteenth birthday, he applied to his Chief Constable for permission to be released. He wanted to volunteer for the RAF; the only service he could apply for because of his reserved occupation. Permission was granted, although unwillingly; Don was a valued police cadet. A month later, a brown envelope marked 'On His Majesty's Service' arrived. The letter required him to report to the RAF recruiting office in Edinburgh three weeks later. Don was delighted.

'I was bored with the police and I wanted to be part of the war. It sounded exciting and I looked forward to the dangers involved. I'd applied to be an air gunner, but they decided I might make a pilot – which I was delighted to hear!'

The hardest part was telling his mother. She already knew about his decision to join up, and when he told her about the RAF, 'she stiffened as if I'd struck her'. But she was a strong, stoical woman, of Hebridean stock, and once she had recovered from the shock, she simply told him that if that *was* his decision, then he'd have to follow it. When the time came to go, it was tougher. 'My mother was upset by my leaving, but she didn't show it. No one showed their fears or concerns at that time: one just got on with one's life and hoped for the best. There was no point in showing fear. Nothing would change. My mother just said, "God bless you, my son – take care."

'We hugged and said goodbye. That was it.'

Don MacIntosh was heading to war.

\* \* \*

Though he'd been an enthusiastic Boy Scout and always rather a good student, Ted Watson knew he wasn't destined for the grammar school in Bishop Auckland, County Durham, since only the top pupil from each school in his area made it there. As he turned fourteen, his thoughts focused on a career. He was excellent at geometry, and his drawing skills were impressive, so he managed to land an apprenticeship with Wilson's, a local engineering firm, which meant that, like Don MacIntosh, he was also in a reserved

*Ted Watson is awarded his King's Scout award in 1943*

occupation. Ted had turned fifteen in 1940. In August that year, during the Battle of Britain, sirens had wailed across the north-east of England as waves of Luftwaffe bombers homed in on Durham and Bishop Auckland, among other targets. It was a daylight raid, and soon after 2 p.m. Ted, who'd been at work in Bishop Auckland, heard the all-clear signal. But his relief was marred by the news that his village had also been bombed. It seemed impossible. Why would they bomb Cockfield?

'I was desperate to get home in case my family had been affected. I cycled the 8 miles as fast as I could, praying that no one had been killed. When I arrived in the village it was immediately obvious that it had suffered from the raid; twenty-eight high-explosive bombs and hundreds of incendiaries had been dropped. One had exploded in Front Street, leaving a crater across more than half the road. Windows had been blown out, the medieval ceilings of some of the older houses had come down. Most of the bombs, though, including the hundreds of 4lb incendiaries, had fallen on the open land of the Fell.'

No one had been hurt, and Ted's family was safe and sound, their house untouched. Completely oblivious to any danger, Ted, along with many other villagers, collected unexploded incendiaries as souvenirs. Ted stuffed two into his saddlebag to show them off at work the next day. The Germans had probably been en route to Liverpool, but, thwarted by the defending fighter squadrons, had dumped their deadly cargoes indiscriminately and beaten a hasty retreat.

'I didn't really have any sense of anger or notions of revenge. We were in a war and this was what was going to happen. It all looked rather adventurous and exciting. I had no idea of the reality.'

When the Air Training Corps was launched in February 1941 to prepare young men aged between sixteen and eighteen for entry into the RAF, Ted jumped at the chance to join, along with the 200,000 others who signed up during the first six months of the ATC's existence. 'Here was a chance to fly when flying itself was a new and novel activity. There was also the issue of patriotism. It was a huge motivator for me and for millions of others during the war. We were desperate to get involved, to do whatever we could to beat this enemy who threatened our very way of life, and everything we held dear.'

Extraordinary times demand extraordinary things of ordinary people. Ted Watson, Ron Needle, Stan Shaw, Maurice Garlick, Ken Trent and Don MacIntosh had set a course that would lead them and the other 125,000 men of Bomber Command to the dark heart of Nazi Germany.

'There were no thoughts of death or danger,' Watson recalled. 'Of course I'd heard about the losses on radio reports and the like. But it all seemed very distant and unreal. Hearing a phrase like "twenty of our bombers failed to return" didn't really mean anything to me. I had no concept that "twenty bombers" might contain over 100 men.'

When Ted joined the ATC in early 1941, the Lancaster bomber was in the process of being born.

## CHAPTER THREE

# 'KEEP IT SIMPLE': THE BIRTH OF A WARHORSE

Thomas Murray was born in Dorset at the end of May 1918, four months after the RAF was created from the army's Royal Flying Corps and the Royal Naval Air Service. Thomas's father, a former Royal Marines officer, had been involved at its inception, setting up the RAF's secretarial branch, and rising to the rank of Group Captain. Charles Murray, however, wanted his son to go into his old service – the navy – and although young Thomas grew up in an RAF family, he hadn't initially felt any great interest in flying himself. Unlike many of his contemporaries, he didn't make model aircraft or read books about the heroics of the early aviators. But in 1929, when his father was stationed at RAF Halton in Buckinghamshire, all that changed.

'I remember the moment I knew I was going to be a pilot. I was lying in a field near my school, right next to the airfield. The sun was out and I was watching a Hawker biplane. He performed a spin right over my head! I was totally captivated – as he spiralled down, he was pointing straight at me. I knew, at that moment, I would go into the Air Force. My first flight was at the age of eleven at RAF Halton. The pilot told me what a wonderful privilege it was to be up in the air, at one with the birds. To show this, he found a heron flying along a stream, which he formatted on!'[1]

Thomas underwent a full medical examination at his father's RAF station and had several hours' experience under his belt by the time he went up to the RAF College at Cranwell in Lincolnshire. On 5 February 1937 he first went solo – 'Fifteen glorious minutes of freedom! – Aerobatics and spinning, with some low flying thrown in for good measure!' He also learned that 'just flying the aircraft, performing aerobatics well, and formation flying, were not the only skills to be mastered for the new era of RAF pilot. The importance of being able to fly on instruments [flying 'blind' in cloud or at night] was becoming a higher priority.'

Thomas joined the RAF at a time when it was expanding and changing. Bomber Command was formed in July 1936, and during the second half of the decade a number of twin-engined bombers were belatedly developed – Blenheims, Hampdens, Whitleys and Wellingtons. But there was a need for heavier, longer-range aircraft that were also capable of carrying a bigger bombload.

The first of these four-engined bombers to enter service was the Short Stirling – notoriously difficult to handle on take-off and landing – in 1940. The Handley Page Halifax followed in November that year. It wasn't the answer either. Crews quickly nicknamed it the 'Halibag'. It could carry a 14,500lb payload, but not high enough to avoid enemy interceptors. More powerful engines were installed, but the capacity of its bomb bay couldn't be increased. The Stirling was withdrawn from Bomber Command service about halfway through the war. The Halifax flew on operations until the end. But something better was needed.

* * *

The Avro Lancaster was something better. It came into existence almost by accident, and as a result of private determination rather than official encouragement, born of its forerunner, the 'Manchester'.

A. V. Roe & Company was founded in 1910 in Manchester by Alliott Verdon Roe and his brother Humphrey. In 1911, Alliott hired the volatile but gifted eighteen-year-old Roy Chadwick as his personal assistant. By 1918, Chadwick, a talented draughtsman, had become a designer in his own right. Avro ran into financial difficulties owing to a lack of post-First World War orders, and by 1935, both founding brothers having left the company, it had become a subsidiary of Hawker Siddeley. Chadwick stayed on as designer-in-chief, and paired up with a new managing director, the energetic and equally fiery Roy Dobson, who'd joined in 1914 at the age of twenty-three. By mid-1940, they were working on a new, improved version of their twin-engined bomber, which they'd named after the city of their birth.

At the time of the Manchester's introduction in November 1940, Thomas Murray was an experienced and seasoned pilot on Hampdens. Thomas flew his first sortie as a second pilot/navigator on 21 December 1939 against the pocket battleship *Deutschland*, holed up in a Norwegian fjord. 'We never found it as we had no radio transmitters then, and had to send each other coded letters via a signal lamp, which made things even more complicated. I remember seeing something which looked like a pocket battleship, so we all roared towards it with open bomb doors. It turned out to be a lighthouse on a low-lying island! We must have scared the lighthouse-keeper somewhat.'

Mine-laying and 'nickelling' sorties (dropping propaganda leaflets over German cities) followed. At this early stage of the war, ops were usually limited to small numbers of aircraft. The crews were trailblazing for Bomber Command – six-hour night flights, with no autopilot, navigating by compass and stopwatch – and the lessons learned would be invaluable later.

When the first Manchesters were delivered to Thomas's squadron at RAF Waddington in Lincolnshire, they were seen as a big improvement on the twin-engined aircraft already in service with Bomber Command. With a crew of seven, it was ultimately powered by a pair of Rolls-Royce Vulture IIs, comprising four cylinder blocks from the earlier Peregrine engine, joined by a common crankshaft and mounted on a single crankcase. They delivered around 1,500 horsepower, about 250 less than anticipated, and once in operational service, from early 1941, it quickly became apparent that they weren't capable of climbing above German anti-aircraft fire. Worse still, the engines were prone to sudden failure, and if one Vulture failed, the remaining engine couldn't bridge the gap. Improvements were attempted, but with little effect.

Thomas Murray took a Manchester up for the first time on 1 May 1941, and then flew them for a week or so to 'really get to grips with its handling', prior to his unit's conversion from Hampdens. 'My first impression was that it was a very *big* aircraft compared with the Hampden. Although it was pleasant to fly, light on the controls, it was colossally underpowered. Our training was on the squadron and not all that methodical – we learned as we went along. These were desperate times, so the aircraft was rushed into service long before it was operationally fit, and while it still had many teething problems. It was light on the ailerons, but unfortunately not at all reliable.'

The authorities had indeed been frantic to get a new, improved bomber into the skies, and turned a blind eye to the Manchester's failings. Always a man of measured judgement, Thomas Murray became increasingly sceptical. 'When you were taxiing out with a full bombload, the centre of gravity was slightly wrong, so that the tailwheel would shimmy and be damaged. It meant changing that wheel before you took off. That delay killed a friend of mine. He was at the end of the runway waiting to have his tailwheel changed. As he took off and climbed away, a [marauding German] fighter took him out.'

He had further concerns: 'The engines themselves were totally unreliable. There were spots where the coolant couldn't reach so the engines would overheat and start engine fires after a few hours' running. The hydraulics system, on which the operation of the flaps, undercarriage, bomb doors and turrets depended, was subject to leaking and consequently failure.'

Thomas felt that flying a Manchester demanded the advanced skills of a test pilot, rather than those of a 'regular' bomber pilot.

Unnervingly, the aircraft were grounded again and again during May 1941 due to recurring engine problems, and when they did fly, 'I remember my first full bombload take-off. I got the thing airborne and that's all I could do. It flew along the runway but it looked as if I'd hit the hedge at the end. So I banged the aircraft back down on the ground and fortunately it bounced back into the air, staggering over the hedge. RAF Waddington is on a ridge, and as I went over the edge I managed to get the aircraft's nose down and increase the speed sufficiently to climb away. We had to fly straight ahead, carrying on for about 5 miles before we dared turn. If you had an engine go on take-off you were a goner.'

A desperate plan was concocted to fly a Manchester continuously around the country until an engine failed, in the hope that the aircraft would nevertheless be able to land safely, the faulty component be identified and sent to Rolls-Royce for examination. On one such flight, Thomas Murray's own squadron commander headed for Land's End before turning north towards the Isle of Man. Hardly had he done so than the starboard engine caught fire. He immediately lost height, and ordered the crew to jettison the guns and the dummy bombload to lose weight. He changed course again – for a fighter base near Perranporth in Cornwall, where the strip was too short to land the giant bomber so they had to retract the undercarriage. Skidding along the runway they smashed through two hedges and across a road before a parked lorry finally brought them to a standstill. 'So Rolls-Royce got their engine and I had to fly down and pick up the crew the following day.'

Thomas Murray flew his last raid in a Manchester over the Krupp's plant in Essen, in the Ruhr industrial area – 'Happy Valley' as the bomber crews called it – with a new navigation system on several of the aircraft. Known as GEE (Ground Electronic Equipment), it received two synchronised pulses transmitted from Britain and determined its position – accurate to within a few hundred yards and effective at up to 350 miles – from the time delay between them. But there were teething troubles. During Thomas's Krupp's raid, the GEE-equipped aircraft marking the target with flares were followed by bombers with incendiaries, which obscured the view of the target, causing the next wave to drop their high explosives to little effect.

'It was one of the worst trips I had to the Ruhr,' Thomas recalled.

*Pip Beck*

This failure added to the increasing despondency of Manchester pilots. Pip Beck, a nineteen-year-old WAAF radio operator at Waddington, summed up the situation: 'Anyone who could survive a tour on a Manchester could *fly*, and was also lucky!'[2]

Further development of Vulture engines was cancelled at the end of 1941 – 'much to the relief of Rolls-Royce', as Thomas said – and the Manchesters were withdrawn in mid-1942, after nearly two years' service, during which they managed 1,269 sorties and dropped 1,826 tons of bombs. Only 209 were built, a disastrous 40 per cent were lost on operations, and a further 25 per cent crashed.

The Ministry of Aircraft Production requested that the Avro plant now be turned over to production of the Halifax, but Avro's Chadwick and Dobson believed that within their failed twin-engined bomber lay the seeds of a much better, four-engined aircraft. And many of the machine tools used in the production of the Manchester could continue to be used in its production, thus avoiding huge extra costs. So it was that Roy Chadwick persisted in the teeth of initial indifference and even obstruction in official circles, and he and Roy Dobson finally won through. Their partnership – overseeing design and production respectively – was, fortunately for Britain, a brilliant one.

*Test pilot 'Bill' Thorn in the Lancaster cockpit*
*at the Avro factory in Manchester, 16 March 1942.*
*'Sam' Brown stands behind him*

After a series of successful test flights at Ringway (now the site of Manchester International Airport) by test pilot Harry Albert 'Sam' Brown, the first four-engined Manchester III BT308 was delivered in late January 1941 to the Aeroplane and Armament Experimental Establishment at Boscombe Down in Wiltshire for evaluation. As well as a distinctive twin-finned tailplane, it boasted an extra fin at the rear of the fuselage. A second prototype, fitted with four improved Rolls-Royce Merlin XX engines, took to the skies in mid-May, minus the middle fin. This prototype, DG595, was to be the model for future production, which continued with little variation, except for adaptation for specific tasks and to carry specific bomb-loads, throughout the war.

The new engine, deriving from a Merlin type that had been in development for eight years and was powering the increasingly successful Spitfire fighter, arrived with perfect timing. The twelve-cylinder, 60-degree, upright V-shape engine delivered 1,280 horsepower and was to become its standard plant, propelling the aircraft and providing the hydraulic power for the gun turrets and other onboard functions.[3] The Merlins drove four three-bladed propellers with a diameter of 13ft, and could get the crew home even if only two were functioning. One engine was enough to keep the bomber airborne, often for long enough to make the difference between capture and safety, death or survival.

There was to be no co-pilot, unlike in the Manchester; a flight engineer would take overall responsibility for the aircraft's mechanical smooth-running, and act as support pilot should the need arise. The Manchester, for all its faults, had paved the way for a revolutionary new aircraft, the most advanced bomber the world had yet seen.

After the Boscombe Down tests, the design was approved and officially adopted, and its new name formally accepted. On 28 February 1941, a new British legend, the mighty Lancaster bomber, was born. Its fuselage was just over 69ft long, and its wingspan 102ft. It stood a little over 20 feet high, and was powerful enough to take off at an overall maximum weight, depending on variant, of 68,000lb. In the air, it could achieve speeds of up to 282mph and could climb to a height of 21,400ft, at a rate of 720ft per minute, carrying a normal bombload of 14,000lb. Protected by two 0.303-inch

Browning Mark II machine guns in the nose and mid-upper turret, and four in the rear turret, the aircraft was designed to carry the largest possible number of bombs the greatest possible distance. It was an airborne bomb carrier, built to the highest specifications, and its business was destruction.

With sleek yet businesslike lines, massive and reassuring to its friends, menacing and deadly to its foes, it was like nothing that had come before. Its fuel capacity of over 2,000 gallons and range of 2,530 miles meant it could take the battle to the very heart of Nazi Germany, and, alongside the young men training to fly her, the Lancaster would have a profound effect on the course of the war.

Thomas Murray had his first crack at flying a Lancaster prototype early in October 1941 and was an immediate and enthusiastic convert. 'It took off like a startled stallion.' It was as light as a feather and handled beautifully, almost dancing in the air. Amazingly manoeuvrable, Thomas found it 'a tonic after the lumbering Manchester'. Very soon, the bomber had acquired its affectionate nickname – the 'Lanc'. And, as promised, 'It flew happily on *one* of its four engines!'

The early-production Lancaster, the B1, took its maiden flight on 31 October 1941. Almost two months later, 44 Squadron, based at Waddington, took delivery of the operational aircraft.

Pip Beck remembered their arrival.

'On Christmas Eve 1941, 44's first Lancasters arrived – a magnificent Christmas present for the squadron. It was with intense interest that everyone in Flying Control watched their approach and landing. As the first of the three taxied round the perimeter to the Watch Office, I stared in astonishment at this formidable and beautiful aircraft, cockpit as high as the balcony on which I stood and great spread of wings with four enormous engines. Its lines were sleek and graceful, and yet there was an awesome feeling of power about it. It looked so right after the clumsiness of the Manchester. Their arrival meant a new programme of training for the air and ground crews and there were no operations until the crews had thoroughly familiarised themselves with the Lancasters. There were one or two minor accidents – changing from a twin-engined aircraft to a heavier one with four engines must have presented *some* difficulties, but the crews took to them rapidly. I heard nothing but praise for the Lancs.'[4]

There was a special feeling of bonhomie on Christmas Day 1941, as the officers, in time-honoured tradition, donned aprons and served the 'other ranks' their Christmas dinner. That winter was a particularly bitter one, but somehow hope had now dared to raise its head. One of Pip Beck's special friends was a Rhodesian named Cecil, after his country's founder, Cecil Rhodes. Cecil had come to Britain to work as an RAF aircraft fitter while waiting for a place on a pilots' course.

'Cecil had a food parcel from home containing all sorts of good things, including a gorgeous rich fruitcake. He decided to have a party, since discipline was somewhat relaxed for Christmas Day. We fell on the contents of the food parcel with great enjoyment and appreciation, demolishing the rich tinned soup, tinned ham, and sweetcorn served on toast – and, of course, the fruitcake and some chocolate. It was all delicious. The only thing not available was alcohol, but I don't think we noticed; our spirits were high enough anyway.'

Hope was in the air. Perhaps Christmas 1941 might be the last Christmas at war?

\* \* \*

Roy Chadwick's aim had been to keep the design as simple as possible. The Lancaster would be built in a series of sections, each fully finished, so that they could be transported – by road and rail – from any given factory to a different assembly site, close to an airfield. Each Lancaster cost around £50,000 to produce – more than four times as much as a Spitfire[5] – but its simplicity made for shorter man-hours, and as 1941 and the first half of 1942 saw the Germans still in the ascendant, the need for a speedy production line was vital.[6]

'Keeping it simple' may have been Roy Chadwick's watchword, but a great deal went into achieving that, involving thousands of male and female workers, huge factories, vast drawing offices and an efficient, smooth-running timetable. The process wasn't always perfect, and simple though its essential design was, each Lancaster was made up of around 55,000 separate parts, if you included the rivets and nuts and bolts that held it together. To assemble a Lancaster took 500,000 different manufacturing processes, occupying over 70,000 man-hours. Nevertheless, 7,377 rolled off the production lines during the five years of its manufacture.

Ted Watson visited a factory and was enormously impressed.

'We could watch the Lancasters being assembled – here were some of the machines I would go to war in. We were even allowed to help on the production line. The process was impressive and it gave confidence that everything was being done correctly! We had a tour round a brand-new Lanc and it looked so smart and pristine, everything was in order, it was clean and calm, and as we looked over each crew position it looked like an impressive workshop – a nice place to work. Of course, I had no idea how that sense of calmness would change when we were working in the Lanc in its proper role!'[7]

The oval fuselage, aluminium sheets riveted onto a light-alloy skeleton, was designed to be produced in five sections, which not only made transport easier, but meant that if one were damaged, it could be easily replaced. The wings comprised fourteen segments. The central sections were attached by massive spar booms which crossed the fuselage at thigh height. Lancasters were built to dispense bombs, not for comfort. The main spar was just aft of the radio operator's seat; the rear one about 8ft further back, near a stowage area for parachutes. This crucial assembly, checked and checked again before release from the factory, was vital to the Lancaster's safety. Tailplanes were also divided into units: the 12ft fins and the 33ft span.

The final touch was the paint; greens and browns on the upper surfaces, matt black underneath. The RAF roundels and the identification numbers and letters were the only bright spots on the entire aircraft. Painting was not an easy job, however. Protective face masks were not yet used, and conditions for workers weren't easy overall. Machinist Lilian Grundy[8] recalled working ten-hour days making bolts for the Lancaster. The conditions were dreadful: 'It was like going into a dungeon and the noise was horrendous. They had you at the machines all the time.' At the height of production, shifts were twelve hours long, and the factories worked twenty-four hours a day, seven days a week.

Chadderton, Avro's massive factory near Oldham, complete with an impressive art-deco façade, was responsible for producing over 3,000 Lancasters. It was built in 1938 with the help of a government grant of £1 million. With a floor area of around 750,000 square feet, it was by far the largest aircraft factory of the time, twice the size of any other, and by 1939 it had become Avro's headquarters. Initially used to build Blenheims, it was given over to Lancaster production from autumn 1941. At night the factory was cavernously dark – the only lights were those used to illuminate the workbenches and the work areas – and the noise was perpetually deafening. Panel-beaters, working without ear shields, had one of the worst jobs. Geoff Bentley, aged fourteen when he started at Chadderton, described it as 'a hell of a factory'.

'You could see the Lancasters for miles, fifty of them lined up at a time. Chadderton was a lovely building at the front, with a beautiful big reception and staircase, a bit like a film set. But the factory was so noisy. The riveters would be going all day. I worked for a while in the machine shop, and when those massive presses dropped down, the whole place shuddered.'[9]

The hard work at the factories soon began to pay off. Thomas Murray's squadron was stood down to convert to the Lancaster shortly after their last disastrous raid on Essen in a Manchester.

'At last we had a reliable aircraft with an excellent bombload, rate of climb, and operational ceiling,' Thomas said. Everyone was more than ready to welcome the new arrival, with new hope and vigour in their hearts. And it wouldn't be very long before the new aircraft would be getting its first taste of action. Early in 1942, Lancasters were being delivered to Bomber Command squadrons for operational use, replacing outmoded models faster and faster as production increased. Thomas could almost hear the aircrews' sigh of relief. The effect on morale was palpable.

George VI and Queen Elizabeth paid a visit to the largest factory at Yeadon, Yorkshire, in March 1942. Two recently completed Lancasters were named in their honour. *The Times* later reported that the King and Queen had both displayed extensive technical knowledge of aviation in their conversations with Chadwick and Dobson – the 'two Roys' as they'd become known.

Triumphantly reported by *Pathé Gazette*,[10] another visit to the Avro factories a month or so later by Squadron Leader John Nettleton and his much-decorated crew from 44 Squadron had an even greater significance for the panel-beaters, pop-riveters, electricians, hydraulic engineers, draughtsmen and everyone else who contributed to the creation of the new bomber. They had recently returned from the Lancaster's first significant venture, during which Nettleton had been awarded the Victoria Cross, the nation's highest award for valour, in recognition of his 'unflinching determination and leadership'.[11]

Kay Mitchell had a newspaper picture of John Nettleton pinned to her workbench instead of the portraits of film stars favoured by the other factory workers. She was overjoyed when the Squadron Leader, looking every bit as pleased and shy as she did, was invited to sign it.

# CHAPTER FOUR

## 'A BAD WAY TO SPEND AN AFTERNOON'

The Lancaster's appearance coincided with the appointment in February 1942 of Bomber Command's most notorious Commander-in-Chief, Arthur Harris, and would play a pivotal role in his most controversial strategy. Harris was two months shy of his fiftieth birthday when he took the helm. Born in Cheltenham, the youngest of three sons, he had been sent to a less prestigious public school than his two older brothers, because 'there was not much money left for number three'.[1] He then emigrated to Southern Rhodesia at the age of seventeen, with the aim of becoming a rancher, in defiance of his largely absent father, who worked in the Indian Civil Service.

Harris was destined to be something of an outsider, a rough diamond, not always ready to take orders without question, and single-minded to the point of blinkered stubbornness – which may well have made him the right man in the right place at the right time. After fighting in the South West Africa Campaign in the First World War, he returned to Britain in 1915 and joined the Royal Flying Corps, serving as a fighter pilot and then commander with some distinction. When the war ended he remained in the RAF. In the meantime he'd married and become a father. He didn't feel his wife[2] would take kindly to life on the veld, so he decided to make his home in England. Never quite part of the establishment, his pugnacity earned him few friends; but his tenacity in office and his devotion to his task were beyond question.

Bombing strategy had been framed a quarter of a century earlier by Jan Smuts, a South African soldier and politician. Twice serving as South Africa's prime minister, Smuts was invited to join the British Imperial War Cabinet in 1917. He expressed his vision of future wars in writing:

'The day may not be far off when aerial operations with their devastation of enemy lands and destruction of industrial and populous centres on a vast scale may become the principal operations of war, to which the older forms of military and naval operations may become secondary and subordinate.'[3]

This thinking wasn't new. As early as 1907, the writer and science fiction expert H. G. Wells had envisaged a German bombing attack on New York in *The War in the Air*.

Harris was keen to put the Lancaster through its paces as quickly as possible but had to resist pressure from the government, the Air Ministry and Charles Portal, Chief of the Air Staff, to use his new bomber in direct support of the navy in the Atlantic.

When Harris took control of Bomber Command in 1942, the worst of the German blitzes had abated, but during the period between autumn 1940 and spring 1941, Britain had suffered severely. London bore the early brunt and suffered around 43,000 fatalities overall. The notorious raid on Coventry killed 554.[4] By February 1941, Hitler had switched the Luftwaffe's attention to British ports; Belfast, Bristol, Glasgow, Hull and Liverpool were among the many affected. Thousands more civilians were being killed. By April 1942, a substantial proportion of the Luftwaffe's forces had been diverted to the Eastern Front after Hitler's breach of his non-aggression pact with the USSR and the launch of Operation Barbarossa. And the USA had entered the war the previous December, in the wake of the Japanese attack on Pearl Harbor.

Harris believed that a direct and dramatic strike-back at Germany was now called for, which would put new heart into the

British public. Under his guidance, 'Most Secret Operation Order Number 143' was produced.

*King George VI inspects Lancaster crews
at RAF Waddington in 1942*

John Nettleton was to play a leading role in the operation. Born in Natal Province at the end of June 1917, the grandson of an admiral, he trained as a naval cadet, then went on to serve in the South African Merchant Marine fleet before changing tack to work as a civil engineer. Combining a sense of duty with a thirst for adventure, like thousands of others from the Dominions of the British Empire,[5] he joined the RAF in 1938. By 1941 he was a Squadron Leader with 44 Squadron, when the first Lancasters were delivered to RAF Waddington in Lincolnshire.

Nettleton had led the Lancaster's debut sorties early in March 1942 – largely 'gardening' exercises, the laying of mines (nicknamed 'vegetables') off the coast of Heligoland and Düne, two small islands in the North Sea, 45 miles north-west of Cuxhaven, used by the Germans as a fortress and harbour.

The pressure was now on to get the still relatively small number of Lancasters into action, to see them prove their worth. Nettleton's 44 Squadron was soon working alongside 97 Squadron from nearby RAF Woodhall Spa, flying several raids on Essen that April. By now a number of the Lancasters were equipped with the GEE[6] navigation system. Navigational and bomb-aiming systems hadn't yet achieved their later sophistication, but both the GEE and the Lancaster itself were still on the 'Secret List'.[7] High-tech devices still sat alongside less sophisticated wizardry at this stage of the conflict. Each Lancaster carried two homing pigeons: one in a coop by the main door, the other near the navigator's desk. They could fly over 800 miles at 80mph, at 8,000ft, so in the event of a successful crash-landing or sea-ditching could carry home a message giving the aircraft's location. The birds were so highly valued that, for many crews, tradition dictated they were called Sidney and Reginald. History doesn't relate whether they were at their crew stations now the Lancaster was heading into action for the first time on its own.

The target selected by Harris for the Lancaster's first great display of bombing prowess was the *Maschinenfabrik-Augsburg-Nürnberg*, or 'MAN', U-boat diesel engine plant in Augsburg, 40 miles north-west of Munich, deep in southern Germany. U-boats were taking a severe toll on the Allied Atlantic convoys carrying badly needed supplies to a beleaguered Britain. The choice wasn't without controversy. The Minister of Economic Warfare pointed out that far more significant targets would be the fuel-pump factory at Stuttgart or the ball-bearing plant at Schweinfurt. However, Charles Portal supported Harris's decision when consulted by Churchill.

This first independent outing for the Lancaster was something of an experiment. The bombers would be flying at low level and would need easily identifiable landmarks to guide them. Augsburg had such landmarks; Stuttgart and Schweinfurt did not. Moreover, an attack on a factory supplying U-boats would demonstrate Bomber Command's direct support in the Battle of the Atlantic. It was the boldest of gambles, but if it succeeded, it would send an unmistakable message. As the war in the air had progressed, the Germans had initiated strategic bombing;[8] planning to destroy Britain's ability to wage war by systematic targeting of military, industrial and economic sites alongside relentless, morale-sapping attacks on the civilian population. Harris passionately believed in the need to pay the enemy back in their own coin.

'The German people entered this war under the rather childish delusion they were going to bomb everyone else, and nobody was going to bomb them. At Rotterdam, London, Warsaw, and half a hundred other places, they put their rather naive theory into operation. They sowed the wind, and now they are going to reap the whirlwind.'[9]

44 and 97 Squadrons were detailed for the landmark operation – codenamed MARGIN[10] – and they undertook low-level flying exercises in preparation from the beginning of April 1942. Still in the dark about the precise target details, by the 14th they were ready for a dress rehearsal. Aircraft from 44 Squadron under Nettleton's command, together with those from 97 Squadron under Squadron Leader John Sherwood, were to fly independently to the south coast, rendezvous, then fly north in tandem as far as Inverness, where they would launch a concerted dummy attack.

Despite their youth, both men were seasoned and level-headed pilots. Nettleton was just two months short of his twenty-fifth birthday. Sherwood, at twenty-three, was marginally the more experienced pilot. He'd been commissioned into the RAF in 1937, had already earned the Distinguished Flying Cross, and added a bar to it after action against the German capital ships *Gneisenau* and *Scharnhorst*.

On the morning of 17 April 1942, the curtains covering the map on the wall of 44 Squadron's briefing room were drawn back to finally reveal the target. The Station Commander, Roderick Learoyd VC, told the expectant crews, 'Bomber Command have come up with a real beauty this time,' adding, 'I shan't be coming with you. I've got my VC already. I've no desire to get another.'[11]

The crews were left in no doubt about the operation's importance. 'Don't be overawed by the distance,' they were told. 'The RAF must strike this blow to help our seamen, and *your* Lancasters are the only aircraft that can strike it – with a fighting chance.'[12]

At nearby RAF Woodhall Spa, 97 Squadron's airmen were to share the honour of proving the Lancaster in battle with those at RAF Waddington. When the curtain in their briefing was pulled aside, the reaction was one of incredulous laughter.

'We all started giggling. We really did. We honestly thought it was a joke. The Group Captain was a bit cross. He stomped about the place and said, "If you'll stop bloody laughing, I'll tell you all about it."'[13]

The plan was bold and straightforward. Six aircraft from each squadron would proceed in two separate groups – two flights of three in an inverted V-shaped, 'Vic' formation (one aircraft in front with the other two following in parallel behind). 44 Squadron would lead. Backup Lancasters would accompany them as far as the final rendezvous point near Selsey Bill on the English coast, peeling off if not needed. Ominously, crews were ordered to bring their steel helmets. Several men foraged for pieces of sheet metal to sit on, aware that they'd need protection from below as well as above. Ernest 'Rod' Rodley,[14] the seasoned 28-year-old skipper of one of the backup Lancs in the 97 Squadron group, aware that the only armour-plating installed for his position in the aircraft was behind his seat, took himself off to the armoury for extra 'padding'. He was told regretfully by the corporal in charge, 'You're too late, sir. We've had quite a demand for armour-plate today.'

Rodley decided to sit on his helmet instead. As a backup aircraft, he knew he shouldn't – probably wouldn't – be flying the full distance, but it was better to be safe than sorry. His real anxiety wasn't for himself; it was for his mother and his wife, whom he'd kissed goodbye at their rented house in Woodhall Spa that morning. For their sake, he was determined to do all he could to return successfully from this disquieting mission. Steel helmets? What were they to expect from the German defences?

At first no one believed the RAF was actually going to send a dozen of their newest bombers 800 miles in daylight. Nobody had penetrated anything like that distance into enemy territory before, let alone in an aircraft that, though it handled beautifully and appeared to be utterly reliable, had scarcely been tested in action. But every precaution had been taken. There'd be diversionary tactics by fighter and other bomber squadrons to draw off enemy attackers, and it was presumed Arthur Harris wouldn't put such a number of his precious new eggs into one basket without having carefully calculated the risk.

After the briefing, as time passed and tension built again, the crews checked and rechecked their aircraft. There was a feeling of tangible relief when the time came to get going. They would set off at 3 p.m., the idea being that they would carry out their task just before dusk, and return under the shelter of darkness. Each aircraft, filled to the brim with fuel (2,154 gallons[15]), carried the relatively light load of four 1,000lb delayed-fuse bombs – an eleven-second delay, designed to give them time to get clear after the drop.

\* \* \*

The good burghers of Augsburg were celebrating the traditional festival of *Plärrer*, which had been held biannually, in April and August, for over a thousand years. Folk in their Sunday best thronged the Exerzierplatz, enjoying the freely flowing beer and snacks from the profusion of little stalls. Children played happily between the marquees and queued impatiently for the funfair rides. The smell of fried *Bratwurst* and cigars filled the air and dance music was played by the local band. It was the time of year when the city came to life, filled with joy and laughter. Thoughts of the war were far from anyone's mind.

Meanwhile, at Waddington and nearby Woodhall Spa, the arc of a Very cartridge fired from the watchtowers lit up the sky. Eight aircraft at each base – two of them backups – started their engines. The propellers began to turn as the giant Merlin engines, one by one, roared into life. High up in the cockpits, the sun warming them through the Perspex, the pilots went over their instruments, waiting for each engine to be ready. If there was no malfunction now, one of the two reserve Lancasters would shut down. At Waddington, all went smoothly. At Woodhall Spa, one of the lead aircraft proved unserviceable, and its pilot shut it down, disappointed.

Rod Rodley, the backup, tensed as he saw the puffs of oily smoke from the port engine of the Lancaster ahead. His instinct had proved correct. He'd be going the full distance. After manoeuvring his aircraft into take-off position, breathing in its strangely comforting blend of leather, glycol, chewing gum and oxygen, he clasped and unclasped his hands on the controls, then made his final checks. Sitting on his steel helmet wasn't exactly comfortable, and Rod tried not to think about how it would feel after several hours in the air, but its protective presence reassured him.

Now he concentrated, easing the throttle levers slowly forward, watching for the Lancaster's tendency to swing to port. If that happened, and you were late correcting it, you might then swing in the other direction, then back again, making the aircraft vacillate. If you couldn't stop it, the undercarriage might break or you might run out of runway – neither a particularly healthy option with a full quota of fuel and bombs.

The huge, dark machine shuddered as it picked up speed and started its take-off run. Listening to the pitch of the engines, Rod pushed the throttle fully forward, and at 105mph they lifted into the sky. His bomb aimer/front gunner, who'd been standing by the wireless operator for take-off in accordance with the official safety instructions, now moved forward – first past the navigator, then squeezing by Rod and the flight engineer, and down through the narrow entrance to the pilot's right, into his own Perspex 'office' in the nose of the aircraft. He adopted a prone position on the padded board below his twin Brownings, looking out through the Perspex nose as the ground fell away beneath them.

Keeping a careful eye on the other aircraft, Rod gained altitude.

They were off. Nerves would be put on hold now until their return. *If* they returned. But no one thought about that. Or, if they did, no one talked about it. Their course took them across the English Channel, flying so low that one front gunner, Bert Dowty, under pilot Bert Crum in *T-Tommy*, one of Nettleton's group, had the unnerving experience of seeing sea spray spatter his turret. Crossing the French coast near Cabourg, just to the west of Le Havre, and lifting their noses to clear the cliffs, each squadron still kept their altitude low, in the hope of avoiding the German *Freya* radar – capable of detecting targets at long range, and therefore alerting defences well in advance. Diversionary operations and fighter sorties over northern France had been organised to distract Luftwaffe intervention, so, with luck, the twelve Lancasters would reach their destination unmolested.

It was a warm day, the sky was clear, and most of the crews were in shirtsleeves as the sun continued to beat down through the large Perspex cockpit. The two squadrons flew 2 miles apart, 97 behind 44. The plan was to head south of Paris to give the enemy the impression that Munich was their target, before changing course over Lake Constance, which straddles the borders of Germany, Austria and Switzerland.

The MAN factory complex was relatively small, hence the need for a low-level visual attack – the best means of achieving the greatest accuracy. Everything seemed set fair, though no one made any presumptions on that score. As they crossed into enemy territory, 97 Squadron noticed that 44 had veered away, slightly north of the prescribed route. 97 stuck to its planned course – providentially, as things turned out.

They'd been right not to take anything for granted, for chance could play a hand in the best-planned operation. Soon after the leading group had crossed the enemy coast, lifting their noses to clear the French cliffs, a section of thirty Messerschmitt Bf109[16] fighters, sent up – ironically – in pursuit of the diversionary activity, was returning to their base near Évreux, west of Paris, when it noticed John Nettleton's Lancasters. Some of the 109s already had their undercarriages down for landing, but now they drew them up again.

*V-Victor*'s pilot, Joe Beckett, was the first to spot them, and shouted a warning over the radio: 'Fighters – eleven o'clock high!'

The 109s plunged down, forced to attack from above as the Lancasters were still hedge-hopping in close formation. Giving each other cover, the RAF gunners fired round after round at the ducking and diving intruders. Nettleton had seen them almost as soon as Beckett. 'There were two or three of them about 1,000 feet above us, but the next thing I knew, they were all around us.' The fighters pounced on Nettleton's second group of three aircraft, hammering ferocious volleys of machine-gun and cannon fire into them. Joe Beckett's aircraft bucked in the air and erupted in black smoke and flames, a nightmare vision of buckled steel and aluminium as it plunged earthwards.

One Lancaster had been downed in a matter of seconds.

As the attackers and the attacked flew on in a furious game of cat-and-mouse, the Messerschmitts focused next on the Lancaster flown by Beckett's friend Bert Crum.

All Bert had heard of Joe Beckett's end was what he could gather from his rear and mid-upper gunners' frantic reports over the intercom against the magpie chattering of machine guns and the roar of the slipstream. There was no time to think about Joe's fate now. Bert and the crew of *T-Tommy* were under relentless attack themselves, and six of the fighters were closing in fast. Bert steeled himself, forcing his hand to keep steady on the controls. He knew they'd be lucky to get out of this. All too soon the closest 109 opened fire. Bert's cockpit shattered and splinters of Perspex whipped through the cabin, cutting his face. But he flew on, his gunners fiercely returning fire.

The other 109s closed in relentlessly, hyenas bringing down a wounded antelope. Both the Lancaster's port engines were now on fire. As the stench of hydraulic fluid and fuel filled the cabin, confused cries filled Bert's ears. He gave the order to jettison the bombs and the aircraft jolted skywards as it was relieved of the weight, but it was too late to save it. In the nose, Bert Dowty watched in mounting fear as the ground rushed towards them. *My God!* he thought. *We're going to crash. Crummy's going to fly straight into the deck!*[17]

The Lancaster wallowed in the air as Bert Crum fought to keep it under some kind of control. By a tremendous combination of skill and muscle power, he managed at last to crash-land safely in a wheat field, not 500 yards from where Beckett had hit the ground.

Two Lancasters down.

Crum's crew scrambled out into the field, and Crum himself followed them calmly. Only one man was left in the aircraft; Bert Dowty was trapped in the nose. The front gunner was beginning to panic; he thought that not only was the Lancaster on fire, but that all the bombs might still be on board. Still calm, a bloodied Crum had taken a crash-axe[18] from its rack in the fuselage, and now used it to break through the Perspex nose. Dowty clambered out fast, panting his gratitude. But Crum was looking across the field to where his friend Beckett's aircraft lay, smoke pouring from it like a Viking funeral.

'You know the drill,' he said to the others. 'Destroy the kite [aircraft] and clear off. I want to see what's happened over there.'

He turned away from them. They were grateful that he'd got them all down alive and they watched in silence as he ran across the field to the burning pyre that had been Beckett's aircraft. They knew what he'd find; there was no doubt his friend was dead. There was nothing more they could do or say.

Individual crews tended to stick together, but close friendships between men on different crews, like the one Crum had with Beckett, were rare. With the chance of death ever-present, there was an unspoken code which discouraged such things. What had just happened was a good example of why that code, though harsh, was also sage. Crum's men knew what their skipper must be going through.

Beckett's crew had not been so lucky. They hadn't had time to jettison their bombs, nor was Beckett able to pull off a controlled crash-landing. His attackers' bullets had hammered along the Lancaster's fuselage and the flames from one of the damaged engines had spread to its body. It had ploughed heavily into the earth and finally been brought to a halt by a copse, by which time the aircraft and its crew were immolated.

Crum's crew turned to the task in hand. The fires on their own Lancaster had fizzled out so, ignoring two German fighters overhead, the navigator fired a flare into the wing of their aircraft. Nothing happened. He fired another, with the same result. Then they attacked the fabric of a wing with their axe, releasing fuel from the tank. Bert Dowty, who, in defiance of standing orders, carried cigarettes and matches in a tobacco tin as part of his escape kit, at last set their own Lancaster alight. It became a funeral pyre itself, taking its secrets and its GEE navigation equipment with it. There was no way either could be allowed to fall into German hands. Splitting into pairs, they made their way to the safety of the woods as the battle above them raged on.[19]

The third of Nettleton's group to be caught was flown by Nick Sandford, who had taught many of his fellow pilots from both 44 and 97 Squadron how to handle the Lancaster. Now he had to put every iota of his skill and experience to the test, and, in a desperate attempt to escape, he took a deep breath and flew unerringly beneath a line of pylons carrying high-tension power cables. But it was no use. Sandford's aircraft – still pursued, all four engines ablaze from enemy rounds, its fuselage ripped apart – could hold out no more. A wing clipped the ground and it cartwheeled, exploding in flames not 2 miles from where Crum and Beckett had come to the end of their raid. There were no survivors.

Three Lancasters down.

Only half of Nettleton's six now remained. The Lancasters' guns were no match for the 109s' 20mm cannon, and during this first encounter the Germans had quickly learned that these unfamiliar British bombers, sleek though they looked, nevertheless carried guns with less firepower and a shorter range than they had themselves. Nettleton now had to watch as a 109 strafed *H-Harry*, in his first Vic, piloted by Dusty Rhodes. The aircraft reared then swooped directly towards him, passing so close that they could see the terrified faces of the doomed crew. 'Smoke poured from Rhodes' cockpit and his port wing caught fire. I thought we were going to collide. We missed by a matter of feet and he crashed beneath me.'[20]

Four Lancasters down.

Nettleton and his wingman, John 'Ginger' Garwell, were now piloting the two remaining 44 Squadron Lancasters. They hadn't escaped multiple hits from the 109s' cannons, which had taken out some of their guns and shredded Garwell's starboard wingtip. Now both pilots tried to avoid the fate of their comrades, flying at breathtakingly low altitude – less than 100ft; sometimes as low as 25ft – following the contours of the land below them, determined not to abandon their operation. Nettleton later told a BBC interviewer, 'You can imagine what that must have been like, 30 tons or so of aircraft, its four engines roaring, driving along at several miles a minute. Horses and cattle scattered in front of us. We saw two German officers out riding. Their horses bolted, and they were still out of control when we last saw them.'[21]

The Lancaster could not be seen to fail. But that very thing seemed more than likely as the fate of the last two aircraft of 44 Squadron's group hung in the balance. Bracing themselves for the worst, putting on as much speed as they could, pounded by gunfire from the pursuing 109s, twisting and turning as best they could and thanking God for their aircraft's brilliant manoeuvrability, Nettleton and Garwell swung through the sky ahead of their hunters, determined to complete their operation against all the odds.

Then fate played another card. The Messerschmitts suddenly pulled away. They were at the end of their flight capacity, and now, short of fuel, had to return to base. A hair's breadth away from disaster, the two survivors of the 44 Squadron detachment were able to fly on. The target was still far distant, but Nettleton knew how much hung on this raid. With enormous dedication, and almost defenceless, he and Garwell kept to their perilous course, often flying at less than 50ft above ground, constantly checking the health of their aircraft, depending on it to survive its battering and win through.

*The view from the Lancaster cockpit*
*while flying in close formation*

97 Squadron, flying behind them on the prescribed route, to the south of the encounter with the Messerschmitts, continued on its way unscathed. Pilot 'Rod' Rodley was able to take note of how people on the ground reacted to the low-flying Lancasters: 'Occasionally you would see some Frenchmen take a second look and wave their berets or their shovels. A bunch of German soldiers doing PT in their singlets broke hurriedly for their shelters as we roared over. The first opposition was a German officer on one of the steamers on Lake Constance firing a revolver at us. I could see him quite clearly, defending the ladies with his Luger against our Browning machine guns.'[22] Passing the eastern end of Lake Constance, they headed north-east towards Lake Ammer, about 40 miles south of Augsburg.

An elderly, bearded Bavarian took pot shots at a Lancaster with a duck rifle as it cleared Lake Ammer. One of the gunners asked the skipper if he could return fire. He was told to leave him alone.

Ahead of 97 Squadron's aircraft, Nettleton and Garwell reached their target without encountering further opposition. They lifted the noses of their Lancasters across low woodland hills and saw the medieval town ahead of them, bathed in the late afternoon sun, the spires of its Gothic churches and the towers of its palaces casting intricate shadows, but Nettleton and Garwell weren't concerned with its beauty; their eyes were searching for a spot where a canal forked north-west from the River Singold to the MAN factory. They saw it an instant later, but their path was impeded by tall chimney stacks, and they veered round to find a clearer approach. As they flew over Augsburg town, the residents celebrating the festival paused in their revelry to look up, point and even wave. The food and beer was set down as delight turned to confusion. Were these Luftwaffe? No one would have seen anything like them before. The merriment was cut short by the sound of anti-aircraft fire. People scattered and fled in alarm. The *Plärrer* festival was over.

Manoeuvring to locate his target, Nettleton closed in, so low that the gunfire from the ground came at him almost horizontally. Nettleton kept his course as if the enemy fire didn't exist, with Garwell close behind him. The factory sheds beneath them, from which workers were running frantically in every direction, looked exactly like those of the models he'd studied back at base, meticulously built using aerial reconnaissance photographs for reference. Nettleton's target was the T-shaped submarine diesel engine shed. As the rooftops flashed beneath them, he and Garwell concentrated on the last push, listening intently to the instructions of their bomb aimers as they closed in. German flak continued to explode around them as they made their final approach.

Nettleton swooped in and dropped his deadly cargo. Now he had to get the hell out of there. He was able to turn for home before the Krupp 88mm anti-aircraft guns managed to draw a bead on him. He couldn't hang around, but after he'd seen his bombs hit their target in a riptide of explosions, he scanned the skies anxiously for Garwell.

'Any sign?' he asked his rear gunner over the intercom.

'Starboard quarter, Skipper – a bit above us. I think he's got a fire in the fuselage.'[23]

Following close behind Nettleton, 'Ginger' Garwell hadn't been so lucky. His aircraft was hit during its approach. As he looked back over his shoulder, he saw that the fuselage aft of the cockpit was an open furnace. The smell of the fire triggered instinctive fear, but Garwell had the courage to overcome it. He struggled to stay on course, determined not to have come so far and fail to complete the job he'd set out to do. Trying not to think of the fate of his mid-upper and rear gunners, whom he was powerless to help, he pressed on through the maelstrom.

The Lancaster reared up as the bomb aimer reported 'Bombs gone'; but smoke was filling the interior as they tried to pull away and follow Nettleton. One of the crew managed to release the ditching escape hatch in the top of the fuselage and the smoke was sucked out amid the scream of the slipstream, but there was no saving the Lancaster. Striving to bring it down safely, Garwell rubbed his burning eyes and saw a row of cottages ahead of him and just below, and beyond them, a railway bridge. Clearing it, he brought the aircraft down in a meadow, sliding 50 yards as the fuselage, destroyed by fire just aft of the wings, broke in two. Garwell and three of his crew survived. The others perished in the flames.

Five of 44 Squadron's six Lancasters were down.

Minutes later, Sherwood's six from 97 Squadron, which had made the journey without interception, flew in for their attack.

By this time, however, the entire German defensive machine was fully geared up, and the two Vics were caught in an inescapable onslaught. Faces set, they made their approach as low as they dared. Sherwood led, closely followed by his two outriders, Brian Hallows and Rod Rodley. Both concentrated on maintaining position and preparing for the final run. 'We were belting at full throttle at about 100 feet towards the targets,' Rodley said.

'I dropped the bombs along the side wall. We flashed across the target and down the other side to about 50 feet, because flak was quite heavy. As we went away I could see light flak shells overtaking us, green balls flowing away on our right and hitting the ground ahead of us. Leaving the target, I looked down at Sherwood's aircraft and saw that there was a little wisp of steam trailing back from it. The white steam turned to black smoke, with fire in the wing. I was slightly above him. In the top of the Lancaster there was a little wooden hatch[24] for getting out if you had to land at sea. I realised that this wooden hatch had burned away and I could look down into the fuselage. It looked like a blow-lamp with the petrol swilling around the wings and the centre section, igniting the fuselage and the slipstream blowing it down. I asked our gunner to keep an eye on him. Suddenly he said, "Oh God, Skip, he's gone. He looks like a chrysanthemum of fire."[25]

At the same time, Rodley's wingman, Brian Hallows, was in trouble. 'I'd just clobbered the sheds we were meant to bomb when we were hit badly, in the starboard wing. A bloody great hole appeared about a yard wide just where the main petrol tank was. And just when I was hoping and praying that he hadn't been hit, I suddenly noticed Sherwood's aircraft was streaming a white plume of smoke from its port wing which soon turned to flames.'[26] Sherwood's Lancaster hit the ground and exploded, but astonishingly he survived. With truly miraculous luck, in the midst of the crash he'd been thrown clear and, still strapped into his seat, landed on a nearby hillside. The rest of his crew were killed.

Six of the twelve Lancasters were now down.

There was nothing for Rodley and Hallows to do but get away as fast as possible after completing their own successful bomb runs. As he turned away, Rodley thanked God for the upside-down tin helmet that he'd been sitting on with such discomfort for so long. It had seen him through a dive down to 200ft as he'd cleared the factory's chimneys and approached the target through a barrage of flak that rattled on the outside of the fuselage like the drumming fingers of a thousand goblins.

Rodley and Hallows kept each other company as they flew back to Woodhall Spa.

The second 97 Squadron Vic now made its approach, but had to bear the brunt of the now fully attuned German gunners. All three pilots had seen Sherwood go down in flames before they made their attack. All three knew last in was always worst off – and all three were badly hit.

Flight Lieutenant David 'Jock' Penman held the first aircraft steady through the hail of flak, listening calmly to the bomb aimer's instructions as they flew in and dropped their bombs, though an enemy shell smashed through the cowling of the inner port engine not 6ft from his seat. Thanks to the Lancaster's resilience, he managed to get away.

Flying Officer Ernest Deverill's Lancaster, the second to approach, was riddled through the starboard inner engine as it flew over the target. The bomber's hydraulic system was wrecked, rendering the gun turrets inoperable. Then hydraulic oil leaked under the mid-upper gun position and caught fire, though this was swiftly extinguished and they too were able to escape.

The third was not so lucky. Warrant Officer Tommy Mycock's *P-Peter* took a direct hit in its forward turret as it made its approach and burst into flames. The bomb aimer must have been killed or at least badly wounded, and the turret's oil supply had caught fire. The burning oil was even now flooding through the body of the aircraft.

That would have been the moment when a pilot might have cut his losses, jettisoned his bombs and found a place to crash-land before the fire took fatal hold. Baling out would have been out of the question. They were far too low. But Mycock stayed at the controls. Ernest Deverill's mid-upper gunner saw him through the open cockpit window as he made the run, sitting calm and upright. Mycock completed his run and dropped his bombs on target. Then his Lancaster reared up, its bomb doors still open, and passed over Penman's aircraft.

A moment later, it exploded in mid-air.

Seven Lancasters down.

Their bombing had been so accurate that the medieval town of Augsburg was spared and there were no civilian casualties, despite the festivities. Twelve-year-old Erika Harbacher was watching the raid from a window of her family's apartment. One of the bombers flew so low that she could clearly see the pilot. His aircraft was in trouble, its fuselage on fire. Erika watched it fly out of sight, trailing smoke and flame. On impulse, she left her building and ran in its wake – until she reached its smouldering wreckage scattered along a railway track. Beside it, she noticed a solitary flying boot. Remembering the pilot, Erika began to cry.

Only five of the twelve Lancasters that had set out would make it home. Four from 97 Squadron, and only Nettleton's from 44. All had varying degrees of battle damage.

Rodley and Hallows had lost contact in the dark, but their flight paths and speeds were so well synchronised that they reached home together. Hallows landed first, adjusting his trim to compensate for his damaged wing, while Rodley held back, giving his fellow pilot time to clear the runway. On landing, they felt relief flood over them at last, irritation at the thought of debriefing, anticipation at the prospect of a hot meal and bed, but also a sense of anticlimax, and the uncomfortable feeling that in less than twenty-four hours they might well be going through the whole thing again.

Well behind them, Deverill's Lancaster was flying on three engines and without hydraulics, but at least he had Penman for company, as a shepherd and guard. As they flew out of the target area, Penman caught the smell of burning from below and wondered briefly which of his companions had been downed there. He couldn't know that the smoke in his nostrils came from the wreck of 'Ginger' Garwell's Lancaster, or that Garwell himself was standing and waving as he flew overhead. They were unmolested on the long flight home, but both pilots knew how much they had to be aware of their exhausted thoughts wandering, of the sensations of relief, even euphoria, that had to be guarded against. For the journey was not over, and the dangers were not past. One slip, one lapse of concentration at the wrong moment, could be fatal.

Meshed with these feelings were those of panic and sudden tension – were those enemy fighters over there, or specks of dirt on the canopy? Then there was the seductive yearning just to fall asleep. On top of all this, the skipper had to keep track of the rest of the crew, calling them on the intercom, checking on them. This was enough to cope with in an undamaged aircraft, but if you had to fly home on three engines and battered hydraulics, as Deverill did, it was ten times worse. At last they were over the British coast and could begin the long descent to Woodhall Spa. Both landed safely, but Deverill was to learn that his Lancaster, which he'd coaxed home with such devotion, was beyond repair.

Nettleton, flying alone and well ahead of the other four survivors, was having navigational problems; his master gyro-compass wasn't working, and he was having to rely on the less accurate P4 compass below the panel on his left in the cockpit. Despite the navigator's best efforts, the aircraft was a long way off track and well behind its estimated time of arrival. To make matters worse, it was running low on fuel. By half-past midnight, and with no idea of their position, Nettleton decided to call for help. His wireless operator leapt into action, tapping out 'SOS' in Morse code. Everyone held their breath. When would they get a response? *Would* they get a response? After seconds that seemed like hours, a welcome crackle was heard.

'They're sending us to Squire's Gate.'

The navigator studied his map. He was astounded; they had somehow missed England altogether and were now over the Irish Sea, south of Blackpool.

They were saved. In the nick of time. Ten hours after they'd taken off from Waddington, they landed safely.

*John Nettleton VC*

Operation MARGIN had been a costly exercise. Not only were eight of the twelve Lancasters gone, but of the original eighty-five aircrew (Nettleton had been carrying a second pilot), forty-nine were missing in action, mostly presumed killed. In the event, twelve of them had survived their ordeal, though were destined to spend the rest of the hostilities as POWs.

At Waddington, nineteen-year-old WAAF wireless operator Pip Beck remembered the moment she heard the news.

'It was not until the next morning that I learned the terrible toll the raid had exacted. There was no way to express the horror that I, like everyone else on the station, felt. The whole camp seemed shocked and silent ... thirty-five men missing – thirty-five empty bunks, thirty-five empty places at the table, shared between the Officers' and the Sergeants' Messes. Many of us wondered if it was worth it.'[27]

Nevertheless, as much spin had to be put on it as possible. Though the damage to the MAN factory hadn't been as thorough as had been hoped, sufficient harm had been done to hold up production, it was claimed, for several weeks. However, Brian Hallows, one of the 97 Squadron pilots, noted in his diary: 'Over half the bombs dropped failed to explode.'[28] In fact, only five of the seventeen bombs actually dropped on the MAN plant failed to go off; but although the others damaged four main machine shops, only 3 per cent of the total capacity of the plant was destroyed, and most of the damage was to roofs and walls, not to machinery.

Hallows concluded that it had been 'a bad way to spend an afternoon'.

\* \* \*

U-boat engine production continued at Augsburg after a negligible interruption, as German newspapers and broadcasts were quick to emphasise. And the RAF's 58 per cent casualty rate was far too high. Daylight raids in normal circumstances were clearly far too risky. On the other hand, the lessons learned paved the way for the establishment of a 'Pathfinder', target-finding and marking, force within the RAF. With more sophisticated navigational and bomb-aiming equipment, Lancasters would be able to operate more accurately and from greater heights in the future. The raid had displayed heroism and fortitude under fire. It also remained the longest low-level infiltration of the war.

The press and British propaganda played up the raid as much as possible. The Ministry of Information proclaimed it a triumph. The popular Sunday weekly, *The People*, hailed it as 'WAR'S MOST DARING RAID' on 19 April. The *Sunday Pictorial* ran 'AMAZING DAY RAID BY THE RAF'; while *The Observer* led with 'AUGSBURG SUCCESS'.

The roles of the men who flew the bombers were highlighted. John Nettleton felt a keen responsibility for the loss of so many under his command and was uncomfortable with the part he and a number of his fellow surviving airmen were expected to play as celebrities in order to boost war morale. He was quickly promoted to Wing Commander.

Nettleton's Victoria Cross had come at the recommendation of Arthur Harris. John Sherwood's Victoria Cross recommendation was to be revised down to the Distinguished Service Order – 'if he is later to be found alive'[29] – a decision resented by Brian Hallows, among others. 'The myth had grown up that Nettleton had been leading the twelve aircraft, but he bloody well wasn't. He led six and Sherwood led six and he did just as much and should have had a VC.'[30] But the fact was that Nettleton had got home, and Sherwood hadn't.

When the news came through of Sherwood's survival, no one was happier than his wife. Who cared about medals, as long as John was safe? He was a prisoner of war, and she didn't know how long it would be before she saw him again; but one day, she was sure, he would come home.

A further slew of gallantry medals were awarded, both to the living and the dead. It was a very public demonstration of the faith Britain had placed and would place in the hands of such men. Winston Churchill said, 'We must plainly regard the attack ... as an outstanding achievement of the Royal Air Force. Undeterred by heavy losses at the outset, 44 and 97 Squadrons pierced and struck a vital point with deadly precision in broad daylight. Pray convey the thanks of His Majesty's Government to the officers and men who accomplished this memorable feat of arms in which no life was lost in vain.'[31]

The urbane Chief of the Air Staff, Charles Portal, wrote, 'I would like 44 and 97 Squadrons to know the great importance I attach to this gallant and successful attack on the diesel engine factory at Augsburg. Please give them my warmest congratulations and thanks.'

Arthur Harris, who always couched his official pronouncements in the most Churchillian way possible, pressed all the most positive propaganda buttons in his contribution, as well as intelligently boosting Bomber Command's key role in the war.

*Convey to the crews of 44 and 97 Squadrons who took part in the Augsburg raid, the following:*

*The resounding blow which has been struck at the enemy's submarine building programme will echo round the world. The gallant adventure penetrating deep into the heart of Germany in daylight and pressed home with outstanding determination in the face of bitter and unforeseen opposition takes its place among the most courageous operations of the war. It is moreover yet another fine example of effective cooperation with the other services by striking at the very sources of the enemy effort. The officers and men who took part, those who returned and those who fell, have indeed served their country well.*[32]

Nettleton himself was specific in his praise of his aircraft: 'In the Lancaster we have got the answer for heavy bombing. We have tremendous confidence in everything about the Lancasters and in the workers who are turning them out in such numbers. We know we are only sent out to attack the most worthwhile targets. We believe that the way to win the war is to have our own spring offensive before Hitler has his, and in places not of his choice but ours.'

Within five weeks of the raid, Nettleton, still keenly aware of the cost of the Augsburg operation in terms of human life, and the reluctant focus of propaganda attention, found himself in command of 44 Squadron. At a London cocktail party on 25 May, he met WAAF Section Officer Betty Havelock, and escorted her home. Less than a week later, he had proposed and been accepted. She managed a transfer from London to a base not far from Waddington, and the couple married in Lincoln on 17 July.

It was not to be a long marriage. A little less than a year later, on 12 July 1943, aged twenty-six, Nettleton joined an operation to Turin, part of the initiative against Mussolini's crumbling regime and a bare fortnight before the Italian dictator's fall. He never returned. Betty Nettleton gave birth to his son seven months later, in February 1944. He would never meet his heroic father.

\* \* \*

In the end, the Augsburg raid had sent the desired message to the enemy. From now on, no part of their occupied territory would be safe from Allied air attack, and the heart of Germany itself would be under threat. The chief of the Luftwaffe, Hermann Göring, a keen huntsman, had been in the habit of boasting that, 'If ever enemy bombers fly over the Fatherland, you can call me Meier.'[33] It wasn't long before a joke was circulating in anti-Nazi Berlin: when the air-raid sirens went off, people said that 'Meier was sounding his hunting horn!'

Göring had been very wrong in his assertion that 'No enemy plane will fly over the Reich territory'. The RAF was to prove that there was a lot worse to come for the Germans, and Bomber Command's Lancasters would be leading the charge.

# CHAPTER FIVE

# JOINING UP TOGETHER, TRAINING TOGETHER, DYING TOGETHER

Ron Needle joined up as soon as he could after his eighteenth birthday.

'I wanted to get into the war in any way I could. I wasn't confident enough in my own abilities to apply for the likes of pilot or navigator, so I decided trying to be a gunner would give me the best opportunity to get involved. I didn't want to set my sights too high, and being a gunner would also mean I'd get into the war quicker.'

Ron's father knew what war meant; it hadn't been many years since he'd been in the thick of it himself, during the First World War. But he and his wife hid their anxiety from Ron. 'Neither of them said a word. They simply thought that families all over the country were going through the same thing and it wouldn't have been right to make a fuss about a son going to war. Of course, I had no idea at all about the risks I would face or the deaths I would see. You just didn't think about those things.' After reporting to the RAF Air Crew Reception Centre in London's St John's Wood, Ron was kitted out then dispatched to Bridlington in Yorkshire where he encountered a 'horrible sergeant' and a 'kindly officer'. The sergeant taught him discipline while the officer 'was a true gentleman'. When Ron's young aunt invited him to her wedding, he applied for a weekend pass and was bitterly disappointed to be turned down.

'Feeling rather low, I went to bed very early and started to write a letter to my girl, Sylvia. I looked up and, to my surprise, the officer had entered the room. He said he realised how I felt and if I promised to be back by midnight on Sunday, I could have my pass after all. I was elated, thrilled to go home and show everyone my uniform. I also made sure I was back to base on time!'

Homesickness was something else the young trainees had to contend with, all the more so if they were far away. From his navigator's course in Canada, where many recruits were being sent for training, Ken Darke, who would eventually team up with Ron's Lancaster crew, wrote to his brother Peter:

> I certainly realise the importance of my job and am doing my best at it. I came second highest in our 6 weeks intermediate exams but naturally it all depends on how you make out in the finals. Naturally, even though Canada is a grand place, I am just longing to get home and see the folks – and to see the familiar sights of London once more. It'll be a great day when it does come, as come it must.[1]

Those left behind would miss their loved ones too. Not only in Britain, but throughout the Dominions. Britain never really stood alone. Men and women from across the world, who had the opportunity of staying safely where they were, were soon volunteering for the RAF, answering the call of what they still thought of as the 'Motherland'. Australia was among the first of those countries to declare war on Hitler's Germany, and Australians were among the first to join the fight. They were swiftly followed by New Zealanders and Canadians, Rhodesians and South Africans. Volunteers came from the United States even before the attack on Pearl Harbor. They came from the Caribbean, from India and Nigeria. Many Poles served valiantly, together with Czechs, Belgians and Frenchmen – all united in their desire to face the common enemy and expunge a great evil from the world.

*Stan Shaw during his early RAF training*

When he walked into the RAF recruiting office, 28-year-old hosiery knitter Stanley Shaw, from Nottinghamshire, was taking the first step on the path that would lead him, and those who followed him, on an astonishing personal journey. His young daughter Elaine remembered: 'I didn't see much of him after he joined – he would come home on leave now and then but they were fleeting visits. I would sometimes go for a walk with my dad when he was home as far as the Hemlock Stone. I felt so proud to be next to him, holding his hand and feeling on top of the world.'[2]

Shaw, a quiet and kindly man beneath his gritty determination, missed Elaine as keenly as she missed him. Elaine had been packed off double-quick to her grandparents in Sutton-in-Ashfield, just outside Mansfield, where her mum hoped she'd be safe from the bombing. Her dad went to train as a rear gunner. From his digs in Blackpool he wrote mournfully about it to his wife, Elsie, but his letter hints at other news.

*Darling,*

*I was a bit surprised when I received no letter yesterday. I hope you are not ill, or Elaine, so that you cannot get out. I am having a pretty rough time just now. I am confined to billets with a septic ankle and vaccinia[3] – neither serious – similar symptoms to flu only a lot worse. Well dear I hope you have got the pram from next door, it will most likely save you a lot if you have. Have you got anything else for Baby yet – you mustn't leave things too late, you know, although I know you won't. I shall bring you some chocolate and Elaine some Blackpool rock when I come home. I know I shall receive a letter from you tomorrow and then I shall know when I ought to apply for leave.*

*I am damned fed up with this place; we were out drilling all Wednesday in pouring rain so there wasn't a chap in the billets or squad for that matter who was not lousy next day. It's bloody ridiculous – it's a wonder we didn't all refuse to carry on, but that would cancel all leave. I didn't write yesterday because I expected a letter from someone but none came so I shall expect a letter tomorrow.*

*Well darling I can't think just now so you must excuse me and don't worry too much about me – I shall be all right I think, after tomorrow, when I get my old socks to wear under these hard things we have now. Tell Elaine I will write her a letter next time. So Cheerio.*

*Best love*

*Stan & Daddy[4]*

He ended his letter with forty-five kisses.

Pamela, Elaine's baby sister, arrived on 25 January 1942, and, after two years with her grandparents, Elaine returned home to help out her mother. Elsie was working, making gas masks at the Boots factory in Nottingham, so Elaine became a little mother to Pam. 'I would pick my sister up from the nursery, and start doing some housework ready for when my mum got home.' Elaine wasn't yet nine. At least their family income had had a boost a couple of months earlier when Elsie received an official notification from the Air Ministry confirming her Family Allowance in respect of Stan's RAF service: one pound, eighteen shillings and sixpence (about £1.95). And there was more good news; when Pamela was born, Stan was given leave to see her. Elaine was delighted.

Letters were important, a crucial link to life away from the brutality of battle, and after he'd returned to training in Wales, Stan wrote to his young daughter.

> Dear Elaine
>
> Your Mummy tells me you are a good girl now that you sleep by yourself always, and that you help her by washing the pots.
>
> Well, pet, I think that is very nice of you and I feel like kissing you for it because your Mummy has such a lot to do with Pamela being a little baby, and I want you to help her always and be a good girl. How is Pamela, is she a good girl? Don't you think she is nice, because I think you both are.
>
> Well, goodbye love
> Daddy

This letter ended with ninety-one kisses.

Stan's square-bashing gave way to gunnery training. They used twin-engined Avro Ansons, fitted with a turret containing two Browning machine guns, often linked to cameras instead of live ammunition, and would practise firing at RAF fighters making mock attacks. Another exercise involved using live ammunition to target a drogue towed by a light aircraft. James Flowers, a 'Tail-end Charlie' like Stan, and also from Nottinghamshire, remembered thinking that 'the pilot of the aircraft was in more danger of being hit than the drogue!'[5]

New recruits arrived in their droves. Ken Johnson was only fifteen when the war started.

'We moved out of Sheffield to Hexthorpe, just outside Doncaster, because of the bombing. The village was on high ground so we could sit and watch all the bombs falling on Sheffield. A lot of family friends were bombed out of their homes so we were all too aware of what war from the air meant.'[6]

Despite Ken's youth – 'I was just a schoolboy and could never imagine what the war would mean to me, and how it would touch my life' – he was eager to enlist. 'I first tried to join the RAF aged seventeen, but they sent me home until I was eighteen; by then I was at work making cables for barrage balloons at British Ropes, a reserved occupation; I was nineteen before they let me go.' At last he was sent to the RAF Induction Centre near Lord's Cricket Ground in London, 'to be kitted out, and also inoculated and vaccinated, walking between two rows of nurses armed with needles which they happily plunged into one's arms'.

Ken was going to be a mid-upper gunner. The next step for him was to join an Operational Training Unit, where he did his share of square-bashing, but also learned about aircraft recognition and the ins and outs of the Brownings; 'stripping them down and reassembling them both blindfold and with gloves on, to replicate the conditions we might be under in action'. They also had to undertake tasks that didn't seem to have much to do with flying: 'We had the worst corporal in the unit. He made us march everywhere at light infantry pace, almost jogging. We were always at each destination ahead of all the others and had to wait for them.'

There was also guard duty.

'The rifles had no ammunition but there was a reason for this. A previous cadet had been on guard with a loaded rifle and a local bobby decided, for a joke, to creep up on him from behind a wall. The lad clocked him and gave the challenge, "Who goes there?" When he got no reply, the cadet shot a hole through the bobby's helmet. We weren't told the state of the policeman's trousers but from then on no live ammunition was allowed.'

At last serious gunnery training beckoned, and Ken's section transferred by train to Dalcross, near Inverness. Here the men were given their first flying suits, and Ken's experience followed the same course as Stan's and James's.

'After a few days in the classroom doing the usual recognition and gun practice, the big day arrived. Clad in flying gear, we marched out to the waiting planes. I'd never been in an aircraft before – what an adventure! The whole process was such an exciting event, from putting your kit on, getting airborne, flying! It was fabulous! Beautiful scenery to fly over, and as it was November the high mountain tops were covered in snow. For a Doncaster lad this was a hell of an adventure! Of course I had no idea what the future would hold, or what risks would be involved. I just wanted to get back at the Germans, and this was my means of doing it. None of us discussed the dangers we might face, or that some of us might not survive. The thought of death didn't enter our heads. We were young, determined, and up for the fight!'

* * *

By May 1942 the recruits noticed that something was brewing. Several crews were being seconded away from training duties, together with their aircraft. Lancasters were coming off the production line in increasing numbers and the tide was turning. In the last days of May, Gordon Mellor, based at RAF Elsham Wolds with 103 Squadron, felt a change in the air.

'Additional aircraft and crew began to arrive, adding to the congestion in all areas of the base. The engineering ground staff were being pushed to get all aircraft up to full flying condition. It looked as if a maximum operational effort was in the wind, but nobody was saying what.'[7]

At Bomber Command in High Wycombe, Arthur Harris was fighting to maintain his reputation and that of his force. He still believed that strategic bombing – targeting every aspect of the German nation; industrial, military and civilian – was the best way to shorten the war. This was a period of trial and error for Harris, who needed to justify these ideas. He had not yet succeeded in persuading his own superiors and the War Cabinet by dint of the Augsburg raid and those that followed. And while Lancaster production was gearing up, it was by no means yet equal to fulfilling the tasks he had in mind.

Working and chain-smoking from dawn to dusk, as well as dealing in his usual brusque manner with the business of the day at his regular briefings, Harris decided to launch a major attack on Cologne. German defences were made up of a series of territorial boxes, each monitored by a radar controller who would dispatch small groups of night-fighters to intercept enemy intruders. Harris planned to amass 1,000 bombers and fly them in a stream towards their target. Some feared the increased possibility of disastrous mid-air collisions when so many aircraft were flying in a close-packed line, but Harris believed it was the best way to swamp the German defences.

Guide aircraft equipped with GEE would pinpoint his chosen targets.

'The stage of the war has been reached when the morale of the German people is likely to be seriously affected by an unprecedented blow of great magnitude in the West at a time when they are experiencing difficulties on the Russian Front. Apart from the effect on morale of such an attack, the unprecedented damage which will be caused is bound to have a considerable effect on the issue of the war.'[8]

Harris knew that the raid could be make-or-break for his strategy, and that not everyone shared his conviction that bombing alone was the key to winning the war. As the great force gathered from hundreds of bases across the country, tension must have mounted in his heart, and the heart of every crewman, every WAAF bent over maps in operations rooms, and many in the corridors of power. The only way Harris could amass such a large number of bombers was by co-opting aircraft from the Training Units, where new aircrew were undertaking their initial preparations for operations. Alex Shaw had already completed one full tour in action, and was now away from the front line, training new pilots, when the call came.

'To find 1,000 crews they had to rope in instructors,' Shaw remembered, and he was ordered to join forces with an operational unit to make up their numbers. 'We went up to Snaith, in the East

Riding of Yorkshire, taking our old training aircraft. The unit there had modern, up-to-date Wellingtons. Our ground staff Flight Sergeant told us that his opposite number was laying bets that none of us would get back, because of our clapped-out aircraft.'[9]

\* \* \*

The night of 30/31 May 1942 saw a total of 1,047 bombers home in on Cologne. It was still early in the Lancaster's career, but seventy-five of them took part – a small but significant portion of the overall force. Few were lucky enough to fly them. The target-finders, flying ahead of the main stream, did their job perfectly. Eight hundred and forty-eight aircraft pounded the city with devastating effect and far greater accuracy than anything achieved the previous year.

One airman recalled his crew's elation: 'This was payback. We had suffered in the Blitz for years and were full of venom and hate for all things German. I was twenty years old, and twice before I joined up I was nearly killed by bombs falling on London. We had a heavy load, hundreds of incendiaries and big high explosives. The incendiaries going off were like sudden platinum-coloured flashes, which slowly turned to red. We saw many flashes going from white to red and then our great bombs burst in the centre of them. The flames were higher than I had ever seen before. Buildings were skeletons in the midst of fires.'[10]

Forty-one aircraft were lost; but 12,000 buildings were destroyed and nearly 500 people killed. In June, Harris followed this success with two more thousand-bomber raids in quick succession, on Essen and Bremen, but it was Cologne that shocked the Germans most. It also confirmed Hermann Göring's loss of standing in the eyes of the Führer, from which he never recovered. Harris and Bomber Command gained the attention they'd fought for; the massive aerial bombardment of Germany would continue apace. The idea of crushing the enemy's morale by bombing their cities and diverting their resources to the business of damage repair and increased defences, including the construction of shelters to protect civilians, appeared sound. But it came at an enormous cost, not just for the German population on the ground, but for the Bomber Command airmen in the skies above them.

More and more recruits were needed to replace the ever-increasing casualties. Huge numbers were going into training, taking their first steps in a process that would produce finished bomber crews, but of the 125,000 men who served in Bomber Command, some 75,000 – 60 per cent of operational airmen – would be killed, wounded or taken prisoner.

Nonetheless, the bombing campaign went from strength to strength. Alongside the devastation of cities and civilian targets, more precise attacks on military strongholds were also carried out. To achieve this, the Telecommunications Research Establishment (TRE) at Malvern worked on more sophisticated radar and navigational equipment, whose development had also been stimulated by earlier criticism of bombing accuracy.

OBOE was introduced at the end of 1942, utilising radio connections between an aircraft and two separate ground stations, which guided the crew by a series of audible 'dots and dashes'. The signals would tell them which side of the track they were on, so they could correct their approach to the target, and when to release their weapons. It was a significant improvement on GEE, and was used throughout the war.

The continuing success of the bombing campaign through late 1942 also saw the formal creation of a specialist Pathfinder Force (PFF) – flying ahead of the main sections of the bomber stream to pinpoint targets and mark them with flares. The initiative didn't meet with Arthur Harris's immediate approval – he didn't want his best men diverted from direct bombing duties – but it wouldn't take long for the PFF to prove its value in the operations that would soon follow. The thousand-bomber raids, however, each took around 2.6 million gallons of fuel – twenty-five trainloads – which made them virtually impossible to repeat.[11] They also drained too many resources from Training Units when they really needed to devote themselves to their essential role: training the vital new aircrew as

Harris began to implement his plan for a frontline strength of 4,000 heavy bombers.

Within a year of the Cologne raid, it was the Lancaster that became, in the eyes of friend and foe, the Allied bomber whose nightly forays were to be either applauded or feared.[12]

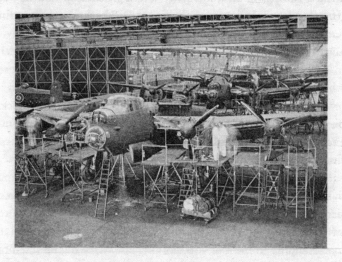

*Lancasters under production at the
Woodford factory in 1943*

As Lancaster production increased, more and more men were needed to fly them.

When the instructors at the Operational Training Units were satisfied that the men in their charge were ready, the time came for crewing up – forging themselves into a unit, ready to take one of the giant bombers to war. The men themselves were shocked by the process – it was simple, unscientific and totally arbitrary. Large groups of airmen gathered to self-select the men with whom they would fly and perhaps die. Casual and swift, the ritual would normally take place in a large hut, hangar or Mess room, cleared for the occasion. It was an unnerving experience for the freshly fledged navigators, bomb aimers, wireless operators, pilots, engineers and gunners, all feeling a bit like girls at a school dance, waiting to be asked to take the floor. It cut both ways; crewmen could approach pilots, but the pilots were the ones who made the final decisions that would determine the makeup of their crews.

Don MacIntosh entered the room to find hundreds of uniformed airmen thronging around, many looking bemused and nervous. After leaving the Glasgow police, Don had become a fully trained Lancaster pilot; at least he had the chance to take the initiative in any encounter and could rely on his own very strong self-confidence to carry him through. Nevertheless, it all seemed pretty abrupt when it came down to it:

'Inside the hut, a grey-haired Warrant Officer rapped his knuckles on the table. "All right, chaps, sort yourselves out. I'll leave you now, and when you have a full crew, go next door and give the names to the WAAF corporal." He paused. "Don't take too long about it."

'Trainee pilots like me now had to find airmen, more ignorant of flying than the pilots, who were willing to entrust their lives to our slender and unproven abilities. All were aware of the Russian roulette in which they were taking part. The only clue for both was the man standing in front of you; nothing else. Crewing up resembled a blind date, but was as important as a marriage, and potentially more lethal.'[13]

Former instructors who hadn't yet flown operationally, and men over twenty-five, were favourites, so Don found that, 'I didn't exactly find people falling over themselves to crew up with me. It may have been my thick Scottish accent, which made them think perhaps I was thick, and the fact that I looked even younger than most of the ex-schoolboys.' Don also had his own ideas. He felt that the two most important crew members were his navigator and rear gunner. The selection of these two specialists was crucial.

But selection cut both ways. A couple of airmen might have teamed up or made friends in training and wanted to be taken as a package. 'Gunners liked to fly with their chums,' Don reminded himself as he trawled the crowded room; navigators in one knot, flight engineers in another, and so on.

So far Don had only managed to get a half-promise out of a wireless operator and a rear gunner, Geoff, a stocky eighteen-year-old with darting eyes who smelt of engine oil. Geoff approached Don in the crewing-up room with a mate in tow. 'Skipper, this is Jock. He's a mid-upper gunner and we'd like to fly together.' Don, already feeling a lot better now that Geoff had called him 'Skipper', shook hands and gave Jock an appraising glance. Jock looked almost too good to be true. A gamekeeper in civilian life, he was dignified, tall and muscular. His keen, grey-blue eyes bore out the general impression. 'He looked as if he'd arrived from the casting lot.'

The wireless operator returned – perhaps he didn't get a better offer – to declare he would give Don a try. Together they scanned the emptying room and found a flight engineer soon afterwards. Now they just had a navigator and a bomb aimer to go. Don made for a group of bomb aimers and approached two men standing together. They politely introduced themselves. George, a big, jovial Irishman, and Peter, who looked as if he'd escaped from a painting of some Elizabethan noblemen, hadn't crewed up yet, but neither wanted to cut the other out when Don made his offer.

'Let's toss for it,' said Peter. 'Your shout, George!'

Peter won, and perhaps fate had sided with him in more ways than one.

Don had less luck finding a navigator. His spirits began to sink.

'I sat in the near-empty hall, stuffing myself with the usual fare of bread, margarine and lashings of Tate & Lyle syrup, thinking what the hell to do. As if on cue, I saw a tall, smart-looking sergeant march in. He turned, displaying the "N" brevet I was looking for. Wasting no time, I addressed him. "Excuse me, but are you crewed up?"

'"No-o."

'"Well, look, I've got a full crew bar a navigator. I think they're pretty good. Would you like to join us?"'

The man looked cagey, perhaps hedging his bets, but he did join Don for a cup of tea.

'What were you doing before?' asked Don.

'I was halfway through a science degree at Oxford. My parents were captured by the Japs in Malaya, and I thought I'd better help win the war and get them home. My name's Nigel Hawkins. Here's my initial.' At last he grinned, pointing to the 'N' on his chest. 'May I ask your name, and your curriculum vitae?'

'MacIntosh – Don. You're baffling me with big words,' Don replied, laughing. 'I left school at fourteen, but I acquired a glancing knowledge of the Classics, taught to me by a baldy old bastard who crept up on me and banged my knuckles with a steel ruler.'

Nigel finished his tea, still undecided, but was friendly enough as he stood to leave. 'See you, Mac. I'll let you know tomorrow.'

The following day, his answer was positive and the future was set for Don's new crew.

*Don MacIntosh as a newly qualified pilot*

Unsurprisingly, with hundreds of men from all parts of the world, all walks of life, all differing characters coming together and matching up as best they could, not all fits turned out to be ideal.

Ron Needle found crewing up daunting – even intimidating. He felt shy in the vast crowd of airmen, and confused. Everyone wanted to be picked, to get it over with, but that desire was accompanied by a curious reluctance. Would Ron dare turn down a pilot whom he didn't instinctively trust?

'It was simply a lottery. A lottery of life and death. You didn't realise it at the time, of course, but you were choosing what would become a new family, people you would live alongside, and ultimately might die alongside. There was no rhyme or reason. Did you like the look of him? The cut of his jib? Did he sound pleasant when he spoke?'

No one even knew if the person they were crewing up with was actually good at his job. Still nervous of his own skills and prospects, Ron teamed up with another gunner, Billy Swift. The two men gave each other confidence, and after a few circuits of the room, sizing up both the competition and potential new crewmates, they eventually found five like-minded – or so they thought – people they could go to war with. At first all went well. They were sent to RAF Bruntingthorpe, not too far from Birmingham, so it was easy for Ron to get home. As many crews did, they socialised together, and taking his newfound friends to his family home was a special occasion.

'I was so pleased. My crew were my new family and I was introducing them to my old family! We all went on the train; the lads were excited to be getting away from the base and doing something different. My mum and dad were very proud to see us all in our uniforms, but I knew I was such a worry to them then. My sisters, aged twenty-five, seven and five, were all there and they were all so excited to meet my crew. Everyone had put on their Sunday best! They pulled out all the stops and scrimped together some food and drink for a celebration lunch, a few beers and lots to eat. We had such a good time; the war seemed so far away. Then we went to the pub nearby with my dad. It was crowded with locals, and as there were no RAF bases nearby it was a novelty for them to see a bomber crew. Lots of people came up to us to talk, and thank us for what we were doing. My dad was very proud to be with us all. I was only sorry that my girlfriend Sylvia couldn't be there.'

But tensions were building back at base. The crew didn't get on with the pilot, who was domineering to a fault. The crunch came on their very first training flight, which would put anyone on their mettle whatever the circumstances, let alone men new to the military and new to flying. Their aircraft was caught in severe turbulence, thrown around and battered in the clouds. The panic on board was made worse by the pilot's intransigence. Ron remembered: 'When the navigator told the pilot to change course to 240, he replied, "We'll change course when I say so." When the bomb aimer was finally able to announce they were ready for a practice target run, the skipper said, "We'll be ready when I tell you."'

Their ill-feeling was cemented during that awful trip, which was crowned by having to make an emergency landing, leaving many of the crew with their nerves shredded. But it showed how vital it was to be in a unit that gelled. Ron's colleagues complained to their Commanding Officer. The upshot was that their pilot – a brave man who would go on to win the DFC, but a bad mismatch here – was transferred. The navigator, mid-upper gunner and wireless operator were also grounded and replaced as well.

But good came out of bad, for it was at this moment that pilot Jimmy Scott, wireless operator Harry Stunell, and navigator Ken Darke appeared. Happily crewed up, Ron Needle and his fellow flyers were ready to take on the world. In a Lancaster. They were not disappointed. As he walked across the airfield, Ron Needle caught his first sight of it: 'It was a wonderful looking machine and I thought we were damn lucky to be going to war in it. With the Lanc, the rest of my crew and all our training and preparation, I was delighted to be part of this complete war machine. I had every faith in us and her.'

Ron's crew may have been eager, but they were all embarking on a journey into the unknown. And fear was something everyone had to come to terms with; it could settle on you at any time. Ken Trent, from Becontree, on the fringe of east London, was aware of his own apprehension when, as a 22-year-old Lancaster pilot, he approached his first posting, at Barnetby le Wold in Lincolnshire.

'It was a beautiful English summer's day, warm and with few clouds. The base which was to be my first operational posting was 3 miles away across the fields. With nothing to do but walk and think, my mind started wandering and suddenly I was gripped with a feeling which until now had never troubled me.

'Fear.

'It came down on me like a black curtain. How does one cope with it? In a few days I would be flying high above enemy Germany, hundreds of miles away. Amid guns and searchlights in the dark, with the lives of six other men depending on me. The terror of what could happen was suddenly very real, there in that English summer lane. The heavy kitbag weighed me down, my feet began to drag, and the confidence which had buoyed me up until now seemed to drain away into the dust. I forced my feet to continue, but as I walked the fear walked with me. The kitbag got heavier, I was hot, shaking and had now completely lost my nerve. *Will I ever walk back down this lane again, or is this a one-way journey? For God's sake, pull yourself together. You have a good crew; you can't just let them down, and yourself down. What's wrong with you? JUST DO IT!*

'But it was no good. I stopped and turned. All around me was typically quaint, English beauty. The enormity of what I was about to do was terrifying. This is what I had striven for, worked and trained for, for years. This is what I so badly wanted. Or was it?

'I knew I had come too far to back out. Hitching my kitbag higher on my shoulder, I gritted my teeth and forced my feet onwards. The gates of the base finally appeared, and, after a final look down the lane, I presented myself at the Guard House. I was in, and there was to be no turning back.'[14]

\* \* \*

The winter of 1942/43 marked a massive turning point in the fortunes of war. In October and November 1942, the Second Battle of El Alamein saw German and Italian forces routed. Soon afterwards, in February 1943, after six months of bitter fighting, the German-held city of Stalingrad fell to the Red Army. Bomber Command followed through with one of the most daring raids the Lancaster ever took part in.

Operation Chastise took place in mid-May 1943. Later known as the Dambusters raid, it was undertaken in great secrecy, using Lancasters that had been adapted to carry the bouncing 'Upkeep' bomb developed by Barnes Wallis to breach the Möhne, Eder, Schwelme and Sorpe dams, which secured the Ruhr's massive industrial water supply. 617 Squadron, a specially created force commanded by 24-year-old Guy Gibson, flew in on the night of 16/17 May. Nineteen Lancasters were involved.

The raid sustained heavy losses; eight Lancasters were shot down and fifty-three airmen were killed. In the end, the Ruhr industry's water supply wasn't badly affected – remarkable in view of the fact that two direct hits on the Möhne dam caused a breach 250ft wide and 292ft deep – 330 million tons of water flooded 50 miles of land in the western Ruhr region as a result. Eleven small factories were destroyed, along with ninety-two houses; a further 114 factories and 971 houses were damaged. Two power stations were destroyed and seven others damaged. Coal and steel production, and hydroelectric power, were severely affected. German resources were stretched to the limit to make good the destruction

The flooding of the surrounding farmland caused chaos and claimed many lives. At least 1,650 people were killed, of whom 1,026 were foreign prisoners of war and forced labourers.[15] But the raid was an even bigger propaganda success than Augsburg and made stars of both 617 Squadron and its commander. Bomber Command, and the Lancaster in particular, was held in the public spotlight of admiration and hope.

Chastise was perhaps the most famous of the precision operations that, despite some misgivings, increasingly went hand-in-hand with strategic raids. Operation Gomorrah became one of the most infamous.

In tandem with the now-UK-based US 8th Army Air Force, Bomber Command planned a massive assault on Hamburg – Germany's second city and the world's largest port. Still trading with neutral countries, it was also a centre for U-boat and other military manufacture.

Although Hamburg was outside the range of OBOE, it was an ideal target for H2S, a relatively new and more sophisticated navigation aid that the Telecommunications Research Establishment had come up with early in 1943. H2S was a ground-mapping system that operated in the same way that radar had been used during the Battle of Britain to detect incoming enemy aircraft. A ground station transmitted a radio wave that would bounce off solid objects at a distance and return to the receiver, which could display the solid object on a screen. By measuring the angle of the transmitted radio wave and the time the signal took to return to the receiver, a picture of the location, height and speed of enemy aircraft could be built.

In Bomber Command, the H2S radar was carried in the aircraft itself, which sent out and received the signals – with the radio beam tilted downwards, it was the ground, and solid objects like dams or bridges, that reflected the signal back to the screen to give an indication of the terrain below. Versatile in the extreme, it could also be used for general navigation since it could identify prominent landmarks at long range. Coastlines were particularly easy to identify, as were large river junctions. Cities were more difficult to pinpoint as any radar beam was also reflected by the ground, but with skilful use of his radar set, a good navigator could build an excellent picture of the target. Hamburg, a large industrial conurbation near the north German coast, at the estuary of the River Elbe, would be the perfect proving ground for this new targeting system.

With the additional help of WINDOW, a new radar disrupting device, the target was a sitting duck. As simple as it was cheap – consisting of thousands of strips of aluminium foil, an inch wide and 14 inches long – WINDOW was dropped in bundles from the bomb aimer's position or down the flare chute by the main door of a Lancaster. Spreading in the air, it confused the German Würzburg radar by reflecting its beams in arbitrary directions so huge areas of the screen were 'whited out', as though in a snowstorm, disguising the exact locations of the individual bombers. Until the Germans found a way of countering it – and they never fully did – WINDOW deceived the Germans' early-warning systems.

It was deployed at Hamburg to devastating effect.

On the night of 24/25 July 1943, a force of 791 aircraft, including 347 Lancasters, attacked the city centre. Weather conditions were ideal – unusually hot and dry. With the use of H2S the target was relatively easy to identify, while WINDOW protected the bomber force from the worst of the German fighters. The firestorm created by the sheer number of bombs dropped completely overwhelmed local emergency services. The results were horrific.

One navigator, keen to see the results of the action, decided to join his pilot in the cockpit. 'All around us and reaching to all heights, were hundreds of searchlights, moving back and forth in ever changing crisscross patterns. Those close to us towered above like huge sword blades. Among them, the small flashes of hundreds of flak bursts appeared and disappeared, leaving only black splodges of smoke against the starlit sky.'

The sight in the air may have been mesmerising, but it was the vision of hell on the ground that gave him greatest pause for thought.

'It was a shapeless mass of fire so far below that it all appeared like a badly focused technicoloured film of lights that seemed to move, twinkle and shimmer in a thousand shapes in colours of yellow, red and orange on a background of black velvet. I could soon distinguish bomb bursts and gun flashes among the blotches of light. I stared and stared. My heart was pounding and I felt I was not getting enough air.'[16]

Another airman, who flew on the subsequent raids, saw the cumulative effect.

'We went to Hamburg three nights out of four. The last night, we could see the fire from 150 miles away; see Hamburg burning. It was just awful, a terrible sight. It was like flying into a holocaust and [it] took several minutes to fly over the fires.'[17]

Individual incendiaries merged and grew into a brutal conflagration. Rising heat created violent up-currents and sucked in fresh air at ground level, which further fuelled the furnace. Wind speeds reached 150mph – hurricane force – on the ground, and temperatures at least 800°C. Wood and fabric blazed, and so did flesh. Glass exploded, metal twisted, stonework glowed red. Packed apartment blocks became shells within minutes, and streets screaming blast tunnels.

One rear gunner was awestruck by what he saw: 'As you turned for home you got the impression someone wanted to grab you and pull you back into the darkness on account of what you'd done. Others simply felt that "you had to black out all thought of civilians being killed".'[18]

On the ground, nineteen-year-old Käthe Hoffmeister tried to escape the furnace her neighbourhood had become, struggling to make headway against the tempest in her street. 'There were people there, some already dead, some still alive but stuck in the asphalt. They must have rushed onto the roadway without thinking. Their feet had got stuck and they had put out their hands to try to get out again. They were on their hands and knees, screaming.'[19]

Elfriede Sindel, then fourteen, saw bombed-out people in the streets after the first attack, begging for food, for water.

'Women were calling for their children, children for their mothers. We managed to get some lost children into a group, their small faces smeared with soot and tears, so that their mothers would find it easier to find their little ones. By noon, all of them had been reunited. Later a man came along, his clothes in disorder, wearing no shoes or socks. "Father! Gesa!" he shouted, over and over again. "Father! Gesa! Where are you?" He was roaring and crying at the same time. We offered him water and bread, but he waved us off and ran away, still screaming, with bloody feet, over the broken glass and tiles, stumbling against brick walls from which iron wires and broken pipes twisted outwards. Couldn't physical pain reach him? Was he not thirsty?'[20]

*The devastation caused by the bombing in Hamburg,*
*July 1943*

The Allied bombers returned three nights later, and again two nights after that. A final raid early in August was frustrated by bad weather, but by then the damage had been done. They had dropped 9,000 tons of bombs and destroyed 214,350 homes, over half the total. The districts of Hammerbrook and Rothenburgsort were obliterated. Two hundred and ninety-nine major industrial and armaments plants were damaged or demolished, together with a further 183 large factories. But raging fires devastated at least half the city and left 42,600 civilians dead, with another 37,000 wounded. Thanks to WINDOW, successfully used as a countermeasure to radar-directed German night-fighters and their controllers, losses on the night of 24/25 July stood at twelve aircraft – just 1.2 per cent of the total force deployed that night.

Operation Gomorrah was also a powder keg at home. Churchill's special scientific advisor, Lord Cherwell, had already advocated a policy of what he called 'dehousing', and Harris sincerely believed that strategic bombing was the one way to catastrophically undermine Hitler's ability to wage war. However, dissident voices were already being raised. The eminent soldier and military historian Liddell Hart condemned such raids: 'It will be ironical if the defenders of civilisation depend for victory upon the most barbaric, and unskilled way of winning a war that the modern world has seen.'[21]

He was joined by another distinguished military thinker of the time, Major-General J. F. C. 'Boney' Fuller, who it must be said was for a time suspected of harbouring Nazi sympathies. In August 1943, Fuller wrote an article for the London *Evening Standard*, edited at the time by the socialist journalist (and later politician) Michael Foot. In it, he writes that 'the worst devastations of the Goths, Vandals, Huns, Seljuks and Mongols pale into insignificance when compared with the material and moral damage now wrought'. Later, the Bishop of Chichester would join the ranks of respected establishment figures who felt the government had gone too far. He told the House of Lords, 'I desire to challenge the Government on the policy which directs the bombing of enemy towns on the present scale, especially with reference to civilians who are non-combatants, and non-military and non-industrial objectives.'[22]

On a more personal level, Thomas Murray, who after his initial stint in Bomber Command spent much of his war flying secretive missions with the Special Operations Executive, found his 'special duties role' a tonic: 'I never really believed in bombing, but it was the only thing to do, I suppose. As the defences got more effective, we would try to hit a target in the centre of a town, effectively hitting civilians. I didn't like that. In the SOE role you were doing something to help.'[23]

The majority of airmen just got on with the job. Many shared Harris's belief that the end would justify the means, but others shared Thomas's reservations. Some took refuge in the darkest of black humour. 'Looks like another mothers and babies run tonight,' one anonymous briefing officer was heard to tell his audience. Arthur Harris had indeed fulfilled his vow that Germany 'had sown the wind, and would reap the whirlwind'.

To ensure Harris's 'whirlwind' could blow at full strength, though, the Bomber Command machine needed to produce large numbers of trained aircrew. And, to do that, it required a huge quantity of young volunteers to enter its training system. In 1943, only one airman in six could expect to survive his first tour of thirty sorties.[24] The training continued, conveyor-belt style, while losses at the other end of the process continued apace.

# CHAPTER SIX

## 'STRIKE AND RETURN'

'Until the night of 24 June 1943, I had lived an uncomplicated twenty years, three months and fifteen days. I was about to keep an appointment with destiny.'[1]

As dusk was falling at RAF Binbrook in north-east Lincolnshire, Gordon Stooke, a twenty-year-old, handsome and cheerful Australian, sat at the controls of his Lancaster, *D-Donald*, its propellers ticking over, one of fourteen from 460 Squadron waiting in line for take-off. Gordon was already a veteran of several mine-laying operations and bombing ops to the Ruhr, not all of which had been run-of-the-mill. On a previous op he'd been shocked to find that one of their ground crew, fellow Australian Corporal Jim Nuttall, had hitched an uninvited lift with them.

'What the bloody hell are you doing here?' Gordon shouted, barely able to compete with the screaming engines.

'I just wanted to do one operation – just one,' Nuttall explained. 'I just wanted to find out what it's like.'

'You bloody idiot, you'll find out what it's like all right. You'll have us all court-martialled.'

But there was nothing to be done. Nuttall had sensibly brought an oxygen mask and parachute with him, so Gordon sent him to plug into the supply by the astrodome. They completed the op and, once home, Gordon sent Nuttall packing as fast as he could. Gordon heard later that Nuttall had confided to a mate, 'They're all crackpots, the whole bloody lot of them. Anyone who does that more than once ought to be certified.' Gordon could only agree with him, but he still went out on another sortie himself the very next night. And the one after that.

*Gordon Stooke's engineer Corporal Jim Nuttall*
*with their driver, Peggy*

So the night of the 24th looked like just another day at the coalface for Gordon and his crewmates.

They'd gathered edgily in the briefing room, on chairs ranged before the still-covered map of their target. It was always like this. The section commanders stood nearby, together with the Met Officer, the Flying Control Officer, the Armaments Officer, the Gunnery Officer, the Navigation Officer and the Intelligence Officer, some by their information blackboards. The Commanding Officer surveyed the scene.[2] The air, as usual, was blue with cigarette smoke.

The moment before you flew took people differently. Tonight, some of the men were taking bets on what the target might be. Others were chatting, maybe overexcited, maybe trying to hide their nerves. Most sat quietly, alone with their thoughts, perhaps forcing themselves to concentrate on the job at hand rather than its possible consequences. While waiting, Gordon thought back to a night/low-flying exercise he'd undertaken a month earlier. He was quite happy. He'd signed the low-flying clearance book which allowed him to drop down to a minimum of 500ft, and was off. Corporal Nuttall had been on board – legitimately that time, as part of an engineering check – and happened to mention a mansion he'd seen a few days before. Maybe they could go and find it? Gordon agreed and followed Nuttall's instructions until, sure enough, the mansion came into view.

'One pass at 500ft brought only two or three people out onto the roof and into the garden. *Not good enough*, I thought, and turned to make another pass, lower. Two more attacks at flagpole height with our four Merlins roaring and soon all vantage points were crowded, everyone waving excitedly. Or so we thought. In fact they were shaking their fists at us, as I was shortly to find out.'

Returning to base and landing, Gordon was directed to report immediately to the Duty Pilot.

'When I arrived at the Control Tower, the Duty Pilot looked grim.

'"Were you just flying anywhere over Yorkshire?" he asked, sternly.

'"Yes," I said, as there was no point in lying. "But I had a low-flying clearance."

'"Did you go lower than 500 feet?" A smile flickered across his face.

'"Do you think I'd do a thing like that?" I said, evasively.

'"Well," he burst out laughing. "Some silly clot has been buzzing Group Headquarters in a Lancaster, and all the Air Marshals in the RAF are after his blood."'

Gordon's reverie was broken as the room quietened and the briefing staff took up their positions by the covered map. The curtain was finally drawn back. The airmen groaned. Not Happy Valley again! The heavily defended Ruhr was all too familiar to them. 'I can't say too much,' the CO told them. 'But we know there are factories in Wuppertal manufacturing parts for secret Luftwaffe aircraft not yet in service. At least you know that it's of the utmost importance that these factories are destroyed.'

There had been a raid on the same target a month earlier and it had met with success. 'Your task is to ensure that this raid is as successful as the first so we don't have to go back. A good strike and a safe return,' he finished, reflecting 460 Squadron's motto: 'STRIKE AND RETURN'.

The Navigation Officer took over, detailing the rendezvous point with other units taking part in the raid over The Wash off the east coast of England, then outlining the route to the target. They'd have to be careful to stick meticulously to it around Düsseldorf and Krefeld, both heavily defended cities, not straying within range of their searchlights and anti-aircraft guns.

'460 Squadron is due over the target at 0035 hours, 20,000 feet. There should be plenty of red target indicators, otherwise bomb on the greens. Route home is south around Cologne and then west back to base.'

The Met Officer followed. There'd be moonlight and light cloud, ideal conditions for German night-fighters. The Gunnery Officer repeated this warning and told the gunners to stay behind after the briefing for further instructions. The Armaments Officer came next, detailing the bombloads: 'You'll carry one 4,000lb high-capacity cookie, two 500lb general-purpose bombs, one delayed-action, six cans 30lb incendiary and seven cans 4lb incendiary.'

The 'cookie' was a large cylindrical blast bomb designed to shatter building structures, leaving them open to allow the incendiaries to do their work on the interiors. Delayed-action bombs could remain dormant for many hours, even days, finally detonating to trap rescue workers or returning civilians in the blast. The aerial war was a brutal, deadly business.

Briefing over, the pilots gathered in the flight office while the navigators attended their own special brief. Then they all went to the Mess for a pre-flight meal, some forcing themselves to eat however disinclined they felt, all silently praying that they'd return safely for the post-op breakfast of real eggs and bacon. It seemed a very long way away. Everyone was supposed to relax during the hour that followed, but few could, and Gordon Stooke left his hut early, telling his crew to join him when they were ready, reminding them to relieve themselves before the long flight.

Nobody liked the Elsan onboard lavatory, the dustbin-like apparatus with the clip-down lid placed in the centre of the fuselage aft, near the main door. It was one of the Lancaster's major design faults, and crews hated them. Apart from the challenges of aim and balance, men who'd used it at high altitude in intense cold had been known to freeze to the seat. And the ground crews hated cleaning them out.

'While we were flying in rough air, this devil's convenience often shared its contents with the floor of the aircraft, the walls and the ceiling, though sometimes a bit remained in the container itself. It doesn't take much imagination to picture what it was like trying to combat fear and airsickness while struggling to remove enough gear in cramped quarters and at the same time trying to use the bloody Elsan. If it wasn't an invention of the Devil, it certainly must have been foisted on us by the enemy. When seated in frigid cold amid the cacophony of roaring engines and whistling air, away from what should have been one of life's peaceful moments, the occupant had a chance fully to ponder the miserable condition of his life instead. This loathsome creation invariably overflowed on long trips and, in turbulence, was always prone to bathe the nether regions of the user. It was one of the true reminders to me that war is hell.'[3]

Gordon had picked up his parachute and caught an early bus to his aircraft's dispersal point. He found the area alive with activity. The armourers, having transported the bombs from the ammunition dump on long, low trolley trains, had done their job, and, looking up at the still-open bomb-bay doors, Gordon thought, not for the first time, that a Lancaster was 'nothing more than a huge flying bomb bay'.

'The massive 4,000lb cookie dominated, surrounded by high-explosive and delayed-action 500-pounders and cans of fiery incendiaries. Transported from the ammunition dump on long trolley trains, one load could blow the whole aerodrome to kingdom come. That any bomber could fit one complete trolley-load into its bomb bay and then become airborne seemed unbelievable. The Lancaster took the lot with ease.'

Gordon ran over the checklist in his mind, watching as the Brownings' ammunition was loaded and the Bedford tankers filled the wing tanks with 1,500 gallons of high-octane fuel – less than maximum, but sufficient for this op. The same scene was being played out, he knew, not only on the thirteen other Lancasters from his squadron that would soon rise in the air with him, but, right across the country, for hundreds of other bombers, as aircrews prepared for another encounter with death and destruction in the night skies over Germany.

At last the Lancaster was ready – or almost.

'The last inspection was done from the aircraft's cockpit by an expert, the ground staff flight sergeant engineer. He checked oil and coolant temperatures, OK. Oil pressure, OK. Bomb doors closed, flaps down and up, brakes operating, hydraulics, all OK. Navigation lights, OK. Instruments, OK. Magnetos – damn! A problem. A drop in revolutions on engine No. 4.'

One of the two magnetos – the electrical generators that used magnets to produce alternating current – on Gordon's No. 4 engine, the starboard outer, was unserviceable. They had forty minutes to replace it. By now the rest of the crew had arrived.

'Get aboard and check your equipment,' Gordon said. 'We have maggie trouble and the Flight Sergeant is doing a slow march.' Soon afterwards, however, he regretted his impatience. The ground crew had worked their magic, and the new magneto was installed with ten minutes to spare.

'Soon, we would again take off for the dreaded "Happy Valley". Anticipation, tension and a hint of suppressed fear began to mount. With a fatalistic shrug, I crawled over the main spar and into the cockpit.'

Nothing to do now but the job. As Gordon ran the engines up, his flight engineer, Col Broadbent, made final checks on pressure, temperature, hydraulics and instruments. He nodded in satisfaction as Gordon checked over the intercom with the rest of his crew, a mix of Australians and Englishmen, older than himself and three of them married. Gordon was always deeply aware of the responsibility he carried for their safety. They, in turn, placed absolute trust in him. It was a perfect combination for survival – if all went well.

*Gordon Stooke*

At last they joined the queue for take-off and time started to race. A green lamp flashed. There was the rush of adrenaline as he released the brakes to give the Merlins their head, and his Lancaster powered along the runway. Gordon had to correct a slight swing to the left by advancing the two left throttles ahead of the right, then, as the slipstream increased, he moved the control column forward to raise the tail, knowing that Col would be watching the engine temperatures like a hawk. Then he pushed the throttles right up to their gate, and with a heave, flexing its muscles against the weight of 11,000lb of bombs, 1,500 gallons of fuel and seven men, the mighty aircraft took to the sky, heading east.

Gordon double-checked their position with his navigator and, as they slowly climbed towards the rendezvous height of 10,000ft, was told that they'd arrive a minute and a half early.

'Without thinking, I made a 360-degree turn to port to lose time. I should have realised that there were dozens of heavy bombers in the vicinity, all streaming east. *D-Donald*, on the other hand, was now for a time flying west against this stream. How we did not collide with another bomber I will never know. I had been very stupid and we had been very lucky.'

Gordon quickly corrected his error. At least they were now on time, and joined the rest of the attacking force without incident off the east coast over The Wash. It was already getting chilly on board, and the air was thinning. Gordon gave the order to don oxygen masks, and, as they rose to 15,000ft, the cold really began to bite. The gunners would be snug enough in their khaki-brown cotton Sidcot flying suits, or at least Gordon hoped they would – 'they were sometimes not too effective in keeping out the cold'. In contrast, the navigator and the wireless operator would be sweltering; the heating duct from the port inner engine entered the cabin near their seats. Gordon and Col were the unlucky ones, wishing they had fleece-lined Irvin jackets, but glad their feet were warm enough in their flying boots.

Flying steadily now, and rising to 20,000ft, this might have been the time to switch to the automatic pilot, nicknamed George. But Gordon had only ever used George once, on a familiarisation exercise. It was never used in action, for obvious reasons, but even on the flight into a raid you never knew when an attack might be coming and you needed to be ready to take evasive action in an instant. They were flying over the Dutch coast now, and German Me110s stationed in Holland might already be prowling the skies. Gordon checked that his gunners were keeping their eyes peeled.

'We were all eyes long ago,' came the reassuring reply.

They flew on. Far to his left and at about the same height, Gordon caught a glimpse of a bright light which flared for a moment and then slowly faded. He pressed his lips together, saying nothing to his crew, but thinking of his error in judgement earlier. What he'd

seen was almost certainly a collision between two friendly bombers. Another fourteen airmen gone. He'd heard that such accidents
accounted for an increasing number of losses, as raids intensified
in size and number. It wasn't just your crew you were responsible
for – you had to make sure you never flew into a fellow Lancaster
and brought another seven men down with yours.

'There were plenty of aircraft in your wave and at your height, so
your life and the lives of thirteen others depended on the competence
and vigilance of all. Quite a responsibility for twenty-year-olds.'

Soon afterwards, he saw another blaze of light, at ground level
this time, a bomber brought down by a fighter. As they approached
the target, Gordon saw a kaleidoscope of colour: the red and orange
of flame, the green and red of target indicators dropped by the
preceding Pathfinder Force, the glare of searchlights and now the
popping of anti-aircraft guns.

'We could see Wuppertal ablaze, in front of us and still 10 miles
away. Dozens of searchlights speared skywards around the now-
familiar barrage of exploding anti-aircraft shells. Heavy bombers
were as thick as flies, thankfully all going in somewhat the same
direction. Some, above us, possibly early or late arrivals, were
getting ready to drop their bombs on the target and possibly on *D-
Donald* as well. Others, below us, silhouetted against the fires, were
positioned in such a way as to receive our load of bombs. The seemingly impregnable wall of fiery anti-aircraft bursts was closing fast.
Probing searchlights, seeking their prey, were much too close. There
were only a few Luftwaffe fighters though. It was too dangerous
over the target for them. Most attacked the bombers either before
they reached the target or afterwards on the trip home. Only the
bravest and most dedicated members of the German night-fighter
units would face their own flak.'

Suddenly, night turned to day as they were 'coned' – caught in
multiple connecting searchlight beams from differing positions on
the ground, which all came together to form a cone – with Gordon's
Lancaster at the pinnacle. Based on prior experience, his reaction
was instantaneous, and he threw the aircraft into a series of violent

climbing and diving manoeuvres in an attempt to free himself from the deadly cone.

'Nose down. Throttles open. Go like hell. The faster you go, the harder you are to hit. Get out as quickly as possible. Fifteen thousand feet and put on speed – better than corkscrewing.'

Heavy with bombs, *D-Donald* quickly dropped from 20,000 to 15,000ft. They were just about clear of the 'cone' when Gordon saw two bright yellow flashes, in quick succession, over the nose of the aircraft.

'I heard the *clump*, *clump* of two exploding flak shells, then a noise like hail on a tin roof, and I swore I smelt cordite.'

'Bloody hell, Skip,' Col yelled. 'The starboard inner's on fire!'

Gordon saw that flame was already licking the wing. The wing that carried the second fuel tank.

'Kill it fast,' he shouted. 'NOW!'

Col throttled the engine back and feathered the propeller, at the same time pressing the red fire-extinguisher button. As if by magic the fire went out and the engine stopped. But they weren't out of it yet. Where else were they hit? What about the bombs? They opened the hatch to the bay. To their dismay, the incendiaries were glowing.

'Jettison the bombload, FAST.'

Bomb aimer Norm Conklin leapt to obey. Gordon 'felt the aircraft jump as 11,000lb of bombs fell away', but they were free of the searchlights at last: 'Perhaps they couldn't hold us any longer, or perhaps they knew they'd clobbered us and went looking for other game.'

A moment of relief, and a moment more when he knew that all the crew were safe. But the other inner engine had stalled now, and they'd dropped to 12,500ft, which meant they were vulnerable not only to the flak from below but the payloads of their fellow aircraft above. Norm reported that the bomb-bay doors were stuck open. They exerted a heavy drag, and couldn't be closed without the hydraulic power from the damaged engines. Then navigator Clarrie Craven, another fellow Australian, reported that he could see the port undercarriage hanging halfway down, and at the same time Col Broadbent said the same went for the starboard 'under-cart'. Without hydraulics, nothing could be done about them either.

The remaining engines screamed at full pitch but the Lancaster went on losing height. In desperation, they jettisoned everything possible, including equipment and fuel, and slowed enough to release a carrier pigeon, though with faint hope it would find its way back home. They were still alive and flying; a Lancaster could fly reasonably well at 10,000ft on two engines, but this wasn't an exercise, and the intercom between Gordon and his gunners was down. If an enemy fighter attacked now, they'd have no means of communicating. They tried unfeathering the dead port engine's propeller to see if allowing it to rotate freely might generate enough hydraulic power to close the bomb doors. No joy.

At least they were out of the battle now, flying north towards home. But they were still losing height, and Gordon knew that they'd soon be too low to bale out safely. At last the decision he knew he'd have to make was taken out of his hands. They were about 20 miles away from Liège, at 2,500ft, when Col, watching the instruments, 'reported that the temperature of the starboard outer engine was off the clock and could seize at any moment'.

That was it.

'ABANDON AIRCRAFT!' Gordon ordered, sending his wireless operator back to tell the gunners as the bomb aimer jettisoned the narrow escape hatch beneath his position and baled out. Col, clipping on his chest parachute, went next, with a brave smile and a nervous wink. Then the wireless operator hurried forward, clambering over the main spar to tell Gordon that the gunners had gone through the main door aft.

'They'll be OK.'

'Thanks. Off you go now. Be quick.'

'Good luck, Skipper. See you in Spain!' He checked that Gordon's parachute was secure and then, with a reassuring glance, dropped into the night sky.

'*D-Donald* and I were alone. Just for a moment the ship's

captain syndrome almost overcame me as I felt sadness and shame because I was about to desert my mighty Lancaster. Soon, *D-Donald* would be no more. It was no consolation to me that many had already gone before, and that there would be many more to follow.'

They were down to 2,000ft. No more time to waste.

'Below, the open hatchway waited and I hurried down and knelt at its edge. Then, for a moment, I thought of the hundreds – no, the thousands of aircrew who had attempted and were yet to attempt to save their lives by abandoning their stricken aircraft as I was about to do.'

Gordon knew he was lucky. He wasn't trapped in a Lancaster spiralling on fire to its doom, its crew trapped with no hope of escape. What would their last thoughts have been? As things stood, he'd got all his crew out safely and now all he had to do was simply roll forward and his Lancaster, still flying straight and level, would let him go. He looked at the narrow rectangle of the escape hatch and prayed he'd get through it. Why hadn't they made it just a couple of inches longer and wider? He fell forward into the blackness, pulling his ripcord almost immediately.

'As I tumbled over in the air, I saw the dark outline of my Lancaster above me as it flew on alone. The slender fuselage, the broad, rounded wings, the prominent four Merlins and the tailplane with its tall twin rudders, was a vision never to be forgotten.'

As his parachute opened and its harness yanked at every bone in his body, Gordon sent a silent prayer of thanks to the WAAF who had packed it. Fifteen hundred feet above the ground, the only sound he could hear was the scream of the Lancaster's engines as it went unseen into its death dive, somewhere beyond him in the night. He imagined for a moment that it was turning back to exact revenge for his desertion, then he heard the screams crescendo, followed by a furious explosion. He could see the inferno, hear the chatter of the small-arms ammunition inside the dying giant.

'*Vale, D-Donald.*'

Now he was truly on his own. Drifting inexorably downwards,

he remembered stories of airmen parachuting into the flames of cities they'd just bombed, or into the hands of civilians whose loved ones had perished or whose property had been destroyed. *Terrorflieger* or *Luftgangsters*, the civilians called them; 'terror flyers' or 'air gangsters'. He thought of the accounts he'd heard of men caught in trees or on high buildings, whom no one would come to rescue because of what they'd done. They were left to dangle there and die. Others had been lynched, beaten to death or shot by the enraged civilians they had been bombing. What would be his fate?

In training, they'd learned that a parachute landing had the impact of jumping 12 feet. Now the ground was suddenly rushing up to meet him. He didn't have time to go into a roll and his heels hit the ground, spraining both his ankles. Wincing with pain, he looked around. He found he could stand up and walk. He was in a field, and he wasn't alone. 'An amazed cow reared back in fright, wondering, no doubt, where the devil I had come from.'

For Gordon Stooke, the war in the air was over; he would eventually be captured and spend the remainder of the war as a POW. For others, it was just beginning.

* * *

Crewed up and fully trained, Stan Shaw could now take the white flash that denoted a trainee out of his forage cap. His own posting was to RAF Dunholme Lodge, one of a cluster of bases near Lincoln, and it was from here that Stan's crew joined the fray. He had told his family that he didn't want the Germans setting foot in England, and was doing something about it now. They'd soon be flying their Lancaster on a major mission to a top-secret German missile site at Peenemünde.

'I remember Mum once telling me that Dad and his friends were "all really afraid, but they went anyway. They had to,"' his daughter Elaine remembered. 'I often think about how many hundreds of thousands of people must have felt that way but never talked about it. My mum also said that during his training Dad saw a Lancaster crash on landing, killing some of his colleagues. That really affected him.'

Stan's periods on leave with his family were precious and happy occasions. Elaine's memories of those times are still strong. 'Once, he took Mum to the pictures to see *Gone with the Wind*. Another time, I remember falling off a wall, splitting the skin near my eye. Dad had to take me to hospital to have it stitched. He did all the normal things a dad would do, even though there was a war on and he was seeing terrible things on the ground and in the skies.'

Despite the brutality of war, the normality of life still went on all around him.

'But he could never stay for long – he had to get back to the war. Often, he'd bring some of his fellow crewmen home with him. His Canadian pilot, Reg Harding, and the other gunner, Peter Pynisky – he was from Canada too – and his bomb aimer, Len 'Mac' McDermott, whose parents had been bombed out in London. My dad was thirty-one, the old man of the crew. I think they regarded him as a bit of a father figure.

'I remember running down Brook Hill to meet him and his mates. It was such a wonderful sight to see them getting off the bus, joking and laughing without a care in the world. My dad came from a mining background where they all chewed tobacco, and he managed to persuade some of his crew to take it up too! They'd bring their sweets ration for me, and Reg's mum had sent my mum a Christmas hamper full of the most amazing food – dried fruit, chocolate, chewing gum. It was such a treat! I was so proud to see them all in their uniform. I would hold their hands so tightly, as if they belonged to me. I certainly had a bit of a crush on them! I would write to them and they would write back and send me photos. I had a little orange desk which I'd got one Christmas where I would sit and write my letters, and keep their replies, and Dad's letters, and the photos of them all in front of the Lancaster in the drawer. They were so precious to me.'

Those letters were never thrown away. The memories of a

much-loved father, doing his duty for his King, country and family, imprinted on young Elaine's mind. But Stan's time as a father had to be shared with his rear gunner duties on a Lancaster squadron in Bomber Command, and he and his crew had to return to the fight.

## CHAPTER SEVEN

# 'IT WON'T BE LONG UNTIL
# I SEE YOU AGAIN'

While Stan Shaw and his crew were flying their first ops during the opening months of 1943, an Air Tasking Order was sent to 430 Squadron's A-Flight at RAF Leuchars in Scotland, far away from their main base in Oxfordshire. A-Flight operated the photo reconnaissance version of the de Havilland Mosquito fighter-bomber, a fast, highly manoeuvrable aircraft adaptable to many roles.

They were to photograph a hitherto unnoticed segment of the German Baltic coast comprising the fishing village of Peenemünde, isolated among coastal flatlands, and two small nearby islands. Some 200 miles north of Berlin and less than 100 east of Rostock, it had once been the site of a Nazi *Kraft durch Freude* ('Strength Through Joy') holiday camp, but seemed otherwise insignificant. The order was very precise, however, and the men on its receiving end jibbed at it, since it involved making several runs through the same airspace, greatly increasing the risk of being spotted and shot down. So unusual was their task that the commander of A-Flight, Gordon Hughes, flew down to Oxfordshire to question it personally. He was told, in the strictest confidence, that 'there were almost incredible anxieties about the Peenemünde area'.[1]

Hughes and his men flew their mission unmolested. Whatever intelligence the higher-ups had garnered about the place was obviously at fault: there couldn't be anything there if it wasn't defended. But when experts looked at the imagery the Mosquitos had captured, they recognised some of the shapes at a site near the village as rockets.

Winston Churchill's chief scientific advisor, Lord Cherwell, never a man to have his authority questioned, had declared roundly that the Germans couldn't possibly have the technology to build rockets – on the grounds that the British hadn't. But British Intelligence Services knew this was wishful thinking. They belatedly remembered information that had come through years earlier, in November 1939. Delivered anonymously through the letterbox of the British Embassy in Norway, it had contained a detailed summary of German rocketry development.

The document, known as the Oslo Report, contained such detailed descriptions – even mentioning Peenemünde – that it seemed too good to be true. Dismissed as a German Intelligence bluff, it was consigned to a back shelf and wasn't resurrected even when other bulletins about Peenemünde trickled through later. Effectively, it was forgotten. That is, until a few months before the reconnaissance mission, when its full import was finally discovered.

Trent Park, a country house to the north of London, had been taken over as a holding camp for senior German officers. They lived there in relative comfort though, unknown to them, their rooms, both public and private, were bugged and their conversations were monitored by the Intelligence Services. One set of recordings featured two generals who'd been deliberately lodged together after being taken prisoner during the North African campaign. The two long-time friends were pleased to see each other and, naively unaware that they might be under surveillance, caught up with each other's news. They openly discussed as much as they knew about the secret rocket programme and the brilliant scientists behind it. One went so far as to say how surprised he was that they'd heard no explosions, and that the attack on London hadn't yet commenced.[2]

The conversation not only confirmed the validity of the Oslo Report, now hastily resurrected, but the other pieces of information that had dribbled in since – the enemy had been quietly developing what came to be known as 'V' or 'vengeance weapons': the V1 flying bomb, which would fall to earth and detonate at a pre-determined range after launch, the V2 rocket, which could reach targets many hundreds of miles away; and the V3 supergun, which would be able to bombard southern England from positions dug into the country-side of northern France.

Tucked away in that nondescript fishing village in northern Germany was part of the development programme that would lead to the V2 – a weapon like nothing seen before: a long-range ballistic missile, nearly 46ft high and 5.5ft wide, carrying a 2,000lb warhead. There was also talk of a crack team of scientists working on the project, including 31-year-old genius Wernher von Braun.

Something had to be done – and fast. Operation Hydra took two months of meticulous planning to prepare, in the utmost secrecy.

\* \* \*

In the meantime, Bomber Command continued its regular attacks, and men like Stan Shaw, oblivious to the looming threat, con-tinued to fly missions with 44 Squadron from Dunholme Lodge. While waging war, they also continued their lives as brothers, sons and fathers.

At the end of June, Stan wrote from the Sergeants' Mess to his brother Vic, in service with the Royal Navy. His humanity and spirit show through in every line.

*Dear Vic*

*Thanks for the letter received the day before yesterday. I was very pleased to hear from you.*

*Yes, it is a beggar when you have set your mind on leave to find it cancelled, however much you were expecting otherwise.*

*Now, apparently, you are to begin what may be a long term at sea. Well, I wish you the best of luck, it is bound to be a hard life, but with the luck of the Shaws and the false courage that always comes to a man in times of stress, you and I will be thinking back in better times, under better conditions, of those ghastly and hair-raising moments we are bound to get, both in your branch of the service, and myself in mine.*

*I am sorry too for all who have to stay at home and worry about us who are in the forces, but I would sooner go out and fight than have to see them being held in ridicule by any persons – or should I say enemy – who may invade and conquer England. A lot of worry now will be nothing to what may have been if that did, or even now, does, happen. Pray God it never does.*

*Yes, the gardens were lovely when I was there last week. We lay on your lawn in the sun most of the afternoon to watch Pam and Elaine* [his young daughters] *with the flowers.*

*We keep doing an odd trip now and again to give the Jerries our regards and although it isn't what you might call pleasant over the Ruhr, I would rather be at the delivering end than the receiving end. It must be plain hell let loose.*

*I am pleased to see everyone looking so well at Sutton. I thought in particular that Ma looked very well, and of course I bucked her up no end by sleeping at home one night. She fussed no end!*

*Well Vic I think that is about all for now, so will you send Doris my regards when you write, and for goodness' sake look after yourself, and the very best of luck. Please write whenever you can. Cheerio. See you soon.*

*Stan*

*Elsie and Elaine send their best wishes and from Pam to their Uncle Vic.*[3]

Ten kisses followed, sent from Stan's daughters to their much-loved uncle.

Vic replied from HMS *Ceylon*, then at Scapa Flow in the Orkney Islands.[4]

*Dear Stan*

*I am sorry for the delay in writing to you. I find it very difficult to keep in hand with any correspondence and I expect you have the same experience.*

*Have you been on any more bombing expeditions? I suppose you have almost completed your tour. I shall be relieved to hear you are on ground duties once more.*

*I have had a very interesting time at my job. We have had the King inspecting the Home Fleet, and the setting was very impressive, as you'd imagine.*

*I was favourably impressed with the King's behaviour. He was very much at ease during the days he was with us, and carried on the inspection with full confidence, chatting freely with officers and men.*

*Well Stan, I hope you are well. Do look after yourself. Please give my regards to Elsie and family.*

*Yours sincerely*

*Vic*

By August, Stan was occupied in raids over Italy. During the first half of that month, 197 Lancasters flew sorties over Genoa, Milan and Turin – the object being to hasten Italy's capitulation following the fall of Mussolini in late July, and her withdrawal from the Axis Powers, so robbing Greater Germany of her European ally. Stan didn't go into detail in conversations with his family when he was on leave, or mention anything much about his war in his letters, but he did once show his daughter Elaine a lucky halfpenny he always carried with him. His mascot.

'He took it with him every time he went off on an operation as his lucky charm to keep him safe, and to make sure he always came back to us. Although I didn't really understand what it all meant, I knew that he and his friends were flying Lancaster bombers and were attacking Germans who had been bombing us. I had a sense that their job was dangerous but I didn't really know how or why. I was only nine. The war didn't really mean much to me at that stage. I certainly didn't know it then, of course, but he was putting his life on the line every time he took off on an operation.'[5]

At the beginning of August, Elaine was again staying at her grand-mother's house while she was in hospital being treated for cancer. Stan was allowed home on a short compassionate leave to see her. It was so brief that he didn't even manage to see his wife Elsie – he only had an hour with his mother before returning to base. At least he was able to reassure his father and his elder daughter. But his time with them flew by.

'He was in his uniform, and I remember walking down to the bus stop on Pepper Street with him. As we waited for the Number 55 bus to arrive, he asked me to be a good girl and look after my mum and my baby sister. I was hoping the bus would be late, but all too soon it arrived. He climbed on board and sat down at a window seat so he could see me. I waved as the red bus pulled away and then stood for a few moments, just staring after it. Then I walked slowly back up the hill to my grandparents' house, already looking forward to his next visit in a few weeks' time, when I'd go back down the hill to meet him.'

Elaine was the only member of the family to wave her father goodbye.

*Stan Shaw and his daughter Elaine on holiday*

Lancasters from Stan's squadron were soon detailed to take part in Operation Hydra – still so clandestine that crews had no idea of its true objective. Not even the briefing officers knew. The word was that new radar countermeasures were being developed at Peenemünde. This was a useful mistruth, since it created a target serious enough to encourage bomber crews to press home their attack, while at the same time keeping the dangerous and panic-inducing truth – that rockets were being developed to attack British cities – from the press and public.

The men tasked with the mission weren't happy about flying in at 8,000ft and lower, especially in full moonlight, but were reassured that this was a soft target, not well defended, and a Mosquito section would fly a diversionary raid over Berlin to draw off (everyone hoped) any German fighters.

The aim was to hit the experimental works within the Peenemünde compound, the rocket production works just to the south of them, the housing estate where the scientists lived, the army barracks and the forced labour camp. There was some anxiety about the forced labour population, largely made up of Polish prisoners of war, but taking out the intellectual manpower was of primary importance. If the labour camp was collateral damage, it would be a necessary evil.

The night chosen was Tuesday 17 August, to ensure that most of the scientists would be in place, rather than away for the weekend enjoying the local attractions (the landscape was of great natural beauty and the nearby Baltic offered ample opportunities for swimming, socialising and relaxation). They would approach by a route that steered clear of the most heavily defended night-fighter areas, and would go in low to avoid the German *Freya* radar, which was thought sophisticated enough not to be confused by WINDOW.

H2S ground-mapping radar would be carried by the Pathfinders to assist in identifying the precise aiming points. They would fly in advance of the various elements of the main stream and mark the targets with different coloured flares, a task that would continue for the duration of the raid.

The battle order was drawn up using the fullest possible resources of Arthur Harris's Bomber Command: 594 aircraft, of which 324 were Lancasters – a measure of how important the bomber had become. The Lancaster group included the new Mark II, powered by Bristol Hercules radial engines instead of the venerable Merlins. There had been early concerns that, with the enormous expansion of the bomber force, and the RAF as a whole, the supply of the incredibly reliable Merlin engines may not keep up with the demand. Such fears did not materialise, however, and only 300 MkIIs were produced.

Thirteen Lancasters were drawn from Stan Shaw's 44 Squadron at Dunholme Lodge, and his aircraft, DV-202, was one of them. Days before the op, on Friday 13 August, Stan found a quiet corner in the Sergeants' Mess to write another letter to his beloved wife Elsie.

*Darling,*

*This will have to be a rush letter. I am tired. I have just returned from Italy so I could go to sleep now, but I want you to get this letter before the weekend as I know you like to receive one if possible.*

*How are you, darling? I hope you are all well, did you manage to get back to sleep the other morning with Pam; I thought by the look of her she had got up to stay.*

*I thoroughly enjoyed being at home again – by the way, our leave has been brought forward to the 9th September so it will not be so long after all, and I am ready!*

*Well darling I am nearly asleep so cheerio and God bless you all. Give Elaine and Pam a kiss for me.*

*Tons of love*

*Stan*

The letter closed with the kisses arranged to form the initials 'RAF'.

As Stan pondered over his words, perhaps deciding how many kisses to add to that particular letter (forty-eight appeared this time), many thousands of other young men across Bomber Command were also putting pen to paper. Some were composing their 'last letters', only to be delivered after an airman failed to return and was 'Missing Believed Killed'. They bade farewell to mothers and fathers, wives and girlfriends, whoever would now be missing them. They were heartfelt and clearly incredibly difficult for the airmen to write. How did one express love, thanks, devotion, sadness and loss – a sense of duty done and a life well-lived – in a few simple words?

At RAF Darley Moor in Derbyshire, pilot Percy Brunt had written a very formal last letter – not to his parents and new fiancée, Rags, but to the solicitors who would deal with his affairs. His normal style was a hurried scrawl, which only his closest family, and Rags of course, could easily decipher. But this letter was for strangers to read, and it was carefully and precisely formed, as if, in his last will and testament, he was trying to emulate the copperplate he had been taught at school.

> *To my fiancée (Miss R. Newman-Newgas) the sum of £50 which she is to spend solely on herself – clothes for example. If she would like any of my personal effects, no doubt my parents will give them to her if at all possible.*
>
> *Thank you very much indeed for all you have done for me, Mother and Dad. No man could ever wish for better parents, and thank you Rags for your love. My only regret is that this should have ever to be read to you. You are my life. Cheerio for now and thank you all for everything. I hope I have done my part as well.*

There were no kisses. Just a very formal 'Sidney P. Brunt F/O'.[6]

Other airmen, like Sergeant J. A. Clough, were far more direct in their instructions to their loved ones:

> *I have no regrets dying for my country, it is a grand country and any man who can call himself an Englishman should be proud to die in the struggle for freedom.*
>
> *Give this message to my friends and yours and to the people*

*of England if it is possible: Let every Englishman fight to the last
drop of blood in his body.*

*Let him keep the golden fields and busy streets clean and
fresh, and let him keep the air he breaths [sic] free from the stench
of Nazism.*[7]

Most last letters to loved ones were written in a similar style to
Percy's; moving and emotional, yet also businesslike:

*My Darling,*

*If ever you get this note one of two things will have happened.
I will either not be alive or will be a prisoner of war. In either
case darling I shall be leaving you a great responsibility with
our two lads, but I know that you will always do your best for
them. Please don't coddle them. Many times they will do things
that make you fear for them & their safety, but if they have the
confidence to carry out their exploits don't try to hinder them.
You must encourage them to be self-reliant.*

*If I should not come out of this war alive I would like them to
complete their vocational training, then travel abroad if possible.
They will in that way gather a wealth of experience and get an
outlook on life that will get them anywhere. Again don't forget
to impress them that they will get nothing without working for
it & that they will only get out of life what they put in it.*

*In conclusion dearest all I have ever done & do is for you &
the boys although I have many times annoyed, disappointed &
let you down.*

*I have always loved you & always will*

*Cheerio dearest*

*Yours Ian*[8]

At this stage of the war, tens of thousands of 'last letters' were
being written in preparation for an event few imagined and no one
talked about – death. Yet many, like all those above, were actually
being delivered to the family homes of those with loved ones flying

in Bomber Command. The heartfelt entreaties for wives to get on with their own lives, to allow young sons, now fatherless, to experience life's dangers, and for the nation to continue the fight against the scourge of Nazism must have been felt keenly by those left behind.

By 1943, a member of a bomber crew had less chance of survival than a soldier in the trenches during the First World War. Bomber Command pilot Denis Hornsey, in the thick of the action that year, reflected on this: 'If you live on the brink of death yourself, it is as if those who have gone have merely caught an earlier train to the same destination, and whatever that destination is, you will be sharing it soon, since you will almost certainly be catching the next one.'[9]

By the same point in the war, only one in forty men was expected to survive through a second tour of thirty operations. Aircraft and men were being devoured by war as surely as they rained death on Germany, and more and more were needed. It was no wonder that Arthur Harris remained aloof from his men – it wasn't that he didn't care for them; it was that he knew what he was demanding of them, and knew he'd earned his nickname 'Butch' or 'Butcher'. He knew too that the nickname was used as often as not with affection. His aim remained unwavering – to pull out each German city 'like teeth' – always convinced that such destruction would be justified by the greater good of bringing the war to a swifter conclusion. Peenemünde – another precision raid – was not his preferred method of operation.

Stan Shaw wrote a letter – not a 'last letter' – to his parents on the eve of the raid. He was clearly cheerful, and looking forward to the possibility of seeing one of his brothers and his wife Elsie and daughters Pam and Elaine when next on leave:

*Dear Ma and Pa*
    *Thanks very much for your letter which I received on the dot today.*
    *I am glad to hear you are both well and that Connie and Alan are also; by the way it is quite possible that Alan may get his*

*leave at the same time as myself if he is about due for it; mine is
on a fortnight next Wednesday. Anyway, I hope so – it would be
grand to see him again.*

*I am glad to hear Elaine was a good girl. Yes, I reckon we are
lucky to have such nice kiddies, I know Pam missed her too while
she was at Sutton – she kept going round the house shouting
'Lane!' Thank you for having her. I know she likes to come.*

*Well, that seems about all just now, so cheerio and God
Bless You.*

*Love*

*Stan*

Stan's thoughts may well have been on his beloved family and
upcoming leave, but there was a battle to be fought in the skies first.

The next day it was on. The bombers' approach run was planned
to start over the beautiful and easily identifiable island of Rügen off
Germany's north-east Baltic coast. They'd make their calculations
for the final approach and the bomb run as the stream flew south
to Peenemünde. All anyone knew was that this operation was of
the highest importance, so much so that there would be a Master
Bomber to direct it. This new innovation enabled full co-ordination
of the entire force, including the Pathfinders marking the targets,
by one pilot directing the whole attack. The Master Bomber had
backup in the form of at least one reserve should his aircraft be damaged or shot down, and Master Bombers and their deputies were
in constant contact, liaising with each other and the main bomber
stream as the attack commenced.

The onerous task fell to thirty-year-old Group Captain John
Searby of the Pathfinder Force, a veteran of some fifty operations.
Searby was clearly struck by the opening words of the briefing given
for the operation: 'If you don't knock out this important target
tonight, it will be laid on again tomorrow and every night until the
job is done.' He later recalled, 'The significance of Arthur Harris's
words were not lost on my elite Pathfinder crews assembled in 83
Squadron's briefing room on the afternoon of 17 August 1943. To

return to a target on successive nights meant stiffer defences and heavier casualties.'[10]

The message was clear: this was do-or-die.

From the low dais in front of the map of Europe, with its coloured tapes and pins marking the heavily defended areas of enemy territory, Searby watched the faces of his crews. 'They were impressed by the urgency, but not worried, for the job would be done to the best of their ability. Against the background of Essen, Berlin, Hamburg, Munich, Cologne and similar bloodbaths, Peenemünde did not, at this stage, make much impression. In fact the reactions of the crews were ones of relief at the prospect of a sortie to northern Germany. The only real hazard lay in the long penetration under conditions of full moonlight with the possible increased fighter activity. No one had heard of this insignificant pimple sticking out of Pomerania, but there was nothing humdrum about the operation.' By virtue of his special responsibility as Master Bomber, Searby was better informed than most of the others at this stage. The previous day he'd gathered his own Pathfinder crew to study a beautifully constructed scale model of the target. Based on reconnaissance photographs, analysed at the specialised photographic intelligence unit at RAF Medmenham, and constructed there largely by WAAFs, the model was key to fine-tuning the details of the attack. Searby and his men painstakingly memorised the key features near the three aiming points, still unaware that this was anything other than an 'experimental station'.

Meanwhile, preparations at bases across Britain were also under way, as ground crews checked every inch of the aircraft each nurtured and cherished. They shared that sense of ownership – and even love – for the Lancaster with the men who flew it. In many ways, the ground crews were the forgotten heroes of Bomber Command and the RAF in general. The 'flyboys' received most of the glory and attention, but without the men and women who ensured the aircraft got airborne, properly armed, refuelled and equipped, there would have been no bomber war.

*Ground crew replenishing a Lancaster's*
*oxygen supply before an operation*

On 17 August, there was little for the air crews to do before their late-afternoon pre-raid briefing, apart from a routine test flight of their aircraft.[11] For the men of RAF Bottesford in Lincolnshire, there was a special treat to distract them, when a visiting 'Entertainments National Service Association' troupe put on a matinée of Noël Coward's *This Happy Breed*, since the timing of the op meant they would be missing the evening show. The airmen enjoyed the production, but then it was down to business.

'Once inside the briefing hut, there was an ostentatious locking of the door – an obvious turning of the key with a clunk.'[12] Guards were posted. The 'whole atmosphere suggested that the operation was going to be something pretty big', and 'there was naturally an atmosphere of special excitement and mystery about the whole thing, with much speculation'.

The speculation was widespread, and intelligence and briefing officers were in the best position to control it. It was also their job to inform crews of the nature of the mission – to the best of their ability, given the secrecy – and to encourage enthusiasm for the job in hand. This wasn't the easiest of tasks when trying to stimulate men who went out to bomb on a nightly basis. And Peenemünde presented very particular challenges. When they were cautiously told about bombing experimental works and production facilities, no one batted an eye, but the news that the housing estate was also a target wasn't well received. This was the first time that the deliberate killing of civilians had been mooted, and the thought of knowingly dealing out death to women and children – for the scientists had their families with them – was deeply disturbing. But this was war, and it wouldn't be enough simply to bomb facilities. The specialised scientists and technicians who worked in them had to be destroyed as well.

Several squadrons were told that there'd be a concourse of evil Nazi scientists at Peenemünde that night and that this would be a golden opportunity to neutralise them. Still, no one was happy about it – 'We weren't too proud about bombing this part of Peenemünde but we didn't dwell on it.'[13]

But the moment had come. Stan Shaw, now a veteran of many ops and looking forward to the end of his tour, boarded the bus to his Lancaster at its dispersal point, as did the 4,240 other aircrew[14] around the country who were sharing his voyage. Every man knew he had a good chance of never returning, though no one spoke of it; no one quite believed it. The last letter had been written, the last supper eaten (the gallows-humour nickname for the final meal before an op) and the final details covered.

The WAAF drivers who took the crews to their aircraft would long remember the impossibly young, schoolboy faces that turned to say goodbye. Some, the women knew, they'd never see again. They'd also remember the smells – of damp kapok, of oil and petrol, and of fear. Some of the WAAFs had boyfriends on this trip, and prayed for their safe return, but the prayer was also partly for their own sake: a girl who dated a flyer who died often attracted the stigma of being a jinx. Those who'd dated two or three doomed men were known as 'chop' girls, and were avoided like the plague.

Some of the men boarded briskly – no question of turning back, let's get it over with. Others mounted slowly and reluctantly, but they had no choice. Better not think about it and crack on.

The final moments before take-off were charged with tension for every unit involved. Master Bomber John Searby knew that after the days of preparation, this was the moment when something could go wrong. Perhaps one of the aircraft would develop a last-minute fault and have to be withdrawn. It often happened. But so far everything was running smoothly. The armourers had worked hard hauling the bombs aboard – a varied load to suit the different targets at Peenemünde: one 4,000lb impact-fused high-capacity bomb, three 1,000lb short-finned, short-delay, tail-armed high-explosive bombs, and a number of 30lb and 40lb incendiaries. Hydraulics, electrics, radio and radar had been checked and checked again. The magnesium flares had been placed in the flare chutes – ground and aircrew worked together to check guns, ammunition, and turret rotation. Flight rations were collected and escape kits, containing the essentials for survival if you were shot down and were lucky enough to survive, packed into buttoned trouser pockets.

Searby said goodbye and good luck to the other Pathfinder crews of 83 Squadron who were flying with him.

'I can remember Maurice Chick and his merry men departing, laughing as usual because with Chick around, nothing could be serious for long. They were clutching the odds and ends of their various trades, the two gunners huge in their padded suits. I waved to Chick and set out myself. It was a fine evening, warm and pleasant, the sun about to set and the long twilight beginning: a time for the river pub down at the ferry, where 83 Squadron foregathered. I suppose there will never again be gatherings quite like that, and to recapture the atmosphere is impossible: all was warmth and friendliness, with much laughter. Tommy Blair, doyen of Pathfinder navigators, red-faced and of powerful build, waving his tankard in time to the singing – but this was no time for the Ferryboat Inn.'

Tomorrow, perhaps. If all went well. For now, Searby concentrated on his job. The whole raid was expected to last forty-five minutes and he'd be in charge of it throughout. If all went well.

There were two deputy Master Bombers ready to take over if he was shot down. Searby fervently hoped they wouldn't be needed.

The first aircraft, heavily laden, took off at 8.28 p.m. Ninety minutes later, the entire force would be airborne. Searby's Lancaster, *W-William*, taxied past the squadron dispersals, getting a wave from the ground crews, then turned into the wind at the runway threshold. The Merlins thundered on full power and the aircraft moved up the wide runway, easily and at increasing speed. This was the moment when the men forgot the anxieties and stress of the preceding days. Up and away!

Searby's Lancaster levelled out at 1,000ft. As they approached the Norfolk coast, they could almost feel the rest of the mighty bomber stream leaving the ground to join them. Dropping to 200ft for thirty minutes to avoid German radar as they passed over the North Sea, the gunners kept a vigilant eye on the skies while the others kept a sharp lookout below for German fishing boats equipped with radio.

All was calm – even the sea. But calm could be deceptive. You could never be lulled by it. The price of that was often death.

They climbed again to medium altitude as they approached Denmark. The worry was always the bright moonlight. It'd be an odd and novel experience, Searby knew, for the bombers in the main stream following him to be able to see each other, and even he found it deceptively peaceful as they flew on undisturbed. But he knew too that the main threat in the early stages would come from the night-fighters equipped with their own radar, based around Hamburg, Kiel and Lübeck. They were organised according to the '*Zahme Sau*' – Tame Boar – fighter-control system. At the sign of any incoming raid, fighters were scrambled and collected together in groups, orbiting one of several radio beacons throughout Germany. Then, controlled by ground controllers, they were ready to be directed as a mass force into the bomber stream. From there they'd use their own internal radar sets to single out individual targets for attack.

Searby knew that the fighters would rise 'like a cloud of hornets' if alerted by radar, and he also knew that sooner or later the enemy would know that the diversionary dummy attack on Berlin was just that. In any case, he couldn't be sure that enough German fighters would have been diverted. As they flew, Searby weaved their Lancaster gently so the gunners, 'huge in their padded suits', could see directly below, checking for any threats. His rear gunner was bunched up in his narrow turret behind his four Brownings and almost certainly perishingly cold despite his suit. His mid-upper, swinging in his suspended hammock seat as the aircraft twisted and turned, scanning the wide sky above him, looking down when he could, alert for an attack from below.

Reaching a higher altitude, Searby 'increased the swing into a full-blooded corkscrewing movement calculated to confuse the radar-equipped night-fighters as they search for us. The corkscrew is sick-making after long periods and calls for considerable effort at the controls, but it's stood us in very good stead and all my pilots swear by it.'

Meanwhile the navigator emerged from his cramped desk behind his blackout curtain to take a sight with his sextant through the Perspex astrodome. It was one of the few occasions he could see what was going on outside. Searby knew his navigator could become 'very bad-tempered sometimes if asked what he deems to be an unnecessary question which breaks his thought processes'. Searby knew why, too. His navigator was sitting alone, his light screened off, cramped and having constantly to think on his feet because 'in a matter of minutes we may be heading into a heavily defended area: and, of course, we are doing the sickening corkscrewing all the time'.

Ever fearful of attack, sticking out in the bright moonlit sky 'like a toilet in the desert', but aware that the spoof diversion raid on Berlin must have alerted enemy defences by now, and praying that they'd be giving their full attention to that, they flew on. At one point their course passed within 50 miles of neutral Sweden, and they could see the lights of the town of Malmö. It was difficult to believe, after having had nearly four years of deprivation, danger and nightly blackouts, that some could still be enjoying brightly lit, peaceful lives. 'There are people down there actually living like human beings!' remarked one of Searby's crew. Many of those flying into danger longed to join them, and the beautiful blonde girls they'd heard so much about.

'Navigator to Captain – five minutes to Rügen Island, where we alter course to one-seven-zero degrees.'

On the ground below Searby, the Commandant of Peenemünde, *Generalmajor* Walter Dornberger, was taking a walk on the perimeter of the housing estate. It was 11.30 p.m. and the night was still and calm. As he strolled, enjoying the pine-scented air, he heard the air-raid sirens in the compound begin to wail. This wasn't a new experience for the occupants of Peenemünde. It was not at all unusual for Allied bombers to gather over the Baltic before heading for Berlin, and so far they had been overlooked. Dornberger even wondered if the enemy was aware of its existence; though reconnaissance aircraft had appeared overhead several times in the recent past, his base hadn't yet been attacked.

'Hitherto we had simply played possum. Our anti-aircraft guns had orders to fire only if we were actually being raided. All was quiet. The blackout was faultless and it was constantly checked.'[15] In the eventuality of an attack, they were covered, since at least one copy of all the production, research and development files had already been placed elsewhere. In addition, dispersal of the various departments was already under way, and all possible air-raid precautions had been taken.

Satisfied all was in order, Dornberger returned to his quarters and turned in.

In the skies above, Stan Shaw sat at his lonely rear gunner position in Lancaster DV-202, tirelessly scanning the skies as he and his crew tensed up for the coming attack.

The exhaust stubs of the Merlins glowed red in the night sky as John Searby's aircraft turned south, feeling naked and alone, several minutes ahead of the main attacking force. Searby was concerned at first to see a ledge of cloud ahead, but it was higher than he'd expected and he found he could fly below it. Soon, the men could see what hitherto they'd only observed as a model back in the briefing room. How unreal it looked, but there it all was – the airfield at the tip and the experimental works and the other targeted buildings, the massive production works and the neatly laid-out housing estate – spreading along the east coast. Searby flew along the line of buildings to check off the three principal targets; the development factory, the rocket assembly plant and the housing estate. But their arrival, after all, was not unexpected. Hundreds of smoke canisters on the ground had already begun to belch out fumes, the wind from the sea blowing the smoke across the target area.

'Light flak opening up, Skipper,' the bomb aimer warned.

'The green and red shells shot past the aircraft and we turned out to sea, where I noticed two ships anchored. As we neared them they both opened up with heavy and light flak,' Searby recalls. But the German gunners hadn't got their aim in and Searby knew they were in no immediate danger. Two minutes to H-Hour when the attack would begin. He pulled off to the north and waited for the preliminary marking of the targets to begin.

'The method selected for that night was one of first illuminating the whole area with powerful magnesium flares dropped by the first Pathfinders using their H2S [ground-mapping radar], utilising the tiny island of Rügen as their reference point – from previous experience we knew this to be the best way of ensuring accuracy.'

It was 12.11 a.m. when the first wave of the attack began; its target, the housing estate. The first markers were dropped inaccurately, however, falling on the nearby forced labour camp. Thus the first wave of bombers followed suit. There were many fatalities before the error could be corrected. Hit by the first wave of bombers at fifteen minutes past midnight, the housing estate very soon looked to Searby's experienced eye like anywhere else 'under massive attack: bursting bombs, masses through which the sliding beams of the searchlights crossed and re-crossed. The red burst from the heavy anti-aircraft fire mingled with it all, and yet we could not say that the defence systems were anything but relatively light in character. This happy situation continued for some twenty minutes, until the second aiming point, the actual rocket factory, was under heavy bombardment.'

Pandemonium already, but so far no sign of heavy defences. Perhaps the Berlin spoof raid had paid off. Perhaps they'd get away with it and make a clean escape. One never knew one's luck.

On the ground, Peenemünde's Commandant, Walter Dornberger, was dragged from his sleep by the unmistakable pounding of the compound's anti-aircraft guns: 'I sprang out of bed and had breeches and socks on in record time.'

Dornberger didn't have time to find his boots as the first bombs exploded, so he pulled on his slippers. 'The first window panes tinkled out. Tiles came hurtling and crashing down the sloping roof, crashing to the ground.' As more bombs fell, 'every window pane blew out and the rest of the tiles came down. The frame of the hall door had been driven outwards and it was jammed. I managed to push through it.'

Once outside, Dornberger saw 'flights of bombers passing uninterruptedly over the works'.

'There was a distant, hollow rumble of many bombs falling, mingled with the noise of the anti-aircraft guns. All my senses were concentrated on the whistle of bombs dropping close. Alternately throwing ourselves down and leaping up again, we reached the west side of the building which housed the Instruments, Guidance and Measurement Department, at the time the most valuable part of the works. Tongues of flame shot, crackling and hissing, out of the shattered windows. Iron girders, twisted and red hot, rose above the outer walls. Parts of the roof collapsed, crashing down into the interior. Help here would be too late.'[16]

Things were moving fast. At 12.31 a.m., Searby turned the attention of the attack, the second wave, made up of 113 Lancasters and their eighteen Pathfinder aircraft, to the V2 production works. The whole target area was now an inferno, and it was hard to distinguish where the works lay. Searby decided to fly in lower in order to identify the targeted buildings precisely. 'To my horror the gunners informed me that they had seen large 4,000lb bombs falling past our aircraft: this was most alarming but was to be expected since many bombers were flying above the height at which we were orbiting.'

Throughout the raid, Searby continued to direct his Pathfinders to mark the various targets with different coloured flares, then allocated the various elements of the incoming bomber stream onto each target. Timing and accuracy were vital, and this performance, though planned in detail, had had no rehearsal. A clutch of red target indicators fell in a dazzling cascade to the ground, but almost immediately Searby's bomb aimer, watching like a hawk, yelled that they'd fallen over a mile south of the target. Another clutch of reds fell wide to the north, but by good fortune or better judgement, a yellow dropped midway between them. This was swiftly backed up by the dropping of green indicators in the correct position. Searby quickly ordered the incoming bombers to use the green flares as their aiming point and ignore all others.

'I broadcast to the main force and warned them of the errors, and successive backers-up brought the marking back again to the correct spot. Some stray greens fell along the coast and I broadcast again to stop the waste of bombs.'

The attack was going as planned and the results could be clearly seen and heard by the next elements of the bomber stream.

'Approaching the target, we could see the raid ahead progressing as the first- and second-wave aircraft bombed the red and green target indicators laid down by the Pathfinders. From our position at the rear of the bomber stream there appeared to be little enemy opposition with only light flak and few searchlights. Over our radio set we heard the calm voice of Group Captain Searby assuring the third-wave crews the raid was progressing in a satisfactory way and to await further orders.'[17]

Then came a new threat.

'Bomb aimer to Captain – look out for fighters. I've just seen a Lanc blow up over target!'

It was 12.40 a.m., and as the words reached Master Bomber John Searby, he saw the burning Lancaster himself. There was no doubt that German fighters had arrived. The bombers were silhouetted against the bright flames and illuminated by the clear moon. The enemy had no need of searchlights to find them now, and the Germans had introduced a second, more unpredictable interception tactic than Tame Boar: '*Wilde Sau*' or 'Wild Boar'.

Generally, in single-engined day-fighters such as Me109s, the free-ranging 'Wild Boar' pilots would seek out the British bombers, sometimes in co-operation with the searchlight crews on the ground. After the fighters had reached the combat zone, pilots tried to identify and intercept enemy bombers visually, sometimes diving from above after spotting them silhouetted against the burning targets. Both were to be feared – the Wild Boars because of their unpredictability and boldness, their willingness to risk being taken out by their own flak; and the Tame Boars because of their accurate and powerful cannon. One short burst was enough to blow off a bomber's wing or kill all the crew in the cockpit.

The bombers, so far relatively unscathed, were in for a deadly surprise.

'After our bombing run, we made two complete circuits of the area – no indication of fighters or flak – when, suddenly, aircraft began to go down. The night-fighters had arrived. Our excitement at a successful operation was immediately squashed as Lancs began to fall out of the sky. It was a perfectly clear night and the Lancs made perfect silhouettes against the brightly lit target areas.'[18]

The fighters had originally been decoyed to Berlin, which had worked in their favour for the first elements of the attack. But then the German controllers realised their capital wasn't the real target and ordered them to refuel. Those that had the range were dispatched to Peenemünde. Ironically, the German pilots had no more idea of precisely what the British were attacking than the British themselves. They were too late to defend the production works, which were now a mass of flame, but they could certainly try to avenge it.

*Oberleutnant* Friedrich-Karl Müller arrived early at the scene in his single-engined Focke-Wulf 190 and attacked at once.

'It was so easy. I could see fifty bombers. I was a bit nervous as I seemed to be alone then, but I picked out a Lancaster. The tail gunner fired back, of course. His first hit was in the spinner in the middle of my propeller, then he knocked out a piece of my engine cowling. It was a quick combat. I tried to hit the fuel tanks between the engines in the right wing, and I think I must have hit both engines on that side, because I saw the propellers windmilling and he kept swinging to the right. He couldn't maintain altitude. I watched him make a forced landing among the breakers off the shore. I didn't see any parachutes. There was a great cloud of spray.

'I flew back to the target area and found another Lancaster, easily visible against the smoke. I attacked again but this tail gunner was not so well-trained or else he was nervous. His first shots went past me on the left. He swung his turret and fired again but I had moved to the left and easily avoided him. His right wing caught fire and about a minute later the wing fell off and he spiralled down. I couldn't see any parachutes again. It was very difficult to bale out when an aircraft is spinning. It fell into the sea.'

Out of ammunition, Müller now withdrew. He'd fired far longer bursts than recommended and had risked destroying his own cannons. 'I thought it made good business sense to make sure of getting the bombers even if it meant putting in new cannon.'[19]

The cost of a Lancaster was far greater than that of an Fw190, let alone its weaponry.

It was close to 1.15 a.m. when the third wave of the attack flew in, its target the experimental works. Mercilessly harassed by German fighters, the bombers drove through a net of lethal tracer shells, their gunners often blinded by the flashing of their own guns. In the melee, escape was never going to be easy.

Confusion reigned in the fire-lit sky as bombers ducked and weaved to avoid being hunted down. One of Stan Shaw's colleagues on 44 Squadron, Sergeant Bill Sparkes, was leaving the target area in his Lancaster when it was hit.

'We kept on going down. I thought we were still trying to evade by a straightforward dive, but we continued on – down, down, down. We got instructions to abandon the aircraft. My job was to get the front hatch open and I had to get the bundles of WINDOW we were carrying off the hatch. It didn't take me long, not the way I moved: I tossed it all forward onto the bomb-sight. I opened the hatch and almost immediately heard the command to abandon the aircraft. Because I'd been so busy, I'd stopped taking note of the altitude, and of what the rest of the crew were doing. I just didn't know what the damage had been or whether any of the others had been hit. I do know that there was no doubt in my mind about getting out – there was no hesitation – so I suppose I must have known the situation was rather dire. Normally, in training, the crew always lined up behind me, waiting to get out, and it has always puzzled me why there was no one there. It never occurred to me that they were all dead.'[20]

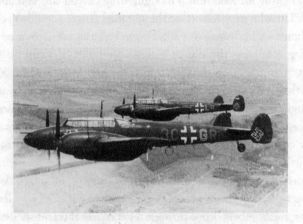

*German Me110 night-fighters*

The bomber crews on the Peenemünde raid were experiencing yet another brand-new and very unpleasant surprise. Two of the Me110s targeting the Lancasters, the bombers most feared by the Germans, were flying beneath them and, carefully positioning themselves, raked the bombers' wings and fuselages from below with a strange new device. The Germans knew Lancasters by now, knew that none had ventral guns positioned beneath the fuselage. They'd therefore mounted diagonally inclined upward-pointing cannon to shoot at their soft underbellies. The Germans called this *Schräge Musik* – 'slanting music', the German slang for jazz.

It could have done even more damage but for the fact that it was brand new, and so far only fitted to two aircraft flown by experienced pilots. Its great success was borne out by *Leutnant* Peter Erhardt, who positioned himself beneath his selected victim, holding steady while his guns strafed the Lancaster from below, shattering the wings and engines before the crew knew what had hit them. He then got clear fast and watched with grim satisfaction as the bomber veered over to the side, belching flame, before arching over and down, plummeting away from the battle. Erhardt listened to the scream of the engines fade and turned his attention to his next prey. His *Schräge Musik* was a triumph. Within the next half-hour he sent three more bombers to their deaths.[21]

The second *Schräge Musik* pilot flew right under a bomber, 'so close I couldn't see the sky, only this huge aircraft. Then I pressed the button, aiming as best I could at the left inner engine. I only fired four or six shots and the petrol immediately came pouring out on fire and the bomber started to go down. I slid out from underneath it and we flew alongside it as it fell because it was our first success and I was determined to get credit for it.' A new fear had entered the souls of the bomber crews. But *Schräge Musik* was not enough to stop the onslaught. On the ground, Commandant Walter Dornberger surveyed the damage.

'The farther south I penetrated, the more bomb craters I found. They rose before me, among the smoking, splintered trees. The view was wide across a strangely altered landscape. Where were the huts, the fire station and the big canteen? Nothing remained but a mass of craters and smoking ruins. The raid had been a terrific one. Our carefully laid scheme, covering all eventualities and rehearsed several times, had failed completely. The dense fog of smoke, the destruction of the roads, the rubble and the fallen trees made it impossible to get through by car or bicycle.'

At 1 a.m. John Searby surveyed the massive destruction wrought below him.

'Nothing more remained to be done at Peenemünde. These fifty minutes of time would remain long after other experiences had been forgotten. We turned for home.'

'Crossing the coast, Skipper,' the bomb aimer said to Searby, who immediately felt a great wave of relief.

'How many times had one heard this simple but significant phrase – the feeling of escape from danger and things that go bang in the night? One felt as if this were the last time, but I knew that tomorrow we were likely to be called again – maybe the Ruhr. If we were lucky enough we might enjoy a free evening. Ours was a strange war – the heavy brigade of the Royal Air Force. There was no glamour in what we did – a long, cold ride spending eight or nine hours in the darkness, shot at and bound to a rigid flight plan. The nature of our task involved crushing fatigue and it is truly remarkable how very few ever cracked up. Staying power was a prime requirement if one flew under Air Marshal Harris's orders.'

Forty aircraft did not reach home, including twenty-three Lancasters, three from Stan Shaw's 44 Squadron. Operation Hydra also cost Bomber Command sixteen Halifaxes, three Mosquitos and two Stirlings. In more than half the bombers shot down, there were no survivors at all. Among those left behind on the ground was Bill Sparkes, who made a safe landing and was taken prisoner. He was treated relatively well, avoiding the fate of many Allied *Terrorflieger* who had the misfortune to fall into the hands of angry victims of their raids. Soon after his capture, Bill had a visit from Peter Spoden, one of the German pilots who'd been involved in the Battle of Peenemünde: 'He looked a typical, clean-looking German, square-cut, trim and blond. He treated me with great respect. He spoke to me in English and told me that he had shot my aircraft down. I felt amazed that I was talking to him. I don't remember my answer.'

Peter had also travelled by motorbike to the site of his 'kill' to collect, in his youthful enthusiasm, some kind of souvenir from the wreck. He was shocked to see the bodies of the RAF men. The image remained with him for ever. Spoden brought down twenty-four British bombers during the war, and recalling those days from the care home he shared with his wife in his later years, he cried at the memory of how he shot down three Lancasters in ten minutes. 'I was going out of my mind! Those young men, in their early twenties, were just the age of my sons today. It all seems like nonsense now.'[22]

But this was the reality. This was no longer a game of derring-do in the skies.

At Peenemünde, buildings had been badly damaged, and the deaths of the chemical engineer and the site's overall chief engineer were among the worst consequences of the attack. Some 180 civilian personnel were killed, out of a total housing estate population of 1,400. The key man at Peenemünde, the leader and prime mover of the V2 project, Wernher von Braun, had been spared. His work would be delayed by four and a half months, and this, according to President Roosevelt, may have seriously helped D-Day's later success.

However, the crucial time bought by the raid on Peenemünde, and those that followed it, meant that the V2 couldn't be used in anger until just over another year had passed, and by September 1944, though it accounted for an estimated 2,750 civilian deaths in London, its appearance as a weapon came too late to affect the outcome of the war.

\* \* \*

On 18 August, little Elaine Shaw was looking forward to seeing her dad again. He'd be back on leave in less than a fortnight now. That day at school, however, 'I was told to go to the headmistress's office. Her name was Mrs Boltrop – she had even taught my dad earlier. I thought I must be in some sort of serious trouble and was very worried! But Mrs Boltrop was very upset, and crying, and she said, "Go home, your mother needs you." I knew something was wrong but I had no idea what it could be. It took me just a couple of minutes to run back to our house.'

Her heart pounding, Elaine climbed the steps to the back door and went into the kitchen. It was empty, and everything looked normal. As she walked through to the sitting room, she saw her mother on her knees in front of the fire, pushing the coals to the back and trying to put out the flames.

'It seemed a curious thing to be doing. As she turned towards me I could see that she'd been crying, and she glanced towards a telegram lying on the table. My little sister was there and there was a bag in the middle of the floor, packed as though we were going somewhere. I just couldn't understand what was wrong.'

Tears in her eyes, Elsie Shaw put her hands on her little girl's shoulders and simply said, 'Your dad's reported missing; he won't be coming home.'

Elaine couldn't understand what her mother meant. This was her dearly loved father; the most important person in her life. 'I was only nine and it was so much to take in. What did "*not coming home*" mean? Surely it didn't mean for ever?'

# CHAPTER EIGHT

## TOWARDS THE BIG CITY

At the recruiting office in the Old Town behind Edinburgh Castle, former Glasgow police cadet Don MacIntosh had waited in a queue with a number of nervous, shabbily dressed young men. Eventually, he was ushered into a room where a small, elderly RAF Flight Lieutenant sat behind a desk. His eyes were bloodshot with age and unfamiliar medals from a forgotten war decorated his chest. After spending some time perusing Don's paperwork through his monocle and quizzing him on aspects of his schooldays and former career, he eventually growled, 'Ha! Keen to fly and fight the Hun, are ye?'

'Yes, sir!' Don replied, with complete honesty, at the same time thinking: *Jesus, is he having me on?* 'I didn't know anyone who talked like that. Maybe he'd seen it done in a film.'

A few more questions, and that was it. He was in. 'I applied to be an air gunner but they decided I might make pilot, which I was delighted to hear! I returned home, surprised and elated at how easy it was to become a flier.'[1]

For the nineteen-year-old, the decision had meant the beginning of many long journeys. The night train from home in Scotland to the Air Crew Reception Centre in St John's Wood, London, was long and dreary, his dirty, smoky compartment dimly lit by a blue bulb – the less light there was, the less chance of it catching the eye of some German intruder high above. But nothing lessened his excitement at the prospect ahead of him.

Arriving at Euston Station on a sunny day in August 1941, he had joined the throng of men and women in their different uniforms – soldiers, sailors, WAAFs, Wrens,[2] Poles, Sikhs, Canadians – looking for the connection to their next destination. Don joined the hundreds of new recruits heading to Lord's Cricket Ground, one of the RAF's reception centres. Everything was new, bewildering and exciting. Induction was a production line – mass inoculations, a bored Medical Officer in rubber gloves telling them to drop their trousers and cough while he tugged their testicles. Then billeting at flats, six bunks in what used to be a single bedroom, and marching in columns of sixty for meals at the London Zoo café.

But he was going to train as a pilot, so Don happily went through the phases of initial training, which would take up his first year of service. London was followed by Cornwall, where there was gunnery, drill, meteorology, aircraft recognition, aerodynamics and navigation.

Training was like getting onto a conveyor belt; finished airmen churned out at one end, as raw recruits arrived in St John's Wood at the other. Not everyone completed the course; not everyone had what it took to be a bomber pilot; not everyone survived. Finally, however, in June 1942, the day came for Don's next phase: pilot training in the USA, where the wide skies, free from the risk of enemy attack, provided the perfect arena. Here, and in South Africa and Canada, future aviators were nurtured and burnished.

Don found himself travelling again, via Manchester and a holding camp where his RAF uniform caught both welcome attention from the girls and unwelcome reactions elsewhere. There was often tension between the army, the navy and the RAF – soldiers and sailors who went to war didn't see their homes for months; RAF crews, they knew, came back to safe beds and billets after every night's action. They were glamorous, too; girls made a beeline for them – hence both the mockery and the envy. Soldiers and sailors didn't always realise just how many airmen were not returning to the comfort and safety of those beds.

Walking two girls home after a dance in the company of a fellow recruit from New Zealand, a weedy-looking soldier shouted from across the street, 'Bloody Brylcreem Boys, poncing about; fuck off back where you came from.' Don's friend, a huge, part-Maori former schoolteacher, went over to 'have a word', and a fight broke out, during which the squaddie proved not to be nearly as weedy as he looked. A major battle seemed on the cards when the police arrived and the combatants scattered.

Don went on to join 799 other pilot cadets on the *Letitia*, a ship designed to carry just 200 passengers, so 'much of our time was spent queuing up for the lavatories and waiting in shifts to eat'.

'We disembarked at Halifax, Nova Scotia, early in July 1942, and were then sent to a vast training camp at Moncton, Ontario, near the US border, where we had to wait several weeks for posting to one of the many flying training schools.'

Moncton was a dismal barracks, but Don's time there was enlivened by a close encounter with a female primary schoolteacher. She made the first move, but when, after coffee at her place, they progressed to the bedroom and started to get to know each other better, Don went a button too far, was hysterically rebuffed and had to beat a retreat. 'Maybe she'd heard of the lurid films about the horrors of venereal disease shown regularly at the camp in glorious Technicolor by the Medical Section. I realised that I didn't understand women.' A few days later he met her again and she wondered why he hadn't been in touch. He told her he'd ring her, but never did. This was early days, and the young Scot had a lot to learn.

As one door closed, however, another opened. The moment for flying school allocation finally arrived in mid-August. Keeping his ear to the ground, Don learned from one of his fellow trainees 'that the best school was in Florida and the worst in Phoenix, Arizona. We assembled in a wooden hangar with an enormous floor and jockeyed to get on the list for Clewiston, Florida.'

Don got the posting he wanted, and boarded the train for the three-day journey to the training school.

'As we neared our destination, there was a tremendous roar as a single-engine Harvard trainer proceeded to fly at the train. The pilot came back repeatedly, the profile of his Pratt and Whitney radial engine growing, then pulling to one side and flying down the length of the train half a wingspan away. On the final pass, he waved two reversed fingers at us, grinning beneath his cloth helmet and Ray-Bans, and shot up into the sky, leaving a trainful of elated and excited cadets.'

Clewiston, run by American civilian instructors but administered by the RAF, was to be Don's home for the next seven months. The new boys sat down to their first lunch only to learn from the senior cadets that the day before their arrival two training aircraft had collided, killing their occupants. Daunting though this news was, there was no time to reflect; that same afternoon Don found himself taking to the air with his instructor, at the controls of a Stearman biplane.

'The novelty and excitement of my first flight were so great that I hardly paid any attention to what my instructor was telling me. It was a joy to be in the air, the feeling of the freedom of the skies, the excitement of being airborne. I felt privileged; flying was still a very novel experience! The weather was beautiful; it was so peaceful and calm. Very different from flights I presumed I would experience over Europe in a Lancaster in the not too distant future!'

Long months of hard work followed, on the ground and in the air, and a progress to solo flying – from Stearman biplanes to Harvard trainers.

Then came the low-flying exercises. Among the others on his course were two former public schoolboys, inseparable friends. To Don's eye, one looked like a Saxon and the other a Norman.

Low flying appealed to Don, and he took to the Harvard like a duck to water.

'Going up with my instructor, I really thought this might be an opportunity to shine and display my skill. I flew over the cane fields, blowing the green stalks flat with my wash and lifting over the low dykes. I found it immensely exhilarating and enjoyable, although I did occasionally feel my instructor pull back on the stick.'

Pleased with himself, Don was surprised to hear that his instructor didn't share his enthusiasm. Don had been flying far too low. Didn't he realise how many people had been killed doing just that? A week later, the Saxon and Norman pilots were sent on a detail together and failed to return. The crashed Harvard was found in a swamp. It appeared that they'd caught a wingtip on a tree, causing them to cart-wheel over and over. Both wings had broken off and the fuselage had come to rest right-side up, and relatively undamaged. The two young men were found dead, still strapped inside the cockpit, inseparable in death as they had been in life.

'The deaths of the two cadets didn't affect me. I thought they were absolutely bloody silly to be taking risks like that. No one discussed what had happened, we never discussed death; nothing would be achieved by that. I didn't concern myself with fears of death; I was absolutely convinced I would survive. That belief would help me through the war. You *had* to believe you would survive; there was no other option. Of course many others told themselves exactly the same thing and didn't survive, but whatever will be, will be.'

A total of 5,327 Bomber Command aircrew were killed in training during the war.[3]

*Jim Penny*

Don's path through training had been smoothed, though he didn't know it, by a fellow Glaswegian. Born in 1922, James Penny was a post-First World War baby and the youngest by far of five brothers. Sons of the owners of a small fish-and-chip shop chain, they were keen rowers and, with Jim as their cox, they were known as the Fourpence-Halfpenny team.

Jim was a bright lad and would have been the first of the family to go to university, but when war intervened, he joined up as soon as he was able. Like Don MacIntosh, he was selected for pilot training.

Jim passed muster in the initial training, and it wasn't long before he found himself on his way to the USA, but his destination wasn't Florida. His training took him first to Alabama, then Georgia. And here he learned another lesson. Meals in the Mess hall, tremendous and plentiful after the austerity at home, were served by black waiters who addressed the trainees as 'Massa Birdman'.[4] One afternoon, long after lunch, Jim was in the sitting room of the Mess hall writing a letter home.

'One of the waiters came in and in a cultured voice asked, "Would you care for some coffee, sir?" I was startled by his tone and choice of words, so different from the usual Mess hall language and subservient attitude of the waiters there. I said I would like coffee, and, as he poured, I commented on his educated tone and language and asked what he was doing there as a waiter. He said he was a graduate of a Negro college and taught at a school for the local black children in the evenings, reminding me, most courteously, that we were in the Deep South, and that the only jobs for black people were menial. He needed his job to support his teaching work.'

Jim had already noticed the white Mess hall supervisor looking their way with a none-too-friendly expression on his face. Warning the waiter not to look round, but to bow and leave, Jim finished his coffee and folded his letter before getting up to go himself. The supervisor approached Jim angrily and, 'in a hectoring tone, he asked me, "What were that nigger and you talking about?" I told him I'd asked for coffee and when he'd brought it, I'd thanked him, as was the British custom when anyone did us a service.' Segregation and discrimination were new phenomena to Jim, but he was in for further surprises, especially when one Southern gentleman asked him about Britain's 'troubles with your Indians', and why 'we didn't put them in reservations the way they had with the American Indians. I tried to explain without much success.'

Pilot training was going swimmingly until the advanced section, when Jim hit a serious snag. Unlike Don, he hadn't gone straight from Stearmans to Harvards but via another trainer, the Vultee, which had far heavier controls. Jim then had great difficulty adapting to the lighter touch the Harvard required. On one flight he inadvertently let the speed drop so low coming in to land that the aircraft came close to stalling and his instructor sent him for two further check-rides. He failed both.

He was told he'd be going back to Canada. Jim knew what that meant: he was 'washed out'. He had failed pilot training.

He was devastated, but he wasn't finished. At the 'Personnel Despatch Centre' in Ontario, where the interview panel would decide which non-pilot role he would now take up, they asked for his opinion of what had gone wrong. Jim's explanation for his apparent failure was clear and honest: the whole thing was his fault; his trouble was adapting from the Stearman to the heavier Vultee and then back again to the lighter Harvard. 'I think it would have been better if I'd gone from the Stearman straight to the Harvard.'

The officer looked at him and smiled. 'We've been worried about the number of wash-outs at Advanced Training and we sent a team of experienced pilots to investigate. They agree with you. I'm going to recommend you go back on flying training. And you didn't blame the Americans. Your admission that it was your fault was your first good mark.'

It wasn't quite over yet. Jim still had to go before another panel chaired by a Group Captain. He seemed to have answered most of their questions to their satisfaction when they came to what sounded like the clincher.

'Do you think you'll make a good pilot?'

The answer, presumably, was 'yes', but Jim didn't want to appear boastful and scrabbled around in his mind for a better reply.

'Good enough to beat the Hun, sir.'

Later, Jim shuddered at how gung-ho he must have sounded, but it did the trick. The panel collapsed with laughter, and told Jim he was indeed back on pilot training. It would be many months before the full ramifications of that decision became apparent.

\* \* \*

Back in Britain, as bombing sorties increased, relentlessly targeting industry, U-boat bases and cities, Arthur Harris pushed for more and more Lancasters. As operations stepped up, so losses mounted, but it was clearly the premium weapon for the war that Harris envisaged as he set his eyes on his next major target.

By 1943, Avro's first factory at Chadderton, near Oldham, had increased its floorspace to a million square feet, and Lancaster production, using a workforce of close to 11,500, touched 150 per month. The factory at Woodford, south of Stockport, had three assembly lines, each a quarter of a mile long. Woodford was an assembly plant for the manufactured sections, with an airfield and test-flight centre attached. As 1943 progressed, production increased to 170 aircraft per month, later peaking at 293. Such a high rate was increasingly necessary. The average 'life' of a Lancaster was a mere twenty-three operational flights. Not many, given that they were undertaken on an almost nightly basis.

The presence of an airfield meant that, after a final lick of paint, finished and tested bombers could be flown directly to the RAF stations that were to use them. This task was performed by pilots of the Air Transport Auxiliary, many of whom were women. Women, too, drove the tractors that hauled the finished Lancasters, on their 5ft 6in-diameter main wheels, out onto the runways from which they began their flights to destiny. There are few records of women flying Lancasters, though they certainly ferried the giant Halifax and Stirling bombers to their operational units. Sometimes the appearance of these women pilots from the cockpits caused quite a stir. Jim Penny clearly remembered the moment one of the aircraft was delivered.

'Several of us were sitting outside the crew-room waiting to fly when a Stirling landed and taxied round to stop on the perimeter track across from us. It was BIG! The door at the rear opened and a ladder was slipped out. A slight figure descended, paused at the foot of the ladder and took its helmet off. Long golden hair fell to her waist and there was a gasp of awe from the watching young pilots. She was flying this monster alone with no crew to help! And my, but she was a bonny lass.'

Another ATA pilot, Mary Ellis, met with similar disbelief when she delivered a Wellington to East Anglia. As she came in to land, the ground crew assembled to see their new bomber complete its journey from the factory to the front line. Gathered at the dispersal point, they watched in admiration as it taxied towards them and came to a standstill. The engines shut down and, as the propellers slowed to a halt, they came forward to greet the pilot. They couldn't believe their eyes. To their astonishment it was not a man but a petite woman who climbed down from the cockpit carrying her parachute.

'Where's the pilot?' they shouted in disbelief.

'I *am* the pilot!' Mary replied.

They simply didn't believe her; it must have been a practical joke. A couple of them clambered in to check the aeroplane for the 'missing' pilot. 'They could not believe women could fly these aeroplanes, so it was a huge surprise for them to see me – a slim, blonde, 5ft 2in female flying such a giant aircraft.'[5]

Regardless of stature, women adopting those major and important roles in the war effort was something new wherever it occurred. When Sophie Pape started work at the Woodford Lancaster factory she remembered that, 'The presence of the first women employees caused some disquiet among the predominantly male workforce. On my first day, two other girls and I had to wait while the union officials met to consider the reaction of their members to our arrival. I was sent to work on the shop floor where the Lancasters were assembled. As my small stature was ideal for working in restricted spaces, I joined the team that fitted oxygen systems into the aircraft. I also did other tasks such as pop-riveting the skin to the fuselage and fitting the rubber seals to the undercarriage.'[6]

Sophie worked long hours under stressful conditions (there were few health-and-safety requirements eighty years ago), but she was a skilled worker. Unskilled workers earned £2 per week at the most for a woman, £3 for a man. This, however, compared quite well with the wage of a Bomber Command sergeant pilot, who received £4.75 a week for the privilege of risking life and limb nightly, taking the war to the enemy.[7] The presence of so many women working alongside men on the factory floor was something everyone had to get accustomed to. The war, with its tensions and threat, supercharged an atmosphere in which traditional social and sexual attitudes were being challenged; added to which, many women missed male companionship with their partners away at the Front. Long night shifts provided a perfect theatre for romantic and sexual liaisons to flourish.

Many of these were sincere, and 'Avro sweethearts' were quite common. Others were more opportunistic. Sophie Pape remembered working alongside a handsome but shy bachelor who stimulated a lot of interest among Sophie's female workmates, while Joseph Barry, a male fitter who started work as an apprentice at Chadderton, soon found himself besieged by female colleagues, some of whom could be alarmingly forward. 'In one job, when I had the duty of collecting tools, there would be girls saying, "Come round here," trying to get me to go with them behind their machines. Some even started to take off their overalls.'[8]

Men were equally keen to form liaisons, casual or permanent. 'There were a lot of babies born at Avro and there were a lot of abortions too. If the lads from the Air Force had known what had gone on in some of their Lancasters – and not just on the night shifts either – they would have been really surprised. Some babies were started in them and a few were born in them too,' recalled a female worker at Yeadon, Avro's other main factory, a few miles north-east of Bradford.[9]

Yeadon was another massive plant – it employed 17,500 workers, 60 per cent of whom were women. But even at its most efficient, Yeadon wasn't enough. Lancasters and their components were produced in factories all over the country. Their manufacture was even expanded to include a plant in Canada, where Victory Aircraft built them under licence. The Canadian Lancasters only differed from their British counterparts in that their instrumentation and electrics were American and their Merlin engines were built locally by Packard. Ford had been approached initially in the USA, but declined, possibly because Henry Ford thought Britain unlikely to win the war. In the meantime, Packard made a huge success of the Merlin concession, and its engines were to equip the Mark III Lancaster. The use of the Packard Merlin 28, capable of delivering 1,420hp at take-off, was the only real difference between the Mark I and the Mark III, and 3,020 Mark III Lancasters would eventually be built, some modified to carry the famous 'bouncing bomb' used on the Dambusters raid.

Many Merlins *were* in fact subsequently produced by Ford in Britain, after cordial talks between the head of the Ford Motor Company in the UK and RAF mandarin Sir Wilfrid Freeman. The reason was simple: demand for Merlins overreached Rolls-Royce capacity. A factory was established a few miles from Manchester city centre, and part of another factory nearby was given over to drawing offices and tool-making. Rolls-Royce was delighted with the arrangement, and the two companies found on meeting that they already held each other in high esteem. However, Rolls was in for a shock when it came to discussing the technical nitty-gritty. Ford was a car manufacturer. Would it have the sophistication for aircraft engines? Stanley Hooker, a young designer at Rolls who was behind huge improvements to the Merlin's supercharger and would go on to pioneer the jet engine with Frank Whittle, was sceptical when he first met them at his Derby offices:

'A number of Ford engineers arrived at Rolls-Royce HQ and spent some months examining the drawings and manufacturing methods. One day, their chief engineer said, "You know, we can't make the Merlin to these measurements." I replied, loftily, "I suppose that is because the drawing tolerances are too diffi-cult for you, and you can't achieve the accuracy." The Ford man replied, "On the contrary, the tolerances are far too *wide* for us. We make motor cars far more accurately than this. Every part on our car engines has to be interchangeable with the same part on any other engine, and hence all parts have to be made with extreme accuracy, far closer than you use. That is the only way we can achieve mass production."'[10]

Hooker was duly impressed, and though the new technical drawings required by Ford took a year to draw up, the subsequent production proved immensely successful. Hooker saw Ford pro-ducing engines 'like shelling peas, and very good engines they were too'.

Precision brought its own problems, however. Specialist machin-ery was needed to make the tools that made the components, and Britain didn't have enough of them. Three attempts were made to freight a crankshaft machining tool from the USA, but two of the three ships were sunk by German U-boats. Their Swiss-made jig-borers could work to within 0.00005 inches. Merlin engines had seventy-two gear-wheels, and under Ford's regime, measurements for their manufacture were in millionths of inches – a higher specifi-cation than would be needed for a chronometer. And *not one* of the 30,400 Merlin engines produced by Ford failed the Air Ministry's standards. Quite an achievement, and a tribute to the automobile manufacturer's production technique, whereby any given worker specialised in one particular part, and each part was rigorously inspected. Of their 17,316 employees (well over a third of whom were women) working on the Merlin, fewer than 300 had any prior experience of making cars, let alone aircraft.

American aid was also enlisted in a very different way. A vital installation like Yeadon, pumping out the one war machine whose use against the enemy could be viewed as all-but-infallibly destructive, had to be protected at all costs. It needed an elaborate system of camouflage.

To do this, Roy Dobson engaged the services of designers from Hollywood, including the young Xavier Atencio. Atencio had joined the Walt Disney Company at the age of nineteen in 1938. After America had entered the war, he served as a photo reconnaissance analyst for the United States Army Air Forces (USAAF), stationed in England. Atencio and his design colleagues from the film world had earth banked up the walls of the factory in a 45-degree slope, ensuring that the sun would cast no shadow. The factory's flat roof, meanwhile, was grassed over. Hedgerows were erected to demarcate fields, and dummy farm buildings were installed on it, complete with stone walls, a duck pond, and moveable life-size model cows and sheep (whose positions were changed by members of the night shift). The disguise was so effective that not only was Yeadon unmolested by enemy bombers throughout the war, but even friendly airmen, who knew of its existence and location, sometimes had a hard time finding it.

*Lancaster nose sections awaiting assembly on the*
*Castle Bromwich production line*

By late 1943, Arthur Harris had built up the quantity of Lancasters he needed for his next major assault – and had the men to fly them. The number of airfields had increased enormously, and thousands of women had joined the WAAF to staff them. Harris was ready for an all-out assault on the German capital.

Concern continued to mount in some quarters about the bombing policy, and major figures were already expressing firm disapproval of civilian casualties. On 27 May 1943 in the House of Commons, Richard Stokes, Labour MP for Ipswich and a powerful independent voice, asked Sir Archibald Sinclair, Secretary of State for Air: 'Is the Right Honourable Member aware that a growing volume of opinion in this country considers indiscriminate bombing of civilians both morally wrong and strategic lunacy?'

There were many, however, who thought Harris's strategic bombing policy was correct. He still had Churchill's support, that of the public, and that of the press. One *Daily Telegraph* article might, from its tone, have been written by Harris himself: 'He who took up the sword shall perish by the sword; and the flames in which he swore he would convulse the world will, in his fall, be the flames of Berlin and the cities of Germany.'[11] And for all Harris's belligerence and awkwardness, and despite the demands he made on his men, he was generally popular with them. Jim Penny thought it was 'appropriate to record the great regard bomber crews had for "Butch" Harris.'

'Black humour was the ethos of the time with us, and we were proud to be the "Butcher's" men. "Butch" was a term of affection. I don't expect those not there to understand that. There is ample proof that the Hitler regime was truly evil, intent on enforcing its will with great barbarity. The bombing campaign was indeed terrible, but in the context of the time it was essential.'

To men like Jim Penny and his Lancaster crewmates, Berlin was the capital of that evil regime and the centre of the Nazi administration. It was also a pivotal transport hub and the location of several key industries. There had been a number of raids on 'The Big City' previously, and everyone knew the Berlin defences would be prepared for them. But after what he perceived to be the success of the Hamburg raid, it was time for a truly massive attack. With the help of the US 8th Air Force, he thought he could bring about Hitler's downfall, saving the wastage of a huge land offensive. It might cost the Allies up to 500 aircraft, and over 3,000 airmen, but it would cost Germany the war.

His pilot training complete, Jim Penny loved the Lancaster he and his new crew would take to war. 'From my very first flight, I knew it was a pilot's aircraft. I had real trust in it; the controls were just right, it was beautiful to fly and it handled perfectly. It was a delightful aeroplane and did exactly what it was designed to do.' Jim and his crew were assigned to 97 Squadron, RAF Bourn, west of Cambridge, where he found there was still a lot to learn; which he did, from his Wing Commander, a law unto himself, who handled an aircraft as if it were a part of his own body.

'What can you do if you get coned in searchlights, sir?'

'Stop and go sideways.'

'You're having me on.'

'Haven't you ever heard of a stall turn, lad?'

The Wing Commander's way of flying the giant bomber, like a fighter, was very different to what Jim had been trained to do. 'You pull the nose of your Lancaster up through a quarter loop until the speed falls off to a point where it won't support the aircraft any longer and the nose drops sharply. Then you kick the full right rudder, which sends you into a steep right dive. You stop and go sideways.'

Not for the faint-hearted.

But that wasn't all.

'Have you rolled your Lancaster, lad?'

'You're having me on again, sir.'

'I've been blown on my back. Find out how to recover.'

So Jim tried it. On a test flight one sunny day, he performed a barrel roll – a manoeuvre normally reserved for fighters or aerobatic aircraft. While flying straight and level, Jim pulled the Lancaster into a climb and, rotating at the same time, his flight path mimicked the shape of a barrel – the upper surface of his aircraft remaining in contact with the imaginary barrel throughout the manoeuvre so, at the top of the roll, Jim, his crew and their Lancaster were upside-down and facing earthwards. Completing the roll to the usual, more sedentary position, the aircraft handled like a dream.

But at a price.

Jim's navigator had managed to get hold of a pound of tomatoes and, not having time to stow them before the test flight, had brought them on board. Jim had warned the crew about what he was going to do, but the navigator had never been in a barrel roll before. None of them had, pilot included. When the Lancaster was inverted, he came off his seat and, held aloft by his safety harness, dangled upside-down. When the aircraft eventually righted itself at the bottom of the roll, he plunged back onto his bag of precious tomatoes.

'I was not a popular skipper with my navigator that day!'

Sitting on a bag of squashed tomatoes was one thing, but the higher you flew, the lower the pressure, which could have an irresistible effect on a man's bladder and bowels,[12] so relieving oneself was among the more usual discomforts to plague Lancaster airmen. It was possible, in extremis, to make use of the Elsan portable lavatory, but not over enemy territory. Leaving a gun turret unmanned, engaging the automatic pilot or handing over control to the flight engineer were never options when you might be obliterated at any moment by an enemy fighter.

Wireless operator Reg Payne paints a familiar picture:

'The gunners either had to hold on to it, or, as was more often the case, just let everything go in their flying suits and then get washed and cleaned up once back at base. On one trip, Don, our flight engineer, noticed sparks coming from somewhere along the fuselage, and, busy with his instruments, asked me to investigate. When I got to the area around the mid-turret, there was some smoke, but no sparks or flashing lights; all seemed well. It wasn't until years later when Jock, the mid-upper gunner, and I were chatting about that tour of ops that the subject came up again and he admitted that he had been the culprit! Unable to hold on any longer, he had wet himself so much that the urine had run down into the electrics around his turret. It was a fairly regular event on those long cold trips deep into Germany.'[13]

Using an empty bottle was awkward, and the risk of missing or spillage made the prospect an unpleasant one. It wouldn't have been applauded by the ground crew either, as they'd have to mop up afterwards, so Jim Penny sought their advice. On his next outing he found they'd clipped a largish funnel to the front of his seat, attached to which was a tube that ran through the metal-work and outside the fuselage. It was a perfect solution, 'though trying to extract the appropriate member through multiple layers of thick flying clothing when strapped to your seat was still quite a problem'.

That clothing was also fraught with other difficulties. The first layer was a vest and scratchy long johns. Jim wore pyjama trousers instead, and his mother knitted him some knee warmers since Lancaster pilots had to put up with a fierce and constant draught. Next came a thick sweater and battledress uniform, and Jim liked to wear an overall flying suit on top of them, though some pilots preferred the fleece-lined leather Irvin jacket. He kept his hands warm with silk inner gloves covered by soft leather gauntlets. His helmet was also soft leather, with connections to the intercom and clips for the oxygen mask. The whole ensemble was topped off by a Mae West lifejacket, the parachute harness and, last but far from least, the parachute itself, close at hand to be clipped on if the worst came to the worst.

Jim and his fellow airmen carried other equipment into battle. A small knife with which to cut down his flying boots so that they'd look more like shoes and be less noticeable if he were shot down. Their escape pack had been designed to fit into a flying suit or trouser patch pocket, and included silk maps, a small rubber water bottle, Horlicks malted milk tablets, a miniature compass, matches, a needle and thread, chocolate, amphetamine stimulant

Benzedrine tablets and chewing gum. Appropriate foreign currency was also issued, depending on the target.

Escape packs became standard issue for aircrews, but many flyers took extra kit. Thomas Murray disliked strategic bombing and was relieved when he transferred to Special Operations.

'One of my greatest friends was my .38 service revolver, and I kept it with one round in the second chamber so you had to click it twice. I kept it in my flying boot. The thing that gave me the most fear was burning to death. You saw a lot of it on operations over Germany; a plume of flames and you knew another aircraft had been shot down. It was pretty horrific and as captain you knew you would never leave the aircraft, at least I never would, since you never knew if your crew were all right. It'd have to be a very controlled operation in which you could be sure that all your crew had bailed out safely. So I never expected to leave. The gun was for me, so I'd never have to face that last bit. It was good for my morale.'[14]

Tail-end Charlie Bill Kiley shared Murray's greatest anxiety.

'I never really worried about death – it almost seemed unreal. I worried about being burnt though. Stationed near Cambridge, I was walking in the town one day and saw six aircrew, all terribly burnt. They were some of the Guinea Pigs[15] – airmen who had been severely burnt and were undergoing pioneering plastic surgery. Their faces were terrible; one had no hands. Yet they were chatting away together, laughing and talking, and they were in uniform. That was the only thing I worried about, the one thing I was afraid of – burning alive.'[16]

Rituals mattered too, as did mascots – a lucky coin, a girlfriend's suspenders, a dab of her scent on the silk scarf worn to protect the neck from chafing when on ops – whatever a man thought might protect him when there was nothing else to turn to for reassurance. Pilot Officer G. J. L. Bate,[17] Jim Penny's popular and efficient mid-upper gunner, wore the battledress he'd donned on his first tour on every subsequent operation; it was his lucky uniform. Battered and frayed, torn in places, it had certainly seen better days, but it wasn't doing anyone any harm and bomber crews weren't sticklers about uniform.

One night, however, just before they were due to set off, Jim and his crew were having a last cigarette near their Lancaster, and Bate hadn't yet put on his flying suit over his battledress. Their Group Captain, who was making his way from aircraft to aircraft to wish his crews well, took one look at the scruffy uniform and told him to get a new one. Bate explained why he couldn't, which got the senior officer's back up, and he was ordered to report to the Commanding Officer the following day.

That night's target was Mannheim, but less than an hour from base Jim's starboard outer engine caught fire and he had to boo-merang – return to base. He managed this with great skill and, left leg aching from pushing the rudder control hard against the pull of the port engines, saved both the aircraft and the lives of his men. Busy discussing what had gone wrong with the ground crew, it wasn't until later in the day that he heard from his Flight Commander that he would be assigned a new mid-upper gunner.

'I protested, saying how much it meant to us having Bate in the crew, how it gave us confidence. He said he quite understood but it was no use, the Group Captain and Pilot Officer had had a stand-up row over that battledress and Bate had been posted elsewhere. We never saw him again.'

Jim found out later that Bate had been promoted to Flight Lieutenant and awarded the Distinguished Flying Cross (DFC). 'I bet he wore that scruffy, lucky battledress on every op. He was a grand chap.' Bate would never know how fortuitous that contre-temps with the Group Captain had been.

There was never time to reflect. Raid after raid, no let-up, as summer passed into autumn and the nights grew longer, which allowed deeper penetration into Germany. Ops to Berlin loomed. Jim's crew soldiered on but the threat of death was ever present, and not just over enemy territory. Reaching the end of a pre-op flying test, Jim was preparing to land when he noticed that the windsock for the runway he'd been assigned was flying at right angles to his approach – blowing across the runway, which made landing much more dangerous. He called the control tower to ask permission to use the alternative runway so he could approach into the wind, but was refused. Three times the controller told him to land, assuring him that another Lancaster had done so perfectly safely a short time before. Jim knew they were on ops that night; he had to get the Lancaster refuelled and loaded with bombs. So he did what he could. 'On the approach I crabbed in at a pronounced angle and, as I rounded out, kicked the Lanc straight and closed the throttles.'

At that moment, however, as Jim had feared, they started to drift sideways – and fast. 'The right tyre burst immediately it touched the tarmac. As we began to slew to the right, I opened up the starboard outer engine to lift the wing and held it up until I'd cleared the runway.' They were now bouncing across the grass. 'I closed the throttles and the undercarriage immediately collapsed. We swung right round with the undercarriage legs sticking through the right wing.' Jim made a quick check. All the crew had already taken up crash positions. They were badly shaken, but otherwise unharmed. His rear gunner was out of the main exit almost before the Lancaster stopped moving. 'He wasn't fast enough, for the fire wagon was at the aircraft as it came to rest, and he met the full blast of its foam as it sprayed over the starboard wing.' Jim scrambled out as quickly as he could and began making his way, fuming, to the control tower.

His progress was stalled by the arrival of the Group Captain.

'Where are you going?'

'To thump that bloody controller.'

'Leave this with me, Flight Sergeant. I'll deal with it.'

As everyone had seen what had happened, the controller couldn't pass the buck. Responsible for wrecking an expensive operational aircraft and potentially killing its crew in the process, he was relieved of duty and left the station that same day.

Accidents in training were all too frequent. While working as a navigation instructor at RAF Feltwell in Norfolk, Reg Davey witnessed one of the worst:

'I was on what was supposed to be a rest period between operational tours. One night two of our Lancasters, with pupil crews, collided and exploded over the airfield. There were fourteen bodies, badly smashed up, and we somehow had to find fourteen coffins from around the local area. It was a most gruesome task for the medical orderlies. We heard that the ones who had to collect the pieces of the dead men and gather them together were in such a bad way that they were drinking formaldehyde to get themselves through it. When they put the pieces in the coffins, they had to make up the weight of a human body by using sandbags. I'd never experienced anything like this before, and it brought it all very close to home for me. We just thought, thank goodness we weren't on those aircraft. But if it doesn't happen to me, it happens to somebody else.'[18]

\* \* \*

On a week's leave home, Jim Penny was able to have lunch in Stirling with his brother Laurie, a private in the Black Watch. Normally Laurie wouldn't have been allowed out without prior permission, but his Regimental Sergeant Major was so impressed by Jim's RAF uniform and credentials that he bent the rules.

'I explained my errand and that I had to leave that evening from Glasgow to rejoin my squadron, which was operational. The Sergeant Major rose to his full six-foot-plus. He was a splendid figure in his Black Watch kilt and his two rows of medal ribbons. Leading me outside, he bellowed a command and a corporal shot out of the guardroom like a jack-in-the-box.'

In a stentorian voice he ordered him to fetch Recruit Penny. Laurie rapidly appeared, quivering at attention, with a tin hat wobbling on his head.

'"Get changed. You'll be going out for a meal with your brother, the Flight Sergeant. He hasn't got much time, so be quick about it!"'

In Glasgow, Jim basked in the comfort of home, and his parents' company. He was twenty-one years old. Inside, he was still a boy – and yet he wasn't. He was a man who had both dealt and faced death on a nightly basis for many months; a man who took responsibility for the lives of six others as well as his own; a man who had travelled further than he could have imagined in his wildest dreams. At home, though, 'there was no discussion about the war, or what I'd seen and done. I was conscious of protecting my parents from the reality of my war – I didn't want them to worry about what I was doing. They didn't ask, and I didn't say anything. They were two very separate parts of my life. Leave was a respite from war.'

This would be Jim Penny's last respite. On the evening of Thursday 18 November 1943, Arthur Harris's planned series of massive raids to smash Berlin began. For Jim Penny, those 'Battle of Berlin' ops were a disturbing experience.

'I remember my navigator stuck his head out from behind his curtain once. When he saw the flak we were flying into, he said, "This is bloody dangerous!" and his head shot straight back. He said he'd never look out again! It was the only time any member of my crew made any allusion to the dangers we faced; but I always had every sympathy for the people whose nerve broke and couldn't go on. But we never spoke about our own fears. You just didn't. There was never any thought of the death and destruction we were causing, either. There was a job to be done, and we had to do it. Our thoughts were concentrated on winning the war.'[19]

Jim Penny and his crew, now chosen to fly with the Pathfinder Force due to their excellent navigation and bombing skills, were at the forefront of raids on Berlin that winter. His second op, on the night of 22 November, was relatively – for Bomber Command – uneventful. Waiting at the end of the runway, he looked down as the station's pipe band played its bombers off on their operation – the tradition at RAF Bourn. Jim couldn't hear them over the sound of his engines, 'but the sight was enough to cheer my Scottish heart'.

Now for take-off. One of the toughest moments of all. If you went wrong in an aircraft full of explosives, the chances were your mission would end before it had begun. Jim could feel rather than hear the sharp intake of breath around him as the Merlins thundered to full power.

They were all right! The slight, passing sense of weightlessness mixed with relief took hold of them all as their Lancaster swept regally up into the night to join the bomber stream. They all knew well enough what a long haul they were in for. They knew Berlin was heavily defended. They'd not only have flak, but groups of fighters to contend with, as well as those armed with the dreaded *Schräge Musik* – the upward-firing cannons.

But now the Lancasters were fitted with a new, defensive onboard radar, Monica, capable of detecting an enemy aircraft approaching from behind far faster than the rear gunner could. Initially Monica was enthusiastically embraced by the crews but, as with so many technological developments, best intentions could have a sting in their tail. Learning of this new detection system, German scientists designed their own '*Flensburg*' device that could home in on Monica's own radar signals.

The war of the airwaves was also gearing up, and here, too, being one step ahead was vital to safety. A new, highly special-ised type of Lancaster was accompanying the bomber stream on these ops that was equipped with 'ABC', or 'airborne cigar' as it was nicknamed by the crews, because of the shape of the aerials involved. Its secret and highly sophisticated radio equipment, operated by a new, eighth, highly trained, German-speaking crew member, could detect the enemy communications with its fighter force, which could then be jammed, or used to direct their aircraft to false locations. The German controllers found both difficult to counter, and one wireless operator reported that they'd resorted to having their instructions sung by Wagnerian sopranos in an effort to convince the RAF eavesdroppers they were just listening to a music station that wasn't worth jamming.[20]

*Reg Payne*

Wireless operator Reg Payne's Lancaster crew was on those same ops to Berlin alongside Jim Penny. He was always on the alert for other radio information being broadcast. 'The half-hour updates from our control at Group would send us new information such as course changes, wind strengths or raid instructions. After a while, I became curious to see what was happening, so I turned out my light and stood up in the astrodome. It was very dark out there, but I could see the mid-upper turret behind me moving around as the gunner kept a wary lookout for fighters – or any of our own aircraft straying too close to us; collision in the stream was a constant risk.'[21] Reg returned to his position to check the broadcasts again, but it wasn't long before his navigator announced that they'd be over the target in fifteen minutes. The bomb aimer then reported from his position in the nose that he could see searchlights ahead, illuminating the cloud base.

'Back in the astrodome, I could see the first of the Pathfinder Force sky markers come into view before drifting down into the clouds below. Then, as if in slow motion, the strings of red and green sausages of flak came rising up through the clouds and burst around and just below us. Looking down, I could see the black shapes of other Lancasters and Halifaxes crawling over the tops of the clouds, silhouetted by the glow of the defending searchlights.'

Reg decided he preferred his own position, where he couldn't witness the action unfold.

Jim Penny could see everything as he flew in at 19,000ft to find Berlin under thick cloud. Searchlights were already probing through it, and as they started their bomb run, flak opened up, bursting around them like giant black snowflakes, and so intense that Jim's bomb aimer, 22-year-old Bob Campbell, cracked the well-worn joke that, 'The flak was so heavy the skipper put his wheels down and ran in on it!' And there were other onboard problems. Jim's mid-upper gunner had broken his oxygen supply, essential for flying over 10,000ft, so he had to move forward to the astrodome and plug in there. He could still keep a lookout from there at least, but it meant that his Brownings were unmanned.

Concentrating hard in his 'office' in the nose of the aircraft, Bob, the bomb aimer, dropped sky markers, used when the ground was obscured by cloud. These would float on parachutes above the cloud, giving an aiming point to others in the stream. All he could see of the city was the reflection of the fires already burning there. Jim studied his instruments as he followed Bob's instructions on this blind bombing run, at the same time keeping a weather eye open for the flak that continued to burst all around and above them.

Bob lay prone below his twin Brownings on a padded board, scanning the fiery night through his Perspex cone. His cool, undisturbed voice had a calming effect on the rest of the crew, and Jim appreciated it. 'I was always amazed because he was looking right down through those flak bursts.'

As part of the Pathfinder Group, they were carrying one cookie and six high-explosive 500-pounders in addition to their six target indicators. Cookies weren't the most popular bombs to carry. Owing to the airflow over the detonators in their noses, they would often explode even if jettisoned unarmed. And it wasn't safe to drop one at any height below 6,000ft, since you risked damage from its immense 360-degree shockwave.

Bombs away, and the Lancaster, freed of its load, leapt upwards. 'If it could have sighed with relief, I'm sure it would have.' Now for the camera run. Jim hated that extra delay, when all his instincts were to turn and get away from the flak bursting so close that he felt the next had to be on target. Then there was the intense camera flash and, once Bob had given the all-clear, Jim performed his now customary and preferred routine of climbing to 24,000ft, corkscrewing from time to time as an insurance against undetected enemy fighters.

After that, the long haul over the North Sea, where Jim made a gentle descent, resting his eyes and his brain for the next difficult bit – the landing. He'd known too many aircraft crash on the home threshold, and he thought with envy of the airfields already equipped with the new FIDO (Fog Investigation and Dispersal Operation) system. The device used two pipelines fitted at intervals with burner jets along each side of a runway, creating a flare path and burning off the fogs that plagued RAF airfields. It burnt untold amounts of fuel – up to 100,000 gallons an hour – but saved many an aircraft from crashing in winter fog. Tonight, at least, the Met Officer hadn't issued any bad news. In a real pea-souper, you couldn't see your hand at the end of your arm, let alone a landing strip.

By the time he came down, Jim had been flying his Lancaster for upwards of seven hours. The effect of the methamphetamine 'wakey wakey' Benzedrine tablets doled out by the Medical Officer as part of the pre-flight routine had long since worn off, and all Jim could think of now was breakfast – if he wasn't too tired to eat it – and bed.

Eleven Lancasters failed to return from that raid, two from his own squadron. Worse, one of the missing crews shared a billet with Jim and his men. Jim had got on particularly well with his fellow pilot. Arriving at their room in the early hours, it was hard to take in the news, and to see the empty bunks. Jim was all too aware that a new intake would be occupying those beds later that day. The machine needed constant feeding, and survivors had to battle on. There was no time to brood, and brooding itself was dangerous.

'It was certainly upsetting, but it was a fleeting moment and you just moved on. You had to. You just got on with it. I was with a brilliant crew and we all trusted each other with our lives. I had no doubt we would see the war through. If another crew got the chop, so be it. The attitude was, *It will never happen to me.*'

Later that same night, 23 November 1943, Jim Penny and his crew were off again. To the same Big City. They were still tired, but at least they were rested. There was always a bit of apprehension because it was a Berlin job and Berlin was always dodgy. Other than that, however, it was just another day on Bomber Command.

Joining the raid again that night were wireless operator Reg Payne and bomb aimer Les Bartlett, who were good friends, and their crew from RAF Skellingthorpe near Lincoln. 'We sat around the aircraft chatting and smoking as we waited for take-off and one of our ground crew polished the cockpit Perspex.'[22] The moment came, as it always did, too soon – and yet not soon enough. The adrenaline was pumped up, but now nerves gave way to concentration on the business of getting to the target and back. The ground crews rushed out to heave away the great wooden blocks in front of their Lancasters' wheels.

'OK, brakes off.'

They taxied round the perimeter track to the end of the runway. 'It was still daylight, and a great sight to see.' Les Bartlett watched from his position in the Perspex nose – the usual collection of ground staff, aircrew who weren't on the battle order for that night, the Station Commander with some visitors and friends, and a bunch of WAAFs waving goodbye to their boyfriends.

Then it was their Lancaster's turn.

'The Aldis lamp[23] flashes green from Control, and with the mighty roar of the four Merlins we give the crowd a quick wave and tear down the runway, Frank Swinyard the navigator giving the airspeed to the pilot, and the flight engineer's eyes locked on his hundred-and-one instruments until we are airborne and the wheels come up.' The old man of the crew at twenty-seven, Frank suffered from acute airsickness – something else to be aware of. Reg Payne had lost count of the times he'd had to clear up.

'Dusk is rapidly falling and at 9,000 feet, still climbing, we break cloud – it's almost dark, yet all around we can see shapes, vague yet resolute, all moving in the same direction. It's comforting to know you're not alone, and we know from the briefing that for every kite we see there are 100 we can't. Up and up we go, and finally at 20,000 feet we level out and settle down to a steady cruising speed. Already we can see the attempts of the enemy to stem the attack – all along the Dutch coast the bright flashes of the German heavy [flak] light up the clouds. Their aim is bad though, and the shells burst way below us.'

They encountered more flak over Hanover, but the route they'd taken was out of range of the guns there. And the clouds protected them from the searchlights stabbing up at them as they flew closer and closer to Berlin. Far ahead, Les could see the first wave swinging into action.

'I get busy, checking my bombing panel – *bombs selected* – fusing switches *on*. Everywhere for miles around us is burning, throwing up pink and scarlet through the clouds, making it so bright that I could have read a newspaper in my bombing compartment.'

As Jim Penny and his crew flew in, they saw that once again the city was covered in cloud. Below them, powerful 128mm *FlaK 40* anti-aircraft guns were opening up. Capable of firing shells up to 48,500 feet, they were one of the most effective heavy AA guns of the era. Through intelligence briefs, they knew that double-barrelled versions of the guns, the *FlaKzwilling*, were mounted four apiece on a tower in the Tiergarten park in central Berlin. There were similar installations on other towers around the city.

Their high-explosive shells weighed 57lb and travelled at 2,890ft per second. You didn't want to get in their way.

Bob's calm voice directed Jim so that he could release the target indicators, but just at the end of their two-minute run in he interrupted his commentary: 'They've re-centred. Carry on straight and level, Skipper. It's going to be about two more minutes.'

Jim and his crew had received new instructions. Tonight, his Lancaster was one of the backers-up to the first Pathfinders, who'd dropped red markers. Bob was now being told to drop his green ones further on.

'Bloody hell . . .'

Jim was not happy, but there was nothing for it. 'We just had to press on regardless.'

The two minutes passed agonisingly slowly, but then they were over the new dropping point. 'Steady . . . steady . . . *steady!*' Bob said, his voice rising once more. The moment was imminent.

But the delay had given the anti-aircraft gunners far below time to latch onto them. They scored a hit. Direct to the bomb bay.

The target indicators exploded immediately. The electrics fused and the intercom ceased to function. Jim had instinctively released the catch on his seat's Sutton safety harness and leant forward to wave to his flight engineer, Dickie Fathers, who'd joined Bob a little earlier in the bomb aimer's 'office' to help him throw out WINDOW. Jim indicated to Dickie that he should come back and get his parachute from its stowage point behind the pilot's seat.

'There was no sensation of being hit, but I knew what had happened because the target indicators were burning and they cast a fiery green glow throughout the aircraft. I also knew that with the bomb bay on fire we had a matter of seconds to get out before the cookie exploded. Bob already had his hand on the release panel, trying to jettison the load.

'I knew my crew could all bale out in around thirty to sixty seconds; we had practised it often enough.'

Jim couldn't give orders to the other men with a broken intercom, and he knew the forward escape hatch wasn't open. But he had full control of the aircraft. He kept the Lancaster steady to give his men the best chance of getting out.

As Dickie moved forward, Jim started counting.

'*One, two and three . . .*'

'I had two thoughts. The first was, *Mum isn't going to like this*. And, the second – very strangely, for I'd never considered this before, and I'd certainly not yet slept with a woman – was, *I wish I'd left a son behind*.

'*Eight, nine and ten . . .*'

Jim clipped his parachute onto his chest.

'I wasn't afraid. I felt perfectly calm in the realisation that I was going to die. My thoughts were for my crew. I needed to sacrifice my life so they could get out. That was my responsibility as their skipper.' The oldest member of the crew was the navigator, who was twenty-eight. The rest were all around Jim's own age – just twenty-one.

Seconds passed slowly, like hours.

'*Fifteen, sixteen, seventeen . . .*'

By now flames were flickering between Jim's body and his instrument panel.

'*Eighteen . . .*'

Dickie had reached Jim's position, and was bending down for his own parachute, when their world exploded.

The next thing Jim knew, he was out in the void of the night, still in a sitting position, arms forward as if holding the control column. The cold air blasted his face as a simple thought flashed through his mind: *Where's my bloody aeroplane gone?*

He cast that thought aside. He had more pressing matters to deal with. For example, should he delay pulling his ripcord until he'd fallen below the flak or do it at once to drift clear of the bombing? As they'd been exactly over target when their Lancaster had been blown to pieces by its cookie, and by now at the mid-point of the raid, he knew what more was to come. Time now passing in a flash, he pulled his ripcord. When his parachute opened, he saw a piece of his fuselage falling past him like an autumn leaf.

'The mind works rapidly in a situation like that. Now, with no one to think about but myself, I was bloody terrified. It seemed like every gun in Germany was pointing at me. The flak was exploding all around me; sparkling white exploding lights surrounded me as I descended through the barrage. The searchlights were still probing and the bombs were going off beneath me. I was gently floating down through the smoke and the explosions into enemy territory. We'd exploded at 20,000ft and I was under that parachute for many minutes. I had no doubt in my mind that my crew was dead and I was the only survivor.'

Jim had made it by pure chance, and his friends' deaths were in no way his fault – he'd been willing to sacrifice his own life to save theirs – but they would haunt him for ever. As he drifted down, another chunk of his Lancaster's fuselage cascaded past him. At last, he saw the ground rapidly approaching. Jim prepared himself to go into the para roll he'd been taught on landing, but his left leg collapsed and he fell heavily. He looked up to confront the head and shoulders of the Devil himself, horns and all, peering down at him against a backdrop of flames.

Then the goat ran off in shock, and Jim could see buildings burning in the distance. He'd landed in a back garden, near a searchlight battery on the outskirts of the city, which his colleagues were still pounding mercilessly. 'I was now face to face with the enemy, but there was nothing I could do about it. Interestingly, I don't remember any fear.'

Ignoring the pain in his head, neck and left leg, he thumped his harness release and prepared to bury his parachute, but it had snagged on a small tree, out of reach. Jim found his way to a road and stumbled along, resting, or sometimes falling down, at each of the trees that lined it. Then he came upon a huge German soldier who picked him up effortlessly and carried him in his arms to an air-raid shelter, murmuring to him on the way. Jim had only understood the word *kaputt*, spoken sympathetically. When the German laid him down, he saw who he'd been carrying by the dim light in the shelter. 'He said, *"Ach, Engländer,"* to which I automatically replied, *"Nein – Schottländer."*'

They weren't the only people taking refuge there. Two women – one old, the other middle-aged – shared it with them. The younger one looked daggers at him. 'I was a symbol of the men who were

killing their kinsfolk and laying waste their city. I could understand
their hostility.' The older lady spoke to him gently, kindly, even as
the bombs were still falling. 'When the raid was over, she took me to
her house. There was a mirror and I could see blood all over my face
from a head wound and that the thick soot from the smoke I had
come through on my way down had collected in the blood, making
me look as if I were badly burnt. I felt very embarrassed about this
old lady feeling sorry for a young man who'd been bombing her.'
But Jim also knew how lucky he was. He thought of his empty bed
back at base. Someone else would be in it tomorrow night – his
replacement. But at least he was alive.

So far, so good.

Summoned by the German soldier, two Luftwaffe officials soon
arrived and took Jim to hospital where a doctor who spoke some
English told him he was going to vaccinate him. The injection was
in the buttocks, and when Jim lowered his trousers, revealing his
pyjama trousers and knee warmers, his guards were highly amused.
Later they took him to a police station, where he was given two
slices of black bread and a mug of hot but unpleasant ersatz coffee.
Then they locked him in a cell for the night.

Another ordeal was about to begin.

* * *

Jim's war was over, but the Battle of Berlin continued for another
four months and another fourteen raids, varying in size from 379
to 891 aircraft; 7,249 Lancaster sorties were flown, 380 of them
were lost.[24]

But had the sacrifice been worth it? The scientist Freeman Dyson
put it succinctly in his 'A Failure of Intelligence': 'The city is more
modern and less dense than Hamburg, spread out over an area as
large as London with only half London's population, so it did not
burn well.'[25]

Two months into the campaign, Bomber Command concluded
that 'less than twenty-five per cent of Berlin had been devastated,

less than the damage caused to other major cities at that time. For example, Hamburg was estimated to be seventy per cent devastated, Mannheim and Hanover fifty-five per cent, Düsseldorf and Essen forty per cent, and Dortmund thirty-three per cent.'[26] When the Battle of Berlin ended, close to 30,000 tons of bombs had been dropped and 6,427 acres of the city had been destroyed. Joseph Goebbels lamented in his diary, 'I simply don't understand how the English are able to do so much damage to the Reich's capital during one air raid. The picture which met my eyes in Wilhelmplatz was one of total destruction.'[27]

From the British point of view – at least publicly – the battle was a success. But the Reich had not fallen, the war had not been brought to an end, and the cost had been high. As plans for a land invasion grew, military minds turned to a better use for Bomber Command, and Harris would be obliged to concede – at least for the time being. He would never lose his belief in strategic bombing.

The battle prompted even the lucky survivors to pause for thought. Wireless operator Reg Payne had returned safely from the raid that had done for Jim Penny.

'We touched down at just turned midnight, after seven and a quarter hours of flying. It was a wonderful sensation to feel the wheels on the concrete as we raced along the runway, home at last, safe. The relief washed over me, replacing tension with excitement; we had made it. The engines were cut and I removed my helmet. The quiet was welcome after the so many hours with the heavy throbbing roar of the Merlins for company. Our ground crew were there to greet us. Friendly voices and helping hands opened the door, then helped us out with our kit. Our two gunners and our bomb aimer wandered off a little way to have a cigarette. Tired, weary, but thankful to be home, we clambered into the bus with all our gear and the WAAF driver headed back to the operations block.

'I handed my Wireless Ops log, codes and so on to the Duty Signals Officer and then took a very welcome mug of steaming hot sweet tea from one of the WAAFs who had volunteered to stay up and wait for the crews to come home. After going to the locker room and putting all our flying kit away, handing in all the foreign money and any of the rations we had left, it was off to the Sergeants' Mess for a meal and then to the washroom to get the grime and rubber marks off my face. At one o'clock in the morning, with no fire in the stove, our quarters seemed cold, damp and unwelcoming. We talked about the raid for a while and then collapsed into bed. The adrenalin had gone and I was suddenly very tired, but sleep just wouldn't come. For quite some time, the reality of what I had just experienced tumbled through my head.'

Reg and his crew had been lucky. This time. But Jim Penny and many others had not, and now the work of a shadowy group of men – the Committee of Adjustment – began. The crews who were listed as missing had to be replaced immediately, and every trace of them needed to be removed from their various stations.

By morning, only the memories of those who were lost would remain. And those, too, would quickly fade.

# CHAPTER NINE

# THE WAR ON THE GROUND

Counting the dead. The Unreturned. Disposing of their personal possessions, readying their bed spaces for their replacements. It was the necessary though somehow pitiless work of the curiously titled 'Committee of Adjustment'; those involved were not part of any *committee*, and they weren't really *adjusting* anything. Their simple, cold task was to clear all evidence of any missing airmen from their RAF station. There was a war to be fought and little time for sympathy or reflection. Although Jim Penny's private war was still continuing on the ground in Berlin, the Committee of Adjustment was in full flow at RAF Bourn clearing away his and the rest of his crew's personal effects. All trace of them would be wiped from the station.

That ritual clearing of dead men's belongings was one of the most harrowing memories for all who survived the bomber war. 'It was pretty horrific, seeing somebody's life being taken out of his locker to be sorted into personal items for his family to collect and the official things, which went back into stores.'[1] One recently qualified wireless operator arrived at his new hut only to find unmade beds and clothing strewn around and the Committee of Adjustment still at work. 'Sorry about this,' they said, 'but those two crews didn't come back last night. You'll have to wait until we have cleared all their kit away.' He was sent back to the Mess to kick his heels.

Some unlucky replacement crewmen arrived even before the

committee had begun their work, such was the desperate need for replacements. They simply removed the personal possessions of the previous crew themselves. 'At the side of the bed I had chosen, its sheets turned down, were photographs of a pretty girl with a signature and sentiment to the absent previous occupant. We tidied up, placing all the items together for later collection.'[2]

The officer in charge of the Committee of Adjustment at RAF Bardney, in Lincolnshire, where pilot Don MacIntosh was stationed, had a nickname: 'the chop man'.

'He was an elderly Flight Lieutenant, who looked like a vicar. He and his assistants worked with the utmost delicacy, unobtrusive almost to the point of invisibility. One call, and they took care of all the needs of the missing airman. Like "Untouchables", they kept a low profile. The chop man sat alone at meals, his head bent, a furtive look on his face, while we avoided looking in his direction. Occasionally, one of the older and more senior officers would say a few words to him, just to be friendly. He was never seen in the evenings, when his presence would have been as welcome as a beggar at a feast.'[3]

Aircrew hated the arrival of the Committee of Adjustment. They rarely delayed their work because beds and lockers had to be cleared immediately to make room for new crews who'd arrive without delay to replace the dead or missing. That survivors might be sleeping mattered not. Lancaster navigator Bill Kiley and his fellow crewmen returned from a mission deep inside Germany, went through the usual post-operation debriefing process, had a meal, then went to the quarters they shared with another crew. Exhausted, they fell into their beds. They didn't sleep long. The arrival of the Committee of Adjustment jolted them all awake.

'We knew people were missing because they hadn't turned up at debriefing; we had hoped they might have been diverted. But then the officers came in and started packing their things up. They didn't really say anything. They just got on with the job, packing the kitbags, going through lockers. We were all a bit shocked. It's very cold to see people's lives being taken out of lockers and put into bags.'[4]

One thoughtful airman left a note in his locker for the men charged with removing his property if the worst happened:

*To the Committee of Adjustment.*
*Dear Sir, Hoping sincerely that I have caused you as little inconvenience as possible. Please accept this meagre gift for doing a job that receives no thanks. I was yours sincerely,*
*Michael C. Skarratt[5]*

The 'meagre gift' was not detailed in the note, but the officer reading the letter must surely have been moved by the sentiment expressed. Here was a young man, prepared, perhaps even expecting, to die for his country, but concerned that the disposal of his few possessions would trouble the authorities.

\* \* \*

Men died. Men were replaced. And the numbers of both increased alongside Lancaster production and new airfields.

'Christ! What on earth have we done to deserve this?'

The advance members of 106 Squadron had just arrived at Metheringham, 12 miles south-east of Lincoln, from RAF Syerston in November 1943. Their language became a lot bluer as they looked around the pockmarked moonscape. At Syerston, their accommodation had been brick-built and centrally heated. RAF Metheringham was one of a profusion of bases under construction across eastern England to provide the longer, concrete runways the Lancaster bombers demanded, and as yet boasted nothing more than Nissen huts – corrugated-iron islands in a sea of mud – with largely ineffective, haphazardly fuelled pot-bellied stoves, and limited electricity and water.

The local farmers heard the bad news from the Directorate of Land and Requisition. The subsoil was silt, but someone upstairs had decided that the site was important enough to merit the time and expense of draining it.[6]

Peter Scoley was a schoolboy when his family had to make way for the RAF. The upheaval which followed transformed the lives of the entire community. 'We were living at Holme Farm, which became the Station Commander's house; it was one of three small farms owned by my great-uncle George – a potato-growing specialist – and farmed in partnership with my father. Their prized land, nurtured for a lifetime, now disappeared under the bulldozers.'[7]

Peter watched with a mixture of excitement and sadness as bulldozers also claimed the beautiful woodland where oak, ash and birch trees grew in long-established profusion, peppered with rhododendrons. A blaze of colour in spring and summer, it was a favourite place for walks, and the home of a multitude of rabbits and pheasant, highly popular with poachers. All this would soon vanish to make way for the arrival of Bomber Command and the Lancasters. One homestead, destined for demolition, lost an avenue of beautiful chestnut trees, together with a single, stunning red elm that took three men a whole day to bring down. Ancient roots had to be blasted free with explosives.

Blitzed Britain had an abundance of the rubble they would use for hardcore. Thousands upon thousands of tons of it were delivered by the London and North-Eastern Railway along with 14 million bricks on forty special trains running at two a day in a single month in 1943. There wasn't the time or manpower to extend the stations, so sidings were constructed at a few key locations to free the main lines for their usual traffic.

Young Peter Scoley looked on entranced as gigantic machinery arrived – tractors, bulldozers, trench diggers 'like great, primeval, spine-plated dinosaurs'. Three massive concrete mixers were installed. 'Tipper lorries and dumpsters scurried back and forth fetching sand and gravel, stone for foundations, bricks for this, pipes for that, until, where once there had been peace and ordered fields, all was now a frenzy like a nest of demented ants, a 650-acre shambles.'

It took 640,000 square yards of concrete to surface each

150ft-wide runway, and once an airfield was up and running, it had to be constantly supplied with fuel, spares, provisions and bombs in staggering quantities.[8]

*106 Squadron aircrew and ground crew*

Similar massive bases were springing up across the country.

As a four-year-old, Maurice Garlick had seen a British fighter shoot down a Zeppelin at the end of the Great War in 1918 and he was now a Lancaster navigator.[9] Arriving at his new base, he recorded his memories:

'Picture the layout of a typical wartime RAF bomber station. First imagine a vast level field, with a strong high wire protective fence all round and only one entrance, with a guardhouse and armed sentries. Two great wide concrete runways at right angles to each other stretch from one end of the field to the other. Before 1940, you would have seen all the aircraft lined up with military precision next to each other. Why not now? Because one day in 1940, at the height of the Battle of Britain, an enemy fighter bomber flew straight down the line, machine-gunning and bombing the aircraft. He destroyed the lot! Henceforth all aircraft were to be spread out at individual dispersal points all round the perimeter track – the road which followed the inside of the perimeter fence. On an op, all our Lancs would taxi along the perimeter track to the take-off position, which varied with the wind. We had to take off into the wind to get maximum lift as we were always so heavily laden.'

The crews would first be bussed from their quarters to the often-distant dispersal points. The weather office and the control tower were close to the junction of the two runways in order to co-ordinate activity on both. The rest of the buildings were as far away from the runways as possible – as a safety measure and also on account of the noise the aircraft engines generated. The CO's office was next to the Adjutant's; not far away were the aircrews' huts, the ground personnel huts, the Mess halls and canteens, games rooms, bath- and shower-rooms, the briefing hut and a car park large enough for the aircrew buses and other service utility vehicles – the 'Tillys'. 'The entire camp was connected to a Tannoy system and from it you could hear messages wherever you happened to be on the site. No excuse whatsoever was ever accepted for not hearing messages.'

The railway stations around RAF Metheringham, and the roads that serviced them, were swamped by the hundreds of workers arriving every day from as far away as Mansfield and Sheffield. As the airfield rose from the mud, more and more workers stayed on site, which created other tensions. The Royal Oak and the Red Lion pubs were packed every night, and locals had to get used to the sight of 'two hundred drunken Irishmen weaving down Martin High Street singing "Danny Boy" after closing time'.

. The contractors' welfare officer was billeted with Peter's parents. He didn't have an enviable job; many of the arguments that broke out among his charges were settled with shovels and pick handles. But 'he bore it all with equanimity and good humour, and became a familiar figure, roaring around the district on a powerful, noisy motorbike, a cloud of thick, oily smoke lingering in the air to mark his passing'.

On the plus side for Peter and his friends was the arrival of US engineers to lay the telephone cables.

'My brother and I began a short-lived but lucrative trade. Some of the early apples were ripening, which we pulled from the trees and threw over the hedge to the Americans, to be showered in payment with pennies and threepenny bits. Unfortunately my mother, suspicious of the noise, put an immediate stop to these activities.'

As the base neared completion, the Lancasters and their crews arrived, as did the many hundreds of airmen and women needed to send them across the water into enemy territory. Everyone had to be housed, fed, watered, clothed, taken care of and, of course, entertained. The NAAFI[10] began to lay on film shows. Two officers organised a classical record club which met every Sunday evening – the squadron's Operations Record Book relates that 'these concerts prove very popular to a small section of the station personnel who attend faithfully'.[11]

A 'Brains Trust' session started, based on a popular radio programme, where a vast range of questions from philosophy to politics were answered by a panel of experts; and neighbouring units began to exchange concert parties and sporting events. RAF Metheringham was able to drum up halfway decent hockey, rugby and soccer teams, and the Canadians on the base had their own softball league. The WAAFs played netball, and in the summer, naturally enough, there was cricket. Bikes were essential for use as transport to work and to local pubs, but woe betide you if you went without lights – against the law, despite blackout regulations. A couple of offending Lancaster aircrew were pulled in by a police officer in a Wolseley.

'To our amusement he said, "Do you realise you could be killed riding without lights?" We were risking life and limb most nights of the week every time we were on a raid. He took our particulars and sometime later we were summoned to appear in Lincoln County Court. I couldn't appear on the date stated as I was briefed to go on a raid. I received a letter to say I'd been fined for the offence. My friend didn't pay his fine – he failed to return from that particular raid.'

Work on the base went on; the Sick Quarters had to be finished, and water supply was still lacking in the technical, administration and squadron sites. Undaunted, the NAAFI installed a proper dance floor and volunteers built a cinema-cum-concert hall, complete with stage and dressing rooms. A gymnasium came next. RAF Metheringham was fast becoming a sophisticated and self-contained metropolis of swiftly erectable Nissen huts housing 1,685 men and 345 women.

*Norman Jackson VC*

Amid the building at home, the destruction of Germany went on and on; the brave always rising to the occasion.

Norman Jackson, a 25-year-old Lancaster flight engineer at RAF Metheringham, had completed his thirtieth sortie and thus, technically, his required tour of duty. But since one had been with a different crew, he decided to join his own on *their* thirtieth and final op, so they could all finish together. He had something else to celebrate too: his wife Alma had recently sent a telegram to say she'd given birth to their first child, Ian; a cherished addition to a loving family.[12]

Shortly before take-off, the crew's rear gunner, twenty-year-old Norman Johnson, had written his own 'last letter' to his parents, not believing – like so many others – it would ever be delivered.

*My dear father and mother,*

*This is just a note I'm writing to you in case anything unfortunate happens to me while I am flying on operations.*

*The only regrets I shall have on my life ending are those of being parted from you all, my very dear family, whom I love so very much.*

*I should like both of you to know, my dears, how very much I have appreciated my home, and all that you have done for me.*[13]

It was never going to be an easy raid. The ball-bearing factories at Schweinfurt in Bavaria were heavily defended, but a crucial target. The Lancasters of 106 Squadron took off shortly after 9.30 p.m., and Norman Jackson and his fellow crewmen were in high spirits at the prospect of moving on to hopefully easier postings on training units. There was less flak than expected, and at 20,000ft bomb aimer Maurice Toft dropped their lethal burden without difficulty. It was when they turned for home that the wireless operator noticed a blip on his Monica radar, closing fast.

Before their skipper, Fred Mifflin, had time to take evasive action, a Focke-Wulf 190 homed in. A burst from his cannon hammered into the Lancaster's fuselage. Immediately, the starboard inner engine erupted. Jackson activated the stricken engine's built-in Graviner fire extinguisher. For a moment the flames died down – only to flare up with even greater ferocity moments later.

In the midst of the attack, Jackson was thrown to the floor with shell splinters in his right leg and shoulder. It looked as though they were done for.

But he now came up with an incredible plan to try to save his aircraft. It would become one of Bomber Command's most remarkable feats of courage and human endeavour.

'It was my job as flight engineer to get the rest of the crew out of trouble. I was the most experienced member, and they all looked to me to do something.' He had previously mulled over the challenge of an unextinguished engine fire and considered the possibility of getting out of the aircraft and crawling along the wing to fight the flames.

It was as foolishly courageous as it was unlikely to succeed.

Getting his skipper's consent for the desperate attempt, he grabbed a hand-held extinguisher from its clip and stuffed it into his Mae West, then reached up to open the midships roof escape hatch. Before exiting, he released his parachute so his fellow crewmen, bomb aimer Maurice Toft and navigator Frank Higgins, could use it as an improvised safety line. Holding onto the canopy silk and long cords attached to his harness, they – hopefully – could pull him back into the aircraft after he had doused the flames. Or, even more improbably, if he lost his footing and was blown away, they would simply let go of the parachute, allowing it to deploy and carry him safely down to earth.

Standing on the navigator's table, Jackson eased out of the hatch into the blast of a freezing 200mph slipstream before lowering himself onto the wing. It is difficult to comprehend how he managed to steady himself amid the force of the wind; perhaps double the strength of what might be experienced in the worst hurricane. His next job was to get close enough to the fire to put it out, but there were no handholds of any kind to get him there. Except for one. He zeroed in on the damaged engine's protruding air intake cover, and knew what he'd have to do to reach it.

Taking a deep breath, he launched himself into the raging head-wind and somehow seized the intake. Now he had to hold on with his left hand taking his full body weight while he extracted the extinguisher with his right. Body battered by the elements, flying suit whipping and flapping, he managed to turn it onto the flames and they began to die down. For a moment it looked as though Jackson's heroic action had saved the day. But then the Focke-Wulf came back to finish its job. As he clung desperately to the intake cover on the wing, the Lancaster twisted and banked sharply as cannon shells hammered into its flank. More shrapnel hit Jackson in the legs and back. His extinguisher was torn from his hand and cartwheeled off into space. Fresh flames leapt from the starboard inner engine, burning him badly and forcing him to let go. He was flung backwards off the wing.

Maurice and Frank tightened their hold on the canopy cords and paid them out, watching in horror as Jackson found himself suspended, as if flying, a few feet from the rear gun turret as his parachute reached its limit. He was now being dragged, flailing, alongside the tailplane. Finally, his fellow crewmen were able to free the canopy and release it, allowing it to whisk through the escape hatch, billow open and drag him mercifully clear.

His ordeal was far from over, though. The lines had caught fire, which now spread to the already torn silk canopy. He smothered the cords as best he could with his already scorched hands, but there was nothing he could do about the canopy – nearly two-thirds destroyed and making his 3-mile descent far too fast. If he'd hit hard ground, Jackson would almost certainly have died. But fortune on this occasion favoured the brave, and he crashed through a thick tangle of bushes, breaking an ankle in the process, before passing out.

He didn't come round until daybreak, numb with shock and cold, knowing that he was in a dire condition. His hands were charbroiled, his legs and back were flayed by shrapnel, and his face was so badly burnt he could only see with one eye. By a supreme effort of will, Jackson dragged himself on knees and elbows to a nearby house and managed to bang on the door. The occupant, recognising him as one of the enemy who had caused so much devastation to his country, spat at him and yelled, '*Churchill Terrorflieger!*'

The enraged man was then pushed aside by his two beautiful daughters, who bathed Jackson's wounds. 'I was lying there like a lord. I began to think I was pretty lucky!'

They patched him up, only to force him to hobble to the closest town, where he became the target of further abuse and stoning.

Finally delivered to the authorities, he spent ten months in hospital before being transferred to a POW camp.

His Lancaster was just one of five shot down out of the sixteen that had taken off from RAF Metheringham that night. Two of his crewmates – Fred Mifflin, the pilot, and Norman Johnson, the rear gunner, who had so recently written his 'last letter' – were killed when it crashed. The remaining four survived. It was only when they returned from captivity at the end of the war that anyone heard the full, astonishing story of Jackson's bravery. He himself had remained characteristically modest about his achievement.

For his incredible courage and fortitude, Warrant Officer[14] Norman Jackson was awarded the Victoria Cross – one of the most celebrated of the entire war – on 26 October 1945. The order of precedence demanded that Group Captain Leonard Cheshire, one of the nation's most highly lauded pilots, should have been at the head of the queue to receive his medal from King George VI, but Cheshire told the King, 'This man stuck his neck out more than I did. He should have his VC first.' Protocol simply would not permit this, so a compromise was reached and the two valiant men were decorated together.

Jackson's mother gleefully announced to the assembled reporters, 'The only other outstanding thing he ever did was to ride in a procession through Twickenham on the smallest bicycle ever made.'

The conflict left Jackson deeply religious. 'Nobody prayed harder than I did before we took off and after we landed,' he recalled. 'So did all the rest of them, though nobody mentioned it.' For the rest of his life, he was periodically haunted by nightmares of his brush with death, and confessed to bouts of melancholy. He often reflected on how fortunate he was, compared to his friends who had either perished, or struggled to adjust after the war. His hands never fully recovered. The RAF awarded him a disability pension of £2 a week.

He rarely spoke of his Victoria Cross.

\* \* \*

The loss of five out of sixteen Lancasters from one base was not unusual by this stage of proceedings, so life at RAF Metheringham carried on regardless.

The Astra cinema opened with *The Life and Death of Colonel Blimp*, and films became so popular that they played to packed houses six nights a week. Once the stage lighting had been installed, the Station Concert Party presented *Chocks Away!*, a revue produced by Jock Wilson that featured eighteen numbers, including 'Anywhere in Bomber Command', 'Joining the WAAF' and 'The Lancastrians' – but the Report on Station Entertainment remained unmoved: 'This had the makings of a good show, but lacked direction.'

When community singing leader Tom Ratcliffe visited the base, his reception was also muted: 'With the rather small audience at his disposal, he achieved a fair measure of success, but community singing has not a universal appeal.'

Wild games were far more popular on any RAF station, especially isolated ones that had little to offer apart from a local pub with rationed beer – though the landlord would usually give airmen a bit of leeway on that count. One such diversion involved piling all the tables and chairs into a pyramid: 'One person, with blackened feet from the soot in the fireplace, would climb to the top and put his footmarks across the ceiling, down the wall, and disappearing into the hearth.'[15] Even flying exercises could be turned to good account, as Pip Beck and her fellow WAAFs found out.

'During the spell of sunny, warm weather, some of the girls had taken to sunbathing behind our huts minus stockings, shirts and bras. The sun and wind on bare skin felt wonderful, but it couldn't last. There was a spate of low-flying aircraft, suddenly – we'd been spotted! That was the end of semi-nude sunbathing!'[16]

For those like Lancaster pilot Ken Trent, stationed near Lincoln, there was the additional attraction of the Theatre Royal and its showgirls.

'It was one of our favourite places to go when we're lucky enough to be off-duty. We head for the front row of the stalls, making sure we have the best view in the house of all the crumpet onstage. There's a bar on the right-hand side of the stage where we meet them during the interval to explore their talents further.'[17]

Sex, and female company, were delightful when you could get it, but if you couldn't, there was always drink. Ken had the good fortune to acquire a motorbike equipped with a sidecar large enough to take two people side by side. He once used it to take all six of his crew out to their Lancaster before a training flight. They got to the aircraft in one piece, but he came a cropper soon afterwards pursuing a pilot who owned an old Austin Seven.

'I was on my motorbike, and he was ahead of me on the roadway leading to the Mess. As I watched, he drove straight up to the building without slowing down, right up the steps, crashing through the doors and into the hall by the bar.' He climbed out and hailed the barman: 'Afternoon. Pint, please.' Determined to follow suit, Ken only realised at the last moment that his combination of motorbike and sidecar was actually wider than the diminutive automobile. Trapped in the doorway, it stopped dead, and Ken was thrown 'head over heels to land on the floor of the bar on my backside, looking up at an appreciative audience'.

Peace and quiet came to be something many airmen craved, even over the pursuit of pleasure. Ken Trent found the pressure of ops so great that his hands were beginning to shake. The rounds of parties and excess ceased to provide consolation, so he found it in his friendship with a nearby farmer and his young family.

'Brackenwood Farm very soon became my second home away from the base. Until then my life in the RAF had been a continual round of training, operations, nerves, pressure, drinking, the theatre, girls. It was becoming a real strain, which was already manifesting itself in my shaking hands. The farm, on the other hand, exuded stability, warmth, peace and, above all, love. My guardian angel had guided me into a place of happiness, where just along the road was war and all those things which involved killing people, and keeping oneself alive. I stopped drinking excessively and found solace in doing all the little jobs there which helped me to unwind.

'I was often there at six in the morning before operations to milk "my" cows, and headed there immediately after any ops which finished in daylight hours. Before landing I would circle tightly over the farmhouse and waggle the wings of my Lanc. Their little girl, Lucy, would run inside calling, "He's back! Kenneth's back," and her mother, with her lovely soft northern accent, would call back, "Gooood!" Sometimes I would arrive still trembling with nervous energy after a dangerous trip, and before I had the chance to tend to my cows, the farmer's wife would pack me off to their spare room. "Leave the cows alone," she'd say. "You get off to bed. You need a good sleep." I would drift off gratefully in warmth and comfort, with the roar of engines and the bang of guns forgotten.'

\* \* \*

Operations went on. Post-flight rituals on the ground went on.

Jean Barclay was approaching her twentieth birthday when she joined the WAAF in 1939. Two years later she was commissioned and posted to RAF Waddington as an Intelligence Officer, where her duties included debriefing returning aircrew. This wasn't popular in the small hours of the morning after ten hours or more in the air, dodging flak and fighters, fighting exhaustion, sometimes after having coaxed a damaged aircraft home, sometimes wounded themselves, often having seen comrades die before their eyes.

They would stagger from their Lancaster to the crew bus, then, drawing on a Woodbine or a Craven A and sipping a mug of more-or-less drinkable tea, dirty, itchy, with the smell of fuel, glycol, sweat and cordite still in their nostrils, wondering when they'd have to go again, they would have to relive the entire mission. Confronted by an officer interrogating them on the fine detail, quizzed on what they had seen and done, there was no room for exaggeration or economies of truth. 'They used to grill you. They'd ask you what you'd seen and then they would cross-check everything. We used to hate the debriefing. It was really worse than flying.'[18] But Jean knew the men she questioned, as she relived their experiences with them, shared their pain when someone failed to return, having 'got the chop' or 'gone for a Burton'. People she'd seen and had a drink with in the Mess, bumped into around the base. Now she would never see them again. A year into her time at Waddington, she wrote,

> *How many faces have come and gone and how few can be seen today that I first saw then? So many ghosts wander around Waddington now. You meet them at odd times and places, perhaps in the deathly silence of the ops room during the hours before dawn when you are waiting for the aircraft to return and you fall to remembering those who used to wait with you or for whom you waited so often. Perhaps in the clamour and bustle of a Mess party on a Sunday morning and a chance name crops up, whose owner seems suddenly dreadfully and overpoweringly absent. Often at the end of a flarepath as the evening darkens and aircraft loom out of the dark and speed away into it again as they have done so often.*[19]

The debriefings Jean conducted affected her deeply, as did the preparation of any operation orders, 'which will send people out to fight and live or die as chance wills it'. Night after night, as she watched the Lancasters fly off, she always wondered which would return and what she would hear from those who did. The account was often the same, whatever the raid, because there was a mundanity about the endless process that went hand in hand with the stress.

'The great story is briefly told and briefly written down . . .'

'Next, please.'

'Get a photograph, do you think? Good show!'

'Oh, bad luck.'

'Yes, I'm afraid the tea is rather foul – we can only get condensed milk.'

'Did the 109 open fire?'

'What a break!'

'Have a good sleep.'

'Next!'

Debriefing over, the crews made for breakfast – the longed-for real eggs, the ones you dreamt about while over enemy territory, wondering if you'd get back to eat them again, but keeping all those thoughts to yourself. Then bed, maybe with pills to help, but rather not; you woke up fuzzy and it took a while for heads to clear. And, as you finally dropped off to sleep, hoping not to be roused by the Committee of Adjustment.

Jean didn't mention relationships in her diaries, but there were close friendships with airmen, and she needed them. One night, waiting for her Lancasters to return from a raid on Essen in the Ruhr, Jake, a Canadian officer, distracted her with the tale of a trip he'd made round Europe before the war. But he had to leave at 2 a.m., so she continued to wait alone. 'We had never, within my memory, sent aircraft to Essen and got them all back'.

At least there was one aircraft she thought she wouldn't have to worry about. Its pilot was as brilliant as he was experienced. It'd be just another sortie for him to enter in red ink in his logbook. But as the Lancasters came back one by one, Jean realised that the only blank space on the blackboard recording safe returns was opposite the name of her friend, Flying Officer Peter Ball.

At last the sickening truth could no longer be denied. Men from other crews drifted in from time to time and asked her if there was any news. She could only shake her head, not daring to speak. 'Finally the Group Captain came in, looked at the clock, and told me to take "Overdue Action". I managed to say, "Yes, sir," but made no move towards the telephone.'

She hoped the Group Captain would leave before she had to make the call she dreaded. He watched her with concern. 'It sometimes brings them back, you know,' he said, with the shadow of a smile Jean couldn't return. Sometimes it *did* work, but this time Jean knew in her heart that it wouldn't. 'Pete had obviously had it. So I rang up the Air Ministry and reported him overdue.' Then she fled, unable to stand people's enquiring glances any longer.

She was awakened around lunchtime by her Canadian friend,

who asked her to show him Lincoln Cathedral. Then they'd have
dinner and spend half the night saying goodbye to 402 Squadron,
which was relocating to Yorkshire the following day. 402 was Jake's
squadron, so Jean would be saying goodbye to him too.

'I'd been suitably shocked to hear that after three months here
he'd never been to see the cathedral. Such peace and such beauty
on this lovely day. We stood silently together in the quiet of the
cloisters and for me the hideous night seemed to recede almost into
impossibility.'

But her thoughts turned to Jake, by her side, his wife in Canada
expecting a baby, and he himself soon due to return to battle and
the risk of never coming back.

'The sky above the cloisters was blue and lovely and high above
the frozen music of the towers the tiny wings of a fighter twirled and
spun and glittered, as lovely as any bird. At a much lower altitude,
a Lancaster roared across the square of blue. Wasn't it ever possible
to get away?'

*Jean Barclay debriefing a crew after an operation*

Unless you were a woman pilot working with the Air Transport
Auxiliary delivering the aircraft, you'd be hard put to get a ride on

The RAF Battle of Britain Memorial Flight Lancaster over Derwent Reservoir. The two ditching hatches, open on this sortie, are clearly visible on top.

Rear gunner James Flowers with the author, John Nichol, in 2018.

Mid upper gunner Ken Johnson in 2015. Ken died in January 2020.

A crewman at the Lincolnshire Aviation Heritage Centre, East Kirkby, demonstrates the difficulty of climbing over Lancaster *Just Jane*'s main spar.

Flight engineer Ted Watson in December 2017. He died in February 2020 aged 95.

Damage to a Lancaster which was involved in a mid-air collision. The rear gunner was badly injured. The crew of the other aircraft were all killed when it crashed.

The Beetham crew in 1943. (*From left*) Fred Ball, gunner; Les Bartlett, bomb aimer; Michael Beetham, pilot; Frank Swinyard, nav; Reg Payne, Wop; Don Moore, flight engineer; Jock Higgins, gunner. Don and Fred were killed after their Lancaster caught fire during a training sortie.

Reg Payne (*left*) and Les Bartlett (*right*) with their wartime skipper Air Chief Marshal Sir Michael Beetham at a reunion in 2004.

Lancaster pilot Don MacIntosh in 2018. Don died in January 2019.

Lancaster *Just Jane* is stripped back to basics for refurbishment at the Lincolnshire Aviation Heritage Centre at East Kirkby.

Pilot Ken Trent in 2016, holding a wartime portrait of himself. Ken died in January 2018.

A close-up view of the crew in the cockpit of the RAF BBMF Lancaster.

Ron Needle with the author at the RAF Museum in 2018 where he spoke to the young children in the background. Ron died in August 2019.

Loading the bomb bay; the huge cylindrical 'cookie' can be seen surrounded by HE bombs.

Ground crew posing with a 'cookie' after Lancaster *S-Sugar*, now in the RAF Museum, completed 100 operations.

Elaine Towlson, whose father Stan Shaw was killed in 1943, discussing her experiences with the author in 2018.

The RAF BBMF Lancaster passes over Tattershall Castle as it returns to RAF Coningsby in Lincolnshire.

TELEPHONE:
GERRARD 9234
Extn...............

Any communications on the
subject of this letter should
be addressed to:—

THE
UNDER SECRETARY
OF STATE,

and the following number
quoted:—

Your Ref. P.407629/13/P.4.B.8.

AIR MINISTRY

(Casualty Branch),

73-77, OXFORD STREET,

W.1.

1 2 JAN 1944

Madam,

    With reference to the letter from this
Department of the 31st December, 1943, I am
directed to inform you that action has now
been taken to presume, for official purposes,
that your husband, 1576142 Flight Sergeant
S. Shaw, lost his life on the 18th August,
1943.

    I am to express the sympathy of the
Department with you in your great loss.

        I am, Madam,
           Your obedient Servant,

             D. Bent

    for Director of Personal Services.

Mrs. S. Shaw,
   Innisfine,
      Bisley Street,
         Stapleford,
           Nottinghamshire.

The letter to Stan Shaw's family on 12 January 1944 which brought the worst
possible news, dashing all hope; he was now presumed dead.

The scene of a wartime crew leaving their Lancaster after a sortie is recreated at the Lincolnshire Aviation Heritage Centre, East Kirkby.

A view of the cockpit in Lancaster *Just Jane*. The entrance to the bomb aimer's compartment can be seen on the bottom right.

a Lancaster. Even on a training exercise, such a thing was strictly forbidden.

But one female driver was determined to experience a Lancaster sortie.[20]

As RAF Scampton geared up for a night raid on two Benzol plants, the Canadian crew of Lancaster *Vicious Virgin* were making slightly different preparations to those of their fellow flyers.

*Vicious Virgin*'s skipper, Bob Purves, was dating the WAAF driver, Iris Price. Bob's bomb aimer, Jim Vollans, was one of the first to discover what had been planned. 'While they were out on their date, Bob dared her to fly on a combat operation with him.'

'Being the daredevil I was in those days,' Iris readily agreed, but with the proviso that he get hold of some proper flying kit for her. Iris and Bob were well aware of the risk they were taking – if they were caught, they'd have the book *and* the desk thrown at them, but Bob's crew were all for it too; they'd all be in it together. Iris had a very good idea of the dangers she'd be facing over enemy territory, but she trusted Bob to keep her safe on her 'joy-ride'. She knew this would be a once-in-a-lifetime experience. Presumably, she also realised it could well be a life-ending one too.

On the afternoon of the raid, while the ground crew were loading *Vicious Virgin*'s bombload – one high-capacity 4,000lb cookie and twelve 500-pounders – Bob organised flying equipment for Iris. She had her own battledress, standard wear for an MT driver, but as she joined the crew at *Vicious Virgin*'s dispersal, he slipped her a helmet, oxygen mask and parachute. Iris's presence at the dispersal was nothing out of the ordinary. Her friend Doris Roberts, another WAAF driver who'd brought the crew out, simply thought she had come to say goodbye to her boyfriend.

'When I saw Iris I just thought she'd come out on the bus to say goodbye to her boyfriend, as she'd done many times before. I didn't see her again, and assumed she'd got a lift with someone else or walked back to the Control Tower.'

But as Doris returned to her section, Iris was huddling down in the belly of the Lancaster, waiting with a mixture of fear and excitement for take-off.

*Vicious Virgin* left the ground at 5.30 p.m. and soared into the darkening sky towards Germany, their route taking them to the Benzol plant at Gelsenkirchen, north-east of Düsseldorf. It was a relatively short and mercifully uneventful flight, though flak over the target buffeted the aircraft as searchlights probed the darkness for a victim. Battling the unfamiliar confinement of a Lancaster bomber at war, Iris must surely have been having second thoughts about her adventure. She remembered, 'At this stage, I was feeling sick.'

At 8.45 p.m. they dropped their bombs bang on target. Iris watched the flames and explosions 17,000ft below with awe. 'We turned for home. Mission accomplished, I calmed down a bit. Then it happened!'

She suddenly felt a pressing need for the toilet. Realising that the Elsan portable toilet, open for all to see, might be asking a bit much, Bob gave her an airsickness bag, and she disappeared towards a more secluded part of the Lancaster for some privacy. She managed to relieve herself successfully and disposed of the bag down the flare chute near the main door. Then, while she was struggling to dress again, something else went badly wrong.

With no sign of her return Bob realised something was amiss. As he couldn't leave his position, he asked the flight engineer to investigate, who discovered Iris lying unconscious on the floor of the aircraft. While getting dressed again, always awkward, and more so for a woman, especially in a battle-battered Lancaster, her oxygen supply hose had disconnected and she'd collapsed. The flight engineer grabbed a portable oxygen cylinder from its clip on the side of the fuselage and placed its mask over Iris's face, cradling her head as she slowly came round. There was much anxiety aboard as Iris still hadn't fully recovered by the time they eventually landed, and had to be helped out by the gunners.

It was 11.10 p.m., and their crew bus, driven as usual by Doris, was waiting for them. 'I was amazed, when the aircraft door opened, to see Iris, semi-conscious, being supported by two members of the crew.' Doris now had to be let in on the secret. She dropped the crew and took Iris back to her billet, but the next morning she was still unwell, so reported to the doctor. To her relief, he put her indisposition down to flu, and told her to take two days off.

The story could have had a much less pleasant conclusion. In the midst of the airborne drama, bomb aimer Jim Vollans had wondered 'what we would have done if Iris had died'.

'Would the whole crew be blamed, or would it just be Purves? We would certainly all have been charged if the RAF discovered Iris had been with us on the flight, and if we'd been shot down with her aboard it could have been a political embarrassment to the Allies. I must confess I had some evil thoughts about how to dispose of the body if Iris had died. Thank goodness she survived and my thoughts were never put to the test.'

* * *

Lancaster pilot Don MacIntosh knew the risks involved, so avoided getting too closely involved with the opposite sex. Sometimes he weakened, though, and sought out female company. Mary was part of the Women's Land Army[21] – volunteer agricultural workers – whose hostel was near his base. The day following a particularly hairy raid, he decided, once he'd calmed down, to give her a call.

They met at the Bird in Hand, an old village pub with low ceilings, oak beams and the usual dartboard and shove-halfpenny table. Don arrived first, ordered a pint and watched the door through the tobacco-smoke haze. 'She came in – not pretty but good-looking. Above-average height, tawny-haired, dark brown eyes, olive skin and curves in all the right places.'[22]

Mary was full of life, well aware of how attractive she was, and tonight she looked stunning in a dark blue pinstripe suit and white blouse. When Don saw her moving towards him, his usual self-possession left him and he felt his throat go dry. 'Hello, Mac,' she said in her flat Midlands accent. 'Sorry I'm a bit late, but Daisy was being a bit temperamental and kicked over her milk pail, so I had to clear up.' She smiled and ordered a pint. Don thought that if she'd been speaking Swahili she couldn't have sounded more exciting. She raised her glass and smiled.

It wasn't as if he hadn't been warned. Mary was twenty-seven, a good few years older than he was, and Geoff Owen, his eighteen-year-old rear gunner, had already voiced his doubts. Mary had said that she'd been married to a Canadian officer who'd lost his life at Dieppe, but there was also a rumour that he was actually a POW. Don really didn't want to know, and he invited her to the local dance that evening. They arrived as the band, led by a tenor saxophone, poured a slow foxtrot into the smoky room, filled with yellow light. Almost everybody at the dance was in uniform. The women were mainly WAAFs, though there was a handful of Land Army girls who waved to Mary and smiled. Among the men, the Poles were the most elegant, hair Brylcreemed and dancing with intense concentration. The Americans chewed gum and danced as if they didn't care. There were no civilian men; they seldom turned up to these dances since they were universally looked down on.

'Mary danced with great verve. Light of foot, floating in my arms, turning and spinning.' Don waltzed with her as if he were in heaven. After a while, taking his hand firmly, she whispered, 'C'mon, Haggis – let's go outside.'

'The music receded as we walked towards the woods and the smell of wild flowers.' Don pressed her against a large oak tree and they embraced passionately. 'I slowly undid her blouse and stroked her warm breasts. Her cheek was burning and she smelt of apples and soap. I slid my hand down to the top of her stockings, where they joined the warm flesh, and undid the front button of her cami-knickers. With a quick, supple movement she locked her legs round my waist, while I held her lovely bottom and pressed her against the tree, as in an Indian temple carving.'

Afterwards they went back to the Bird in Hand, clinging to each other, and sat in an inglenook by the fire. Don lit his pipe content-edly, but Mary kept squeezing his hand, her eyes appealing with a faraway look, and shaking her head. 'At the time I couldn't think why. I was later to realise that the survival outlook of pilots was bleak and that she didn't expect me to return.'

Off-duty, Don went on seeing Mary, once risking all when he took her back to his quarters in his on-base Nissen hut – taking advantage of the fact that most crews had gone home on 48-hour Easter leave passes. 'I had never spent all night with a woman before, and after the initial excitement, I began to think that this hadn't been such a good idea after all. My bed was very narrow and I couldn't sleep.' Mary, far more mature and sophisticated, thought the whole thing an enormous joke, but as she had trouble sleeping too, removed herself to Don's navigator's bed. 'He'll be pleased about that,' Don thought.

It had been cold when they went to bed but then at least they had each other to cuddle up to. Don woke before dawn, suddenly very sober and very worried. When he woke Mary, she wanted to pull him into bed with her, but he was in too much of a panic. She dressed and he sent her off on his RAF bicycle, wearing his uniform cap and raincoat, so that if no one looked closely she'd pass for a WAAF. Had they got away with it? His heart sank when all officers were summoned to see the Group Captain, who furiously informed them that, 'it has come to my attention that some officers are having women in their Nissen huts and, in future, anyone caught will be severely dealt with!' He paused and seemed to fix Don with a glittering eye, but he had escaped by the skin of his teeth.

He wasn't to continue long with Mary. Though they stayed in touch, his transfers to other bases meant they no longer saw each other. It wasn't long before he'd met someone new at another dance – Molly, a young widowed mother with a baby. They arranged to meet at the Roman Wall near Lincoln Cathedral, and headed for a drink at the Saracen's Head. There was the usual crush in the pub and Molly, black-haired, tall and attractive, was one of the few civilians there. Molly held Don's hand and looked at him wistfully as she asked, 'Do you have a girlfriend back in Scotland?'

Don said nothing about Mary, since she didn't live in Scotland, but he could see that he was already being 'sized up in the marriage stakes'. Molly told him her husband had been shot down and killed three months after their marriage, which did nothing to shake Don's own opinion of wartime marriages. But he arranged to see her again.

On his second date he ran into his crewmate Geoff Owen, so left Molly briefly to say hello. Geoff detached himself from his own girlfriend, a WAAF parachute packer, drawing Don aside.

'I hope you don't think I'm being silly or interfering, but do you know you're with the Black Widow?'

'I don't understand.'

'She's a "chop lady". Since she lost her husband, two other pilots who were going steady with her have been shot down.'

'All right, Geoff, thanks for the tip. Anyway, things go in threes. Perhaps that's the lot. And I haven't been going steady with her.' Don went back to Molly, thinking, *That's how witches got burned.* 'It wasn't the girl's fault that three blokes she teamed up with got shot down. Lots of people were being shot down. Still, three *was* a lot.' Molly, who was looking strangely guilty, asked Don what he'd been talking about. He put her off and, when the evening was over, walked her home, but when he wanted to take things further, it was her turn to put him off, telling him it was too soon.

They didn't meet again for many weeks, and when they did, at her request, it was for her to tell him she'd got engaged to an Australian flyer. Don knew that Australians were prone to spinning yarns of wealth and sunshine to English girls, but there was something about Molly this time that didn't ring true, especially after he'd accepted her news with good grace and bought her a Pimm's to celebrate. Don was in for another surprise when, despite being recently engaged, she took his hand and looked into his eyes. 'Darling, you know I'm very fond of you. We'd make a great team together. You do love me, don't you?'

Later, after a few more Pimm's, Don walked her home. By then they both felt an irresistible attraction, and as they were passing Lincoln Cathedral, he pulled her into a cloister, where they made love for the first and only time – passionately. When it was over, she kissed him, said 'Goodbye, Don', and hurried off into the night.

Don walked the 14 miles back to RAF Bardney, arriving at 4 a.m.

'My feet hurt and all the alcohol and romance had worn off. I got to the Mess, which was always open, switched on the light, looked at the notice board and found my name on the battle order for that day. I went to my hut, washed, shaved, changed into battledress, lay down for an hour and had an early pre-flight breakfast.'

He never saw Molly again.

*James Flowers*

Love's arrow pierced others so thoroughly they could think of nothing else. That was how it was for James Flowers.

'She was such a cracker! I have no idea how I landed her. I wasn't thinking about the war – it was all just living for the moment. Where she was, she was surrounded by bomber bases and had plenty of admirers – so I just wanted to get her while I could!'[23]

James, not yet eighteen, first met Eunice Oakley at a dance in

Sutton-in-Ashfield in 1942, before he had joined the RAF. He was working twelve-hour shifts at a munitions factory, and once he'd seen Eunice he fell so completely in love that he moved heaven and earth to make her his. Furiously jealous of his innumerable rivals, all of whom were in the seductive blue uniforms already, and frustrated by her teasing attitude that he and she were, after all, 'just friends', he was devastated when she announced that she'd volunteered for the Land Army and was being posted to Gringley on the Hill, far away from him and dangerously close to Lincolnshire – Bomber County. 'When she came home at weekends I had to listen to tales about the lovely evenings spent with other Land Army friends in a hotel near their hostel, having singsongs with the local airmen.'

James's life was a misery, and he longed for the day when he could join up and put on a uniform. He didn't give up on Eunice and saw her as often as he could to reduce the risk of her being swept off her feet by someone else.

'I decided I had to make the effort to see her during the week. I could only do this when I was working on day shifts. After leaving work at 7 p.m., I would pedal furiously home, have a quick snack, then set off to cycle the 37 miles to Gringley.'

James used to keep his spirits up on the journey by reciting *She loves me, she loves me not*, but he'd often come close to falling asleep in the saddle. When he eventually arrived around 10 p.m., he'd only have half an hour with her before setting off home again. Arriving in the small hours, he'd creep into bed, only to be woken by his alarm clock at 5.30 a.m. for another twelve-hour shift. But he was making progress. On one of their weekends, which Eunice spent at home in Sutton, they were getting on so well that on Sunday she missed the last bus to Gringley. Not arriving back in time for work at eight the following morning would mean trouble. James leapt to the rescue, persuading his older brother to lend him his tandem. They would both cycle to Gringley early on Monday morning, arriving in time for Eunice to get to work. Fate seemed to be smiling on James; he'd just changed shifts from day to night, so he'd have all

Monday to get back – plenty of time before his own shift began at 7 p.m. Another huge advantage was that he'd have all the rest of that Sunday evening with Eunice, and her company on the way back to the Land Army hostel. He was in seventh heaven.

They set off together in the early hours on the 37-mile journey.

'It was hard work. Eunice always said that she pedalled hard at the back. I've always felt that I did all the work! By the time we climbed the steep hill to Gringley, I was completely whacked. After stopping outside the hostel I just collapsed on the ground and Eunice immediately rushed in to report. Lying there, I thought to myself, *Well, blow me! After all that effort, not even a blooming kiss.* I lay there for some time, feeling quite dejected.'

But Eunice soon reappeared, with a cup of tea and a kiss. 'Spirits now high, I set off for the 37-mile ride home.' He sped down Gringley hill with a light heart – but at the bottom the tandem's rear chain snapped. He couldn't go back – Eunice would be away at work by now. The only thing to do was walk, pushing the bike to a garage which might be able to fix it. But the only one he came across was 5 miles down the road, and it was then that James discovered that, in his haste that morning, he'd forgotten to bring any money with him. Despite his pleas, the mechanic refused to help unless he was paid, so, forlornly, James set off with his bike to walk the remaining 32 miles.

He got home at 6.30 p.m. – just in time to change for work and get to the factory to clock in. By the end of his twelve-hour shift, he felt like a zombie.

'The things we do for love!'

\* \* \*

The realities of love, and lost loves, were experienced across Bomber Command in late 1943. After the raid on Peenemünde, when Elsie Shaw had received the telegram informing her that her husband, rear gunner Stanley, was missing in action, her nine-year-old daughter Elaine was confused and frightened by her mother's misery.

'Your dad's not coming home. We're going to Grandma's,' her mother had told her. 'You need to go upstairs and pack a bag.'

Elsie picked up her younger daughter Pam, still only a one-year-old baby, and gave her a cuddle. Elaine thought about her mother's words as she went upstairs to pack. She didn't want to leave. It was upsetting and hard to understand. What did 'not coming home' mean? For ever?

Once she'd packed, trying not to panic or cry, Elaine joined her mother and baby sister.

'We walked down the street to the bus stop where I'd met my dad and his crew so many times. When we got to Sutton-in-Ashfield, Mum had to tell her parents the news. They were simply devastated – they loved my dad as if he were their own son. Seeing all the tears and the sorrow, I began to understand what it all meant. Then Mum had to go over to Dad's parents and tell them. There were no phones, everything was done by bus, and in person. Dad was so loved by them all that the shock was totally overwhelming. But there was no more information – that was it. There was nothing else to say. There was a war on.'

Stan's Station Commander at RAF Dunholme Lodge sent Elsie a sympathetic letter as early as 19 August 1943:

> As you are probably aware, it often takes some time for news to be received of those who are captured as prisoners of war, but as soon as any such news is forthcoming, I will immediately inform you by telegram. The Committee of Adjustment Officer is dealing with your husband's personal effects, and he will forward them to the Central Committee of Adjustment, RAF Colnbrook, when the officer in charge of that Unit will communicate with you.

There was little time for grief. Men died, life went on, money had to be earned.

'A few days later Mum went back to work making gas masks at Boots in Nottingham, and I went back to school. I went on doing my chores, and dropping off and picking up my baby sister at nursery. We couldn't afford to pay the nursery fees weekly, so I had to pay each day, waiting for a member of staff who could take the money, which sometimes made me late for school. One day, running all the way, I tripped over and cut my knee; I was in tears. Where was my dad? There was no one to pick me up and to tell me everything would be OK. My headmistress, Mrs Boltrop, called me in to find out why I was late yet again and asked about my bleeding knee. When she heard what we were going through, she allowed me an extra half-hour to get to school each day.'

On 24 August another sympathetic letter arrived for Elsie, this time from the managing director of Stan Shaw's old firm, Johnson and Barnes:

> *We are extremely sorry to hear of the news that your Husband is reported missing from operations. We all join with you in sharing your anxiety and do sincerely hope that you may soon hear that he is safe and well as a prisoner of war.*
>
> *We should be glad if you would let us know as soon as you have any further news of him. In the meantime, we should be pleased to do anything we can to assist you.*

This was reassuring, but Elsie Shaw had another problem to contend with. She was pregnant with her third child. Elaine watched over her mother anxiously.

'I'm not even sure my dad knew he was going to be a father again, as it had never been mentioned. But she had a miscarriage after the news that Dad had gone missing arrived, because of all the shock and distress. It was a boy. I remember my mother being sick and being looked after by a friend. She just told me, "I haven't got a baby any more." That was it, another life over. It was devastating, but she never really talked about it.'

The uncertainty and heartache continued throughout the rest of the month, though a further letter, from the Air Ministry's

Casualty Branch in Oxford Street, London, on 3 September, reassured Elsie that although her husband was missing,

> *This does not necessarily mean that he is killed or wounded,*
> *and if he is a prisoner of war he should be able to communicate*
> *with you in due course. Meanwhile enquiries are being made*
> *through the International Red Cross Committee and as soon as*
> *any definite news is received you will be at once informed.*

By then, Elsie and Elaine had their hearts in their mouths every time a brown envelope dropped through the letterbox.

'Had Dad survived? We hoped we might get news that he was a prisoner of war. It was a terrible time but we just had to get on with our lives, like thousands of others who were getting the same news. We just carried on.'

A colder letter arrived from the Air Ministry's Director of Accounts on 27 September. Just because a man was reported missing, it did not mean that financial regulations could be ignored.

> *Madam,*
> *I have to refer with regret to the fact that your husband has*
> *been officially promulgated as missing on 18 August 1943 and in*
> *the circumstances you will wish to be informed to what allowances you are entitled under Air Ministry regulations.*
> *The records of this Department show that you are in*
> *receipt of family allowance and allotments totalling 63s.0d.*
> *per week, and this rate of payment will be continued until 9*
> *December 1943.*

The minutiae of wartime administration was no respecter of personal grief or individual circumstances. The same department sent another letter on 25 October:

> *Although your husband is still, unfortunately, officially*
> *regarded as missing, the regulations do not provide for payment*

*of temporary allowance to be continued at family allowance*
*rate for more than a period of twenty-six weeks.*

   *In these circumstances I am to inform you that unless further*
*information is received regarding your husband, the temporary*
*allowance will continue [until] 10 February 1944, after which*
*the allowance will be reduced to 58s.6d. a week, but if further*
*information is received, it may be necessary to reduce your*
*allowance from an earlier date.*

It is difficult to come to terms with the cold brutality with which
officialdom dealt with the many tens of thousands of grieving relatives across Bomber Command and the other services. Elsie was
being told that if her husband remained 'missing', her allowances
would eventually be reduced anyway. If he was actually declared
dead, they could be reduced sooner.

Like the war itself, the necessary admin simply churned on. And
still there was no news of Stan.

'It was all so overwhelming for my mother at a time when we still
didn't know what had happened. But that was the war; everyone
was receiving all this official correspondence and no one had time
for sympathy. Money would be tight because of the reductions, but
the RAF continued to pay for my school dinners and milk.'

Then, on 22 November, after three months of uncertainty, pain
and heartache, the letter Elsie Shaw dreaded arrived from the Air
Ministry's Casualty Branch.

*In view of information now received from the International Red*
*Cross Committee, your husband, Flight Sergeant Stanley Shaw,*
*Royal Air Force, is believed to have lost his life as the result of*
*the air operations on the night of 17/18th August 1943.*

'*Believed*' to have lost his life – this surely meant there was still
some hope that Elaine's father might still be alive somewhere?
At the back of her mind, little Elaine hoped it was some sort
of mistake.

'In the street, I would see someone from behind in RAF uniform and think it might be him, that he would turn round, and I would see his face again. I used to hope that perhaps he had lost his memory and would turn up one day. Silly, really.'

Les Bartlett

While the grieving were forced to move on with their lives, the fifth Christmas of the war approached.

Wireless operator Reg Payne was stationed at RAF Skellingthorpe, not far from Lincoln. Christmas was always important on the bases, a key point in the diary, to take a break if you could, take stock, and prepare for what the coming year had in store. Would Christmas 1943 be the last Christmas of the war? Or the last Christmas altogether? Hopes rose and sank by turns. Twenty-year-old Reg was hoping for at least a brief respite from operations over the holiday when he'd be able to join his girlfriend, Ena Goodrich, at the ATS[24] dance and buffet in Lincoln's council offices. All his crew, including bomb aimer Les

Bartlett and Reg's close friend, rear gunner Fred Ball, had been invited.

To celebrate the festival and the break from ops, the Officers' Mess was thrown open to all, offering drinks on the house, so as lunchtime approached everyone was pretty well oiled. But then one of the catering officers arrived and asked for volunteers to serve Christmas dinner to the WAAFs. Reg and several others felt they could hardly refuse. 'The girls were already there and seated, duly wearing party hats, and waiting for their meal.'[25]

Serving the soup wasn't too much of a problem, but each WAAF had been given two bottles of beer to go with dinner and that was too much for some of them, so they asked Reg and his fellow waiters to help them out. 'By the time the pudding was due to be served I was having great difficulty in focusing on the table, the WAAFs, and where to put each dish.' Somehow they got through it, however, and made their unsteady way back to their own Mess for their own dinner. They were too late; it was long finished. Feeling rather fragile by now, they went back to their billet and tried to sleep it off. Waking at 6 p.m. feeling somewhat better, they needed a good wash-and-brush-up before they were ready for the dance. 'Ena would never have forgiven me if I'd forgotten: this was our first Christmas together.'

Grabbing a pair of bicycles to carry the five of them, they set off for Lincoln.

'To say we were given a frosty reception by the army lads at the do would be an understatement. The dance had already begun by the time we arrived, but as soon as we walked into the room a number of ATS girls, including Ena and Fred's girlfriend Joan, left their dancing partners and came straight over to these five young RAF aircrew chaps. For the rest of the evening we had all the company we could wish for, which didn't go down at all well with the lads in khaki, but with several officers present, we knew there wouldn't be any trouble.'

Christmas came and went – then it was back to business as usual. Both Reg Payne and Fred Ball carried lucky mascots on their operations; small 'Lincoln Imp' badges (the mythical monster featured in carvings in the cathedral), given to them by Ena and Joan, which were pinned to their battledress. One night, as they set out on a mission to Berlin, their skipper Michael Beetham was easing their Lancaster onto the perimeter track when Fred yelled in desperation from the rear turret, 'Reg, I've left my Imp in the billet. I can't go without it.' There was nothing anyone could do. Michael had already joined a line of Lancasters making their way to the runway to prepare for take-off. Luckily, help was at hand. Reg noticed a ground-crew corporal not far away in a car and signalled to him with his torch. The NCO quickly cottoned on and got behind their aircraft, from where Fred was able to shout instructions to him above the roar of the engines through the open panel of his turret. As was common practice among some gunners, he'd had a section of the Perspex removed for better visibility.

The corporal sped off towards the living quarters. Meanwhile, their Lancaster was slowly but surely moving up the queue for take-off. Closer and closer they came to the front, and there was still no joy. They turned onto the runway and came to a halt, now only waiting for the flash of the green Aldis lamp to send them on their way. Just as the skipper was running up the engines to full pitch, the corporal roared up to the rear turret. 'He's here!' Fred called out frantically. 'Don't go yet! He's got it!'

The corporal leapt from his car and, bent double against the backwash from the Lancaster's Merlins, reached up with the tiny golden badge.

'There's the green, Fred – we've got to go,' Michael called to him over the intercom.

'Skip – it's OK – I've got it,' a hugely relieved voice replied.

The rest of them were relieved too. 'The last thing we wanted was a rear gunner who was convinced we were going to get the chop!'

The raid passed without incident, yet they were not always so lucky.

Three weeks later, Beetham's crew were preparing for a routine 'fighter affiliation' exercise where they would practise tactics to counter attacks by German fighters. They would be taking two other gunners and their skipper from another crew for the experience. It was so run-of-the-mill that their flight engineer, Don Moore, a family man in his late twenties, didn't even bother to bring his parachute with him.

'It's only another training flight,' he told Reg Payne. 'I'm fed up with having to keep carrying it about.'

'You should always have your 'chute with you, Don,' Reg replied, alarmed.

'You worry too much, Reg.' Don laughed and slapped him on the shoulder. 'I'll be OK.'

They took off and rendezvoused with the fighter – a Spitfire – near the Humber estuary. Both pilots, liaising over their radios, went into the exercise of attack and evasion.

'Above the clouds in the bright Yorkshire winter sunshine, the Spitfire attacked us from different directions. Michael climbed, dived and rolled our Lancaster – *Q-Queenie* – through corkscrew manoeuvres, while our gunners practised shooting the fighter down, their efforts recorded by cine cameras fitted to the gun turrets. The rest of us simply hung onto our seats and tried not to be thrown about too much.'

After half an hour, Michael radioed the Spitfire pilot to hold off while he, the spare pilot and the gunners changed places. The exercise recommenced, with the Spitfire diving in for another practice attack, the new rear gunner shouting instructions.

'Fighter, fighter, starboard quarter, up! Prepare to corkscrew starboard. Corkscrew starboard, GO!'

Reg and Les clung on as the Lancaster went into a steep dive, at which point Don Moore anxiously yelled, 'The port outer's on fire!'

Reg looked quickly out of his side window and saw a mass of orange flame engulfing the engine and wing. Once the fire extinguisher was activated, Beetham, the senior officer in charge, gave the order to prepare to abandon the aircraft. As Reg reached for the bracket close to his table to grab his own parachute, he caught sight of Don Moore, who had left his parachute on the ground. 'Just for a second, he paused and looked at me, fear in his eyes.

'My heart was pumping fast as I turned my attention back to the fire in the engine, and it was with some relief that I watched the flames die down and then go out. But as soon as the extinguishers were empty, the fire blazed up once more and quickly engulfed the engine again. The outer wing was starting to glow as the fire grew in intensity. Soon, the flames, fanned by the wind, were licking at the whole length of it.

'We had just a few seconds to get out before it dropped off, and sent Q-Queenie into her final dive.'

Skipper Michael Beetham had been watching the fire too. Now he knew the Lancaster was doomed. He gave the order to bale out, not knowing that Don Moore didn't have a parachute. Les and Beetham got out through the forward escape hatch. Reg stood by the open main door with Fred Ball and the two extra gunners, but they hesitated, transfixed by fear.

'We hadn't trained for this; we had never jumped out of an aircraft before, never stepped into that abyss.'

Reg yelled to Fred to jump, straining his voice against the roar of the screaming engines; but he and the other two held back, indicating that Reg should go first.

'There was no time to waste. The whole wing was on fire now, and the moment it dropped off the chance to get out would be gone for ever. We'd be trapped, helpless in the plummeting aircraft.'

Don Moore, parachute-less, was standing with them. 'The blood had drained from his face, his hands were shaking, and although he was looking at me, it wasn't me he saw. His eyes were wide and glazed over – he was staring through me at someone or something behind me, perhaps the image of death itself; but I hope it was his wife and young daughter whom he would never see again. I put my hand out and touched his arm in farewell, sat on the step and rolled out. My last sight of Don was of him scrabbling his way back along the fuselage desperately searching for a spare parachute.'

Reg felt a surge of relief as he fell clear of the aircraft. A moment later he was horrified to find himself back on board. The slipstream had thrown him back through the open main door. Instinctively, one of the gunners pushed him back out again and this time he was clear, falling faster and faster, still above the cloud.

He counted to three, and pulled his ripcord.

'Nothing happened. I pulled it again. Still it wouldn't open. In desperation I pulled again and again as I plunged and somersaulted through the wet mist of the cloud layer, the cold wind ripping at my flying suit and tearing at my face. After falling for around 3,000ft I burst through the murk into clear air.'

He called on God for help, and, as he did so, realised that he hadn't been pulling on the ripcord, but on part of his harness. With a gasp of relief, he released the parachute and felt the life-saving jolt as the silk bloomed out above him. But it wasn't over yet.

'When I put my parachute harness on, I hadn't tightened it properly. So, as the canopy caught the air, the parachute pulled my shoulders out of the harness, leaving only my legs secure. In the nick of time, I managed to duck back under the straps and grab hold of the flapping straps, hanging on for dear life. If I failed to hold on, I'd be tipped forward and out of the harness, parting company from my parachute, and this world.

'Content that I was now secure, I drifted down. I could see for miles around me and my thoughts returned to Don Moore, and how he should have been floating down as well, instead of being condemned to die in the Lancaster. Then, some distance ahead of me, I saw a great orange flash and a large pall of thick black smoke, followed a few moments later by a muffled boom.'

Reg knew that Q-Queenie had breathed her last. Don had died too. He prayed that Fred Ball had managed to get out in time. Then his attention was caught by something new. 'I turned my gaze upwards, just in time to see the outer port wing from Q-Queenie following me down, lurching backwards and forwards like an autumn leaf gently falling from a tree. I watched it see-saw through the sky, mesmerised by the beauty of its motion.' Below him, not far from where his Lancaster had come down, Reg could now see an aerodrome. He was close now, and soon he was bracing himself for the moment of impact.

'The jolt, a flurry of soft earth under my boots, then I was rolling on the ground. I was down. I was safe. I had survived.' He later learned that four men were still in the Lancaster when he'd seen it crash – the two extra gunners, Don Moore, and his dear friend, Fred Ball.

Reg returned sadly to his own base, and, once in his billet, looked across at the neatly made beds where Don and Fred should have been lying, knowing that he'd never see them again and wondering how he was going to be able to break the news to Fred's girlfriend, Joan. The Christmas dance, two months earlier, seemed a million years ago.

Fred's blue tunic was hanging on a peg near his bed as Reg stared emptily across the room. A shaft of sunlight passed over it, catching a glint of something in the lapel.

'I realised it was Fred's lucky mascot; the golden Lincoln Imp. I flopped back on my pillow, a lump in my throat. I glanced at my own Imp, still pinned securely on the breast pocket of my battle-dress jacket. Do lucky charms work? Who knows? But I do know that I had worn my Imp and survived; Fred had left his behind, and he hadn't.'

Joan was inconsolable when she heard of Fred's death, but they shielded her from the whole truth. They'd managed to extricate what was left of Fred from the wreckage and transfer the shattered remains to a coffin to be taken home to his family in Birmingham. Reg and Michael Beetham accompanied the coffin, under the strictest instructions that on no account should it be opened for the funeral.

Joan, and Fred's parents, would join the legions of people already grieving for lost lovers and lost sons.

\* \* \*

There had been no happy Christmas for Elaine Shaw, still waiting in desperate hope that her father, rear gunner Stanley, might eventually be discovered, injured in a POW camp, perhaps even on the run and heading home. But official advice had declared him *believed* dead after the Peenemünde raid and administration to reduce Elaine's mother's allowances continued. Stan's brother Vic had written to Elsie on 23 December, the prelude to a wretched Christmas. Angry at the way his brother's wife (despite his own words, not yet officially a widow) was being treated and that her allowances were being cut, he wrote:

> *I know you must feel very sick at heart and frayed of temper. It is a disgrace to the British Government that widows with two small children like you have to turn out to work to supplement the income. The sacrifice evidently is not enough.*

Finally, in the bleak days following Christmas, and as New Year 1944 opened, Elsie Shaw received the letter she dreaded most on 12 January. It came from the Air Ministry's Casualty Department:

> *I am directed to inform you that action has now been taken to presume, for official purposes, your husband, 1576142 Flight Sergeant S. Shaw, lost his life on 18 August, 1943.*
>
> *I am to express the sympathy of the Department with you in your great loss.*

There could be no more hope.

A standard note of sympathy from the King followed:

> *BUCKINGHAM PALACE*
> *The Queen and I offer you our heartfelt sympathy in your great sorrow.*
> *We pray that your country's gratitude for a life so nobly given in its service may bring you some measure of consolation.*
> *GEORGE R. I.*

It was a heartbreaking time for the family, especially young Elaine. 'Obviously there was no funeral or any sort of service. No chance to say goodbye. My father was gone. That was the reality of war. There were many thousands like us. We just moved on.'

But there was no let-up for the family. On 27 January, the Director of Accounts wrote again to confirm that Elsie's allowance would be reduced as previously notified.

The following day, the local newspaper *The Free Press* carried an article in tribute to Stan.

### BURIED IN GERMANY
#### News of former Sutton Resident

Flight-Sergeant Shaw was 31 years of age, and had been in the RAF two-and-a-half years. At the time of his death, having been over enemy territory 22 times. In civil life he was employed at Messrs. Johnson and Barnes Ltd. A letter from Messrs. Johnson and Barnes to Mrs Shaw states: 'We at the factory had a very high opinion of your husband, and I can say, on behalf of his fellow-workmen in the fully fashioned department, that he was very highly respected by them.'

In the meantime, the Committee of Adjustment at Stan's squadron had done its work, packing up Stan's possessions, clearing his bed and locker for his successor. He would leave no physical trace behind.

On the same day as *The Free Press* article appeared, officials from the Central Depository at RAF Colnbrook, where the personal effects of all missing airmen were stored, wrote to Elsie to let her know that Flight Sergeant Stanley Shaw's possessions would now be forwarded. The enclosed inventory detailed: '3 pairs Braces (2 pairs damaged); 1 Tobacco Pouch; 1 Swim Suit; 1 Fountain Pen Golden Platinum; 1 Pipe; 1 India Rubber; 1 Air Gunner's Brevet; 1 Razor Gillette; 1 pair Pants; 4 Handkerchiefs; 1 pair Socks.'

It took the Director of Accounts until 9 March to let Elsie

know 'the out-turn of your husband's Service Estate'. It came to £28.8s.8d.

Some laundry, a few pounds, some toiletries and meagre possessions; all that remained of a husband, son, brother and father.

One of Stan's friends had also written to Elsie to tell her he'd been on the same operation to Peenemünde. He'd heard the news about Stan, and he promised to pay her a visit as soon as he got leave, when he would tell her what he knew about the trip in the hope it might provide some comfort. He never made it; he too was killed on operations soon after writing.

Stan's few possessions arrived home, bundled up in a parcel.

'This was all that was left of my dad, wrapped up in brown paper. As we unpacked it and checked everything, a halfpenny dropped out of his wallet. It was the lucky charm he'd told me he always flew with to make sure he got back to us safely. He had forgotten to take it on that flight. I remember my dad's last words to me, "Look after your mum and baby sister," so that's what I tried to do. My mother was truly heartbroken, but Dad was rarely mentioned in the house afterwards. It wasn't hard-hearted – there just wasn't much to be said. We still had to see the war out and hopefully survive. There were pictures on the wall, but that was the only reminder. Our tragedy was a small, individual tragedy in the midst of hundreds of thousands of tragedies and everyone simply had to get on with their lives.'

# CHAPTER TEN

# PILOTS OF THE CARIBBEAN

The onslaught continued, the casualties mounted, and the search for new recruits to feed the Bomber Command machine expanded across the globe.

During the First World War, Jamaican-born William Robinson 'Robbie' Clarke had arrived in Britain as a nineteen-year-old volunteer in 1915. He eventually become a sergeant, the Royal Flying Corps' first black pilot, and a shining example to those who followed in his footsteps.

On the morning of 28 July 1917, he was attacked by enemy fighters while on reconnaissance in an RE8 biplane over the Western Front. He described the experience in a letter to his mother:

> *I was doing some photographs a few miles the other side when about five Hun scouts came down upon me, and before I could get away, I got a bullet through the spine. I managed to pilot the machine nearly back to the aerodrome, but had to put her down as I was too weak to fly any more.*[1]

Robbie had more than proved himself – and some 16,000 First World War West Indian volunteers were to follow his example. They wanted to show their loyalty to George V – and to demonstrate that they deserved better treatment under British rule, paving the way for independence.

The 1917 Air Force (Constitution) Act had restricted entry into the RAF to men of pure European descent. The official line was: 'Although sections of the Act permitted voluntary enlistment of *any inhabitant of any British protectorate and any negro or person of colour* in exceptional circumstances, no such "aliens" were to be promoted above the rank of Non-Commissioned or Warrant Officer.'[2] After 1940, because of the losses of some 3,000 aircrew in the Battles of Britain and France, the RAF changed its policy, and many from the Caribbean and Africa willingly left the safety of home to join up.

It wasn't always an easy path.

Among the early volunteers was Cy Grant, who came to Britain from Guyana in South America to join the RAF in 1941. Born in 1919 in the sleepy village of Beterverwagting in Demerara, Cy was the son of a Moravian Church minister. The family lived in a huge mansion complete with servants. When Cy was eleven, the family moved to New Amsterdam, the capital of Berbice. Although such place names survived, British Guiana, as it was then, had passed from Dutch hands in 1815, and his bourgeois education had 'implied that everything black was inferior – the only language we spoke confirmed this. History lessons taught us nothing about ourselves or tried to explain the great diversity of our population.'[3]

Despite his growing reservations about the moral and ethical stance of the 'Mother Country' towards its colonies, he jumped at the chance of recruitment to the RAF in 1941, when 'suddenly the cream of West Indian young men was being exhorted to join the distinguished ranks of The Few. I was one of the first Guyanese to be selected to serve as aircrew, and how proud I was. My decision to join up had been prompted solely by a desire for adventure and to get away from what I foresaw would be a dull colonial future.'

Next came the first of many new experiences for Cy and his fellow volunteers on their way to do battle in the air.

'We sailed from Georgetown to Halifax, Nova Scotia, anchored in the harbour for a few days as a convoy of ships gathered, before we set sail on the hazardous journey across the Atlantic.

'The passage lasted for many days in freezing weather, with a constant lookout for the U-boats which were causing so much havoc in
the Atlantic. We were all pressed into service to stand watch, by day
and by night. The night shift was the most arduous, the dull, relentless throb of the engines as we tried to stay upright on the heaving
deck, cold and damp from the freezing spray stinging our faces. How
many ships were in the convoy? I hadn't the slightest idea.'

*Cy Grant*

Safely in England, Cy went through the usual induction process
at the Air Crew Reception Centre in St John's Wood, London. He
experienced the jolt of alienation when a middle-aged Englishman
expressed surprise at his fluent command of the language. 'Many
were not aware that literacy in British Guiana then was much higher
than in Britain.' On another occasion a doctor commented on 'the
toughness of my skin when administering the prescribed injection
for servicemen from overseas'.

Despite these disquieting experiences, life in training dis-
pelled any further misgivings about prejudice. Most of what Cy

experienced, he realised, was due to ignorance and unfamiliarity. He transferred from St John's Wood to a training unit near Nottingham, where 'there was strict discipline but a relaxed and friendly atmosphere and no hint of colour prejudice'.

A fellow crewman, Sam King, a future Mayor of Southwark (the first black mayor in London, and one of the founders of the Notting Hill Carnival), remarked that, 'The RAF taught me two things: the importance of discipline and the importance of honesty.'[4]

* * *

Cy's friend, eighteen-year-old William 'Billy' Strachan, had left school in Kingston, Jamaica, in December 1939 and started work as a Civil Service clerk. Like so many of his contemporaries, he still regarded Britain as the Mother Country, even though there had been nothing particularly motherly about her administration in the Caribbean.

There had been some slow improvement in the twentieth century, but colonial rule had been divisive and discriminatory. By the mid-1930s, the seeds of independence were already sown, but when Billy heard appeals on the radio to members of the Empire to take part in the war effort, he was inspired by the spirit of adventure and the desire to prevent an evil regime from imposing itself on humanity. He duly presented himself at Up-Park Camp, the local headquarters of the British Army since 1774, to volunteer for the RAF.[5] After being passed medically fit, Billy asked when he'd be sent to Britain to join the RAF; surely they would be extremely keen to get him into service? 'They laughed at me and told me to find my own way there. So I went to the Jamaica Fruit Shipping Company and persuaded them to let me have a passage for £15.'[6] Exasperated, he wondered how he could raise what, at the time, was a huge sum of money in order to get to England and be part of the war.

He sold his bicycle and precious saxophone, raising £17.10s., and took a berth on the steamer which, by a stroke of irony, had docked in Port Royal a short time earlier with a large number of well-to-do Britons escaping to the safety of the Caribbean. The only passenger on the journey back, he was given a First Class cabin, which saved the shipping company having to open and clean the main accommodation suite. But Billy didn't live the First Class lifestyle, spending a large part of the voyage on deck, flattening used tin cans to provide metal for the war effort.

He arrived in Bristol docks on a wet Saturday in March 1940, in the middle of an air raid, with nothing to his name but £2.10s. and a suitcase with one change of clothes. He made for Temple Meads railway station, where the first person he encountered was a uniformed porter. Billy took him for an officer, stood to attention and saluted. After paying for his ticket to London, he was left with £1, some of which he spent getting from Paddington to a hostel near Tottenham Court Road. It had been an expensive journey.

The following day, not understanding the need to enlist at a local recruiting office, he simply presented himself at Adastral House, the Air Ministry headquarters. 'The guards thought I was taking the mickey.'

'What do you want?' a corporal at the entrance asked him.

'I'm here to join the RAF.'

'Piss off!'

Billy's plan to serve the King was not going well.

A passing sergeant asked him where he came from.

'Kingston,' he answered.

'Well, son, you'll have to go to your local recruiting office there.'

There was a difficult moment, before a young RAF officer who had overheard the tail-end of the conversation realised Billy didn't mean Kingston in Surrey. 'You're from Jamaica,' he cried. 'One of our colonial friends. Welcome! You know, I did geography at university and I've always been impressed with you West Africans.'

Billy wondered whether the newcomer had managed to complete his degree, but he clearly meant well, and went on to organise his recruitment. Not long afterwards, Billy found himself as the only non-white airman training as a Bomber Command wireless operator in Blackpool. The others were amazed that he should have chosen to leave the warmth and peace of the Caribbean for cold, damp, wartime Britain.

There was little trace of prejudice towards the Caribbean recruits, though when Billy turned out to be the fittest of his group during physical training, their instructor, who'd been a circus acrobat before the war, announced, 'Darky, I'm going to make you my deputy.' Billy's family was light-skinned – he was known as a 'Red Man' at home, part of an elite – and it was the first time he'd been addressed in this way. He found himself torn between what seemed at best patronising and at worst racist, and pride at being selected.[7] Billy was destined to fly Lancasters, but his first tour would be on Wellington twin-engined bombers as a wireless operator and then navigator.

As well as volunteers, the Caribbean colonies also provided natural resources such as aluminium, oil, coffee, rum and bananas in such quantities that it led to rationing at home. Nigeria supplied cocoa, and Sierra Leone iron ore. British dominions in West Africa donated £1.5 million (nearly £70 million today) to the war effort, and the West Indies £500,000 – no small sums at the time.[8]

All volunteers arrived in the UK feeling a mixture of 'excitement and fear'.[9] They found the weather 'bloody cold and gloomy', but most locals were only too glad to welcome people from far away who were prepared to risk their lives fighting for the common cause. At the time, few white Britons had ever seen, let alone met, black people, and though prejudice wasn't widespread, ignorance and insensitivity played their part in creating misunderstanding and conflict. An airman from Jamaica was approached by 'a darling old couple who humbly begged to be allowed to shake my hand for good luck. Up until then I thought that kind of superstition was confined to uneducated colonials.'

The new arrivals were meeting white people of all kinds for the first time, and fellow West Indians from different islands; there, too, antagonism and mistrust could erupt. Sport, especially cricket, helped break down barriers, but other activities could create them. One Jamaican radar operator rejoiced in the fact that 'black men could dance and swing their hips, which the white women loved. This caused envy and fights; but the white women stood up for the black men and defended them with their stiletto heels as weapons.'

Another Caribbean airman was verbally abused by a pair of Scottish soldiers who clearly failed to understand the irony of their jibes, aimed as they were at someone who was fighting Nazism: 'You're dancing with white girls. If this was Germany they'd have you shot for that.'

Having completed his tour of thirty operations on Wellingtons – his was the only crew in his squadron to complete a full tour intact[10] – Billy Strachan had the chance to leave the front line and become an instructor, but 'I was cocky and self-assured, in perfect physical and mental condition, and, being young, quite arrogant!'[11] He decided to retrain as a pilot.

It was not without its setbacks. While under instruction in Cambridgeshire, the Tiger Moth he was flying crashed. Billy ended up in Ely Hospital with a fractured right hip, a broken nose and cheekbones. He was in a coma for three weeks, in plaster for longer, and had to hobble about for several more after that.

But there was one big consolation. He'd met Joyce Smith, a young north Londoner, at a dance shortly before the crash. They married while he was still on crutches, and honeymooned at the Palace Hotel in Torquay. Their romantic respite, however, was soon shattered by a German bomb. Joyce came to no harm; Billy fell through two floors, but limped out of the wreckage and eventually returned to active duty.

Like most of his fellow airmen, Billy enjoyed the high regard of the British public. But there was always the *awareness* of being black in a white world. During pilot training at RAF Cranwell, Billy had his first batman – a member of the Mess staff appointed to look after him – whom he described as a 'real smooth Jeeves type. I was a little boy from the Caribbean and I instinctively called him "sir". "No, sir," the batman hastily corrected. "It is *I* who call *you* sir."

'My own experience, together with [that of] most of my colleagues, showed that whenever one black person arrived anywhere he was always welcomed and treated well. If there were two of you, the other men could still cope. It was when there were three or more of us that racism really got sharp. When you arrived anywhere as a black man you were treated like a teddy bear. You were loved and fêted. I know that some of us fared badly; but I had no problems in that respect.'

Training complete, Billy took charge of his first Lancaster, leading an all-white crew who trusted him completely. But as time passed and the number of operations under their belts increased, the stress was getting to them, and on his fifteenth sortie as skipper, Billy knew he would become more of a liability than an asset if he continued.

'I remember it so clearly. I was carrying a 12,000lb bomb and we were destined for some German port. We were stationed in Lincolnshire and our flight path was over Lincoln Cathedral. It was a foggy night, with visibility down to about 100 yards. I asked my engineer to make sure we were on course to get over the top of the cathedral. He replied, "We've just passed it." I looked out and suddenly realised that it was just beyond our wingtips. It was sheer luck we hadn't collided with it. I hadn't seen it at all – and I was the pilot! That was the last straw. Then and there my nerve went. I knew I simply couldn't go on – that this was the end of me as a pilot! I flew to a special "hole" we had in the North Sea, which no Allied shipping ever went near, and dropped my "big one". Then I flew back to the airfield.'

In view of his record, no action was taken; but Billy's Lancaster days were over.

* * *

Cy Grant first took to the sky in a Tiger Moth biplane at Elementary Flying Training School in Ansty, near Coventry. 'This was something special for a young lad fresh from the Colonies. It was a heady experience, but exhilarating – the rush of air in the open cockpit plus the noise of the aircraft itself – none of which dulled one's senses to the wonderful scenery of the English countryside in good weather. Learning to use the controls was really challenging, even though the instructor was extremely patient. About the time I was to do my first solo flight, I was informed that I had been selected to be a navigator, and no Spitfire for me!'

*Billy Strachan (left) and his crew. Their aircraft was named* Vizagapatam *after the town in India that paid for it*

It was a bitter pill to swallow, and he couldn't help wondering why, at that time, so few West Indian and black African volunteers were selected to be pilots. But, like Billy Strachan, he had 'personally never experienced any racism in the RAF. I had accepted the reason given for me to train as a navigator, never suspecting that, in my case, it had been anything but genuine. I still had not been subjected to any form of overt prejudice. A war was on and I was wearing a uniform. People were generally very friendly. Outside in the streets I occasionally heard a child say, "Look, Mummy, a black man." That always brought me up sharp. Before coming to England I didn't think of myself as black – a salutary shock!'

In the long run, around 5,950 people of colour from the Caribbean, Africa and Britain volunteered to join the RAF; 5,500 as ground crew and 450 as aircrew. They served with all UK-based units except Transport Command, whose personnel visited some countries intolerant of such integrated crews.[12]

As the war progressed, the RAF proved themselves more enlightened than other employers of the day. An Air Ministry Confidential Order of June 1944 stated that, 'All ranks should clearly understand that there is no colour bar in the Royal Air Force. Any instance of discrimination on grounds of colour by white officers or airmen or any attitude of hostility towards personnel of non-European descent should be immediately and severely checked.'[13] And this was generally observed. One Nigerian wireless operator/gunner not only experienced no problem with his crew; they even named their bomber in honour of him, painting on its nose: 'ACHTUNG! THE BLACK PRINCE'.

Eighty per cent of Afro-Caribbean airmen served in Bomber Command, but so liberal was the official attitude that it is impossible to tell their precise number, since race did not feature on their personal records.

Cy Grant completed his training in February 1943 and crewed up with Alton Langille, his French-Canadian skipper, 'who chose me as he was to choose all the other crew members – because we were the best at our respective trades. On 19 June, we were ready for ops.'

Their first raid was on Mühlheim near Frankfurt, three nights later.

'As navigator, one was kept continuously occupied. The navigator's station was just aft of the pilot's position, with a small table on the port side of the cabin on which sat the chief navigational aid – the GEE radio navigation system. You did not see much of what was going on below. It may have been completely different for my pilot, having to fly the Lanc through all that flak, or for the gunners looking out for fighters. For myself, my sense of responsibility for getting us there and back was paramount, and that may be why the obvious dangers of the situation did not seem to get to me. In the Lancaster the navigator's position was screened off, so my light couldn't betray our aircraft's position to enemy night-fighters. In any event, whenever I had a peek, and that was only when we were over the target, I was only too happy to get back to my station to work out a course which would get us away from the scene; away from the noise of the battle, the flares, the searchlights, the inferno below, and the unnerving jolting of the aircraft while we were over the target.'

Like many of the Lancaster crews wreaking destruction on the enemy far below, the reality of the bombing prompted conflicting emotions in Cy.

'I don't think aircrew were fully conscious of the havoc and destruction they were causing. All they were thinking was, "Drop those bombs on the target and get out of there." Warfare denudes you of humanity. Yes, I had sought adventure, an escape from a dull future in a British colony, but, reflecting on it afterwards, I feel no sense of pride.'

The following night, twenty-four Lancasters from his squadron joined a group of 473 bombers heading for the Ruhr. It was one of the shortest nights of the year, and they rendezvoused with the rest of the stream over the North Sea near Harwich at 10.42 p.m. The excitement was high as they flew east towards Bochum and Gelsenkirchen.

Cy's aircraft was straggling behind the main force, so they arrived when the targets were already ablaze.

'Even amid the deafening drone of scores of other aircraft, the glow of the target area, the flak, the sweeping searchlights and the sudden bumps as the aircraft rode the frenzied skies, I never

questioned what I was doing there. I cannot remember feeling particularly frightened; the thought of imminent death did not cross
my mind. It was as though we were in another state of consciousness, emotionally switched off, yet our minds were functioning
clearly as we got on with the things we each had to do.'

Just after they released their bombs over the target, flak burst
through the now empty bomb bay and out through the other
side of the fuselage, but without causing any serious damage.
Everyone had the cold feeling that if the flak had struck seconds
earlier, it would have been the end of them. It seemed unreal. On
the way home, still some distance behind the rest of the stream,
rear gunner Joe Addison yelled over the intercom that a fighter
was closing in on them. 'The German fired a long volley and a jet
of tracer spat out towards us.'

Joe returned fire immediately, and the fighter veered off to
the right, bringing it within range of the mid-upper gunner.
Meanwhile the skipper pushed the nose of the heavy aircraft into
a dive. 'In a moment the world was turned upside-down.'

Alton Langille took evasive action, corkscrewing down and
away. As suddenly as it had started, all became quiet once
more.

The fighter had disappeared.

Had they shot it down?

They must have!

'"Great work, guys!" Alton's Canadian accent betrayed both
the strain we were all under, and the relief.' He levelled out the
aircraft. There didn't seem to be any serious damage, and no one
had been hit.

Cy checked their position; they should now be just west of
Amsterdam. Could they make it across the Channel and to
safety?

'Starboard outer's on fire, Skipper!' the mid-upper gunner
shouted.

They'd been hit after all, but the fire seemed to be a small
one. Alton put the Lancaster into another steep dive in an effort

to smother the flames, but they had spread to the dinghy stored beneath the starboard wing by the time he levelled out again.

'Now we *were* up against it! Without our dinghy we couldn't ditch in the sea.'

They didn't dare jettison the burning dinghy for fear that it would be carried back into the tailplane by the slipstream, fouling the controls. Then they realised that the overall damage was far worse than they'd thought. One of the undercarriage wheels fell away from its housing in an incandescent spiral, and fire broke out on the port wing. Their Lancaster bomber was breaking up.

'The situation was tense and worsening as each moment went by. Both wings were afire now; we were a flaming comet over the Dutch sky.'

It became impossible for Alton to control the aircraft, so, still over enemy-occupied Holland, he give the order they least wanted to hear: 'Well, guys, this is it. Bale out and good luck! Get to it!' Cy moved forward to the escape hatch below the bomb aimer's position. 'I had never contemplated being in this situation. We had been instructed in the use of parachutes but never had to practise leaving an aeroplane by one.'

He saw that the bomb aimer and the engineer, who should by now have already left the aircraft, were struggling to release the hatch. The pilot, having seen Cy go forward safely, and knowing that his wireless operator and two gunners would make for the main door aft on the starboard side, set the Lancaster on a steady course and followed Cy forward.

'The four of us were soon piled up one on top of the other, tossed from side to side in the cramped space in the nose of the aircraft. Though not comprehending why we were unable to escape the now fiercely burning aeroplane, I do not recall any sense of fear or panic. We seemed locked in a timeless moment of inertia when suddenly, with a deafening blast which lit up everything, our craft blew up and disintegrated, freeing us from each other – a free-fall into Eternity. On reflection, I realise that the whole sequence lasted less than thirty seconds. I found myself swallowed up by the silent stretches of space. My chute opened readily and I felt a sudden jerk and the strain of the harness on my shoulders as the wind snatched at the canopy. Except for the rush of wind I was now in an unreal world of mist and utter silence. It was quite light up there above the clouds, which stretched like a white ethereal sea below. To add to the unreality, it seemed as if I was suspended in the air, for at first I experienced no sensation of falling. The canopy of my parachute spread above me like a sinister shadow and I felt as if I were being borne swiftly aloft in the claws of a gigantic eagle.'

Cy also became aware of distant searchlights, and saw the glow of an isolated fire far below. Was that their Lancaster? What had happened to the rest of his crew? Had they survived? Would he link up with any of them?

There was no time to think about that now.

'It still seemed as if I was drifting aimlessly, with only the sound of the wind swelling the silk of the 'chute above me. Then came the sudden rush of a shadow coming towards me at immense speed. It was the ground reaching up to gather me. Instinctively, I grabbed for the release knob on my harness, turned it and slapped it hard. The next thing I knew, I was running on firm ground with ghostly, billowing folds of silk collapsing all about me. Amazingly, I had made a perfect landing.'

Cy clambered out of his harness, his heart pounding. He checked his watch: 2.38 a.m., and the sky was already lightening. The countryside around him was flat, crisscrossed by canals, not unlike the landscape thousands of miles away back home in Guyana. The silence was broken by the distant barking of dogs. The Germans must be searching for them already. 'I knew I had to get away – fast.'

The escape lectures had always stressed that in this predicament a downed airman should head south and travel by night.

'We'd been given maps of the Continent printed on silk handkerchiefs and a few other aids in case we did have to bale out.

We were to make for Spain, and, once there, contact the British consulate, who would make speedy arrangements to get us back to England and back onto operations. How I looked forward to that!'

Then he heard the dogs again. Were they getting closer?

Cy knew that for him the war was by no means over – yet.

It was time to make a move.

## CHAPTER ELEVEN

# 'FOR CHRIST'S SAKE, DO SOMETHING, OR WE'RE ALL GOING TO DIE'

The war in the air could be traumatic, but for the German civilians on the receiving end of the Allied bombs, it was simply terrifying.

Seventeen-year-old Ils Mar Garthaus was working as a ballerina with Tanztheater Bremen when 217 Lancasters raided the city's port in early 1944.

'A stream of enemy bombers made their way through a barricade of searchlights raking the sky, causing the ground to tremble with the sound of their passage. Flak bursts of red, yellow and white travelled up shafts of light, hitting their targets, or moving beyond them skywards. Then a bomb came down close by and every one of us made for the door of our apartment block, where another bomb, or, the pressure from its explosion, swept us down the stairway. Stumbling down ahead of us were the two French girls who helped in the kitchen of the downstairs restaurant. *Chéri! Chéri!* Their screams mingled with the spine-chilling whistle of the falling bombs, as stark naked they ran after their lovers, nightly visitors from a labour camp in the vicinity. When it was all over but for a candelabra of flares hanging above the chaos, I felt I had survived a game of Russian roulette.'[1]

In the skies above, mixed emotions abounded. Some airmen

thought the Germans deserved everything they got; they'd started it and were now being paid back with interest. Others were far more nuanced.

'If we could have seen what we were doing, if we could have seen little babies and women burning to death, screaming in agony, we wouldn't have been able to do it. It's sheer distance that allows you to do these things. You don't see the people you're blowing to smithereens, you don't hear the shrieks and screams. All you hear is the propaganda. You were taught to hate. They never mentioned people in targets. They just said "targets". We had to aim at the flares and drop our bombs. All I thought of was, not the people below, but, *For God's sake let's get home*. When you are facing death, your primary object, right from your very guts, is survival.'[2]

One of the aims of the bombing was to weaken the morale of the civilians on the receiving end. But how effective was it? At Bomber Command HQ, Arthur Harris was undeterred by the fact that German morale appeared to have been undermined as little by the bombing of their cities as British morale had been during the Blitz. Meanwhile, casualties were mounting on both sides. During the Battle of Berlin alone, between November 1943 and March 1944, the RAF lost more than 7,000 aircrew and 1,047 bombers. A further 1,682 aircraft were damaged or written off.[3] But the cost to the Germans was greater: 25 per cent of Berlin was destroyed, and 75 per cent of Hamburg.[4] On the ground, many tens of thousands of civilians had lost their lives.

An Air Staff Intelligence Report from early 1944 summed up the material damage inflicted:

It will be seen that the enemy has irretrievably lost *1,000,000 man years* [of labour]. This represents no less than 36 per cent of the industrial effort which would have been put out by these towns if they had remained unmolested. A Lancaster thus only has to go to a German city once to wipe off its own capital cost, and the results of all subsequent sorties will be clear profit.[5]

By the beginning of 1944 the Luftwaffe was losing up to 1,000 aircraft a month, mainly on the Eastern Front. Allied attacks on oil refineries meant that fuel shortages added to the Luftwaffe's inability effectively to counter air raids with fighters – at best they could muster around 350 fighters for the night defence of the whole of Germany. But they could still pack a lethal punch.

December 1943 had seen Eisenhower's appointment as Supreme Commander of the Allied Expeditionary Force in Europe, and Churchill, Roosevelt and Stalin had discussed Operation Overlord, the cross-Channel invasion of northern France, at their Tehran Conference the previous month.

Preparations for Overlord now obliged Bomber Command to focus on the bombing of military and transportation targets, but one more major strategic raid was launched soon after the Battle of Berlin. On the night of 30 March 1944, Harris ordered a massive attack on Nuremberg, 110 miles north of Munich. A centre of German industry, the city was also the iconic site of Hitler's notorious pre-war rallies and the eponymous birthplace of his anti-Semitic laws. It would turn out to be Bomber Command's worst night of the war. Of the 795 aircraft sent to Nuremberg, ninety-five failed to return, including sixty-four Lancasters. Five more Lancasters were so damaged they had to be written off, and many more needed extensive repairs. Lancaster losses for the raid stood at 12.1 per cent – a huge proportion. Five hundred and forty-five RAF airmen were killed on that single operation – more than the number who died in the whole of the four-month-long Battle of Britain.[6]

But there was no time to reflect. In Bomber Command, as the cycle of life and death, fear and relief continued, thinking too much could be bad news.

* * *

Aircrews faced two kinds of fear. Firstly, the fear of the raid, which most found just about manageable, as navigator Reg Davey remembered: 'Our fear was generally under control, but we were also absolutely terrified, knowing that a lot of us wouldn't come back each night. You didn't talk about the fear, you kept it to yourself and put yourself in the hands of God. Everybody had his own assessment of the fear. Some could stand it, some couldn't. I became a bit of a zombie: do the job, get the aircraft back. Carry on.'[7]

The other fear was of 'cracking up'; having a mental breakdown and being unable to continue on operations. However hard they tried, this possibility was out of their control. For some, as raids proliferated, the increased stress was too much to bear.

Such a breakdown, accompanied by a refusal to carry out operations, was designated 'LMF': 'Lack of Moral Fibre'. Far from being treated with sympathy, many men who could no longer bear the nervous strain were harshly disciplined. Some commanders, who depended on the willingness of their airmen to sacrifice themselves, employed the LMF label as a device to encourage others not to give in. To be stigmatised with it was akin to bearing the mark of Cain. The top brass were well aware of the superhuman strain brought on by their demands, so they hammered out the message of stoicism, of British grit, of the ethos of the stiff upper lip. This in turn exerted pressure not to express any feelings of doubt or fear, but it was nevertheless impossible – as it is in any war – for some fighting men not to suffer some kind of psychological collapse.

No one knew better than their commanders that this was a personal struggle that could be allowed to have only one outcome. Fear had to be conquered. Arthur Harris knew that the best and bravest would never be more than a quarter of his manpower. But the air war could not be won by them alone. The less bold had a job to do too. He once wrote in a note to his boss, Sir Charles Portal, Chief of the Air Staff:

> It is inevitable in war that the best are the keenest to go back to operations and they are the ones who, when they get there, hit the target. There are perhaps 20 to 25 in each 100 who can

*be classed as the best. The remaining 75 to 80 divert the enemy*
*effort from the destruction of the best and receive a certain*
*number of casualties, so saving the best from being picked off*
*by the enemy. At the same time, the weight of bombs they drop,*
*some of which hit the target some of the time, all help to add*
*to the damage but to a smaller degree than the bombs of the*
*best, which will normally land on the target. This is true in any*
*service in any war and in any operation.*[8]

Some eighty years later, this might seem a cold, inhuman way to
view one's subordinates, but it was total war and the task at hand
was to make sure the airmen conquered their fear and did not
desert their posts. The way to do that, or so the reasoning went in
the higher echelons of the RAF, was to make them fear something
else even more. And that 'something else' was the fear of being
exposed as a coward; of being branded 'LMF'.

It worked. Mostly. One bomb aimer felt the burden of those
dreadful initials throughout his time in the RAF.

'It wasn't so much the admission of fear and loss of self-respect
that deterred men from going LMF, it was the awareness that they
would be regarded as inadequate to the pressures of war in a country totally committed to the winning of war. In this atmosphere,
the man who opted out was a pariah, an insult to the national
need. He was conscious of bringing shame to his family, and that
most of his friends wouldn't wish to recognise him, or at best they
would be embarrassed and awkward on meeting.'[9]

The treatment of some of those who refused to carry on was
arbitrary and brutal. Public disgrace and humiliation. The 'guilty'
crewman would be paraded in front of his peers to have his badges
of rank and aircrew insignia torn from his uniform. One airman,
made to watch the 'sad, sad sight' of a comrade being humiliated
for having had enough, recorded in his diary:

*The entire strength of the station was on parade. By order. No*
*exceptions. This sergeant had refused to fly an op. He had been*

*accused and found guilty of LMF. There he was standing out
in front, all on his own, in full view of every person in the unit,
to be stripped of his wings and then his sergeant's tapes. They
had all been unstitched beforehand so they came away easily
when they were ripped from his uniform. He was immediately
posted elsewhere.*[10]

Some viewed the LMF label as relatively humane, pointing out
that in the First World War soldiers who fell victim to shellshock
and could no longer fight on were likely to be shot. Others thought
the treatment of those who could not carry on to be vile and
unnecessary. One pilot, a Flight Commander on 617 Squadron,
could see both views:

'There were obviously occasions when most of us would rather
have gone back to bed. Two o'clock in the morning on a bleak
airfield, a twelve-hour flight into unknown conditions with a
German fighter squadron waiting for you isn't nice. It's not a
Sunday afternoon trip along the Thames. But I think if people had
been allowed to say, "I'm sorry, I can't go," it would have spread.
If one chap was allowed to pull out of ops, then why not another?
We were at war, it was a tough business, and unless someone was
really medically unfit we all simply had to soldier on.'[11]

Ken Johnson, a mid-upper gunner with 61 Squadron at RAF
Skellingthorpe, had direct experience of LMF. By his sixth
Lancaster operation, he had been through a great deal.

'I'd be flying along keeping a good lookout when suddenly
there'd be a massive explosion lighting up the skies; and you
knew it was a Lancaster with seven fellow airmen aboard, gone
in a flash, a mass of tumbling flames, then nothing. Perhaps later,
during the debriefing, as you described what you'd seen, it would
suddenly hit home; but you couldn't let it affect you.'[12]

Ken's ability to step back and observe proceedings, often with
humour, was a great aid to self-preservation.

'My cousin Ivy had given me a green silk scarf when I first
started flying. It was meant to prevent chafing round your neck

as you turned around searching the skies for enemy fighters, but we all thought we looked a bit dashing in our scarves, and they became a necessary item of flying kit. It became my lucky charm and I insisted on wearing it every time I went flying. Once you had started with a lucky charm, you couldn't stop. Even though it was all nonsense, no one would be willing to take the risk of challenging it! Death was always close by, but it seemed unreal. I suppose I was young and naive. If I felt anything, it was that at last I was getting back at the Germans.'

Amid getting back at the Germans, flying operations on an almost daily basis, the relentless pressure of battle was relieved by the few hours they were allowed to rest and an occasional day off to enjoy some light relief.

'After our first six ops, we were given a 48-hour leave pass. Harry Watkins, our skipper, went home to Manchester. The rest of the crew were too far away from their own families, so they all came home with me to our little village outside Doncaster. Mum and Dad were overjoyed to meet my mates, and after a good chinwag and a meal, we went down to my local. Dad was never a drinking man, but he came along too; proud to be part of the group. I didn't count our intake, but Dad told me later that we had downed nine pints and nine whisky chasers each! It was a huge celebration, a relief to be away from the war. We were living for the moment. When you were on ops, you just never knew when any moment could be your last.'

Ken trusted his crew and they all worked well together as a team – a life-saver in itself – but he was particularly close to their rear gunner, Carson John Foy, a Canadian known to everyone as Jack.

'Jack was a bit of a ladies' man, and that evening he soon discovered the Snug where the women drank. He kept buying them drinks and they returned the favour. Then he came back and downed the drinks we'd lined up for him. You can imagine the state he was in!'

The crew put Jack to bed and carried on the celebrations, but the next morning he was nowhere to be found. They had to catch a train back to Skellingthorpe and, just as panic was setting in, Jack turned up, grinning from ear to ear, dressed in a smart civilian suit, a brown-paper parcel tucked under his arm.

'Jack had wandered off through the blackout in search of us and got lost. In the darkness he'd fallen into a nearby canal lock, quickly sobered up and clambered up the steel rungs to safety. Cold and lost, his calls for help were heard by a young lad who took Jack home and put him to bed. In the morning, he gave him a hearty breakfast, lent him a suit, wrapped up his soaked uniform in a parcel, then set him off in the right direction. After that, we spent a lot of time together and became good friends; Jack used to come home with me regularly. We spent many happy hours social-ising and he became a bit of a fixture at our house. My mother treated him like her own son.'

*Ken Johnson*

The war ground on and Ken's eleventh operation was a daylight raid on the airfield at St-Cyr on the southern outskirts of Paris. It would be marked by tragedy.

After taking off in Lancaster *O-Orange* from Skellingthorpe's main runway at 5.30 p.m., they joined up with ninety-seven other Lancasters to form a loose formation heading across the Channel. Over the target the raid developed into a concentrated attack, with aircraft jockeying for position on their bombing runs. Watching the busy skies, Ken noticed another Lancaster above theirs opening its bomb doors to reveal two rows of rusty munitions.

'I warned Harry Watkins, our skipper, but he said we were hemmed in and that the Lanc above would surely have seen us – which I took for wishful thinking. I had to keep quiet because we were on our own bombing run and the pilot needed to hear Ed Day, our bomb aimer's instructions.

'Just as he called out "Bombs gone", the Lanc above us released hers. They fell towards us, mercifully quickly flipping to a vertical position. It was like watching a horror film unfold in slow motion. I could see every detail of the bombs as they fell towards our Lancaster. I shouted another warning to the skipper, but there was nothing to be done. I was a matter of a second or two from death and I could only watch what was happening.'

They seemed to fall harmlessly around the aircraft, but then one struck the rear of the Lancaster, breaking off the starboard tail-fin rudder. They plunged earthwards, Harry Watkins fighting to regain control.

'Our aircraft bucked around and the intercom had gone dead but then we seemed to be steadying, so I sat tight. Never in my twenty years of life had I felt more lonely. As I rotated my turret, I saw that a second bomb had fallen through the starboard wing, breaking away four feet. The broken end dangled for a moment like the wing of an injured bird, then fell away. I suddenly realised I hadn't seen Jack's rear turret moving. I was able to bend down in my swing-seat and look aft between my legs. To my dismay, all

I could see at the end of the aircraft was a gaping hole. We had lost Jack – lost him for ever in the most horrible way. My stomach turned over. It was almost impossible to understand. My mate and drinking partner, the man my own mum had hugged, and regarded as her own son, had simply disappeared and ceased to exist.'

With the intercom still out of operation, the flight engineer was sent into the astrodome to check the damage.

'As he looked back towards my turret I managed to signal to him and a moment later he tugged at my trouser leg. I bent down so he could yell in my ear. He told me to put on my parachute in case we had to bale out. There wasn't time to say anything else. He had to get back to his instruments. At last the intercom spluttered into life, a real blessing as at last I was in touch with the others and could speak to our skipper:

'"Harry, we've lost Jack."

'You could feel the distress in the aircraft, but there was nothing to be said.'

Harry Watkins coaxed the crippled Lancaster back to safety and once on the ground he was ordered to taxi to an isolated area and stop with the Lancaster's tail pointing away from the domestic buildings.

'As we left the aircraft, the silence was unbelievable. Normally the three-foot jump to the ground wouldn't have bothered me, but this time my legs were so shaky that I felt, if I jumped, I'd land on my face. I waited for the ground staff to come and lend a hand. Having seen the damage and the missing gun turret, they too were silent. It'd been a warm day and Harry had flown in his shirtsleeves, but he was soaked in sweat from the effort of getting us home.'

Ken and the surviving crew didn't speak much until the Station Commander arrived to check what had happened. Concerned at their grief and to cheer them up, he offered the crew a slap-up meal in the Officers' Mess. But as the crew bus arrived to take them to debriefing, the meal was forgotten.

'At the debrief it seemed unreal to be talking about the death of a friend. The sorrow was palpable but we had to move on. A friend was dead, but there was a war to be fought and we had to fight it. That was that.'

Their skipper, Harry Watkins, would eventually be awarded a DFC for his incredible actions that day. But Ken couldn't move on just yet. The cold, unfeeling administration of Bomber Command needed to be completed.

'The next morning we were driven back to our aircraft for damage-assessment photographs. I was the smallest crew member so had to creep along the fuselage to the damaged tail and point to Jack's parachute, which was still in its stowed position. I then had to sit in the torn opening to provide perspective for the photos. I was back at the very spot where my friend had perished only a few hours earlier. I wasn't very happy, but there was nothing I could do about it.'

Telling his mother was no easy task either.

'The next time I went home, the first thing she asked me was, "Where's Jack?" The question I'd been dreading but couldn't avoid answering. I simply shook my head and said, "We've lost him." She burst into tears. No one said anything, but we knew it could so easily have been me. It was a harsh reminder of the reality of the war we were fighting. No one was immune from death.'

There was no time to mourn their friend. The following night, Ken and the surviving crew found themselves on the battle order yet again, targeting the railway marshalling yard at Givors, south of Lyons. That there was no respite for the traumatised crew is an indication of how the strain of battle could contribute to mental collapse. An ability to shut down normal emotional responses was vital. And no respite carried real risks.

Ken and his crew were joined by a new rear gunner, also in his early twenties. He was an unknown quantity. Crossing the French coast, they flew into a thunder cloud. Torrential rain hammered the aircraft, oozing through every weak joint. At the same time, 'St Elmo's fire', the glowing weather phenomenon that can occur during electrical storms, danced on the Lancaster.

'The four props had a foot of orange flame, the radio aerials were festooned in blue fairy lights, orange flames leapt from each gun, and to cap it all the aircraft was thrashing around in the turbulence.'

It was too much for the new rear gunner.

'He began to scream and shout; nothing anyone could say would calm him down. He simply lost control and had some sort of breakdown. It was a terrible noise and it was affecting the whole crew – it was also putting us in danger as we couldn't communicate with one another. This got so bad that the skipper ordered his intercom to be disconnected. We managed the raid safely but the return flight led us back through the same storms, and they didn't let up until we'd crossed the Channel. Nearing home, our radio operator reported ahead on the state of the lad in the rear turret.'

The crew were ordered not to leave their positions on landing until two military policemen had escorted the trembling rear gunner to a waiting white van. Only then could the rest of them disembark.

'Two days later we were sent on leave. This was very fortunate because on our return we were told that the poor lad was paraded before the whole station; his stripes and gunner's wing were torn from his uniform, he was reduced to the ranks, and LMF was stamped on his papers. It was a cruel thing to do to someone who had had some sort of breakdown. It did nothing for our crew morale to know that someone, badly affected by their experiences, was treated this way by High Command. We were disgusted.'

They were to learn later that the rear gunner had been badly shot up on a previous operation and had only just been discharged from hospital to join their crew that night. However, there was little chance of any sympathy or understanding for those affected by the brutalities of the ongoing war. It had to be fought, sometimes viciously, until the Nazis were defeated and the Allies had won.

*Dennis Wiltshire*

Ken saw the effect of mental trauma at close range; Dennis Wiltshire, who'd joined the RAF in 1939 at the age of eighteen, experienced it directly.

Involved in a near-disastrous crash in the wilds of Canada while an aircraft engineer servicing the Commonwealth Air Training Scheme in the depths of winter 1943, Dennis didn't connect his later experiences with the incident, but it is hard to see how it could not have affected him:

'I was an engine-fitter on a flight test of a recently repaired trainer. My pilot was an instructor and it was a job I'd already done several times before. After completing the air test, the pilot, in his exhilaration, decided to "shoot up" a few fir trees before turning for home. It was then that we saw that the radio aerial had come adrift and was lashing about dangerously near the tail-plane. We were out of contact with base, and, to make matters worse, our compass needle was now flailing about in all directions; we were totally disoriented. We had plenty of fuel and it was still daylight, but the weather was closing in. I moved from the co-pilot's position to the wireless operator's seat to better assess the damage. The pilot signalled me to ensure that I was strapped in, indicating he was going to take the aircraft down. He seemed full of self-confidence, lowered the undercarriage and started to edge the control column forward. But we were descending into the unknown. A recipe for death.

'My heart was in my mouth, my stomach was near my boots; I was scared stiff! I sat rigid in my seat feeling terribly sick. I could see nothing but a blanket of white ahead. I thought we were going to die. I'm not a particularly religious person, but I began to pray.'[13]

Dennis's worst fears were confirmed moments later when they crashed into trees and the aircraft was torn apart. 'There was utter confusion: wood, canvas, pieces of tree, snow, Perspex and a terrible biting, cold wind. Then the smell of oil, hydraulic fluid, blood, and the most dreaded of all: petrol.' The pilot was slumped over the controls, apparently lifeless. Dennis was hanging from his harness, looking at the co-pilot's seat, where he had recently been sitting. It had been torn from its mount and pierced by a large, broken branch.

Dennis realised he was screaming for help.

'I simply wasn't trained for any of this. I kicked and screamed and pressed and twisted the harness quick-release. I fell forward and was wedged between the co-pilot's seat and the control column. Blood was dripping onto my face and I thought, *Oh, God, now what have I done!* It was the pilot's blood.'

Once his panic died down he managed to release the pilot, who had suffered a severe head laceration. As he regained consciousness, Dennis dressed his wounds, struggling to prevent him from sleeping. They were now stranded in the freezing snow and could only hope that a search party was looking for them. 'I thought there was little hope and that there was a real possibility that we might die out there. We could do nothing but wait.'

It would be a harrowing forty-eight hours, but eventually a search party found them and led them to safety.

Dennis finally joined Bomber Command as a Lancaster flight engineer in early 1944, at the age of twenty-three.

'Before the first op I was very apprehensive about even taking off. We hadn't seen or done anything like this before, and I think everyone was nervous. The worst time was waiting. You know you've got to get up there and face whatever it is. Is it fear, or the fear of *facing* fear? At first I was so involved with my job that I didn't really think about much else. Even though I was stationed up front and could see what we were flying into, it didn't bother me unduly at the time. When the first flak exploded it seemed so far away that you couldn't imagine anything actually happening. Then, when it explodes close and rocks the aircraft – then you get scared. It's then that you realise the dangers, and they begin to play on your mind. I think it must have affected me, and how I went about my day-to-day life.

'There were always guys not getting back home, always plenty of empty beds, and new faces to fill in the gaps. It brings you up to a bit of a halt when you think about it. I think it was all this previous build-up which resulted in the problems, but I wasn't aware before that of fears and apprehension gradually growing. It must have been building up underneath without my knowing.'

What was simmering just beneath the surface of Dennis's psyche would affect the rest of his life. On his third operation, they took off for Cologne as part of a 300-aircraft raid.

'I went through all the pre-flight checks with Leslie, our skipper,[14] and soon afterwards we were given the all-clear to start. Each engine burst into life, the combustion gases belched from the exhaust stubs, the earth seemed to tremble into life with us. Pitch-black outside, the navigator had his map table illumination on, and there was a subdued light from the instrument panels.'

After take-off, Dennis went through his usual routines with Leslie. They were ready for action. Then, 'my stomach went into knots. I felt terribly sick, I longed to be going home. I tried to say the Lord's Prayer but it wouldn't assemble itself in my brain.'

As they approached the target and the orange glow ahead was

turning red with the light of the Pathfinders' target indicators, their rear gunner became nervous, firing off several rounds.

'Bloody hell!'

'Sorry, Skip – I thought I saw a fighter.'

'Don't think – look! You'll have one of ours down in a minute.'

Then came the flak and the searchlight beams. Flashes of light illuminated their aircraft. Anxiety began to overwhelm Dennis.

'I'd been scared before, but this was different. I felt absolutely defenceless and naked. You can't do anything about what's happening. Flak was exploding very close to the aircraft. Too close; the fragments peppered the fuselage, rattling like stones against a metal shed.'

Everyone concentrated on their job. Dennis imagined they were as scared as he was, but at least they had something to do.

'The situation didn't really help because, as the flight engineer, I had no specific duty when on a bomb run. I was just waiting until we headed for home. I tried to concentrate on the Pathfinders' markers. I tried to concentrate on the actual target. Just something to think about, to keep me going.'

There was no respite as the bomb aimer's instructions came slowly over the intercom.

'"Steady, steady . . . Right a bit . . .! Steady . . ."'

'His instructions were so calm and collected I wanted to scream! I was feeling pretty awful. I always felt sick over the target, but this time I was in a cold sweat and feeling very light-headed.'

The pilot yelled at the bomb aimer, 'For Christ's sake, Jim, hurry up! What in God's name are you doing?'

Finally, Dennis heard the longed-for words: *Bombs gone!*

Their Lancaster made a steep turn for home, and Dennis looked down on the carnage. 'Fire everywhere – Dante's *Inferno*. You don't realise what's going on on the ground, what's happening to the cities. You don't think about it normally. But now I *was* concerned about what we had done to the human beings below.'

Suddenly, there was a huge explosion and a chunk of shrapnel crashed through the Perspex nose. It buried itself in the cockpit floor, bringing the sickly smell of burning phosphorus.

'As soon as the shell exploded I was back in the present. I was OK. Something had to be done and I was the only one to do it. It brought me out of my fear. Jim, our bomb aimer, was screaming, "Fire! For God's sake, my suit's on fire!"'

Dennis grabbed an extinguisher and headed from his position next to the pilot, down into the bomb aimer's station. 'I aimed the extinguisher at the flames, stamping on them at the same time. But I was beginning to panic again. Jim kicked and scrambled away from the flames, then, quite suddenly, crumpled up, lying perfectly still.

'I saw the blood streaming from his nose, his mouth, his ears. I pulled his helmet off. He was gone. It turned my stomach and I really went to pieces. I just had to leave him.'

Dennis returned to his own position in the cockpit as their Lancaster continued to take hits. 'Suddenly there is a horrendous, blinding flash. The whole aircraft shook like a fish in its final thrash of life.' Freezing wind blasted in from the smashed nose as the pilot struggled to wrestle back control of the aircraft, staying calm as the bomber was hit once more, then twice. Leslie caught Dennis's eye and winked encouragement. They would still get out of this. It was a comforting moment.

'"Check the fuel levels, Den. I don't know what the situation is. The poor old kite's like a bloody sieve."'

Dennis looked at the fuel gauges, hoping to God they'd got enough to get home.

But then his world dissolved.

'I am not truly aware of what happened. I recall the inferno below us. I remember a Lanc minus its tail, all four engines on fire, hurtling to earth.'

After that, nothing.

He later learned that he'd released his harness and walked silently aft, oblivious to screams and shouts to come back and sit down. He fell over the main spar and lay still on the fuselage floor. The navigator had come to help him, but there was no blood or obvious wound, so he'd returned to his desk to plot the course home. Despite its extensive damage, the pilot brought the aircraft back safely. Dennis was taken by ambulance to the sick bay while the rest of the crew went to debriefing. They came to visit him later, but he was unaware of their presence.

Dennis stayed in the sick bay for four days, unaware of anything, lying in bed, neither eating nor drinking. No one could get through to him. Eventually he was transferred to the RAF Hospital at Matlock in Derbyshire, known to its patients as 'Mad Hatter's Castle', for psychiatric treatment. His blackout continued for weeks. He was completely unresponsive, except once when a nurse accidentally knocked over a steel dish of medical instruments. 'It seems I sprang to my feet, then fell flat on the floor because of my weakened physical state, screaming, "There's another poor sod going down! Let's get the hell out of here!"'

He had suffered a complete mental breakdown, and over the coming weeks, as he returned to full consciousness, he listened to the anguished yelling and howling that came continually from another – distant – part of the hospital where the worst cases were held. Dennis himself was interviewed gently, given endless tests – instruments up the nose, in the ears, rubber mallets striking knees and elbows – and, unforgettably, since the initials remained stamped on his brain: ECT – electroconvulsive treatment, where seizures are electrically induced in patients to provide relief from mental disorders.

Beyond psychotherapy and tests, life at Matlock was dismal.

'Everyone there was in a similar condition to mine, or worse. Above all there was no RAF *camaraderie*. You don't want to talk about where you are; you don't want to talk about why you're there. We were all in a world of our own.'

But Dennis did think his treatment was fair, and that the staff really tried to help. The term LMF was never used by staff at Matlock and Dennis himself was discharged honourably, diagnosed with psychoneurosis – 'though a local psychiatrist told me when I got home that, "I've never heard such bloody rubbish in my life – if you're a bloody neurotic, my cock's a kipper."' Even psychiatrists are not always endowed with tact.

With no sense of dishonour, no 'LMF' stamped on his papers, the war was over for Dennis by late 1944. But his experience would cast a very long shadow over his life.

*Ground crew preparing a Lancaster for operations*

The majority of aircrew were lucky enough to escape the perils of LMF, but, like death, avoidance was a matter of chance. On some raids, nerves could be put to the severest of tests.

On the afternoon of Wednesday 3 May 1944, Maurice Garlick, now thirty-one years old and a seasoned navigator, was enjoying a leisurely game of snooker with his skipper, Peter 'Maxie' Maxwell, when the Tannoy sprang to life. 'All operational aircrews to report for briefing at once!'

The two men looked at each other in mild surprise.

'Hello, that's early,' said Maxie. 'Something's up!'

They joined the rest of the crew in the briefing room.

'This one's a real piece of cake,' the Intelligence Officer began.

'An audible groan went up,' remembers Maurice. 'We'd heard it all before. It usually meant something tricky, dangerous, or a target hard to find. With his usual panache, the Briefing Officer flung back the curtains covering a huge map of the whole of German-occupied Europe which covered the entire wall. When we saw the line marking tonight's route, a huge sigh of relief went up. It seemed to be only a three-hour trip. Somewhere east of Paris, in the area of Champagne.

'"Cor, champagne," shouted our Tail-end Charlie, Bert. "What a place to tumble into!"'[15]

Bombing of military targets in France in preparation for the upcoming invasion was already well under way in April 1944, when a unit of the French Resistance noticed unusual German activity at a tank base just north of the small town of Mailly-le-Camp, about 80 miles east of Paris. The Germans had taken over the base as a training centre for tank crews destined to replace those lost on the Eastern Front. But columns of tanks and lorries were now arriving with their battle-hardened crews, clearly destined to bolster German defences in France. Their presence would not only make the work of the upcoming Allied invasion considerably harder; it could even turn advance into retreat.

Immediate action was demanded from Bomber Command.

So important was the target considered, that Leonard Cheshire, the highly experienced 27-year-old commander of 617 Squadron, was ordered to oversee the raid, leading a group of Mosquitos to fly in first, dropping the initial target indicators in an effort to limit collateral damage to nearby French villages. Cheshire had already acted as 'Master of Ceremonies' on similar operations, and this one wasn't considered particularly challenging. Their objective was to hit the target immediately after midnight, the hour of curfew for the tank crews. The main force would be led by Wing Commander Laurence Deane, aiming at the eastern end of the German base. There were no serious land defences, so flak was expected to be light, but to ensure complete destruction of the new tank force, an unusually substantial force was deployed: 346 Lancasters and fourteen Mosquitos. Cheshire's designation was Marker Leader;

Deane's was Main Force Controller, with Squadron Leader Neville Sparks as his deputy.

They took off at 9.45 p.m. on the night of 3 May 1944, crossing into France and heading for their assembly point. It was meant to be a straightforward operation.

\* \* \*

'Two of my crew are dead already,' someone shouted over the radio. 'For Christ's sake, do something, or we're all going to die.'

The plea was answered out of the blazing night by a harsh Australian voice: 'Die like a man, then, you yellow bastard. And do it quietly.'

That shut people up for a moment, but soon more desperate questions were being broadcast:

'What the hell's happening?'

'Where are the target markers?'

A Canadian pilot interrupted, 'I'm halfway to going LMF.'

'Shut up!' someone else rebuked him. 'What are the Jerries going to think of the RAF, hearing all this?'

'Fuck you *and* the RAF – I'm RCAF!'[16]

Another crewman cut in: 'I don't mind dicing with death, but this is bloody suicide!'

'Come on, Master Bomber [*sic*] – pull your finger out!'

'What the hell is going on?'[17]

Confusion and panic reigned around Mailly-le-Camp.

Though it wasn't known at the time, sections of the strike force were operating on different radio frequencies and were not in communication with either the leaders, or each other. If that wasn't bad enough, *all* radio communications were continually blocked by a powerful transmitter of an American 'Armed Services Radio' mobile station broadcasting US news punctuated with big-band hits by the likes of Bing Crosby and Glenn Miller. The disastrous sequence of mix-ups meant that most of the aircraft were unnecessarily backed-up at the raid's assembly point, 15 miles north of the target, awaiting the instructions to attack that Cheshire, having dropped his markers, was unsuccessfully trying to broadcast. The Lancasters circled in growing frustration. Orders given on one frequency were not getting through to the other.

Frustration soon turned to panic when German fighters were scrambled from nearby bases. It was like shooting fish in a barrel for the *Nachtjagdgeschwader*[18], which were soon sending Me110s and FW190s to tear into the hapless Allied bombers. In desperation, Leonard Cheshire, watching the slaughter over the assembly point but unable to communicate with the beleaguered crews or hear their cries for help, now tried to contact Deane again. He ordered him to break off the attack and return home, but to his horror found he still could not reach him. All the while, more Lancasters were being shot down.

Cheshire later recalled that 'the combination of the attack going wrong with the sight of aircraft being shot down convinced me that it was my duty to order everyone back to base as soon as possible, for in my judgement the further damage the aircraft were likely to do to the target would not justify the large losses we were likely to suffer. In the whole of my operational career I had never seen so many aircraft going down in so short a space of time. To this day I can remember my near despair at finding no way of getting through either to Deane or directly to the aircraft themselves.'[19]

Deane had seen Cheshire's accurately dropped markers over the target and had himself instructed his wireless operator to give the order to attack. But Deane *couldn't hear* Cheshire, and the main force *couldn't hear* Deane. Deane's deputy, Neville Sparks, couldn't hear him either, and, assuming the 'Boss' to be out of action, gave attack orders himself. But Glenn Miller still ruled the airwaves, intermittently blocking the RAF radio transmissions.[20]

Cheshire was furious.

'That a planning staff could contemplate, or a commander countenance, any plan of action in which a possibility existed – even a remote one – of several hundred fully laden Lancasters orbiting a marker in bright moonlight, within striking distance of at least four night-fighter bases, staggers the imagination. Luftwaffe Headquarters, given the chance, could not have planned it better. If the seeds of havoc had already been sown in the groundwork of the plan, here were the rain and sunshine to ensure their germination.'[21]

In the midst of this chaos and confusion, Maurice Garlick sat at his navigator's desk.

'Our Lancaster was a sitting duck. By now the fourth and fifth waves of German fighters had arrived. There were explosions to port and starboard, and acrid smells of cordite wafting through the fuselage. I saw explosions, collisions, aircraft going down like ninepins.'

But pilot Peter Maxwell and Maurice were both sure that wireless operator Harold 'Taffy' Lloyd 'was being extra vigilant, hoping against hope for a message cancelling the trip. That message from Cheshire never got through.'[22]

Despite the monumental confusion, some of the Lancasters had heard garbled orders to attack and headed for the tank base. Other Lancasters followed them, bolting like greyhounds from the traps. Maurice Garlick's aircraft was one of them, relieved to get away from the pounding by the German night-fighters. They were soon lining up in tight formation for the bomb run.

Lancasters ahead of them were already dropping their loads and bouncing in their slipstream, but Maxwell concentrated on his bomb aimer's instructions. Lying prone in the nose, closing his mind to the closeness of other aircraft and the long streams of tracer shooting up around him, Taffy fixed his target in the crosswires of his bombsight.

'"Steady – steady – left – steady – that's it!" A second later – "Bombs gone!"'

'We all felt the great aircraft lift as they fell away. A huge sigh of relief went up all round.

'"Let's get the hell out of here!"'

Maurice had already plotted their course for home. They set off, away from the inferno in the sky and on the ground, Maxwell tipping his wings at frequent intervals to give his gunners a view of what might be lurking below them. Seconds later, their Lancaster gave a sudden shudder, and flames exploded from both port engines.

Despite their precautions, an unseen night-fighter had crept up on them. Maxwell immediately pulled back the port throttles and turned the rudder to starboard to counteract the drag, at the same time ordering the flight engineer to cut the fuel supply to the port engines. He feathered the port engines as the flight engineer activated their fire extinguishers. To no avail. The flames swept on.

'No good, Skipper – the electrics have gone. Can't control it. I reckon it's a case of jump or roast.'

'Crew from Captain,' Peter announced over the intercom, keeping his voice steady. 'Jump! Jump! Jump! Good luck, lads.'

No one wanted to say goodbye to Q-Queenie. Their Lancaster had been their home through thick and thin. But now it was a simple question of living without her or dying with her. The flight engineer clipped Maxwell's parachute onto his chest, nodded in farewell, and made his way forward.

As the call came to bale out, Maurice was still working at his charts, plotting a route to safety.

'It was the order we had all been trained for but never expected to hear; it came as a mighty shock to our cosmopolitan, rather naive crew. I grabbed my parachute, drew the curtains of my navigator's office, looked back to check I hadn't left anything of significance for the enemy to discover, and made for the forward hatch. Everyone had baled out safely except for Maxie, our valiant captain, still at the controls and flying level and steady. He reminded me of Edward Poynter's painting *Faithful unto Death* – the Roman centurion staying at his post amid the destruction of Pompeii.'

Maurice knew that, having got everyone off safely, Peter would leave the aircraft himself. On his way through the cabin to the nose and the forward escape hatch, he shouted in Maxwell's ear, over the screaming noise of the dying aircraft, 'We're just south of the target I reckon. Get out and walk south-east.' Soon afterwards, Maxwell called each crew station in turn. There was no answer. His friends were all out safely. His job was done. It would be every man for himself from now on. Silently, he wished them luck and dived out of the aircraft.

As Maurice Garlick drifted down in the dark skies above the province of Champagne, he could see the whole horizon ablaze to the north. His senses lulled by the gentle descent, he luxuriated in the feeling of relief that he was alive, that his parachute had spread its protective wing over him. Below, there seemed to be no towns or villages. If he made a safe landing, he might well be in with a chance of successful evasion.

'Suddenly my reverie was broken by a terrific explosion overhead. Flames, sparks, white-hot metal tumbled down. Our great aircraft was engulfed in flames from end to end. All at once it seemed to turn, spin and dive to earth. As it hit the ground there was the loudest bang of all as shards flew up and sank down again to what had become a glowing red heap. I thought of the Zeppelin I'd seen as a child all those years ago. No Viking ship ever had a better funeral pyre than our Lanc, nor so worthy a send-off from the field of battle!'

By now the ground was approaching rapidly. Maurice bent his knees slightly, as he'd been taught. It looked like he was going to land in a wheat field.

'Then my luck ran out, and my life changed for ever. There was a blinding flash, a thunderous explosion, and I knew no more.'

\* \* \*

Of the 346 Lancasters that had set out to attack the Germans at Mailly-le-Camp, forty-two were shot down, and another was written off after returning.

Maurice's crew, all of whom parachuted successfully, were among the lucky ones. At 11.6 per cent, the loss rate was prohibitive. In all, 258 airmen lost their lives that night.

Nevertheless, the Mailly raid was claimed as a success. One hundred and fourteen barracks, forty-seven transport sheds, sixty-five vehicles and thirty-seven tanks were destroyed. Two hundred and eighteen German military were killed, and another 156 wounded.[23] The threat posed by the occupying German forces had been slightly reduced, but the overall strategy for Bomber Command dictated that there was still much work to be done before the Allies would be ready to set foot on French soil.

# CHAPTER TWELVE

# FACE TO FACE WITH THE ENEMY

'It was like coming to after an operation, as if rushing down a long, narrow tunnel with a bright light in the far distance. So I wasn't dead after all? There was an acrid smell of burnt flesh and excruciating pain in my legs and feet. What a welcome to Champagne!'[1]

As the surviving Lancasters of the disastrous raid on Mailly-le-Camp headed for the safety of home, Maurice Garlick fought his way back into some semblance of consciousness. He heard another explosion, then a dog howling dolefully in the distance. As the fog in his head began to clear, he found himself lying on his back, looking up at the sky. He pushed himself into a sitting position and gasped in pain as his legs scraped the ground. He was in a wide field with young crops but no cover; he'd need a hiding place before daybreak. He tried to get up but the pain overwhelmed him and he collapsed. Severed steel cables snaked across the ground, and when he looked up, he realised how lucky he was to be alive. He'd crashed through electric power lines, and his legs and feet had borne the brunt of a massive electric shock. The three pairs of socks inside his fleece-lined flying boots had saved him.

But someone would soon notice the damage.

Maurice knew he was lucky to have fallen into France, but it was still occupied territory, and he and his friends had all heard stories of downed airmen – the hated *Terrorflieger* – being shot out of hand by some in the German military. It was time to get away. He would head south-east in the hope of making it to Switzerland; the same advice he had given Maxie, his friend and pilot, as they abandoned their Lancaster. He took comfort in the memory, and in the fact that he now had a plan.

There was no burn cream in his escape kit, so he tried to bind his legs with strips torn from his parachute. He buried the rest of it as best he could. 'After half an hour I'd done a reasonable job. Little did I know that the local Resistance lads would soon dig it up and give it to their girlfriends to make silk undies.'

He crawled to the edge of the field, where he could see a glint of metal in the moonlight. It turned out to be a railway track. He dragged himself over, then through a hawthorn hedge, which tore at his scorched flesh. Across another vast field, he saw what he was looking for – the sanctuary of tree cover. He struggled to his feet, trying to banish his rising panic, reminding himself he was alive; he hadn't gone up in flames with his aircraft. But it was hard to suppress the fear – alone in the dark, badly injured, the silence of the indifferent countryside made more menacing by that damn dog's dismal voice. He missed the racket and roar of flying, the camaraderie, the reassurance of his crewmates. All that had gone.

'Crawling and staggering in turns, I reached the middle of the field. I could go no further. I slumped down and lay on my back, staring at the moon. Suddenly there was a mighty roar and a great Lancaster flew low overhead. Was he lost? Was he part of another raid? I hoped they reached home safely. How I envied them; hot coffee, rum and clean sheets. I thought about my own crew. I hoped they had all got out and landed safely. Such was the way of things in the forces flying into the "Valley of the Shadow of Death"; all together one day, then never to meet again, but never, ever forgotten.'

Dawn broke and he slept through most of the long day that followed. The only signs of life were a labourer alone in a faraway field, and a horse and cart trundling along a country lane to a distant farmhouse. Two stones dug insistently into his back. Flints. He stuffed them in his pocket and, as the sun set, forced himself onward to the trees.

'With a huge sigh of relief I parted two hazel bushes and stumbled under cover. The undergrowth was thick, the untamed bushes at the feet of the trees made excellent homes for pheasants and partridges, and excellent hiding places for me. I managed to break off a large branch and made a splendid staff. A short time later, I came across a dry ditch and collapsed, wound up my navigator's watch, which by some miracle had survived with me, pulled handfuls of fallen leaves over me, and passed out. Thus ended Day One of the saga. The most traumatic day of my life.

'The sun was high in the sky when I woke. I took better stock of my situation, but I was reluctant to leave my ditch. It felt safe.'

The long sleep had rallied him and he ate one Horlicks tablet from his escape kit. But how to slake his thirst?

'Delayed shock was beginning to take effect. I knew I needed seventy calories an hour just to survive, let alone do anything strenuous. One could survive for a little while using up the food stored on one's body – but what then?'

Maurice, however, was better equipped than most to endure his ordeal.

'My brother and I had helped in our father's immaculate garden and on his allotment. There we learned which weeds could be eaten and which were poisonous. Chickweed was full of vitamins and minerals. All members of the buttercup family were dangerous.'

The Horlicks tablet had dried his mouth and he found himself yearning for one of his mother's cups of tea. He'd better find an alternative fast. He forced himself out of the ditch and further into the woods. Once he felt safe, he fished out the flint stones and cautiously struck them together until he'd created two sharp edges. He cut at the bole of a young willow and prised the bark off, revealing the rising sap.

'It wasn't champagne, but it moistened my mouth for the time being.'

The next job was to put more distance between himself and his crashed Lancaster. Maurice discovered he was able to walk a little better now, with the aid of the staff he'd trimmed smooth with one of the flints; and by cutting a notch in the wood every evening when he wound his watch, he'd be able to keep track of time. A routine would also help keep his mind steady. 'I took a hefty chip out of it to mark the first day – not that I'd ever be likely to forget it.' The sheer need to press on helped him fight the pain, and as the day progressed, he came to a road around a much larger, denser forest.

'Then I heard the sound of martial singing. Suddenly, round the corner came a long grey troop carrier with half-a-dozen soldiers sitting facing each other in the back, belting out the chorus of some drinking song. They didn't seem to be putting their hearts into it, and I was reminded of some of our lads having a go at "On Ilkley Moor Baht 'at" to keep their spirits up on dreary training exercises. But were they looking for me? They didn't have any snarling Alsatians with them, so I doubted it. They were probably on their way to a garrison. It was a big shock and I only just had time to spring back into cover as they passed. Once they'd gone, I scudded across that road like a wounded and rattled rabbit.'

That night, he sheltered from the rain under a huge pine tree, which kept him dry but painfully studded his back with fallen needles. The shower allowed him to gather some water, cupping his hands in the puddles which gathered in the ruts and hollows. 'I resolved to tell the penguins at their desks at home to include some sort of collapsible drinking vessel in future escape kits.'

Maurice carried on in the direction of the Swiss border, lonely and afraid, for many more long days and nights.[2]

'I still hadn't got used to all the strange noises which go on in a forest at night: the rustling of the leaves, the shriek of a rabbit caught by a stoat, the outlandish cry of a vixen. One night I awoke to the sound of an unfamiliar grunting and snorting, and much rustling of dry leaves. I felt hot breath on my cheek and opened my eyes to see another pair of eyes – large, fierce and yellow – staring back at me over a pair of great, curled, threatening tusks a foot above me. I lay frozen to the ground. But after a few seconds, the huge, grizzled head turned, and with a final snort of derision trundled off, followed by a smaller mate and seven or eight piglets.'

Maurice knew he had to put as much distance from the boar's territory as he could. He'd got this far; he wasn't taking any chances. He packed his pockets with chickweed and sucked on stems of young grass to quench his constant thirst.

About a week into his trek, he heard a rumble in the sky and looked up through the canopy to witness the war in the air carrying on without him.

'Hundreds of Flying Fortresses were high up in the sunny sky. Their attendant fighters were wheeling around as droves of FW109s and Me110s bore down on them as the force flew relentlessly on. Now and again a white moth would appear high in the sky – someone's parachute had opened. I wished them well, and it gladdened my heart to see the USAAF – we weren't alone!'

But Maurice was alone and had no choice but to press on – though the forest did offer its own rewards. 'I bent down and picked up a shiny, serrated leaf, which I knew belonged to the sweet chestnut. Pictures of cold winter days in London and red-hot braziers with street vendors crying, "Chestnuts! Hot chestnuts! A penny a bag!" came flooding back to me. Sheer ambrosia, and the only protein for days!'

The pain of his wounds had deadened, but the weakness of his left foot and leg made him veer left, so he had to constantly correct his course. Little could quell his increasing loneliness. A fortnight would pass before he made any direct human contact, so when he smelt smoke from a bonfire, he headed towards it, throwing caution to the wind. 'I came to a large open space with a little path leading to a pretty little woodsman's cottage. An elderly forester was tending the fire. He leapt to his feet uttering some French expletive when I stealthily touched him on the shoulder.

'"*J'ai faim – j'ai beaucoup soif*," I said in my schoolboy French.

'He looked at me for a moment and then called, "Clotilde!" An elderly woman appeared at the door of the house, summed up the situation at a glance, and went back inside, soon to reappear with milk, eggs and cider.

'"*Pauvre garçon*," [poor boy] she said, handing me the food and drink.'

Maurice couldn't risk compromising them. If caught, he would become a prisoner of war; they would almost certainly be shot. They were half-starved themselves. He knew what they were sacrificing to help him.

'I smiled, said "*Merci*", and added, "*Vive la France*." I saluted the valiant couple and trundled off.

'I was now very lonely. A day or so later while bending down to pick some succulent grass stems, I discovered a huge Roman snail and put it in my pocket.'

Maurice had no means of cooking it and in any case shared the reserve most Britons experienced when confronted with the idea of eating such 'delicacies'. He decided to keep it as a pet, christening it 'Chicago'. Later, he came across a tempting crop of wild mushrooms under a tree, but knew nothing about them, so decided to put his trust in the toss of a coin.

'The only round thing I had was Chicago, my *escargot*. I found a small piece of chalk nearby and did a head on one side [of his shell] and a sort of Britannia on the other. I told Chicago my life was in his hands, took a deep breath and threw him as far as possible into the air. I waited and waited. He never came down. There were some branches overhead. He must have lodged there; I took it as a sign not to eat any of those fungi.'

Maurice had been on the run for almost three weeks; he was filthy, ragged, dead on his feet. In desperation, he swallowed the only edible thing left in his escape kit: a Benzedrine (amphetamine stimulant) tablet. Half-starved and dehydrated, it had an unexpected effect.

'About an hour later, I began to hallucinate. In front of me was a big waterfall, lots of fresh drinking water. Out of the woods came Pan, the Greek god of nature, playing his pipes and accompanied by nine nifty, nubile wood nymphs who pranced after him. I heard my heart thumping. I dived down under the protecting branches of an oak and lay there. At long last sleep rescued me until noon the next day.'

It is difficult to imagine the determination and courage needed by those Lancaster airmen, blasted from the familiar – though clearly dangerous – environment of their beloved aircraft to parachute into enemy-occupied territory. They had little training and almost no real skills or knowledge to prepare themselves for their ordeal. Yet they had no choice but to endure, to press on regardless into the unknown.

Maurice was now very weak. He knew he couldn't go on much longer, but the trees were beginning to thin out. At last he was surrounded by farmland – a few sheep in the fields and a low farmhouse in the middle distance surrounded by outbuildings. With remarkable fortitude, he made himself wait, to assess the situation, for two more days. As soon as he thought it was safe – by now he had run out of options – he approached the front door and knocked.

Eventually he saw a curtain twitch at a nearby window, and the door opened a tiny fraction.

'"*Faim. Soif.*" I pointed to my mouth; *hungry, thirsty.* "RAF. *Vive la France.*" The door opened wider and a huge man bearing a great wooden club gently guided me into his domain. I thought, *Now my troubles are over.* I felt completely bonkers with relief. Little did I know my adventures were just beginning.'

*Maurice Garlick*

Listening intently for the sound of the men and dogs that might already be tracking him, Guyanese navigator Cy Grant looked around the bleak landscape, assessing his chances of escape. His Lancaster had been shot down by a German fighter over Haarlem, 15 miles west of Amsterdam. He was alone in enemy territory.

'I wondered what had happened to the other members of my crew. Had they survived the blast? I walked, ran and trotted, but my legs and lungs were giving out with the stress of the situation. I estimated that I should be somewhere in the region of the small town of Haarlem – well within the area of coastal defences, where there'd be plenty of Germans. I prayed that the Lanc had crashed north or west of where I'd landed, for I presumed the Germans would start their search for us from that point outwards. It'd be ironic if, in trying to evade them, I was in fact running straight into their arms.'[3]

Cy made his way across an oat field and finally arrived at a road. He wondered if he dared risk crossing it – it was already getting light and he had no idea what lay ahead. He hoped he was heading south-east, but he couldn't be certain. Then the sound of a vehicle made his decision for him: it could be the Germans, already hot on his trail.

'That settled it. I hid instead. The oats were tall enough to give me cover, and I was already very tired, even though I hadn't travelled very far. The vehicle passed, and the sound of dogs was getting fainter. I knew I couldn't attempt to travel further until I'd got some rest and eaten some grub.'

There was a village in the distance and he pondered stripping his loosely sewn badges from his uniform, trying to conceal himself as a local worker. He decided against it; there was no way a black airman could pass for a Dutch civilian.

The best plan was to rest and eat, so he hunkered down to wait.

'It was close to dawn, and I watched the sleepy Dutch village awaken. Had these people been able to sleep at all, with the aerial battle going on over their heads? As it grew lighter, a sense of *déjà vu* suddenly overwhelmed me. Had I been here before? The Dutch countryside was so familiar. It reminded me of the country districts of Guyana, low-lying and flat, with canals everywhere. And there were the same early-morning sounds: a cock-crow, a man shouting, the clatter of a pail, a dog barking.'

There was another sound – gentle, mechanical – on the road. Then someone whistling. Cy took a cautious look through the foliage and caught his first sight of the enemy – a German soldier cycling along, 'blissfully unaware that I was lying only ten yards away'. Cy decided to stay put, but it began to rain, soaking him and making it impossible to sleep. His thoughts returned to the rest of his Lancaster crew; might there be a chance, even a remote one, of joining forces with any of them and making it to Spain?

Wishful thinking, he told himself.

'I was wet, miserable and hungry, though I dared not come out into the open. But I needed some grub and to know my exact position and where the Germans were stationed. I also needed somewhere to stay overnight. A barn would be ideal.'

On his hands and knees, Cy crept cautiously around the edge of the crop. 'I was leaving a long, muddy trail behind me, I was covered in mud, but at least I discovered that to get anywhere I'd have to cross that road.' His only hope was to contact a friendly local. Or simply give himself up. He'd already noticed a large, detached building towards which the German had been cycling. A barracks, perhaps? As dusk fell, Cy saw his opportunity. A solitary farmer in an adjacent field, not far away. 'I crawled on my stomach towards him. When I was near enough I made small pellets of mud and threw them at him.' The man reacted in astonishment – 'his face was a poem of bewilderment' – then he caught sight of Cy and immediately recognised him as RAF. He signalled him to move further away from the road.

There was a 6ft-wide ditch separating the two of them.

'I threw myself at the other bank and clambered up to the man. He thrust a shovel towards me and immediately I knew I was in safe hands. From the road we'd just be two workers. He spoke no English but showed me where I was on my silk escape map. I was not far from where I expected to be; south-east of Haarlem.'

The farmer didn't need to be told that Cy was exhausted and famished. He took him to a large barn full of labourers and their children.

'A shot-down airman would always arouse people's curiosity, but there was something else here. I'd encountered a similar kind of curiosity in parts of England where the natives had never seen someone of my colour close up. It wasn't going to be easy for me to escape.'

The Dutch who surrounded Cy were warm-hearted and friendly. The farmer's pretty young wife took him to their cottage and tended his head wound, then gave him a hot meal. His spirits had lifted considerably when a new visitor arrived – a small man in an ill-fitting pinstripe suit who spoke reasonable English and translated the questions the locals fired at Cy. They were all anxious to know when the invasion would begin.

'"How long will it be before it will commence?" they asked of me as if I was the War Office. I thought I should give them some hope, so I replied, "Soon now. It will not be long before your country will be yours again." That seemed to cheer them up; they turned excitedly to each other. My plight was forgotten by all except myself and probably the interpreter, for he soon broke the bad news to me.'

Cy had hoped to stay with the farmer that night, but the interpreter reluctantly told him that if the Germans didn't already know about his presence, they soon would. Cy had been seen by too many people, and there was always the risk of an informer among them. If he wasn't handed over, the farmer and his wife would be shot. They'd taken a huge risk already.

'I caught the look in the eyes of my benefactors. They were obviously distressed by the grim choices which faced them. This came as a great blow. I pleaded that I simply had to get away, that surely everybody there could be trusted. I looked about me, they all seemed so concerned for me – but I also detected concern for their own safety. I asked the interpreter to help me find another way out, but all he replied was that "it was quite impossible in the circumstances".'

Soon, a large, amiable Dutch policeman arrived, who beckoned

Cy to follow him. He put him on the pillion seat of his motorbike and drove off along a lonely country road.

'His manner was so warm and comforting that I entertained the irrational hope that he was helping me to escape in some way. But at the same time I was feeling emotionally drained and apprehensive. I was still in a state of shock from the events of the past twenty hours and was becoming resigned to my fate. Then I became aware of the huge revolver protruding from its holster by his side. It seemed to be inviting me to grab it. It would have been very easy. Perhaps my friendly policeman was intending me to do just that. All sorts of thoughts tumbled through my mind.

'Was I up to it? I was not a very tough individual, and I didn't know how to ride a motorcycle. And how would I hold him up at gunpoint and ride away on his bike? At that moment he turned towards me, smiling, and said something I didn't understand, but it could well have been, "I wouldn't try that if I were you." His nonchalance was very off-putting!'

They arrived at a quaint little village where the policeman took him into his house. Cy was told to make himself at home while his wife prepared tea and his daughter rushed to put on a pretty dress especially for the occasion. Their friendliness was warm and unfeigned, but the policeman told Cy that the Germans would soon arrive to collect him. He was apologetic, even embarrassed, and showed Cy the short-wave radio they had hidden, to listen to the BBC every night – perhaps to demonstrate his solidarity. But what could he do?

Sure enough, a Ford V8 drew up soon afterwards and two *Gefreite* – Lance Corporals – got out, frisked Cy and drove him straight back to the scene of his rescue. The farmer and his wife seemed to have been expecting this and stood by their front door as one of the Germans harangued them, drawing his pistol. The couple seemed to be vigorously denying whatever allegations were being made. Cy, horrified, expected the *Gefreiter* to shoot his rescuers at any minute, but eventually everyone calmed down and the German gave up. Cy had caught the word '*Fallschirm*' during the row without knowing what it meant, but now it occurred to him that the Lance Corporal was questioning them about the whereabouts of the parachute. Silk was a valuable commodity, and the Germans were beginning to feel the pinch as much as those they had conquered.

'To my relief the soldier put away his gun and soon we were off again, but for a brief second my eyes had caught those of the young wife and I knew that she would have run the same risk all over again if need be.'

They took Cy to a holding unit in Amsterdam for interrogation, where he ran into Geoff Wallis, his Lancaster's mid-upper gunner. They hugged each other in happy relief, but it was short-lived. Geoff only had time to tell him the rear gunner and the flight engineer had been killed, and that there was no news of the others. Then the Germans roughly pulled them apart and led Cy away.

Days of questioning followed, but despite glaring lights, solitary confinement and barked questions in grim, claustrophobic rooms, 'I was never threatened with any form of torture, though I always imagined that that time would inevitably come. Then one day I was dragged out into the bright sunshine and made to sit on a chair in order to be photographed. That was all. I was led back to my cell and left to wonder what use would be made of the photograph. Perhaps it was just routine.'

On the morning of the sixth day, Cy was shoved onto a train with scores of other prisoners. 'Geoff Wallis was nowhere to be seen – perhaps because he was a sergeant and so not destined for an officers' camp.'

Despite the appalling conditions on the two-day journey it was a great relief to Cy to be among fellow flyers again. Their destination was one of the largest air force prisoner-of-war camps, and one of the most famous: Stalag Luft III.[4]

'My arrival at the camp created a bit of a stir among the Germans. A black officer! The Commandant sent for me and I was ushered into the presence of a very handsome middle-aged man. He had an intelligent, dignified manner and was extremely polite. He asked me where I came from and thrust a page of a German newspaper in front of me. It featured the picture of me, taken after five days of solitary confinement.' The newspaper was the *Völkischer Beobachter (People's Observer)*[5] and the caption below the photo read: *'Mitglied der RAF unbestimmbarer Rasse'* – 'A Member of the Royal Air Force of Indeterminate Race'.

Life in the camp was generally humdrum, often boring. But all prisoners were well aware that they were still at war, and had a duty, if possible, to escape. They knew that although they were prisoners, they had a fair chance of surviving if they stayed put; but they were young, and had no idea how long their freedom would be forfeited, or how many years of their youth would go to waste. As the air war continued, and many more bombers were shot down, new arrivals arrived at the camp each week. Cy always joined the rest of their fellow prisoners at the perimeter fence to welcome the newcomers, constantly on the lookout for any members of their old crews.

'Each time I'd gone down to join the reception committee I'd been disappointed, but at last on one of those arrival days I thought I saw a figure who vaguely reminded me of Al Langille, my pilot. Surely that couldn't be him! As they flooded through the gates, amid our cynical greetings, one of them separated himself from the rest and came towards me. Could this pitiful-looking specimen, after all, be Al? He sported a heavy beard and his head was leaning heavily to one side, but his voice was unmistakable.

'"Hi, Cy," he greeted me.

'"Al!" I blurted out. "Man, whatever happened to your neck? A great improvement, I must confess!"'

It transpired his pilot had actually broken his neck during the bale-out.[6]

'I was bursting with happiness and joy. Al was probably the only person who could have broken his neck and survived! His head was to remain listing to one side for ever, but to have him with me in the same camp was the best thing to have happened to me since I was shot down. He was the most charismatic person I've ever known – warm, witty, cheerful – a born leader of men. Even in his weakened state he took charge. He formed his own Mess, just as he'd chosen his crew. There were twelve of us – ten Canadians, an Irishman, and myself. We had the cleanest, best-organised Mess. At first we had no pots and pans, but in the end we even had cups and plates. Al could do anything with his hands and built a radio from the bits and pieces he scrounged from other prisoners and from the guards, usually older men, who weren't averse to a bit of bribery, and were happy to be suborned by cigarettes or chocolate from Red Cross parcels.'

Above all there was a certain pride in establishing order and discipline in the daily routine – something which helped bolster self-respect.

Cy was the sole black officer in the camp, but only once did he suffer any racial abuse. 'An American airman called me a nigger! He was from the Deep South, I gathered, and just couldn't understand that I was an officer in the Royal Air Force.'

Because of the Geneva Convention governing the treatment of prisoners of war, officer prisoners were not obliged to do any form of work, so the ample leisure time – apart from escape planning – was filled with sports, games, putting on shows, the establishment of libraries and, in Cy's case, a jazz band. He was also a good portraitist, and was in perpetual demand to paint pictures of his fellow prisoners' girlfriends from photographs. 'We were able to organise ourselves into a highly efficient community.'

Incarceration proved to be a time for deep reflection on the fact that, if one hadn't been shot down, one would still be on operations, and it was hard to live with the constant reminders that you were a prisoner.

'All day, every day, you had to be aware of the ferrets – guards who conducted spot searches, who might pop up at any time. But even though it was not unbearable for the *Kriegies*[7] [prisoners of war], the absence of freedom and the absence of women were constant reminders not to grow accustomed to it.'

He and his fellow prisoners were to endure eighteen months as '*Kriegies*' before they would face a fresh, potentially deadly challenge.

* * *

Cy Grant had been relatively well treated after his capture. Not all those who were blasted from the skies over occupied Europe were as fortunate.

Lancaster pilot Jim Penny had been shot down a few months after Cy during the Battle of Berlin. After a night in a police cell he was collected by two Luftwaffe personnel and taken by car to a small airfield, where other downed airmen from the previous night's raid were being assembled. On the way they had made a short detour to collect a map of Berlin; the bombing had changed the landscape of the city so much that the Luftwaffe men couldn't find their way without it.

It already seemed an age since Jim's Lancaster had gone down when the cookie it was carrying blew up, throwing him clear but engulfing the rest of the crew.

Jim immediately noticed one young Allied airman on a stretcher and learned that he'd parachuted through the glass roof of a factory, where he'd been found by the women workers when they emerged from their air-raid shelters. He'd been badly beaten before some soldiers arrived and rescued him.

Intimidated by the young man's experience, and feeling sorry for him, Jim volunteered to be one of his four stretcher-bearers, when a large escort took the prisoners to a nearby railway station. There, an elderly man spat at one of the stretcher-bearers and the surrounding crowd turned ugly, but the German corporal in charge hit the man with his gun before turning it on the rest to keep them at bay.

Later, as they were waiting for their train, the same corporal ordered himself a beer, then, noticing the expressions of the stretcher-bearers, ordered the same for them.

'That *stein* of beer was an example of the camaraderie that can exist between disciplined soldiers even when they are enemies. I thought too of the old woman in the shelter who had taken pity on me despite what I'd done to Berlin, and I thought of the innate decency of many Germans. I learned to make a distinction between the evil regime that controlled Germany and the significant number who opposed the Nazis, many of them ending up in concentration camps or being killed. I became aware that despite many supporting the regime it was likely that even more simply feared the consequences of showing any disapproval.'[8]

Jim ended up at Stalag Luft VI – the northernmost camp in the German Reich, near Heydekrug in the Memelland, now Lithuania – after six days packed into filthy, freezing cattle trucks with little sanitation or food. Dirty, emaciated, their clothes often reduced to rags, they would not give in. They had ridden the skies in Lancasters, and they dreamt of the day when they might be able to escape and return home to do their duty once more.

Confined behind the wire of a regulation prisoner-of-war camp, Jim and his comrades were now relatively safe. Not all those who were shot down would be so lucky.

*Tom Tate*

As Allied bombers poured increasing death and destruction upon Germany, with civilians bearing the brunt, Hitler had decreed in spring 1944 that '*Terrorflieger*' should no longer enjoy the protection of the German military. In effect, he actively encouraged the murder of captured aircrew. Then, in a front-page article in a May issue of *Völkischer Beobachter* – the newspaper of the National

Socialist German Workers' Party – Joseph Goebbels had issued an edict stating that air attacks on Germany were no longer warfare; they were to be considered murder and that German troops should no longer protect the lives of downed enemy pilots. Their fate should be left in the hands of the 'sorely tried population'.[9]

Wireless operator Tom Tate, shot down returning from an attack on the synthetic oil refinery at Lutzkendorf near Leipzig, would witness the full brutality of the German people's rage. Quickly captured, he had been taken to a civilian prison in the nearby town.

'My escorts knocked on the front door and it was opened by a woman jailer who grabbed my hair and began pulling it out. I was terrified. She was vicious, shouting at me that I was the enemy. I thought she was going to kill me. Eventually I was put into a cellar already inhabited by six others from my crew. But this was no jolly reunion. We were all tired and depressed and probably in shock. Eventually a conversation got going. The wife of one of the crew was about to have a baby back in England and he was worried for her, so we talked a lot about that. It was strange talking about the birth of a baby in those circumstances. I suppose we were concentrating on something other than our own dreadful predicament. The cellar was foul. There were no facilities and we had to use one corner as a toilet. The smell was awful.'[10]

Tom and his friends spent a terrible night there before being collected. Unfortunately, they had no transport.

'The five guards took us out on the road at gunpoint and thumbed a lift for the twelve of us. Things were so bad in Germany it was their only means of getting around. It was comical, all of us waiting by the side of a road. Finally a lorry stopped and we got in. Driving along, everything seemed fine, so normal, as if life was just carrying on as usual. There was no sense of being in danger, nothing to concern us. We passed through a few villages. And then, after 20 miles or so, we came to Pforzheim.'

What the seven airmen did not know was that a few weeks earlier, the Black Forest town had been hit by one of the most punishing Bomber Command air raids of the entire war. More than

360 Lancasters had pounded it, dropping close to 2,000 tons and setting off a firestorm that killed some 18,000 people – a quarter of the population. Barely a fifth of the town's buildings were still standing after the Lancasters left. The rest was a wreck, as Tate and the others could see only too well when the lorry dropped them on the outskirts.[11]

'I had never seen anything like this before; a whole city in ruins. The shock was tremendous. Our escorts walked us down a hill towards what had been the centre. The main roads had been cleared and there were narrow paths between the rubble on each side. When the people recognised our blue RAF uniforms they started bombarding us with anything they could lay their hands on. I didn't blame them. The utter devastation was awful to see. There is a difference between talking about targets and then seeing the reality of what it was like on the ground. This was complete desolation. This was the awesome power of the Lancaster bomber. Strangely, I didn't think those people in the middle of Pforzheim were going to kill us. They were beaten as people, and when they threw rocks and stones at us it was more an act of defiance. But the guards did well to shelter us. They spread out with their rifles ready and we finally got to the far side of the city. Then we climbed the hills out of the city until we came to a village called Huchenfeld.'

The village was thronging with people who had been bombed out of Pforzheim, and their feelings were being inflamed by members of the Hitler Youth under the direction of the local Nazi Party leader. Tom Tate and his fellow prisoners were locked in the basement of the village school.

'We didn't talk; there was nothing to say. We took our boots off and lay down. The next thing I remember was being dragged up the iron staircase out of the cellar. I didn't even have time to put my boots back on. Lots of people were milling around. Three men were holding me. Were they men or were they boys? I don't really know. All I remember clearly is being forced down the road with the others. I was half asleep and I thought to myself, *What on earth is going on now?* Then someone hit me across the head and cut it open. And that was when the truth dawned: this was a lynching.

'We turned off the main street and I found myself facing the church. To the left of it was a big barn. Its main doors were shut but there was a small door in the middle that had been left open, and through it I could see inside. A single bulb was burning and from its light I saw a massive beam with ten ropes and nooses dangling from it. I realised instantly that they were going to hang us. That glimpse saved my life. I would have gone passively into that barn if I had not been forewarned what they had in store for me.

'Knowing that this was my only chance, I burst away and ran like mad, even though I was in bare feet. One of my crew saw me go and he put his head down like a rugby player and ran too. Someone fired a shot. For a moment I hesitated. Perhaps I had better give myself up? But then I remembered the ropes and the nooses. I darted between houses and across fields until I came to the forest. I dug myself into the mounds of dead oak leaves on the ground and waited. In the distance I heard a long burst of automatic gunfire. I could hear people searching for me but they didn't come very close. Finally I fell asleep. When I woke in the morning, I just kept walking to get as far away from Huchenfeld as I could.'

Later that day, Tate came upon a group of German soldiers. He decided to surrender. His gamble paid off. 'I was taken down into an underground bunker where an elderly officer was sitting at a table. He invited me to sit down and listened to my story. He had my feet attended to, gave me some bread and water, and I was then marched to a barracks, about half an hour's walk away.' While he was being held there a woman brought some shoes for him. They had belonged to her now dead soldier husband. Tate could only wonder at the different sides of human nature he was encountering. One group of Germans wanted to murder him, and here was one going out of her way to help, even though she had as much reason to hate him as the others. He was then taken from the barracks to the railway station.

'Escorts sat on each side of me. We had been waiting about an hour when a dozen men came in and began talking. I realised they had come for me. My life was being threatened again. One guard took off his cap and put it on my head, either to try and disguise me or to make it clear I was one of them. Then an army officer arrived and confronted the crowd. He stood in front of them and told them I was a prisoner of war and that I was protected by the Geneva Convention. Just then the train came in and I was hustled on board. My escort stood at the windows with their guns in their hands until we had left the platform behind and were on our way. I asked one of the escorts what had happened to my friends and he said: "Your comrades are safe." Eventually I arrived unharmed at a POW camp.'

Tom Tate's German guards had lied, perhaps too ashamed to tell their prisoner the truth. He later heard that the mob that had arrived at the railway station had blood on their hands and were thirsting for more. Tate was one of three who ran from the nooses at Huchenfeld when they realised they were about to be lynched. One of the others, his flight engineer, had been recaptured the next day. He was held in the police station until a mob of Hitler Youth dragged him outside and beat him up. Then a fifteen-year-old boy, half-crazy with grief and anger, was given a gun. Just weeks before he had dug through the rubble of Pforzheim and found his mother's crushed body and those of his five brothers and sisters. Egged on by the others, the distraught boy shot the flight engineer in the head.

Hearing of Tate's capture, the mob had then made their way to where he was being held and would have murdered him at the station if his guards had not stood their ground. The other four who had failed to get away at Huchenfeld were dead too. In the chaos after Tate's escape, the plan to hang them had been abandoned. They were gunned down in the churchyard. That was the firing he had heard from the forest.

The bodies were left where they lay overnight, their eyes still open, as one witness recalled. The congregation stepped round them as they arrived for Sunday service the next day.

* * *

In the French region of Champagne, Maurice Garlick was having more luck, although exhausted after three weeks on the run through the forests. Jacques Dédion, the giant of a man carrying a wooden club, made Maurice supremely welcome in his home.

Jacques gently guided him to the end of a large wooden table where eight farmworkers were already seated. The warmth enfolded Maurice like his mother's arms. A delicious smell filled the room, and soon Jacques' wife Yvette was serving large bowls of lamb casserole from a bubbling tureen on the wood-burning stove.

'My host took his seat at the head of the table and poured me a glass of a delicious local red wine which I disposed of in one quaff, with three weeks' thirst behind it. He smiled knowingly and poured another, raising his in silent toast. I no longer had to look over my shoulder all the time! I thought, now my troubles are over. Of course they must have known I was the genuine article. Three weeks' beard, stinking, limping, dirty battledress, hair all over the place, scuffed shoes, torn Mae West lifejacket, and a well-notched walking stick. The Real McCoy!'

The long sticks of crusty French bread and more tumblers of *vin ordinaire* were blissful after Maurice's weeks living off the land. The farmworkers, culled from conquered countries to produce food for the Reich, finished their meal and retired, saying respectful goodnights. Yvette produced a green bottle of ten-year-old cherry brandy. '*Vive la France*,' Maurice toasted them, and they returned the compliment. 'When I told them I was making for Switzerland, they both laughed their heads off. Jacques said it would probably take me two years!'

They gently explained that Maurice could not stay there, since they were already sheltering two USAAF airmen among the labourers and couldn't take any further risks. The Germans stationed locally were constantly calling to requisition food, and there weren't enough hiding places for everyone. Jacques would, however, make other arrangements for their new friend. Maurice was not to worry. 'You are going to stay with some good friends of mine, Champagne Charlie and his family.' Maurice was glad of the reassurance. He'd taken stock of the disposition of the farm and knew there were too many wide-open fields to make a run for it, since he was in no condition to run anywhere. He had stretched himself to the limit and his feet were screaming with agony.

If he went back to the forest in his condition, he could die.

Jacques explained that the Germans often arrived to requisition a pig, sheep or a few chickens, and 'they'd soon notice that the number of my labourers was getting too big. Or someone, sooner or later, would talk. I'm at my limit. You mustn't think I don't trust you.' Far from it; after only five hours in their company but equipped with just enough French to converse, Maurice had already taken Jacques and Yvette into his heart. 'I felt an immediate empathy with them, which I never lost.'

At 3 a.m. there was a soft knock on the door and a slightly built, middle-aged, unassuming man with a Gauloise in the corner of his mouth appeared. Jacques introduced him as Josef Delacroix.[12] Maurice came to think of him as 'Uncle Joe'.

He was the local postman, perfect cover for a Resistance courier. He took Maurice out to a battered old Citroën adapted to run by a small wood-burning stove which heated a boiler. They drove for an hour through the night, to the home of Marius and Blanche, who lived with their two children in *La Belle Maison*, a large bungalow surrounded by outbuildings. Marius turned out to be a great wine connoisseur, and as Maurice had parachuted into champagne country, he was well entertained for the three weeks or so he was the family's guest. His hideout was a 'room', constructed in the middle of stacks of cardboard boxes, in a warehouse within the bungalow's compound, and his hosts swiftly provided him with civilian clothes.

'About noon the next day, Marius entered my hideout with a short, tubby, smartly dressed, middle-aged man carrying a Gladstone bag. This was Dr Diderol. We shook hands and had what had by now become the usual tipple of champagne. He asked me to show him my wounds. There was a sharp intake of breath and a mumbled "*pauvre garçon*" – poor boy. He said the wounds must be kept covered to prevent infection and produced a bandage, but first he asked Marius for a large glass of brandy. I thought the sight of my wounds must have made him feel sick, but not a bit of it. With considerable aplomb, he dashed it all over my feet and legs. I almost jumped out of the window!'

Dr Diderol covered the wounds with medicinal powder, pronounced the right leg to be healing nicely, bandaged both, and promised to return in a few days. Gradually Maurice began to recover. He repaid his hosts as best he could by teaching English to their thirteen-year-old son and his sister, a brave 21-year-old who carried messages for the Resistance rolled up in the handlebars of her bicycle. But despite the constant flow of good wines and the friendly company, inevitably he began to feel confined and bored.

But that would change. Very soon Maurice had more companionship.

'About three in the morning, I was awoken by a noise outside my door, which opened to admit two men in scruffy, muddy battledress.'

He immediately recognised their voices – the bomb aimer and flight engineer from his own crew!

'As soon as I heard their voices I poked my head out from under my blanket and growled, "Get fell in, you 'orrible erks! Kit inspection in five minutes!"

'"Good Lord, it's old Maurie! Trust you to get a cushy number! Fall on your feet all the time!"

'Considering what I'd been through, I thought that was a bit much, but how could they know? They were dying to tell me their adventures, and we were all pleased and relieved beyond description to see each other again. The following morning over breakfast, I heard what had happened to them since our Lancaster crashed. They'd had the good fortune to fall in with a Resistance cell with whom they'd been living for the past six weeks, but after a shoot-out they had been spirited away to find sanctuary with Joe. But they had some sad news too. They'd heard that our mid-upper gunner had died of his wounds.'

The revelation was a huge blow to the normally upbeat Garlick, but better news followed. About ten days into his stay, Blanche and her daughter burst into his room.

'"Monsieur Maurice, Monsieur Maurice! Your friends come and search for you."

'I looked mystified.

'"The soldiers, sailors and airmen, they all come to find you."

'From their excited, happy faces I knew something big had occurred. Then the penny dropped – it must be the long-awaited invasion of occupied Europe, probably the most important date of the twentieth century, and very soon, we hoped, the end of the war. Instead of my being up there helping, I was lying in bed!'

They'd heard the news of D-Day on a forbidden radio soon after 6 June. The French were filled with new hope, and that had to be celebrated, in defiance of the Germans.

'I think it was only two *extra* bottles of the best champagne that evening, and Blanche declared she'd prepare a "Victory Banquet" for the following Sunday. I'm sure she thought she'd see our soldiers coming down the street right now if she parted the curtains. What a pity her wish couldn't come true.

'On the day, their dining-room table was set for fourteen and covered with a crisp white tablecloth. The other guests included Dr Diderol, a couple of men I knew to be from the Resistance, and other friends from nearby. We all drank a Pernod aniseed-flavoured aperitif, then settled down to Blanche's haute cuisine. She'd really pushed the boat out. The banquet began with some crisp, crunchy radishes, followed by chicken soup, then crayfish. Next came some red-hot fireclay pots of some sort of spiced meat in garlic butter which you ate with a funny little fork. I filled my glass with some delicious Sancerre Blanc and ate up the lot. Delicious!

'Then I noticed everyone was watching me intently, finally breaking into uproarious laughter.

'"Hurrah!" they shouted. "Maurice has eaten snails! He is a true Frenchman now!"'

Blanche, Marius and their friends may have hoped to see British

Tommies and American GIs marching into Champagne the day after the D-Day landings – but it was, of course, an impossible wish.

Nothing was certain, and the game was far from over.

It was time for the mighty warhorse, the Lancaster bomber, to play a most crucial role.

# CHAPTER THIRTEEN

# 'I NEEDED TO KILL HIM BEFORE HE COULD KILL ME AND MY CREW'

As Maurice Garlick prepared for D-Day while on the run in France, Lancaster wireless operator Bill Low was flying back across the English Channel from a sortie on 4 June 1944 when he saw a huge gathering of ships and invasion craft massing in the sea below. 'We knew something was happening. Was this it? The moment we had been waiting for, for so many years?'

The tension was broken when, on the 6th, RAF Metheringham's Station Commander broadcast the news over the Tannoy system. 'The invasion had started! There was great excitement and everybody's morale soared; nobody dreamt that it could fail.'

Bill had just turned nineteen when he joined up in August 1941. His father, a First World War veteran, sent him off to the recruiting office with some sage advice ringing in his ears: 'Be a good chap and go and fight for your country.' With the nation's very existence under threat, it was what was expected, and what Bill and all of his friends wanted to do. 'It was our dream, in a way. I thought it was going to be a big adventure; I certainly didn't have any fears for the future.' Now, as the Allies finally set foot in France, he dared to think of what might lie ahead, of a time when he wouldn't be risking his life every day. 'What could I do after the war? Perhaps go into the Civil Service and have a cosy, secure, quiet job?' The talk was of a new era, a chance to live normal lives again. Even at the time, Bill knew he might be tempting fate.

As 150,000 Allied troops stormed the beaches or parachuted inland of Normandy, some 10,000 dying to secure the precarious foothold in mainland Europe, Bill's crew was tasked with what they thought would be an 'easy op'. As D-Day itself came to a close, they took off to bomb the bridges at Caen, 10 miles from the coast, where the fighting was already fierce. 'It was going to be a low-level attack, drop the bombs and come out. It wouldn't take more than ten minutes from Cherbourg – ten minutes there and back. Just a short trip – a piece of cake. I didn't even put my flying boots on.'[1] The light was beginning to fade on what was already being called 'the Longest Day' when they crossed the Channel at 8,000ft. As they dropped down towards the target, Bill could see the flashes of ground artillery.

'It was an amazing sight. We felt quite safe by comparison with the guys on the ground. But then, as we prepared for the run into Caen, all hell broke loose. Out of the blue, German anti-aircraft guns got a bearing on us and let fly. The aircraft was hit in the port wing and in the fuselage. The skipper just shouted, "Abandon ship!" My job was to go and tap the mid-upper's legs, to tell him to bale out. Then I had to go down to make sure the rear gunner had got out. But the back of the aircraft was on fire. There were flames everywhere, and I couldn't get through. I sometimes feel I should have tried harder, but I just couldn't get there, so I fought my way back up to the front.'

He found his skipper about to dive out of the forward escape hatch.

'Luckily for him I got there before he went, because his parachute was only fastened on one side. There was so much noise, flames, confusion, but I can remember stopping to say, "That's not right," and clipping him in properly. It can only have taken a few seconds, but it seemed so slow at the time. We were meant to count to ten before pulling the parachute ring, but we were so low that panic set in and I pulled it as I dived out.'

With the German flak blasting the sky around his parachute, Bill had no time to contemplate his fate as the ground rushed up to meet him. He bounced off a roof before hitting the ground, knocking himself out.

'When I came to, the pain was intense. I was very frightened, but also very surprised; I had always presumed this would never happen to me! I took the parachute off, hid it and began to hobble away. Suddenly, I bumped into a German patrol – about eight of them. I was amazed. It felt unreal. This is what I had seen in films, but these were real Germans, not film Germans. One of them dropped his rifle. Another ran away. I suppose they were more frightened than I was. The others took me inside a building, took my cigarettes, my escape pack and my chocolate – then they threw me down some stairs.'

Bill's war was over. He'd fractured his spine and shattered most of his teeth on landing, but he still regarded himself as one of the lucky ones. He was transferred to a field hospital, where 'for the first time in my life, I realised what the war was all about. I saw German soldiers lying around, bits missing, blood all over the place. It was a sobering realisation. There were 1,160 sorties that night and only eleven aircraft lost. It was never meant to happen to me – but that was life in Bomber Command.

'I spent the rest of the war as a POW, but others weren't so fortunate. Both gunners went down with the aircraft. The mid-upper always carried a special scarf for safety, and part of it was found near the wreckage. He wore that scarf every time he flew. He said it was part of his routine, to keep us all safe. It didn't work that time.'

\* \* \*

Bomber Command, working in conjunction with the USAAF, had been under the orders of General Dwight D. Eisenhower, the Supreme Allied Commander, since the planning for Operation Overlord had begun. Enemy oil refineries, the continental transport system – roads, railways and bridges – and military targets now took priority. German oil production fell from 673,000 tons in January 1944 to 265,000 by September. Tank and aircraft production was cut by 30–35 per cent.[2]

Despite everything possible being done to avoid it, between 15,000 and 20,000 French civilians perished during the Normandy campaign, mostly due to Allied bombing. And although Allied boots were now on French soil, the Germans were fighting hard – and preparing to deploy another, more destructive weapon in an attempt to turn back the tide.

A week after D-Day, on 13 June, the first VI 'flying bomb' struck London. Eight people were killed in the blast by the railway bridge on Grove Road, Mile End. Two days later, the British capital was hit by seventy-three of these 'phantom planes', as they were first called. Londoners were mystified. This wasn't the familiar drone of the heavy bombers that they knew from the earlier blitz. Instead, they heard a sound more like a light aircraft, then nothing, followed by an explosion. For the citizens of south-east England, it was a terrifying new development, as one unnamed child described:

'"Look out! It's coming down!" I heard my father shout. The next moment there was a bright flash of light through the window, and then the house crashed down around us. I curled myself into a small ball as the bricks and mortar tumbled down, burying us in a sort of cave. The stairway still stood, making a roof. The bricks stopped falling and there was silence, except for my father's faint voice calling. He had ducked in under the sink. I sat [as] still as I could and listened to my sister reciting the Lord's Prayer. I kept thinking about my chocolate cake and wishing I had eaten it. Gradually the sound of digging came nearer until I could hear my father's voice telling me to sit still. At last there was a light in the hole near my head. Slowly it grew bigger until I could see my father's grimy face through it. A few minutes' more shovelling and my father was lifting me out into the sunlight. All that was left was a heap of rubble, except for the chimney, which was still standing.'[3]

From 15 June, the attacks became more numerous, and Londoners grew to fear the buzz of the flying bomb's engine, and the sudden silence that told them it was about to drop out of the sky. Before long, that fear prompted a mass exodus as morale was badly hit by these new harbingers of doom.[4] The VIs, despite earning a derogatory nickname – 'Doodlebug' – were achieving what the earlier air raids somehow had not. The novelist Evelyn Waugh wrote at the time, 'No enemy was risking his life up there. It was as impersonal as a plague, as though the city were infested with enormous, venomous insects.'[5]

After nearly five years of war, deprivation and stress, they were breaking people's spirits. Two thousand barrage balloons were deployed around the capital, in the hope that the V1s' wings would be severed by the tethering cables, but their leading edges were equipped with cable-cutters, so no more than 300 were caught. RAF fighters and anti-aircraft batteries also did their part, but aggressive counter-measures were needed, and fast.

A force of 400 aircraft, including 236 Lancasters, attacked four V1 launch sites in the Pas-de-Calais on the night of 16/17 June, and over the next month a dozen raids were aimed at further launch sites, fuel dumps and storage facilities. Further operations, against seven sites, took place on 24–26 June. The clear night sky afforded the bombers no cover, and German night-fighters claimed twenty-two of the 535 Lancasters involved. Four hundred and seventy-seven Lancasters were deployed to finish the job three nights later, of which only three failed to return.

* * *

The threat posed by the V-weapons showed what Germany was still capable of, and it made the success of Operation Overlord even more imperative. Everything hung on the progress of the invasion, and the Lancaster squadrons were vital in its support. Losses continued to climb, and new crews continued to feed the Bomber Command production line. The gap between life and death was narrow, and luck was often all that separated them.

Canadian pilot Jack Thompson – 'Tommy' to his predominantly Canadian crew – joined 12 Squadron at RAF Wickenby in the summer of 1944.

'My first impression of the famed Lancaster was of a big bird of prey crouched and ready to spring into the air. The massive undercarriage appeared like great talons and the dihedral, the up-bend in the wing just past the inner engine, gave the Lanc a rakish, devil-may-care appearance. While massive in size it seemed sleek and streamlined. And we soon found out that the Lanc's eager-to-fly appearance was no misrepresentation.'[6]

*Jack Thompson*

After a couple of 'warm-up' operations flying as a second pilot, Jack was ready for his crew's first operational sortie. He knew that each time they entered the briefing room and the curtain was drawn back, everyone's attention would be riveted on the red ribbon tacked across the vast map of Britain and Europe. What would they face that day? 'A relatively easy flip across the Channel into France and back out again, or a dreaded long voyage through the dark skies over Nazi Germany? Every time, that first view of the op stirred a quiet sigh of relief or a deep gut-wrench which was never allowed to surface beyond a muttered, "Uh-oh."'

Jack often reflected on how unbelievable it was that a group of 'kids' were involved in an almost dreamlike, often nightmarish, activity.

'When we should have been going to school or working at a first job, driving the family car, taking girls to dances, swimming, skating or skiing, we were instead flying through alien skies preparing to wreak havoc. All young fellows craved some excitement and adventure. We were being given that chance but the odds for survival were not all that inviting. Perhaps this great adventure might prove to be more exciting than we had bargained for in those far-off romantic days of enlistment. But, like marriage, we were firmly caught up in it for better or worse, and the ending of the drama we were enacting had not yet been written.'

Their first mission was a daylight raid to the Forêt Ducrocq, near Valenciennes, about 30 miles south-east of Lille. A short run to take out a feared V1 site. It was 6 July, a month after D-Day.

'We were trucked out to Lancaster *J-Jig*. The assigned aircraft was of no significance. We simply hoped it was in good shape and able to carry us and our load of destruction to our target and then back to Wickenby with no problems. We never believed in mascots or chance. We believed in working tightly together. Arnold Cowan, our navigator, at the age of thirty-three, was an old guy by aircrew standards. He arrived loaded down with maps, charts, paper and pencils. He'd be a busy man during the operation, keeping a running log, plotting our courses and times on his chart and keeping me up to speed as well. My wireless operator, my flight engineer and my bomb aimer all had to be really clued up. My job was to get us there and back, no forms to fill in or calculations to make, thank goodness! The gunners' job was also pretty straightforward and didn't need any paperwork. We stormed off down the runway, the speed gradually increased, the tail came up, and we finally shook ourselves free of the asphalt and kept the nose down to gain precious speed. An aircraft is never more vulnerable than when close to the ground, so after a slow and cautious climb away, we breathed more easily.'

They then joined the long, strung-out gaggle of Lancasters heading for France and the V1 site.

'I suppose we wondered if we'd be attacked by enemy fighters, or hit by flak, but nothing momentous happened at all, apart from the sheer personal drama of being over enemy territory for the first time and carrying out the duties for which our long training had prepared us. I think we all felt it was a bit anticlimactic, since we were all psyched up to press on regardless through fire and brimstone, only to end up on a milk run. But, anticlimactic or not, we thankfully accepted the ease with which we'd accomplished Operation Number One, while being very well aware that they wouldn't all be pieces of cake.'

\* \* \*

'*July 18, Lancaster E-Easy PB201, ops Caen SE – 0400 hours.*'

The simple note on the first page of Jack Thompson's pilot logbook bears testimony to one of the major air operations of the war. Jack's second operation was in support of the advancing Allied land forces – and Bomber Command's heaviest offensive since the Battle of Berlin.

'Soon after take-off that early morning we joined together in a mighty stream which seemed never-ending. Like migrating hawks, the Lancasters and their sister bombers all streamed southwards, and the mighty roar of their passing was heard by all who dwelled or worked far below. In all, 1,000 heavy bombers of the RAF, Lancasters and Halifaxes, flew to Caen that day. The Land Army girls in the fields, the village postmen on their rounds, the factory workers returning from the night shift, all heard the thunder of the mighty armada and gazed upwards in awe. The Britishers were used to the sound of air-craft both friendly and hostile; but never before has a sound of such magnitude and a sight of such awesome proportions greeted their eyes and ears. They must have felt a great surge of pride and satisfaction as the bomber force poured southward, on a path of destruction against a foe which had shown no mercy. No doubt many minds joined in the thought, *Old Jerry's going to get it today!*'

Jack and his crew had been disappointed to miss D-Day, but this operation looked just as important. After their initial successes, Allied troops, predominantly British and Canadian, had been stalled outside Caen for some time. This pivotal hub was heavily fortified, and the enemy had put up a tenacious defence.

'Now High Command had ordered a bomber force to break those defences and allow the armies to move ahead, and sweep through France. Long before we arrived at Caen we could see the heavy concentrations of flak we'd have to fly through, but the menacing black puffs of exploding shells didn't lessen our determination to add our load of fifteen 1,000-pounders to the 7,000 tons the Allied bombers were to drop on Caen and the German division defending it that day. I'm sure the view from ground level of the multitude of aircraft high above, coupled with the terrible destruction as the bombs fell, struck terror into the hearts of the troops at the receiving end. I'm sure they must have wondered if the hellish nightmare would ever stop as the Lancasters and Halifaxes droned steadily above in what must have seemed an endless procession.'

On the ground, it was a hellish nightmare indeed. Cecile Leclerc was a student nurse working with her sister at a hospital in Caen.

'It was terrifying, we could hear blasts everywhere. We were told to stay in the corridor, as only a direct hit from a bomb could crush us. But as for the rest of the clinic; when the raids started, everything disappeared. There was fire and screaming everywhere. It was terrifying. The clinic no longer existed; everything was flattened. I never saw my sister again.'[7]

André Heintz, a 24-year-old Resistance fighter, resorted to dipping sheets in blood to create a red cross, and placing them on the roof of a makeshift hospital to stop it being struck from the air. He later recalled, 'After the bombing, I carried wounded people on stretchers for three days and nights. I was haunted by what I saw; it was terrible to see so many wounded.'[8]

With the Allied advance stalled, were the attacks on French towns, and the subsequent casualties, justified? Military historian Antony Beevor describes them as 'stupid, counterproductive and above all very close to a war crime. The bombing was a double disaster. It failed to destroy most of the German positions around the northern fringe of Caen and instead inflicted massive damage to the city. Worst of all, the attack, like the German bombing of Stalingrad, turned much of the city into a mass of rubble which impeded the advance of vehicles and provided an ideal terrain for the defenders.'[9]

Not everyone agreed, including some of those French civilians on the receiving end of the Allied bombs. Colette Marin-Catherine was involved in the Resistance around Caen and helped nurse wounded civilians.

'The British did everything in their power to protect and warn us; they were extraordinary. Even with an arm or a leg less, I would have been delighted to see the British arrive. You can see the photos of civilians jumping into the arms of Allied soldiers even though they were injured. Our house was emptied, pillaged. We were ruined. But I would have given a French kiss to the first British soldier I came across. You mustn't let anyone in the UK or elsewhere say otherwise.'[10]

Seventy per cent of the town was destroyed during the assault, and around 2,000 of its inhabitants perished, alongside many more thousands of Allied and German troops. But as ever, the men whose job it was to wage war from the air had little time to contemplate the stark reality of what was going on beneath them. As Jack Thompson recalled:

'We gave little thought to the lives below us and concentrated mainly on the precision of our work and our own safety. We took pride in being part of a great battle which was slowly and surely bringing us closer to victory over a foe sworn to destroy and enslave the people of our world. To have been part of such a giant operation, which destroyed a major stumbling block for our ground forces, was pretty inspiring for a very new, very green crew. None of our other thirty operations were a patch on this one in terms of the tremendous pride we felt in having been there.'

Jack and his crew had been lucky yet again; no enemy fighters came to the defence of Caen. The Luftwaffe was by now all but mortally affected by a lack of fuel, experienced pilots and aircraft. The German air force might have been down, but it was far from out, as Jack would later discover.

As mission followed mission, night flights lonely and isolated, day flights exposed and vulnerable, the most rewarding moment for the Thompson crew was always their return.

'In daylight we could see the magnificent towers of Lincoln Cathedral, high on a hill, just 10 miles from Wickenby. The cathedral was a comforting and reassuring landmark, a reminder that we had come home unscathed from another sortie against the enemy.'

At night, the relief of homecoming was even more palpable. All RAF stations had a call sign used by pilots to contact the control tower for landing instructions.

'Wickenby probably had the most appropriate designation in all of Bomber Command: "Grateful". There is no question that we were more than grateful to catch our first glimpse of the aerodrome after an operation. But at night, long before our arrival at Wickenby, our return to friendly shores was heralded by the sudden appearance of a myriad tiny red, green and white lights, which suddenly blinked on in the blackness like the beacons of fireflies. As we all arrived over England we switched on our navigation lights – green on the starboard wing, red on the port side and white on the tail. The little lights which appeared all around us were a reminder that we had not been unaccompanied during our lonely night vigil.'

Caution was always the watchword for Jack and his crew. They worked in unison to ensure the success of the mission, and their own survival. Halfway through their tour their expertise was rewarded by the opportunity to join the elite Pathfinder Force. Such invitations were only made to highly regarded, skilled and reliable crews.

A decision had to be made quickly.

'We talked it over and decided that if we managed to complete a regular tour we would be doing well. A Pathfinder tour consisted of fifty trips, which seemed like starting all over again. So we said, "Thanks, but no thanks," and continued to slug away with 12 Squadron.'

Perhaps not the response the Pathfinders were expecting, or usually got, but Jack's crew was simply sticking to the philosophy that had carried them through this far: safety first; don't press your luck. And slug away they did, growing fond of what became their regular Lancaster, *G-George*, which took them safely through nineteen of their operations.

Finally, on 6 November 1944, they were scheduled for the final mission and a daylight raid. It turned out to be one of the most hair-raising of their trips.

'Our target [was] the Gelsenkirchen petrol plant in the heart of the heavy industrial area of the Ruhr – "Happy Valley" as we called it. It was a clear blue sky but as we approached our target its beauty was marred by myriad puffs of black smoke from exploding anti-aircraft shells. I remembered the advice I'd been given at the very beginning of my operational service – "Don't worry about the black puffs: they're already done."'

But some shells were finding their mark.

'Suddenly the Lanc a few hundred yards to our right disappeared! All that remained was a small cloud of black smoke, and some odd bits and pieces spinning through the air. The poor sods didn't have a chance.'

Jack could only think to himself, with the brutal acceptance they'd all had to develop, *Better them than us*.

Moments later, the Perspex encasing the bomb aimer was pierced by flak. No injury, but too close a call. Tight-lipped, they completed their bomb run and headed back.

'Home ground had never seemed more desirable. Nothing could go wrong now, we told ourselves, on this, our last trip. We droned our way back as quickly as possible! I'm afraid that when we got home we were all so relieved and happy that we didn't really bid our faithful Lancaster *G-George* a proper goodbye. We just pulled away in the transit bus from the big bird without so much as a backward glance, leaving her standing stalwart and alone. It would be the last time any of us would ever see her. We had undergone enough fright, enough tension, enough "adventure", as well as some exhilaration, and had seen enough awe-inspiring sights to last us a lifetime – and all in a little more than four months. At the party that night we drank and sang and reminisced with a feeling of sheer relief – which was so different from the artificial bravado at other, earlier Mess parties. The Station Commander wasn't too happy about losing one of his most experienced crews, but we didn't mind. That was his problem! We'd all made it, we were all happy.'

Jack's crew had been lucky. Amid the thousands of casualties, they had survived a tour of Bomber Command relatively unscathed. They had done their duty and were more than content to get away from the war. As Canadians, they could return home, and there were few backward glances as they departed.

'We said goodbye to RAF Wickenby and we five Canadians were on our way home. I don't know how the others felt as the war continued in Europe for another six months. Personally, I was pleased to be home, but at the same time felt strangely lost in Canada. Most of all I regretted not being in Britain at the end – that great day in history which saw the final collapse of the Nazi Empire which all of us Allied servicemen and women had helped bring about.'

\* \* \*

As Jack Thompson's career with Bomber Command had begun, Maurice Garlick's adventures as an RAF evader south-east of Paris were entering a new phase.

They had pushed their luck by openly celebrating D-Day, and it was now a time for caution. After two hazardous but comfortable months, Maurice and his fellow fugitives parted company with their generous hosts and protectors, Marius and Blanche. Two members of the local Resistance arrived, under cover of darkness; their chauffeur and transport were ready and waiting. Postman Joe in his wood-burning, steam-driven Citroën drove them deep into the forests west of Troyes, where they were introduced to another Resistance cell and two downed American airmen who were hiding out with them.

Later, in the high summer, Joe brought news that the Americans were advancing steadily northwards from the Mediterranean coast. The advance from the south, Operation Dragoon, the counterpart to Operation Overlord, was under way, and it was time to try to join them. Ever-resourceful, Joe managed to organise two wood-burning trucks, which Maurice and his companions draped with French flags, and, together with an escort of *maquisards* – members of the French Resistance – they drove cautiously towards the last reported American position.

'We traversed many side roads and back streets, refuelling more than once from the many log piles stacked at strategic intervals along the country roads. Our hearts were in our mouths and our fingers on our triggers, but there was no sign of the Germans. At last we rounded a long bend, and there in front of us we saw the Stars and Stripes billowing in a sunny sky. We also found ourselves staring down the barrels of a number of very businesslike machine guns.'

One of the American evaders in their party quickly cried out, 'It's OK. We're on your side!'

'His heavy Southern drawl instantly broke the ice. Soon my crewmates and I, and our French saviours, were being treated to bottles of Coca Cola, chewing gum, Lucky Strike cigarettes, bars of chocolate, and, best of all, mugs of steaming hot, real coffee.'[11]

Liberation!

They were not yet in the clear, however. The Germans may have retreated, but they were expected to reform and make a stand, perhaps at nearby Troyes, south-east of Paris. Meanwhile, such chaos reigned that the US Army could only take responsibility for their own men. The Britons – Maurice and his two fellow crewmen – would have to stay with the French Resistance until their own forces arrived. Dispirited, and not relishing the prospect of waiting, Maurice and his crewmates, Danny and Mac, eventually made their own way to Paris, arriving late on 25 August, the very day that the German governor, General Dietrich von Choltitz, having defied Hitler's orders to destroy the French capital, surrendered it to the Allies.

'We didn't realise, as we drove along the Champs-Élysées on that warm summer evening amid the cheers of the crowds, that we were present at one of the great moments of history. We forgot that we were hungry, dirty and in desperate need of a loo. Suddenly I spotted a solitary Union Jack flying from a building facing the Arc de Triomphe.'

They presented themselves to a British Parachute Regiment officer, sitting behind an imposing desk.

'Shot-down flyers, eh?' he said. 'Well done, lads. Look, this place is a mess. Utter chaos. Come back tomorrow at 9 a.m. and I'll try to get an RAF liaison man for you. You'll have to fend for yourselves tonight. Oh, by the way, the Para officers are drinking at the Ritz Bar tonight and I'd be honoured if you'd join me.'

They were all longing for home, so when they heard they had been booked onto a noon flight a few days later, they started to count down the hours.

'Two smart US Army coaches took us to the airport, and there waiting for us was a beautiful RAF Dakota. I thought what a pleasant way this was to end my European Odyssey, but not without pausing for a moment and thinking about and mentally thanking all those very brave ordinary French people who nursed me back to health, and without whom my evasion and eventual escape would not have been possible; and most of whom I would never see again. Such is war!

'The flight home took about an hour. I'd made the big mistake of sitting between Danny and Mac, who regaled me and everyone else on board with long tales of their exploits as evaders. I'm sure all the other soldiers being repatriated on that trip were bored stiff. But a cheer went up when we saw the White Cliffs of Dover. We all crowded to the portholes and the pilot had to adjust the Dakota's trim. Danny said it felt rather like coming back from a raid. You more or less felt safe again. At last we landed gently at [RAF] Hendon. We three were the only ones to thank the pilot and his crew for a safe, comfortable and enjoyable trip. Camaraderie of the air, I suppose.'

They cleared military formalities then said their cheery goodbyes; like so many others, their friendship was broken up at the end of their tour and they went their separate ways. Maurice would never see his crewmates again. He had his burns checked, was issued with a new uniform, given a fortnight's pay, a fortnight's leave, and a rail pass.

Then he rang home.

'"Hello, Mum, how are you? This is your long-lost son Maurice speaking." I expected to hear *thump* as she fainted on hearing I was *back from the dead*.'

But Maurice's mother, like so many of the wartime generation, was made of sterner stuff. 'Goodness me!' she replied. 'Where have you been, you naughty boy?'

After a long bus and Tube journey, then a half-hour walk,

Maurice finally arrived back at his family home. It seemed dream-like. But the welcome was real enough, with flags and bunting flying, and neighbours gathering to wish him well.

'After much hugging and kissing, Mum produced the "Fatted Calf": roast beef, Yorkshire pudding, runner beans, new potatoes, and tomatoes fresh from Dad's allotment. I wondered how Mum had done the meal on the strict wartime rationing – it looked like a month's supply on our dining table. We opened a bottle of the best red wine, followed the meat with cheese, then one of Mum's specialities: rhubarb crumble. Once we'd finished, and Dad and I were nursing glasses of Armagnac, I told them a little of my escapades. "You certainly have the knack of getting adventure thrust upon you," my dad said!'

Maurice raised his glass to his mother in salute. 'Nothing, simply nothing, could match that meal.'

His war was finally over. It was Wednesday 6 September 1944, four months since Maurice had been shot down. He too was one of the lucky ones, the survivors.

Not all his comrades would enjoy the same fate. And it wasn't just enemy action they needed to fear; sometimes their beloved Lancaster could present perilous dangers.

*Ken Trent*

Soon after his twenty-second birthday late in 1944, on a night raid to destroy the railway yards at Aschaffenburg near Frankfurt, Ken Trent realised something was very wrong with his Lancaster. 'The kite was beginning to feel sluggish and the engines were struggling to push us any higher.'[12] He could see light glittering on the crust of ice building up on the wings. The ice thickened, changing their shape – and hence their aerodynamics – as they climbed. It was starting to coat the propellers too, which the engines now laboured to turn.

Their Lancaster was struggling.

'It felt tired as I tried to keep it at altitude, like a man with a huge pack on his back trying to climb up a mountain but sinking to his knees with the effort. The weight was building up alarmingly, with layers of frozen water adding to the weight of the bombs we were carrying. Ice had also formed on the control surfaces of the ailerons, making them stiff and hard to move; and there was a risk that their mechanisms could freeze up and go completely solid.'

Ken knew that if things got any worse, his Lancaster would soon be impossible to control. There was only one thing for it: descend and hope the warmer air would solve the problem. But the process was far from simple.

'If we descended too fast, the ice could still be frozen on the control surfaces and I might not be able to pull up in time. Too slowly, and the ice might become even thicker. The altimeter unwound as we dropped through the cloud in a shallow dive, but the layers of ice on the wings disturbed the airflow and the extra speed started shaking the kite as it tried to cope with the extra stresses being placed on it. Down, down, down into the all-obscuring darkness, and I found myself wondering what the hell might happen to us. We had coped with flak, fighters and searchlights, but tonight Mother Nature was our worst enemy. I was beginning to think the gamble might not have paid off when a loud crash against the fuselage shook the kite, and lifted my spirits enormously. "Don't worry," I reassured the crew. "It's just the first ice coming off the props. It's exactly what I wanted to hear!"'

More crashes and bangs followed, as melting shards bounced off the fuselage. The noise was music to Ken's ears. 'The aircraft began to respond to the controls again, and the Merlins started to sing as the weight came off the propellers.'

A similar, daylight sortie to Cologne was equally perilous for Ken and his crew. His rear gunner, little Clarence Dalby, known to all as Clarrie, was looking a little off-colour but declared himself fit to fly; it was just a spot of stomach ache.

'Take-off went smoothly and as we crossed the coast, climbing steadily, we spotted the unmistakable anvil-headed shape of a huge cumulonimbus [thunder] cloud straight ahead.'

Ken wrestled to keep the aircraft under control as it forged its way upwards through fierce gusts of wind and pelting rain. The crew felt like they'd been squeezed into a giant cocktail shaker, and when they were clear of the worst, Clarrie realised he was about to pay the price. His strangulated voice came over the intercom.

'"Sorry, Skip, but I need the bog."

'To ask this early in the mission was no doubt due to his tummy problem, but also probably to the pressure reduction at 22,000ft – which often turned a simple call of nature into a need for immediate action.'

To get to the Elsan toilet back in the main body of the aircraft, behind the two sets of doors isolating his position, the rear gunner had to align his turret precisely before sliding open the doors that encased him.

Then, suddenly, a bloodcurdling scream reverberated across the intercom.

'"Help me! HELP ME!"

'"What the hell's going on? Clarrie?"

'"Help me! My legs! HELP ME!"

'He sounded like a stuck pig, screaming full-blast into our ears – a dreadful sound. It terrified me, and I froze for a few moments in confusion. What on earth had happened to him?'

Ken concentrated on keeping the Lancaster level as Clarrie's heart-stopping shrieks continued. Noel Wadsworth, the bomb aimer, headed aft with a portable oxygen bottle, joined by the mid-upper gunner, Ricky Riccomini.

Noel soon reported back. It wasn't good news.

'Skip, we've got a problem. The turret wasn't locked open properly, it's rotated and trapped his legs. He's caught halfway out of the turret.'

As Clarrie had pushed himself backwards through the doors, the power-driven turret had swivelled and was still trying to turn, but his trapped and shattered legs were jamming the mechanism. It was possible they might be severed if his crewmates couldn't do anything, and his anguished cries continued to drown out the roar of their engines.

Ken made his decision.

'Right. I'm going to feather and stop the port outer engine, the one which drives power to the rear turret; it will stop trying to turn, and you might be able to push it round and free Clarrie's legs.'

The job would have to be done quickly; closing down the engine might freeze the coolant, risking a fire when it restarted. It also meant a temporary loss of height. But there was no other option. The screaming stopped, and Noel reported that Clarrie had passed out, but they'd been successful.

'Got him, Skip. Ricky and I are going to put him on the rest bed and get him back onto oxygen quick.'

Ken restarted the port outer, but their troubles were far from over. His worst fears were realised as it burst into flames. Is this what it would come down to? They had survived so much danger in hostile skies, but a sequence of unimagined events – nothing to do with the enemy – was now putting them in mortal danger. The fire extinguisher eventually doused the flames, but Ken was immediately faced with yet another decision. He was one engine and a rear gunner down.

'Should we go home? We'd passed *over* the storm front and would be unable to climb over it again on just three engines. On the other hand, we could dump the bombs, lose height, and return safely under the clouds. Or we could carry on.

'"OK, everyone. We're going to go ahead, bomb as planned. Is Clarrie OK?"

'"He's quiet now, Skip. Think his legs are broken, but he'll live."

'"Make sure he's strapped in safely, Noel, then go back to the nose. Ricky, you go back too. And keep your eyes extra peeled."

'Not one of them expressed any sign of doubt or disagreement. We were as one.'

With one engine down, they were steadily losing height, but they made it over the target at 15,000ft and dropped their bombs successfully, only two minutes behind schedule. Ken called, 'I'm putting the nose down to get low and fast. We want to be under 1,000ft by the time we reach the cloud.'

Luck was still on their side and they made it safely back to base.

'They took Clarrie out carefully, nursing his injured legs, as my flight engineer and I went through our post-flight shut-down drill in silence. We had been in the air for five and a half hours. The rum I'd been looking forward to tasted even better than I imagined. I could finally exhale and start to relax.'

But there was more to come.

A few days later Ken was approached by his Wing Commander, hand outstretched.

'"Congratulations, Ken," he said, handing me an envelope. "You've been awarded the Distinguished Flying Cross." Naturally, I couldn't wait to get the DFC ribbon sewn onto my tunic, but I was very aware that the award was something I shared with my crew. Without their dedication, bravery and skill, it could all have ended very differently that day.'

\* \* \*

Autumn 1944 saw Bomber Command released from most of its commitments to support the advance through France, to begin one of the most controversial episodes of the air war. Arthur Harris remained determined to refocus his men and machines on the only mission he had ever really believed in – destroying German cities and the factories, homes and people that were their lifeblood.

As Ken Trent was being awarded his DFC, freshly fledged, eager airmen were arriving at their new bases, ready to join the fray. At RAF Metheringham, a newly formed crew took stock of their quarters. Among them were rear gunner Ron Needle, wireless operator Harry Stunell, and navigator Ken Darke. They were impatient for action, but first had to learn their place; they were the new boys, mere replacements for those who would never come home again. Old lags sat round a table, smoking and playing Monopoly. The atmosphere was tense.

'Everyone seems a bit flak happy [jittery] round here,' said Ron, hoping to break the ice. He was mistaken. One of the veterans growled, 'You'd be bloody flak happy if you'd had shells up your arse.'

Ron's enthusiasm, however, was undiminished.

'It was a nice hut with an iron stove, and we had sheets for the first time in the RAF! It was plain and spartan, no wardrobe or cabinet, just a bed. I didn't need much space because I didn't have much except for my RAF uniforms and a few civvies in a kitbag. I liked RAF Metheringham; it was a decent place, but I suppose that's because it was my first real base with my first real squadron. I felt happy; ready to get on with the war.'[13]

They were joining Bomber Command at a time when it was approaching the size and power that Harris had always dreamt of. More aircraft were coming off the production lines. More men were being trained to fill the new squadrons, and navigation and bomb-aiming equipment was improving. The first time he'd put a thousand bombers in the air, Harris had had to throw in virtually anything with wings to get the numbers up. Now he had men and machines to spare. But where should this immensely powerful force be directed? Harris still believed he could make the bloody conquest of German soil by ground troops unnecessary. Not everyone agreed, but he believed that by devastating the cities far away from the front line, he could visit the full horror of war upon their inhabitants, weaken their resolve, and encourage the mindset that would lead them to surrender. He sent his bombers out on all fronts. As a result, 'the crews of this period certainly had variety. They could fly by night or day. Their logbooks might contain details of raids on gun batteries near Calais, old-faithfuls like Essen and Cologne, the dykes on the Dutch island of Walcheren, oil refineries, canals or the railway yards in some German town they had never heard of – all in rapid succession.'[14]

In the middle of October, Harris sent a force of 1,013 Lancasters, Halifaxes and Mosquitos to Duisburg as part of Operation Hurricane, a deliberate exercise to intimidate the enemy and demonstrate the overwhelming air superiority of the Allies.

'It felt unreal to be over Germany in broad daylight, but it certainly made for more relaxed navigation. The Rhine was easily visible and pinpoints could be obtained, which made life easier. It was nine in the morning when we came over our target, Lancasters as far as one could see. Thousands of angry black puffs filled the sky and the going got a bit rough. By 9.15 the city was under a pall of smoke and looked like a burning wreck as we headed home.'[15]

Bomber Command returned to Duisburg that same night to pulverise what was left after the morning run; the new crews could see the fires of Duisburg a hundred miles ahead.

'Poor Duisburg received another huge battering and the immense smoking fires could again be seen all the way back to the Dutch coast. We all thought that perhaps it was a case of gilding the lily a bit but, after all, Happy Valley had harassed, killed and wounded us for years, so the feeling basically was that we had got some of our own back.'[16]

British and American bombers had flown 2,589 sorties to Duisburg, with the loss of just twenty-four aircraft. Nearly 9,000 tons of bombs fell on the city, killing around 2,500 civilians; it was shock and awe of a type not experienced since Hamburg in 1943.

Operation Hurricane was another nail in the coffin of Nazi industrial and production infrastructure, but they weren't yet beaten. Battle-hardened German troops would soon make a comprehensive stand in north-western Europe over the bitter midwinter, launching a month-long counteroffensive – the Battle of the Bulge – which brought the Allied advance to an unexpected standstill. Their new jet fighters were making the first forays into battle, and although the threat from V1 'Doodlebugs' had disappeared as Allied land forces overran the launch sites, the more terrifying V2 rockets were still targeting south-east England, killing and maiming thousands.

After five final training flights on their new squadron, Ron Needle, Harry Stunell and Ken Darke were ready to take their own war to the enemy by mid-November. Their first few ops were relatively uneventful, but then they ran into their first German fighter: a solitary JU88 over the railway yards in Heilbronn, north of Stuttgart. Rear gunner Ron was scouring the skies when he spotted the dark shape lurking on their starboard side.

'I shouted over the intercom to take evasive action. I remember opening fire, but in truth I can't remember using my gunsight or working out any angles. Then, to my horror, the guns jammed. According to my training I should have freed the jam by carrying out certain drills. But I didn't attempt to do any! All I could think of was to shout instructions to Jimmy, our pilot, so he could take evasive action. Six times the enemy fighter attacked us, before breaking off and flying away. In the heat of the moment I was reacting instinctively, without thought. There was a sense of fear hovering in the background but the reality was that this was what we had to do – all I could see was the shape of an aircraft heading in to try to kill us and I needed to do something about it. It was a bit of a shock! Here was my enemy and I needed to kill him before he could kill me and my crew. After it was over I had a chance to mop my brow and think, *Wow, we were lucky there!* I felt very proud that, after we landed, the whole crew came up to congratulate me. I was pleased to be part of this group – we were all growing together amid our shared experience of war.'

Ron's long-time girlfriend, Sylvia Valente, had to celebrate her birthday without him on 21 December. He missed her terribly while on operations. 'She was the love of my life, the girl of my dreams! Always well dressed and a great dance partner.' They didn't get to see each other as often as they wished, and Ron, like almost all of the bomber airmen, was determined to keep love and war apart.

'When we were together I never spoke to Sylvia about what I was doing or seeing during ops. The war was kept compartmentalised, I never mentioned it and she never asked. We wrote regularly about day-to-day life; any parties or family events, but nothing about the war. I suppose we just didn't want to voice any fears or concerns: you just got on with it. Perhaps we just didn't want to tempt fate?'

Thoughts were turning wistfully to the festive season. Could they dare hope that Christmas 1944 might be the last of the war? Though the mood lifted when the weather closed in and operations had to be cancelled as the big day approached, most still tried to banish the idea from their minds. On Ron's base at RAF Metheringham, preparations for the Yuletide season had been in progress for some time. The WAAF handicraft classes were increasingly popular, with airmen making soft toys and other Christmas gifts for children.[17]

Entertainment geared up too, starting with the Dramatic Society's production of *George and Margaret* by Gerald Savory, 'directed by Corporal Jordan', then a Canadian show, presented by another RAF station's visiting troupe. The latter performance was not a success with Metheringham's Operations Record Book; its 'Report on Entertainment for December 1944' recorded rather severely, 'This was an all-female party, well-dressed and at moments spectacular, but lacked the downright comedy flashes which one expects from these Canadian shows, probably due to the absence of males in the party.'[18]

\* \* \*

The last operation of Ken Trent's first tour – an attack on the railway yards at Bonn – fell on 21 December, Ron Needle's girlfriend's birthday. As they put their nose down and turned for home, they were buzzed by something small and ultra-fast.

'"My God, did you see that? Did you get a shot at it?"

'"No chance. Did you see the speed it was going at?"

This was Ken and his crew's first encounter with the Messerschmitt 262, the world's first operational jet-powered fighter aircraft, and another sign that there was plenty of fight left in the Nazi machine. With their incredible performance and a top speed of around 540mph, if they could be produced in numbers, and be kept manned and fuelled, they could prove to be a game-changer.

'Having failed to shoot us down with conventional, propeller-driven fighters, the Germans had launched their new jet interceptor and our gunners were stunned. They were much faster than anything else in the sky and they tore into any bomber foolish enough to poke its head out of the clouds. As the jet came back my gunners made our kite vibrate with the recoil of their guns as I pointed us into the nearest cloud cover.

'"I think we got him, Skip! He's on fire! He's on fire!"

'But the jet didn't seem to be damaged, apart from the huge plumes of smoke and fire shooting out from the engines on either wing. It was just going faster. We reached the cloud then headed for home as fast as our Merlins could carry us.'

They were still not out of the woods. Before they reached home they were rerouted because of lack of visibility to RAF Ludford Magna, which was equipped with FIDO – fuel pipes with holes in them that lined each side of the runway. When ignited, they lit up the landing area and dispersed some of the fog.

'As we got closer to Ludford, I could see the glow separate into twin lines of fire, showing that we were dead on track. Startling amid the darkness and the fog, the flames made it appear as if we were landing in one of the burning cities we had left behind us. I took care to align the Lancaster's long nose exactly with the centre of the runway. The smoke and flames licked up to meet us as I took the aircraft slowly down. The final operation of my tour ended amid fog and flame on an unfamiliar runway, with relief at having made it back safely.'

But Ken was in for an unpleasant shock. As soon as he landed, he was informed that his mother was dangerously ill in the Middlesex Hospital in London. He was to leave immediately. A car had been arranged to take him to the nearest railway station and a travel pass was thrust into his hand. He just had time to take off his flying gear and hand it to a fellow crew member before he was off, all thoughts of Christmas obliterated.

He arrived to devastating news. 'Mum had terminal cancer. The doctors had operated but there was nothing they could do. She was fifty-eight years old, and had just been told she had three months to live.'[19] It was a terrible blow to a man who had spent the previous months fighting off death in the skies. Now, there was nothing he could do to shape the future. But the stiff upper lip would still be important. 'Be bright, be chatty, be normal,' the nurse advised him. 'She's so proud of you being a pilot. Don't let her see you upset.' Ken made himself smile while he was with his mother, who also sought refuge from grief in cheerfulness, declaring, 'While there's life, there's hope.'

It was a frustrating and deeply worrying time for Ken Trent, and all of his comrades who had begun to hope that – just possibly – an end might be in sight. Now, to compound his terrible personal news, it all seemed to be touch and go again. Vicious winter weather continued to make flying all but impossible, so much of the fighting was being done on the ground.

The Germans had launched their counterattack in the Ardennes. Fierce conflict raged across the forests of eastern Belgium, northeastern France and Luxembourg throughout the winter, involving over a million combatants. Awaiting his new posting after a successful first tour, Ken reflected, 'As we slept in our chilly but safe beds in Lincolnshire, thousands of American and British soldiers were dug in under attack in sub-zero temperatures. The Germans pushed a huge gap into the Allied lines and caused many units to retreat in confusion. We were powerless to help.'

*Ted Watson ready for a flight*

Flight engineer Ted Watson's thoughts were also turning to Christmas as he returned from a raid on two pocket battleships, the *Admiral Scheer* and the *Lützow*, moored at the northern Polish port of Gdynia. Flying low at 200mph to avoid radar and fighters, he and his crew were suddenly aware of an eerie sight.

'A call from Jim in the rear turret made me look back over the top of our Lanc in time to see a bright, luminous vapour trail rising up and arching high into the sky over our heads. Higher and higher it went, until eventually lost to my sight. It was a V2 rocket on its way to London – the first of several I would see.'[20]

It hardly seemed possible to Ted that only nine years earlier, as a schoolboy, he'd been so impressed by his very first sight of an aeroplane of any kind. Now, rockets were bringing death and destruction to Antwerp, Paris, London and Maastricht. Just a few weeks earlier, one had detonated at a Woolworths department store in the south-east London district of New Cross, killing 160 people and injuring a further 108.

Tony Rollins, just thirteen at the time, was in the area selling the model aeroplanes he constructed to make a few extra pennies.

'Since there were few toys around I was able to sell them to a shop in New Cross Gate, opposite Woolworths. I had started to walk the few hundred yards home when there was a huge explosion. The V2s always exploded with two "crumps", one quickly followed by a second. I knew immediately it was a V2 and as I looked back in the direction of the noise I saw a huge tower of smoke with all sorts of pieces turning, twisting and glinting, heading skyward. I turned and ran back to the scene. I shall never forget what I witnessed. The front of the shop I had just sold my aeroplanes to was completely blown in, and on the other side of the road was a huge smouldering crater. Sheets of corrugated steel had been placed along some of the gutters to cover what was left of people and blood was seeping out from beneath. There was debris everywhere. I saw several people dead beneath telegraph poles and there were bodies and wounded and maimed laying randomly all over the place.'[21]

Ted Watson shuddered at the thought of how much more death and destruction they might suffer before the Nazi menace was finally crushed. Others wondered if it ever would be. They reached the English coast without incident, but fog, the great winter downside for the Lincolnshire air bases, had rolled in from the sea, and their Lancaster was diverted from their own base at RAF East Kirkby to RAF Woodbridge near Ipswich.

So Christmas Day 1944 began badly for Ted and his crew, still stranded some distance from home.

'With no prospect of flying back to East Kirkby, the CO sent some transport to pick us up along with the other marooned squadron crews. We piled into the back of the three-tonner and set off at a frenetic pace, our driver obviously anxious not to miss the festivities and his Christmas dinner. The lorry lurched left and right around the bends while we clung tightly to the canopy supports. Predictably, we crashed. There was a huge bang, the lorry left the road, ploughed through a hedge and hit a tree.'

Fortunately most of the passengers, though badly shaken up, got away with cuts and bruises. Ted and his compatriots were finally ferried the last few miles to RAF East Kirkby, where they arrived just in time for Christmas dinner and the subsequent dance and party.

Christmas Day at RAF Metheringham saw many of the aircrew awakening with steaming hangovers after a party in the Sergeants' Mess the night before. All the officers had been invited, so Ron Needle, Ken Darke, Harry Stunell and the rest of their crew could celebrate the relative peace of the festive season together.

'What a party it was! Towards the end of the evening, when most of us were rather tiddly, we were singing bawdy songs and cutting each other's ties off below the knot. It was such a nice escape from the reality of war; a chance to let off steam. We were just grateful to be alive to enjoy it. Of course nobody ever said any of this, not even among my friends in the crew; there was never any discussion, no mention, of previous deaths or the loss of friends.'

Alcohol was always a good way to numb any pain and allay any concerns for the future, so the party went on late into the night.

'Afterwards Harry and I made our way back to our beds. We awoke on Christmas Day feeling less than first class and certainly not wanting to attend the mandatory parade. We both agreed that our Flight Commander would be suffering from a hangover and therefore unable to take the parade. Not a bit of it! Ken Darke, our navigator, came into our billet, sent by the Flight Commander to get us up. Everyone looked terrible and the parade was eventually dismissed.'

Ron Needle and his Lancaster crewmates were free to enjoy the rest of the day.

'A day to forget the war and remember the good things in life. There were no presents from my family; we just didn't do that sort of thing in the war, but the food was wonderful! A full Christmas dinner with all the trimmings: turkey, sprouts, roast potatoes, gravy. What a wonderful way to celebrate the end of that year and look forward to the next.'

Ken Trent allowed his thoughts to be diverted briefly from his sick mother, who had rallied a little.

'Come the day, the draughty old Nissen hut which was our Mess was transformed into a nightclub. Spruced up in our best togs, we arrived to find the bar already doing a roaring trade. The squadron padre was already well oiled, propping up the bar and chatting up a couple of local girls whom we knew – by reputation only! – to be prostitutes. I've often wondered whether he knew, and whether he managed to get his end away.'

Crewmen were dancing with local girls to music blaring from a gramophone, and a blazing fire, piled high with logs, was creating a wonderful fug.

'The atmosphere was very happy, enhanced by the presence of the girls and the realisation that we'd survived to celebrate another Christmas. Group Captain Donkin performed his party trick of drinking a pint of beer while standing on his head, and there were all sorts of other games and challenges typical of any group of young, sloshed people.'

The night wore on, and dawn was approaching when they realised that Group Captain Donkin was no longer with them. Ken had dropped a heavy plant pot on his foot earlier, which he'd taken in good part, but had the drink and the injury been too much for him? The answer came soon enough with his reappearance, sober and grim. His voice cut through the noise and brought the party to a rapid halt.

'Right, chaps. I'm sorry, but that's it for tonight. The party's over. Ladies, would you please leave the Mess and make your way home. All flying personnel to the crew room immediately.'

Donkin had laid on jugs of hot coffee. Not a good sign. The weather had cleared. They were to attack the town of St Vith, near the Belgian frontier, which the Germans had recently retaken from the advancing Americans and turned into a heavily fortified citadel, standing in the way of further Allied advance through south-eastern Belgium. The war was far from over, so hangovers took a back seat, and the work of Bomber Command continued.

Boxing Day at RAF East Kirkby also saw the fog lifting, and it was business as usual for Ted Watson's crew.

'We all wondered what the New Year might bring. The war was

going in our favour, but there was certainly no discussion about it nearly being over. The notion that victory might possibly be in sight was simply never mentioned. There was still plenty of fighting to be done before the Nazis would capitulate.

'The Lancaster was the thing which bound us together – she was the constant in our lives. She was always there, rain or shine, and every day we would climb aboard her and entrust our survival to her, to our own skill, and to a good deal of luck.'

Ron Needle hadn't seen his beloved girlfriend, or his family, over Christmas. 'The last time I'd seen Sylvia was months before, in September, when I was back home on leave.' And there were certainly no thoughts about the future, or what 1945 might bring.

'There was no discussion about any end of the war – we were under no illusion that there was still much to be done, and we just took each day as it came. We never took anything for granted; people were still dying and we didn't know if the war would be over by the *next* Christmas, or if we would be alive to see it! We lived life to the full because we didn't know how much life we had left to live.'

Ron's navigator, Ken Darke, wrote to his sister, another Sylvia, whose birthday was on New Year's Eve:

*I hope you get the book* – Everybody's Political What's What,[22] *by Bernard Shaw – on 31st and with it I am sending my love and very best wishes for your birthday. Having been back at this desolate spot for ten days I am starting looking forward to my next leave, which is due on 22 January. Things are OK as usual up here but I have not flown for a week so it is about time I did something to earn my keep.*[23]

Ken, Ron and Harry would all be back in action and 'earning their keep' soon enough.

# CHAPTER FOURTEEN

## SAVED BY THE BELL

The death throes of Ron Needle's flaming Lancaster, crashing through the dense woodland, still rang in his head. From where he lay, he could see the silhouette of the ruined aircraft. Wings torn off, back broken, still smouldering; his friends presumably dead inside.

'It was no longer a beautiful machine, it was dying before my eyes, blackened and charred; it was a wreck in the forest. I felt a personal loss as I gazed at her but I thanked her for my survival – if it hadn't been for the strength and determination of this Lanc I had no doubt I would not be alive. She saved my life.'[1]

As dawn broke in the silence of the snow on Monday 8 January 1945, Ron had a moment to reflect on how much had happened in the past twelve hours: the previous night's raid on Munich, the near-collision with another Lancaster, the terrifying attempt to keep their aircraft from going down over the target, then the crash itself. The fire, the exploding ammunition, his friend Jack Elson's legs, shattered, bleeding and burned, hanging from his hammock seat, still suspended in the mid-upper turret. His desperate and agonising escape from the wreckage. The belief that he was the only survivor. It all floated through his mind like fragments of a half-forgotten nightmare. Now, badly injured, helpless and alone at the edge of the forest, it was small comfort to remember they'd come down in a part of France already liberated by the Allies, for he knew if he stayed where he was much longer, he would die.

'As the night stretched on I prayed that someone had heard the crash and would come to our aid. I was freezing, but, strangely, much of the pain had disappeared. It seemed no help was coming, and my own sense of survival took over. There were no other thoughts – friends, family, my wonderful Sylvia – I just knew I had to find help.'

Seriously injured (it later transpired he had suffered a broken ankle, punctured lung and dislocated shoulder) and unable to stand, he dragged himself along a nearby track, hoping to escape the dense forest.

'Suddenly I heard church bells ringing! That spurred me on. Making a supreme effort I started to crawl in the general direction of their peal. I suppose I must have crawled about 200 yards towards the sound. Then, feeling I could go no further, I began to call out feebly, "Help! Help!" Thank God, looking up I saw my saviours rushing towards me. Not knowing how they would react, I kept repeating, "RAF – English." But the sense of relief was overwhelming – I was safe and had hope of survival again. Badly injured, vision fading, I didn't realise how significant this moment was to become.'

One of his rescuers, twenty-year-old André Fromont, was the man who'd been ringing the 7 a.m. bells, the Angelus call to prayer, in his village church.

André remembered that morning well.

'During the night it'd been snowing heavily and it was freezing cold. I'd taken some milk to my grandfather who told me that maybe an aircraft had crashed nearby during the night – he lived close to the forest, and he'd heard bullets exploding and seen lights and sparks. When I left Grandfather's, I ran into my cousin Albert and asked him if he'd heard the noise of a crash, but the storm during the night had made such a noise that he hadn't heard a thing.

'We decided to walk towards the spot my grandfather had indicated. André Bouchot, the deputy mayor, came with us; but we were cautious – maybe a German aircraft had crashed, and we were afraid they might shoot us. We'd had bad treatment from them and were very hungry. There was often nothing but swedes to eat so we couldn't take any food but we did take a stretcher and a pocket flask of *Mirabelle* plum liqueur.[2] Finally we arrived in a grove and saw a young man leaning back against a small tree. He was very cold, shivering, crying out for help. At first we thought he might be a German and shoot us, but he was making signs with his hands to tell us he was a comrade. I gave him the velvet muffler my mother had made, and some *Mirabelle* to keep him warm. Not too much, in case it might make him sick. Then we carried him back. How heavy he was! My shoulders were sore, and it wasn't easy, walking in deep snow. But he was lucky. If they'd crashed a few metres further along, on the other side of the hill, they wouldn't have heard the bells.'[3]

Ron's French rescuers carefully carried him, barely conscious, to Monsieur Bouchot's house in the tiny village of Méligny-le-Grand, where the bells had been ringing in the Roman Catholic church of St Evre. It was a small community of just 120 people, some 40 miles east of Nancy. Bouchot's wife Mariette gave Ron a boiled egg, and the men who'd carried him to safety fortified him further with more plum brandy. They'd called an ambulance, and while they waited, Ron used sign language to ask Mariette to cut the boot off his injured right foot. 'I could tell by her expression that she didn't want to destroy the boot, but my foot hurt so much when she tried to remove it, that she gave up and cut it away.'

There was further bad news. After dropping Ron off, André had returned to the forest and found the wreckage of the Lancaster.

'What a horrible sight we found! The cockpit was still there but the wings had been torn off the aircraft and it was a burnt-out shell. There were no survivors; just mangled corpses. There was nothing we could do so we sadly returned home.'

Ron was devastated to hear André's news. 'The confirmation that my crew were all dead came like a physical blow. We had been brothers, and losing them was like losing my family.'

Despite the trauma still ahead of him, Ron was very lucky indeed. Méligny was only a few miles south-east of an American military hospital in nearby Commercy, where he was soon lying in a warm, clean bed. Though his own recovery was still in the balance. His injured right foot had frostbite and gangrene was setting in, and an American doctor explained that part of the foot might have to be amputated. But the doctor had also brought some truly wonderful news.

After his own escape through the burning Lancaster's astrodome, wireless operator Harry Stunell had struggled to his feet in the snow, amid the stench of burning rubber and his own burnt body. His face had escaped the worst effects of the fire, thanks to his helmet and oxygen mask, but his legs and hands were seriously burnt.

'My neck had been jarred by the impact. My trousers had burnt away apart from the crotch area thanks to the protection of the stout parachute harness straps. Embers were still glowing in my flying boots and fuel and ammunition continued to explode.'[4]

The quiet of the forest was also shattered as bursts of crackling flame blasted from the Lancaster, scorching the upper branches of the trees. The fierce, bone-chilling wind was taking no prisoners. Harry staggered away from the dying beast and collapsed into a shallow ditch, totally spent. But he knew that if he didn't now drive himself on, he could die where he lay.

'I was freezing cold, stumbling along aimlessly, with tattered strips of skin flapping about in the high wind. I craved rest but could not stop. I had to keep my central engines running, my lifeblood circulating. I was naked from the waist down and I knew what would happen if I collapsed in such arctic conditions.'

Harry reached the top of a mound and, exhausted, surveyed his surroundings. In the distance, he saw a tiny pinprick of light. It was about 2 a.m., three hours after the crash. He shuffled through the drifting snow, desperate not to lose sight of the light, when he found himself caught in a barbed-wire fence. Hauling himself through it, he made his way to a low stone building from which the dim light seemed to be emanating. It was a sheep-pen. The anxious animals backed away as he tried to get among them for warmth. He buried himself in the dry straw instead, and finally allowed sleep to overcome him.

Harry awoke to the tolling of a bell. The same Angelus church bell that was guiding his friend and crewmate Ron Needle to safety. Crawling out of the pen, hardly daring to believe he was still alive, he headed in the direction of the sound. And straight into the prongs of a pitchfork. He found himself surrounded by a group of grim-faced men. Two of them held him fast.

'*Boche*,' they growled.

Not impressed when he called out, '*Anglais*, not *Deutsch*!', they looked at him without pity, jabbing the pitchfork at his chest.

Harry had forgotten his dog-tags, so he couldn't prove who he was. Then he remembered he had a couple of British coins in his breast pocket. He signalled his captors to check. Still suspicious, one of them fished out the coins. A florin (10p) and a shilling (5p); the King's head on both! The coins were passed around, and gradually the Frenchmen's expressions softened. The man with the pitchfork lowered it, and reached out a helping hand.[5]

Back in the village, André Fromont and his friends soon learned about the second survivor of the crash.

'We were told that another person had spent the fatal night in the sheep-pen at the edge of the village. This airman had heard the Angelus bells too, and managed to reach the pond. Monsieur Giroux found him when he took his horses there to water them. The young man was badly wounded and burnt. Giroux took him home, where his wife used a warming pan to heat a bed for him, since he was chilled to the bone. Then of course she had to return the warming pan to the neighbour she'd borrowed it from, since it's the only way we have to warm our beds in winter and the bedrooms are not heated.'

That same afternoon, American medics from the nearby hospital arrived to take Harry Stunell, still traumatised by his experience, to the same hospital where Ron was already being treated.

Ron was overjoyed to hear the American doctor's news that his mate Harry Stunell was alive, albeit badly burnt, and now being cared for in the very same place. But there was no time for a reunion.

'I didn't actually see Harry in hospital because we were both so badly injured. I wouldn't meet him again until many years later.

My leg was in a very bad way, the gangrene had taken too strong a hold and when the doctor told me they would have to amputate, I just told them to get on with it. There was nothing I could do.' The American surgeons removed half his right foot, carefully sparing the big toe, so he'd have a chance of being able to walk again.

A few days later, better news about Harry arrived – the burns to his face were superficial and would leave no scars. The damage to his hands and the backs of his legs was far more serious and would need extensive treatment. They would affect him for the rest of his life. But they had both survived, and still had their future ahead of them.

Their thoughts now turned to their friends, whose lives had ended in a freezing French forest: Jim Scott, twenty-three, the pilot and captain; Bob Dunlop, also twenty-three, the bomb aimer; mid-upper gunner Jack Elson, just nineteen; Ken Darke, twenty-one, the navigator; Les Knapman, the flight engineer and 'old man' of the crew at twenty-six. Five friends gone, five families receiving the worst news. But just five of over 55,000 of the men of Bomber Command who didn't make it home.

\* \* \*

Soon after the operation, Ron was shipped home to England, first on a hospital train which had an overnight stop in Paris. Unable to visit the fabled City of Light, Ron promised himself he'd come back one day. He had no idea how or when that might happen.

He eventually crossed the Channel on a Liberty ship,[6] where the two German prisoners of war carrying him up the gangplank on his stretcher slipped, tipping all his belongings, including the addresses of his American and French rescuers, into the sea. It would be many years before his thoughts would return to those who had saved his life.

Ron would spend many weeks in hospital recovering from his injuries, determined to bear them, by example, with stoicism. Among his fellow patients was a navigator who'd lost both his arms and legs, amputated at the scene of an aircraft crash in an effort to save the man's life. 'Surely this man had faith in God and a grateful heart. He never grumbled and was so glad to be alive. I doubt that I could have coped as well as he did.' There was another amputee with Ron who had been injured in the legs when an unexploded bomb went off. The doctors told him he'd never walk again, but by pure grit he progressed from bed to wheelchair to crutches, and finally managed to walk with no more aid than a walking stick. 'I was, and remain, proud to have known those men. Ever since that time, I have grown intolerant of moaners!'

By mid-February Ron was well enough to be visited by his family. They had received a telegram to let them know he was alive and in an American hospital in France, but it had given them little other information. There was a war on, and keeping the relatives of the injured informed simply wasn't possible or, with many tens of thousands of casualties, particularly important. Nevertheless, after weeks of detective work, letters and phone calls, they'd been able to trace him, and one early morning Ron looked up from his bed to see his mother and father.

'We all tried to hold back the tears. My mother hugged me but she didn't cry – I think none of us knew how to react; we'd never been a particularly emotional family. Everyone was trying their best to keep the feelings of joy and relief suppressed!'

The next day, one of his sisters turned up with his beloved Sylvia.

'I was over the moon to see her, and she *certainly* shed tears! We hugged and held each other tightly in our relief. We didn't really talk about the future then, but the crash and my amputation certainly brought us closer together.'

Ron's initial amputation, however, hadn't stopped the gangrene.

'The doctor had screens put round my bed, and very kindly broke the news that even if they could save my foot I would always have trouble with it. He recommended I have it amputated just above the ankle.'

The news might not have come as a surprise, but it was still dreadful.

'It was only then that it hit me – all I could think about was that I'd never be able to play football or dance again. I really felt sorry for myself and I cried unashamedly. A young nurse who'd been told my bad news came over to me. "Please have something to eat," she said. "I've brought you a boiled egg with bread and butter."

'I couldn't eat it, I told her – even if the King asked me to! But moments later I *had* eaten it.'

Ron ended up with a right leg that extended only 7 inches below the knee. On 17 March he celebrated his twentieth birthday. Ron and Harry were on the road to recovery, but for the relatives of his friends and fellow Lancaster crewmates, the arrival of telegrams had delivered the worst news possible.

*Ken Darke*

Sylvia, their navigator Ken Darke's sister, was no stranger to the agony of waiting.

'Neither Peter [Ken's brother] nor Kenneth were home for Christmas, nor for my birthday on New Year's Eve, but I had a birthday present from Kenneth. The parcel contained a book by G. B. Shaw, one of Kenneth's favourite writers and mine. I put the book aside meaning to read it later. I was to find that I could never read it.'[7]

There would be little time for reading in the Darke family; their world was about to be turned upside-down. As Ron and Harry were being assisted away from the wreckage of their Lancaster by their French rescuers, the Bomber Command casualty reporting machine was swinging into action.

'7 January 1945 was a Sunday,[8] and after the midday meal the five of us were all sitting around the fire. The weather was icy and snow covered the ground.

'Suddenly there was a loud knock at the door. I was the nearest, and left the room. As I opened the door, there stood a telegraph boy looking rather frightened. Nothing was said. The boy handed me the telegram, addressed to my father, and I thanked him. I went straight back into the drawing room and every face looked up at me expectantly. I suppose we all knew the telegram contained bad news, as did the boy who'd delivered it.'

The telegram was short and similar to the ones that had already been received in tens of thousands of homes.

'"Regret your son missing believed killed." I cannot forget that in the silence Father handed the telegram to Mother and buried his face in his hands and wept. I had never seen a man weep before, let alone my father. Mother held the piece of paper firmly for a few moments without moving, then passed it to us. She was sitting absolutely still, hands clasped in her lap, face as white as paper. No tears, no movement, but shocked and almost disbelieving. I guess she was remembering her baby's birth. Nobody spoke for some time. We were all enclosed within our own private thoughts.

'Later that afternoon I set off in the snow for the nearby woods. There were no other people. The silence was intense and the wood very beautiful and peaceful.

'That night, I had a vivid dream of Ken. It awakened me and I was weeping bitterly. I sat up in bed at once. Kenneth was standing at the bottom of my bed, alive, smiling, dressed in his uniform, looking happy. For a moment I believed he was truly there in the flesh, but as that thought came to me, he disappeared. But the vision comforted me.'

On 13 January, by which time the family had received a letter from Ken's Commanding Officer containing more details and stressing that Ken had been one of their very best navigators, Sylvia's other brother Guy wrote to his twin, Peter, also serving in the RAF.

> *We are wondering at home whether or not you received Father's two letters, posted on Tuesday and Wednesday last. If not, then I must break the bad news to you.*
>
> *Poor old Ken was killed last Sunday night. His aircraft crashed in France returning from a heavy raid on Munich. He crashed at Méligny-le-Grand, south-west of Commercy, about thirty miles west of Nancy. Five of the crew were killed and two injured. He was given a military funeral and was buried. We shall hear further details from his CO.*
>
> *I will not say more. Drop a line to Ma, Peter.*

The carcass of the Lancaster that had carried Ken, Ron and Harry was a boon to the deprived local French community. Once the bodies had been removed from the wreckage and buried, André Fromont and some of the villagers began to salvage some of its valuable parts.

'Many people went to the site of the crash out of curiosity and took pieces from the aircraft – it was war and we had nothing. My friend Jean took a wheel and made a watering-trough for his animals out of it. A woman picked up a smaller one for a wheelbarrow. As for me, I picked up some aluminium parts from the cockpit. I have a good friend who works in a foundry and he made three cake tins, which I still use.'

Parts were also used to construct crosses placed at the crash site. Ron's Lancaster bomber, a deadly weapon of death and destruction, became a source of sustenance to the local community she and her crew had helped liberate, and a memorial to those who died in her. Perhaps it was a fitting end. And as one Lancaster died and was reborn, thousands more were still heading into action in pursuit of the final destruction of the Nazi war machine.

*A snow-covered Lancaster in early 1945*

Through early 1945, the RAF was once again being deployed by high command to attack German cities. This initiative came not from Arthur Harris, though he embraced it with enthusiasm, but from the combined Chiefs of Staff and the Air Ministry, who saw it as a way in which the Western Allies could show support of their Russian allies advancing from the east. The new operation, code-named 'Thunderclap', was launched in late January. It would bring about one of the most controversial episodes of the entire war.

In some ways, operations were becoming tougher rather than easier. Targets were deeper into Germany, involving gruelling flights of nine hours and more, which were being attempted in weather that would previously have been considered unflyable. Nor was there any let-up from the hierarchy in its demands that the airmen should 'press on regardless'. The men generally responded with as much determination as ever, and for the new arrivals, there was an eagerness to be involved, to be part of the war effort.

Freddie Hulance was among the new intake getting operational for the first time. An expert pilot, he had spent most of his war teaching recruits to fly. But he was desperate to do the real thing. 'I felt we were winning the war and I had a growing feeling that it would be over in a matter of months rather than years. I didn't want to finish the war without some combat experience. I wanted to be able to say afterwards that "I was there". At the same time, I also wanted to survive!'[9]

Most of those involved hoped the war was in its end stages, but few doubted there would be many more months of fighting before it was won, and Hulance was typical of many of the crews joining the fight in the early months of 1945. He was caught in the late-joiner's dilemma: anxious to do his bit but also desperate not to die. The fatalism with which some men had flown into battle earlier was now replaced by a new, unnerving sensation – hope. But as the end of the conflict began to look like a serious possibility, climbing into the claustrophobic space of a Lancaster to fly against an increasingly desperate enemy and facing the prospect of never coming back called on ever deeper reserves of courage.

On 13 February 1945, Freddie Hulance flew his Lancaster to Dresden, alongside over 1,250 other British and American bombers.

By all accounts, old Dresden was magnificent – a city of rare beauty. Its elegant palaces and churches inspired comparisons with Venice and Florence. It had been hit before by American bombers, but the previous attacks could not have prepared the citizens for the savagery of 13 and 14 February. The instructions to the crews at briefing, and the composition of the bombloads they carried, left no doubt about the intention.

Freddie Hulance remembered being told the precise reason for the attack at his briefing.

'The target had been nominated by the Russians. Dresden was being used as a supply centre and was expected to hold up their advance. Our bombload was a mixture of incendiaries and high explosives. It was just a routine target.'

Rear gunner Peter Twinn had no doubts on that score either: 'We were told before we took off that we were doing this operation at the request of the Russians, who were advancing from the east.

Churchill agreed that we should bomb it. They also made armaments there.'[10]

Twinn's briefing had been correct. Despite some contemporary accounts declaring Dresden to have no military value, the reality was very different. The city's own yearbook of 1942 boasted that it was 'one of the foremost industrial locations in the Reich'. It had 127 civilian factories which had secretly been switched to war work, producing bomb-aiming apparatus, searchlights and parts for V1 flying bombs, to name but a few. The city's chamber of trade admitted that 'the work rhythm of Dresden is determined by the needs of our army'.[11]

And it was also about to take a more active role in the fighting, whether its citizens wanted to or not. The German High Command had designated it a military strongpoint, part of the defensive line along the River Elbe, at which the Soviet advance had to be held. A vital link in the German rail network – twenty-eight military transports a day came through with troops and tanks to fight off the advancing Soviet army – 'peaceful' Dresden was in reality a war factory, a fortress and a transport hub; it was, therefore, a thoroughly legitimate target for the bombers. But there were many civilians on the ground, including some 150,000 refugees fleeing the Russian advance, and a substantial number of Allied prisoners of war.

To many of the 8,500 British and American airmen who made the 900-mile round trip to the ancient capital of Saxony, close to Germany's eastern borders, it was just another in a seemingly endless run of operations. By the time Peter Twinn's Lancaster got there, the area beneath them was ablaze.

'But it didn't stand out as something special. It was just another target. I didn't think about the people down below or the devastation we left behind. We were there to do a job. It was purely impersonal. We were spared the horror of fighting hand to hand or seeing the enemy in front of you. It was our job to get there, drop the bombs and get home in one piece. Dresden was no different; one town on fire is very much the same as another – only the acreage was greater.'

On the ground at Dresden, death and chaos reigned. In the first quarter of an hour of the raid, the Lancasters dropped 880 tons of bombs. One man recalled 'a series of whistling sounds, then the building shook from a quick succession of steadily more powerful explosions, which drove us into the corner of the basement. The roaring crash of the bombs just didn't seem to stop. We hunkered down ever lower as one shudder succeeded another.' When the shaking stopped and the drone of the first bombers had retreated, he ventured upstairs and looked out on a scene from hell. It was eleven o'clock at night but the flames rendered it as bright as day. He went out into the street.

'Everywhere we turned, buildings were on fire. The spark-filled air was suffocating. Chunks of red-hot matter were flying at us. The more we moved into the network of streets, the stronger the storm became, hurling burning scraps and objects through the air.'[12]

One fifteen-year-old boy remembered 'people wandering about helplessly. I saw my aunt, who called out to me to make for the river but the firestorm strangled her last words. A house wall collapsed burying people in the debris. A thick cloud of dust arose and I could not see. A friend grabbed me and pulled me away across the rubble. Time and again, we stumbled over corpses.'[13]

And this was only the beginning; the death and destruction would continue for many hours.

Freddie Hulance's bomb aimer had no difficulty finding the target.

'We were on our way home when my rear gunner got terribly excited about the fires we had left behind. He wanted me to turn the plane around and take a look for myself but I said it would be too dangerous. Anyway, I thought it would be a waste of time. When we landed back at base, a few people were talking about the fires, but we had seen worse. It was just another target and it faded into the memories. Only years later would it come back to haunt us.'

The horror of the attack is undeniable and the arguments over the numbers who perished that awful night continue. Disposal of the dead began immediately, and the ruthless Nazi efficiency helped – SS men from the Treblinka concentration camp were called upon to employ their expertise in the disposal of bodies. A month later, an official report announced that the known number of fatalities was 18,375, estimating that the final figure would be in the region of 25,000. It remains the only official figure, and is undoubtedly a minimum. Absolute precision is impossible, but as many as 15,000 should be added to cover the unknown number of refugees whose deaths must bring the toll to somewhere between 25,000 and 40,000. Nazi propaganda and post-war mythology should not have needed to inflate that number tenfold. It was already a staggering total, a calamity by any standards.

Arguments had already raged about the rights and wrongs of the bombing campaign in general, and they now focused upon Dresden in particular, as did the demonisation of those responsible. Churchill and his counterparts among the Western Allies now realised that if such onslaughts continued, there would be little left of a Germany liberated from Nazism to form any basis for reconstruction. He also became vigorously aware of the stigma of the most recent cataclysm. Within six weeks he had distanced himself from the event, from Harris, and by extension from Bomber Command. By 28 March he had drafted a memorandum for the Chiefs of Staff Committee and the Chief of the Air Staff. Subsequently toned down, the original read:

*It seems to me that the moment has come when the question of bombing of German cities simply for the sake of increasing the terror, though under other pretexts, should be reviewed. Otherwise we shall come into control of an utterly ruined land. We shall not, for instance, be able to get housing materials out of Germany for our own needs because some temporary provision would have to be made for the Germans themselves. The destruction of Dresden remains a serious query against the conduct of Allied bombing. I am of the opinion that military objectives must henceforward be more strictly studied in our own interests rather than that of the enemy.*

> *The Foreign Secretary [Anthony Eden] has spoken to me on this subject and I feel the need for more precise concentration upon military objectives, such as oil and communications behind the immediate battle-zone, rather than on mere acts of terror and wanton destruction, however impressive.*[14]

Arthur Harris responded in his habitually nineteenth-century manner: 'I do not personally regard the whole of the remaining cities of Germany as worth the bones of one British grenadier.'[15]

Churchill, also born in the Victorian era and subject to fits of Victorian thinking himself, was nevertheless enough of a political realist to see that the stability of the post-war world depended on rebuilding Germany as a democratic industrial economy. And the continued bombing of cities which would soon fall into the hands of Allied land forces was becoming counterproductive.

Should the bombing have been stopped? The harsh reality of the time was that only total war would bring Hitler's Germany to its knees. Those fighting could not soften their stance because of an untested notion that the enemy might be on the verge of capitulation. The end was far from visible in those early weeks of 1945.

Arguments raged then, and still do today. But some of those involved are in no doubt about the realities. At the time of the raid, a Dutch woman, Elka Schrijver, was one of 4,000 political prisoners in a jail south-west of Dresden where the male inmates were tasked with digging a huge hole in the ground. She wrote, 'After our liberation, documents found by the Red Cross showed that this was meant to be a mass grave and that orders from Dresden had been received to shoot all of us. Subsequent to the Dresden raids, nobody had the courage to execute these orders. Those of us who were political prisoners in Saxony at the time directly owe our lives to those air raids.'[16]

\* \* \*

*Freddie Hulance*

Lancaster pilot Freddie Hulance had little time for those who judged his actions with the benefit of hindsight. 'I once heard someone describe the bombing of Dresden as a "holocaust". Well that was a word that I had never heard until the end of the war when we were shown what the Germans had done to the Jews. Knowing now the real meaning of *holocaust*, I am even more proud of what I did. I helped to shorten that war, a war that we simply had to win.'

Many simply accepted the rationale they were given. Ken Trent was in the process of transferring to 617 Squadron at the time of the raid, so missed taking part.

'I was sorry after the war to hear so many people decrying the attack. To my mind it was a legitimate target, with the aim of killing Germans and destroying their transport and production centres. I'm also sure that if they'd managed to complete the atomic bomb, which they were very close to achieving, they wouldn't have hesitated in using it on us.'[17]

Whatever one may make of the arguments, it is always easier to rationalise with hindsight. At the time the war was still raging, its outcome far from certain, and the Germans had shown themselves well capable of counterattacks. The journalist and historian Götz Bergander was then an eighteen-year-old Dresdner. He later wrote of the significant shift in his nation's mindset: 'The shockwave triggered by Dresden swept away what was left of the will to resist, as the Germans now feared that such a catastrophe could be repeated daily. Awareness of inevitable defeat increased, and the belief in miracles disappeared. Above all, there was a growing realisation that it would be better if the end came soon.'[18]

The firestorm unleashed by Bomber Command was a warning of how bitter that end could be.

* * *

As the flames of conflict continued to burn, life, in and out of battle, went on for the Lancaster crewmen.

'"Should we get married?" I asked. "Yes, let's," my darling Eunice replied. Just like that! For a moment, I was quite taken aback!'

Courting his beloved Eunice had been a long haul, but trainee rear gunner James Flowers was unceasing in his pursuit of love. Now, at last, he had his reward. Even then he'd only made the big day by the skin of his teeth. Bad weather delayed their flying exercises, so he and his best man Taffy didn't get away from base until 6 p.m. the night before. 'We began the 100-mile journey as soon as we could. We had to go through a succession of poor bus services, slow trains, several changes, and long waits. It took all night!'[19] They finally reached James's home town of Sutton-in-Ashfield, about 15 miles south of Chesterfield, at 8 a.m. on the big day. They then faced a 2-mile walk from the station to his house.

'I didn't get a wink of sleep before the wedding, I was just glad I'd made it! 2.00 p.m. saw us in a taxi making our way to St Mary's Church in Sutton. By now the tensions of the last few days, along with no sleep for thirty-six hours, were really beginning to tell. The wedding was planned for 2.30 p.m. The bride of course was late!'

Eunice's taxi had had to make two detours to avoid funeral cortèges. She later confessed that she regarded this as a sign they might be making a terrible mistake; who knew what the uncertain future would bring?

'It was a strange contrast. We were in the midst of war, people were fighting and dying near and far, and this was the best day of my life. There was no talk of the future; we simply lived one day at a time. It was unsaid, of course, but the reality was each day could be your last! People thought aircrew getting married was a daft idea, and a fast route for a wife to become a widow; so we never spoke about the war at all. We only had short periods of time together and we didn't want to waste those moments on war! We ignored it and talked about the good things in life, the things we'd enjoyed and the things we could look forward to.'

It was now March 1945 and James could look forward to getting through his thirty ops as a rear gunner.

'The first time I saw a Lancaster I was overawed by her grace and power. The skipper and the engineer would rave about her – how she was responsive, almost like a fighter, reliable, a dream to fly. But all I needed her to do was get me in and out of Germany and provide a platform for my guns! I loved my rear turret, that was my office, and I was confident I'd make it through the war in a Lancaster.'

His very first raid was on the synthetic oil refinery at Böhlen, a few miles south of Leipzig. The sooner the Germans were deprived of what fuel remained to them, the sooner even the Nazi diehards would give up the fight. His Lancaster was one of 248 on the mission, which set off at 5.15 p.m. on Monday 5 March. He was intensely excited, but it was to be a baptism of fire. He hoped the tension might leave him as he climbed into the aircraft and made his way aft to his lonely position in the rear turret.

Checking his equipment carefully, he paid special attention to the tried-and-tested Barr & Stroud GJ3, which consisted of an upright sight head and a detachable lamp unit whose brightness James could control with a dimmer knob. The unit could be removed by pushing a button at the bottom of the housing to reveal the sight's circuitry and the bulb that projected the reticule – the fine 'crosshairs' in the eyepiece – through a lens onto a glass reflector.[20]

The whole sight was designed for compactness, measuring just 4 by 3.5 by 3 inches, and James would later be thankful he'd familiarised himself with this crucial piece of equipment.

After the relief of take-off, and long before they approached their target, he scanned the skies ceaselessly for enemy fighters. His skipper swung the Lancaster deftly from side to side to afford James and his fellow gunners the opportunity of looking below them for Ju88s armed with upward-firing cannons – the dreaded *Schräge Musik*. All navigation lights were off, but James was acutely aware of the dim presence of the other aircraft around him. It didn't feel like safety in numbers; anything could happen as they flew so closely together. Suddenly two Lancasters below them collided and disappeared in a mass of roaring flame.

'The blast washed over us and I wasn't sure our own aircraft would survive as it juddered and shook. Here was my first op, we weren't even at the target, and I'd just seen the death of fourteen fellow airmen. I was shocked, but there was no time for fear; you had to close your mind and move on. You couldn't allow yourself to be affected. You just had to get on and do what you'd been trained to do.'

There was no let-up. Soon afterwards, James saw an Me109 on their tail, coming in fast. Inexperienced as he was, he failed to call a warning to his skipper before firing, but since the German fighter was directly behind him, his four Brownings found their mark and it fell away vertically. As they lined up over Böhlen for their run, a second Me109 moved in. James's gunsight fell apart when he opened up once more, filling the turret with dazzling light. It only took him a matter of seconds to repair, but it was many minutes before his night vision returned, by which time the skies were clear. They completed their bomb run and took their photograph. It was time to go home.

'As we landed at Skellingthorpe, all the tension of the past twelve hours drained out of my body and I felt shattered. All I thought was, *How am I going to survive another twenty-nine trips like this one?!*'

But James, like all those others, simply had to get on with the task in hand. There would be no respite; the war would be fought until the bitter end.

'I had to put a barrier between what I was seeing and doing in the air, and my life with Eunice. I didn't mention the deaths I'd seen or the battles we'd fought with attacking aircraft, or dodging the flak, for fear of worrying her.

'Eunice was a rock for me, a stabilising force amid the chaos of war. I spent every free moment I could with her. The others would go out drinking but I wanted to be back with my wife. It was around 40 miles home but I would cycle, hitchhike, walk or run – whatever was needed to be back in her arms. Sometimes, after a long op, I might make it home in the dark in the early hours of the morning and slip into bed, cuddle up to her for a few hours while she was sound asleep, then give her a kiss as she woke up and head off back to camp to fly again. It was really important to have her there for comfort; she was my escape from the war.'

*James and Eunice Flowers on their wedding day*

James Flowers' first raid on Böhlen was to be flight engineer Ted Watson's last. His war was coming to an end and, as a veteran flyer, he thought he knew what to expect. He was wrong.

Keen as ever on Hollywood blockbusters, he'd recently been to see *Thousands Cheer*, an MGM musical designed as a wartime morale-booster, featuring a host of big names like Lucille Ball, Judy Garland and Gene Kelly.

His East Kirkby squadron's official motto was *Nocturna Mors* – 'Death by Night'. But the crews had their own motto: 'Home is when the props stop spinning.' No one was under any illusion; life in Bomber Command was not like the movies.

As they took off in the gathering dusk on that March evening in 1945, Ted experienced that strange feeling of flying both by day and by night. Below, the earth was already dark, and as they crossed the Belgian coast, only the breaking surf indicated the meeting of sea and land. From the Lancaster cockpit, where Ted stood by the pilot, scanning the instruments to his front and right, the sky was tinged with the pastel shades of fading day. It seemed tranquil, but you could never, ever, be seduced by that false sense of security on a mission. After the sun had fully set and the moon risen, there'd be a grim reminder never to relax. He could see outlines of other aircraft nearby, but they came and went like ghosts. Now an unreal orange fireball lit the sky. One had changed direction too soon and flown across the stream, colliding with another. Ted had witnessed the same mid-air crash as James Flowers.

'As the glare subsided, I could see the flaming mass split into two halves which fell away from each other, burning fiercely. Then, in quick succession, the bombloads of the two doomed Lancasters exploded, sending a cascade of burning fragments of aircraft tumbling to the earth. Fourteen young lives wiped out.'[21]

Everyone in Ted's crew felt the shock, but the only person to say anything was their passenger, Pilot Officer Duggan, a rookie pilot flying second dickey to gain experience of what to expect on his own ops.

'"Oh my . . . God . . ." The words were gasped rather than spoken.

I had forgotten all about young Duggan, standing quietly at the back
of the cockpit. I had no words of consolation for him. He would just
have to get used to it. This was my last trip; hopefully I wouldn't
need to worry about any of this again!'

Böhlen, a vital source of fuel, was still well defended, and by the
time Ted and his crew arrived, they flew into furious flak. They
could do nothing but hold steady and pray. The overpowering,
gagging stench of cordite mixed with burning oil seemed a portent
of disaster, but they made their run unharmed then turned, with the
usual mixture of relief and apprehension, for home. A contented,
vigilant calm settled upon the crew. Then they were caught in a
blindingly intense searchlight beam. Gerry Monk, the skipper,
immediately threw the aircraft into a turning dive, but two more
searchlights followed suit. They'd been coned. Murderous, focused
flak battered their aircraft. While Ted feverishly worked the throttles, the pilot strained every muscle in his arms and legs to coax the
giant aircraft into a desperate series of twists and turns.

'The aircraft trembled in the shockwaves of exploding shells,
the fuselage pinged, rattled and thudded at the cascade of shrapnel,
much of which came straight through, and the wings groaned under
the strain of the pilot's demands for ever more violent manoeuvres.'

Ted and his crewmates knew all too well that their lives now
hung in the balance.

'This was not like the Hollywood films I loved. There would
be no chance of crawling up the floor to reach the escape hatch in
a dramatic last effort to slip out of the burning aircraft and float
to safety. Once the pilot lost control, the window of opportunity
swiftly closed and the obstacles to a safe exit were too many and
varied: fire, smoke, loss of oxygen, injury, bits of equipment littering
the fuselage floor, hatchway damage, the aircraft's angle and rate of
descent, the desperate needs of other crew members, time, courage,
fear and bad luck, to name but a few. For eight interminable minutes
we battled on, wriggling this way and that in desperate moves to
escape the web of light that held us in its grip, and the intense hail
of fire directed at us. In the cockpit, my skipper and I instinctively

knew that time had run out, that we had one last chance, just one more card to play. If it worked, we would escape; if it didn't, all eight of us would die in the next few moments.

'I pushed the levers forward through the throttle gate[22] to boost power as Gerry Monk dropped the Lancaster's nose and banked her hard to port. The engines drove the aircraft swiftly down towards the earth, the speed increasing to 300mph. I kept the power full on as we hurtled through a hail of flak and gunfire, passing 360mph, knowing that at this speed the wings were very likely to be ripped off. Down the blinding shaft of light we plunged, engines shrieking and the airframe vibrating in sympathy. Buildings seemed to rush up towards us. I don't think anyone drew breath in those moments.

'It was now or never. I eased the throttles back as the skipper pulled the Lancaster out of the dive and we flashed across the rooftops at an unimaginable speed. Then suddenly everything was dark again. We were out. Even through his goggles I could see how wide young Pilot Officer Duggan's eyes were. We all settled down again, but it took time, especially after our navigator told us that at the end of our dive we had reached the astonishing speed of over 400mph.'

All they had to do now was get home! No one was seriously injured, though everyone's nerves were shot. No time to worry about that now, though; professionalism and survival instinct drove them on. The damage to the aircraft was severe, and the oxygen supply was unserviceable, which meant they'd have to fly below 10,000ft – riskily low over enemy territory – to breathe unaided. The engines were still running, but it looked as if they had a fuel leak. Did they have a chance of getting as far as liberated France and finding an emergency airfield? Perhaps.

At last the navigator announced they had crossed the border. The Lancaster was rumbling ominously. Did they have enough fuel to make it across the freezing Channel? Cautious hope crept into their hearts as they left the clouds on the mainland and flew over the waves at a few hundred feet, under a starlit sky. Finally, they crossed the English coast.

After flying for ten and a half hours, they finally made an

emergency landing back at East Kirkby. Home was indeed 'when the props stopped turning', and as they slowed into stillness the shattered crew climbed down to be greeted by an anxious ground staff.

'The fire tender and the ambulance at the side of the runway were a reassuring sight and our ground crew had dutifully stayed out at dispersal to await our return. Even in the dark it was plain to see that our Lancaster had suffered significant damage, hardly surprising in view of what she'd been through. But the very fact that she had survived that dive and got us home was a remarkable testimony to Roy Chadwick, the Lancaster's designer, and the women who had built her at the Woodford Avro factory. Rarely had I been more pleased to see the smiling young WAAF holding out my mugs of steaming hot tea and rum. As I slumped into a waiting chair at the debriefing, utterly exhausted, I looked around at the faces of my crew and knew we all felt exactly the same. The whole trip had been a complete nightmare and a baptism of fire for young Duggan; he had it all ahead of him, but I also knew he would be able to cope with anything after that.'

Ted and his crew had been to hell and back, but at last they'd flown – and survived – their final sortie.

'A feeling of immense relief washed over me. I had survived a total of thirty-seven missions,[23] and now it was all over. No more long hours waiting for the thudding vibration of cannon shells to rip into our aircraft, no more contemplating the fleeting seconds between life and death. It was done. But, unlike so many of our friends and fellow airmen, we would, after all, have a life to live.'

Now they would disperse, and each would be alone again.

'Even as we stood later in the spring sunshine, I knew a page had turned on a chapter of my life which would see no equal. Never again would I experience anything remotely like the past seven months.'

They looked back at their battle-weary Lancaster for the last time. By a strange coincidence, it was the very aircraft they had flown on their first mission, what seemed like a century earlier.

* * *

In early 1945, after a brief respite from his first tour, Ken Trent had volunteered for a second with the elite 617 Squadron. It was the pinnacle of his ambition, so he was shocked when he arrived to a cool reception in the Officers' Mess. 'As I sipped a subdued beer, I felt a chill which never truly left me for my whole time in the squadron.'

The dampened atmosphere was due to the high losses being experienced on what some had dubbed 'the Suicide Squadron' because of the complex and dangerous operations they were undertaking, but Ken soon put such concerns out of his mind, as he found himself flying specially adapted Lancasters – modified Mark B.1 'Specials' equipped with more powerful Merlin 24 engines.

Flown by a crew of just five, the wireless operator and mid-upper gunner were redundant as these new aircraft had been stripped of their front and mid-upper turrets, bomb doors, armour plating and much of the usual wireless equipment, which by now had been largely superseded by the introduction of sophisticated radios operated by the pilot himself.

The overhaul had been necessary to enable them to carry Barnes Wallis's latest contribution to the destruction of what military hardware the Germans had left: the massive, eye-wateringly expensive 22,000lb, 26ft-long 'Grand Slam'. Perfectly forged from a single piece of chrome molybdenum alloy steel, it could reach speeds of up to 715mph and penetrate deep underground before detonating. Tests in the New Forest in southern England produced a crater 124ft wide and 30ft deep. Armed with molten Torpex, an explosive 50 per cent more powerful than TNT, which took a month to set, production was slow and only forty-two were ever dropped in anger.

Ken Trent got to drop his first Grand Slam on 27 March.

Their target was the Valentin U-boat factory at Farge, about 20 miles north-west of Bremen. The massive concrete structure had been under slave-labour construction by 10,000 men since early 1943. Inside, the Germans were preparing the very latest U-boats, which would head up the River Weser to the North Sea, ready to continue the fight. Even at this late stage of the war, they could still wreak havoc on Allied shipping. The submarines were protected not only by strong anti-aircraft defences, but with reinforced concrete walls and roof, 23ft thick in places. Allied Intelligence had delayed any attack until the building works were all but complete, so that the massive resources employed could be destroyed in one fell swoop. Only the huge Grand Slams, with some backup Tallboys (its 12,000lb 'little' sister), could blast their way through. But the timing had to be perfect: once complete, the Valentin pens might well be impregnable.

Ken ran through the take-off drill carefully before they pulled onto the runway at first light.

'I could feel the extra power from the enhanced engines shaking the airframe, but also the enormous drag of the bomb beneath our belly. On the ground, it looked brutal hanging in its special cradle. Flying alongside a Lancaster armed with a Grand Slam, one could see wingtips flexing upwards in a bow shape under the strain.'[24]

Twenty Lancasters took off at 10.20 a.m., flying the all-too-familiar route across the North Sea. They lined up to follow the Weser upstream at 14,000ft. Visibility was good. No enemy aircraft opposed them, and soon the factory and pens came into view.

'Got it clear, Skipper. Dead straight now. That's it. Bombsight on!'

Ahead of them the first Lancasters were already dropping their bombs. Some were near-misses, but at least one found its mark, smashing down into the western end of the structure. The scale of the explosions was breathtaking.

At last it was Ken's turn.

'OK, that's it. Steady! Whoa! There she goes!'

They'd just about got used to how the Lancaster reacted when they dropped the somewhat smaller Tallboy bomb, but nothing could prepare them for this. Relieved of its 22,000lb load, 'the souped-up aircraft shot upwards like a rocket, leaping 250ft skywards, and pushing us all into our seats while the engines blared. I felt as if I was being squashed to just a few inches tall as my head pressed down through my shoulders; my arms felt like lead on the control column. Fortunately there was no other kite above us, or it could have been disastrous.' Nevertheless, they'd completed their mission unopposed, and as all twenty bombers turned for home and settled into a steady rhythm, Ken had time to enjoy his new aircraft. 'The enhanced Lancaster was so powerful and full of fun, as light as a feather to fly, and felt like a single-engined fighter. A true dream machine.'

617 Squadron dropped eleven Grand Slams and seven Tallboys that day. Sixteen fell among the buildings around the complex, obliterating them. The remaining two, both Grand Slams, scored direct hits on the target and bored down through the half-set concrete roof to bury themselves deep inside the structure. For some minutes nothing happened as the delay fuses did their work. The guards and slave labourers were emerging from their air-raid shelters when the bombs detonated, shaking the complex like an earthquake, killing the 300 men inside and throwing those outside off their feet.

Ken Trent was happy: 'The damage was so bad that the Germans had to abandon the site after two years of work and thousands of tons of concrete and steel used up. Another job well done; anything to bring this seemingly endless war to its conclusion.'

After delivering death from the skies, Ken had a more personal task ahead of him as he took leave to visit his dying mother in London.

'I arrived home wearing my smelly battledress to find Mum weaker than she had been, resting as much as possible, but still helping with the books in my parents' little shop and sub-post office. It was terribly sad. I think she knew she was dying, but when she felt well enough she set about giving the whole house a thorough spring-clean. It was as though she wanted to leave everything clean and tidy for my poor dad, who would have to carry on after she went. She even gave my dirty uniform a good scrubbing, and returned it to me free of the dirt and stink of my Lincolnshire friends' farm, where I'd found such comfort away from the fighting. She was always so proud to see me with my pilot's wings.

'Five years of war had had their effect on the shop too. There was now almost nothing left to sell: cigarettes and confectionery were all strictly rationed and the customers who did come in were there to collect their pensions or the allowances made to the wives of servicemen. Sometimes someone wanted to buy stamps or send a telegram or a postal order, but the business was really suffering. When my leave came to an end, I left with a heavy heart.'

Ken went back to work. There was plenty more to do before he could hang up his flying helmet.

*Ken Trent after he was presented with his*
*DFC by King George*

Easter Day 1945 fell on 1 April. In the previous months, the Russians had entered Silesia and Pomerania, while the Western Allies had crossed the River Rhine north and south of the Ruhr. In an attempt to protect his last oil reserves in Hungary, Hitler launched a major offensive against the Red Army near Lake Balaton, but was repulsed after two weeks of fighting.

The Allies pushed northwards through Italy while Russian

forces took Vienna and Königsberg (now Kaliningrad) in Prussia, on the southern shores of the Baltic. The Western Allies captured Hamburg in the north and Nuremberg in the south of Germany. The net was tightening.

On 21 April, three days after an operation to bomb the gun batteries on Heligoland off the north German coast, Ken Trent attended his mother's funeral.

'It was one of the worst days of my life. I made the now-familiar train journey in my best uniform, wearing my wings and the medal ribbons she had been so proud of. I was so sad that she had died only a week before my actual investiture with the Distinguished Flying Cross. How wonderful it would have been for her to see me presented to the King; but now that could never be. With terrible sadness we climbed into the black limousine which took us behind the hearse the short distance to the church. It was a dark and threatening day. With shaking legs I followed her coffin, and to my amazement saw that the pews were packed with people, many of them customers at my parents' shop. Their loyalty touched me, and I was able to hold myself in check during the service, but at the end of it, when the pallbearers carried the coffin to the hearse for the last journey to the City of London Cemetery in Wanstead, I started to cry uncontrollably. Here was I, an RAF officer in full uniform, with wings and the DFC on his chest, blubbing at a time when the stiff upper lip was expected in even the worst situations.

'By the time we reached the cemetery I had managed to compose myself, but I gripped my sister's hand tightly as the coffin was lowered into the grave, and sobbed again when the first earth was gathered up and thrown down onto her. It was the last time I would be physically close to my mum. A major part of my life had gone for ever.'

But there was no let-up for Ken; no time to grieve or reflect. He was on the battle order again for 25 April. A few days before, the concentration camp at Bergen-Belsen had been liberated and 60,000 starving prisoners freed. A hundred and twenty thousand enemy troops had been taken prisoner in the last campaign of the war in Italy.

The final phase *had* to be in sight. Didn't it?

'We were called to the briefing room at a very late hour, and sat chattering, waiting for it to start. The Station Commander came in to the scraping of chairs as we all stood up, waiting for the news. With a dramatic flourish, the Intelligence Officer pulled back the curtain. The tell-tale strand of red wool snaked across the map in a different direction from any we had flown before. Some 600 miles to the south-east, it appeared to end in the Bavarian Alps.

'"Berchtesgaden," said the officer. "Hitler's hideaway. Your aim today is to take it out. We want it flattened. It's going to be a big one."'

The briefing officer went on to explain that before the war, Hitler had built a holiday haven, the Berghof (Mountain Court), in the mountains near the market town of Berchtesgaden, south of Salzburg, a spot that he loved for its stunning views and crystal-clear air. He had visited many times, and now the RAF were going to destroy it, and perhaps him. The Berghof itself, over time, had been greatly extended, to include railway access, substantial SS barracks, communications and support centres, and Allied Intelligence believed that it may have been intended as an alternative seat of government. Senior Nazi Party members such as Bormann, Goebbels, Göring, Himmler and Speer also took time off there.

On the same day, 25 April, the Russian forces encircled Berlin, while at Torgau on the Elbe they met and shook hands with their American counterparts. And in San Francisco the delegates of fifty countries met to found the United Nations.

The attack on the Berghof may have been founded on the possibility that a last stand might be made there. Allied Intelligence interceptions of German communications reported an increasing amount of talk about 'the Alpine Fortress'; and on 24 April 1945 a message was intercepted from Hitler ordering, with typical bombast, one of his generals to head south from Berlin to prepare 'a last bulwark of fanatical resistance'.[25]

But how significant could that resistance possibly be? Perhaps it didn't matter; bombing the Berghof was also a splendid piece of PR, with the possible bonus of killing the Führer. Two targets were nominated: the Berghof itself, and the Kehlsteinhaus, known to the Western Allies as 'The Eagle's Nest'. Built on the summit of the 6,500ft Mount Kehlstein, it was a chalet-style luxury guesthouse for entertaining visiting dignitaries which had previously included Neville Chamberlain and the Duke and Duchess of Windsor.

The Berghof was heavily fortified and protected by flak batteries. Three hundred and fifty-nine Lancasters from twenty-two squadrons were deployed, and their Mustang fighter escort alone greatly outnumbered the 200 still-operational German fighters.

'THE ARCH-CRIMINAL'S HIDE-OUT' was how one RAF Intelligence Officer described it in his notes for the briefing he'd give to the crews for the mission; 'the target we've been waiting for, for five and a half years'. Here was something to inspire them. He would also stress the 'importance of accurate bombing', as 'it is important to finish the job in one blow'. He needed more capital letters for his conclusion: 'MAKE A NEAT JOB.'[26]

Lancaster pilot Don MacIntosh was incredulous: 'When they announced the target, everyone laughed. The trip to the Berghof had been a standing joke for years. Although it was obvious that the war was nearly over, the fear of launching into the unknown and not returning was as strong as ever, heightened by the thought that another, new life, a new beginning, was almost within our grasp.'[27]

Ken Trent was also sceptical about the whole exercise: 'For the first time in any operation I really couldn't see the point in what we'd been asked to do. To fly all that way with Tallboys just to knock out someone's house right at the end of the war seemed an odd and rather petty mission. Nonetheless, orders were orders, and I prepared for the raid with just as much care as the others on 617 Squadron. After squeezing into our flying gear, we were on board and ready for take-off shortly after 4 a.m.'

Weather conditions for the op were perfect.

'It was a beautiful morning,' remembers Ken. 'The sun appeared over the horizon as we climbed to meet it. Here we were, in all the splendour of the dawn, while it was still dark on the earth 20,000ft below us. Approaching the target area, the alpine peaks stretched out before us in all their glory – a picture postcard which seemed ill-suited to our warlike purposes. Mountains topped with white snow hid deep, dark valleys, many of which were in shadow in the morning sun. As we stooged around, trying to locate the Eagle's Nest, I was more and more aware that our time would be severely limited – we were towards the end of our range.

'"Where the bloody hell is it?" snapped our bomb aimer in frustration at our inability to find what we were supposed to be aiming at. Then—

'"Hold on," said the bomb aimer, suddenly. "I think that's it. Yes! That's it! Got it! OK, now, left a bit, we're nearly bang on. Wait. Steady."

'We began our run in. Ahead of us, the small complex of Adolf Hitler's mountainside home grew closer. We'd all seen the news-reels of him there before the war, greeting politicians on the terrace which looked out on the splendid view, and now we were intent on its destruction.'

The uninterrupted flight over Germany to the Alps was no less spectacular for Don MacIntosh's crew: 'We flew across the Reich, the air clear and still in the spring morning. No smoke rose from the factories below us as twin-engined Mosquitos buzzed along the bomber stream, checking up on us like policemen, ready to take the numbers of any strays. The snow-capped Alps were rising steadily on the windscreen as we approached.'

Don watched the handful of other Lancasters ahead of him. There seemed to be no flak and they delivered their bombs with no opposition.

'"Springtime in the Alps, fellas. Have a look," I said as we wheeled left out of the traffic and saw the rest of the bomber stream flying in. I had a mental picture of Chamberlain arriving back from Berchtesgaden over five years earlier, waving his piece of paper and saying, "I believe I have brought peace in our time." Had there been a communications breakdown? Something lost in translation?'

Ken and Don may have had reservations about the operation, but it all seemed to be going well. There had been no casualties so far, and they were on their way home. Could the luck hold out for those who followed?

Freddie Cole, a 21-year-old flight engineer, had none of those reservations; he was keen as mustard to go on the raid.

'When we heard the squadron was going to Berchtesgaden we really wanted to be part of it, to get back at Hitler. It was going to be a prestigious operation but it was going to be a bit different for us because we'd hardly done any daylight raids. The main thing was to get those arrogant shits, who needed to be dealt with ruthlessly.'[28]

Freddie and his fellow crewmen were a highly experienced team, having completed twenty-seven ops by the time of Berchtesgaden. It looked as though they were going to make it through the war unscathed. Their regular, trusty Lancaster, *F-Freddy*, was piloted by 24-year-old Wilf de Marco, a skilful and admired flyer, with a reputation for being a bit of a daredevil. Large, muscular and boisterous, he hailed from Timmins, Ontario, where he'd been a decent ice-hockey player. 'Wilf was a brilliant pilot. His sharp reactions got us out of trouble many times,' remembers Freddie.

Long barrack buildings betrayed the Berghof's location, and as they homed in, the flak batteries stationed high in the surrounding peaks were now alerted and focused, finding their targets with more ease. There might be trouble ahead.

Arthur Sharman, the 26-year-old bomb aimer, was lying on his belly in the nose.

'I'd just released the bombs from 12,000ft. I'd watched them fall and was pleased to see one land in the middle of a square and another hit the SS barracks. The photoflash had just gone off when our aircraft was hit. There was a big explosion and the intercom went dead. I couldn't see Wilf, but it was clear we had only a short time to get out of it.'

Not waiting for the order to bale out, not knowing if the others were alive or dead, but certain that the pitching Lancaster was doomed, Arthur clipped on his parachute, opened the escape hatch below his position, and dropped out – the first to do so. At least he was alive.

His Lancaster's navigator had never before emerged from his cubby-hole to experience the full force of a raid, or to witness the beauty of the surrounding views. On what was likely to be his last opportunity of the war, he stood near Freddie Cole with his head in the astrodome, marvelling at the scene around him. His pleasure was short-lived. Seconds later, shrapnel burst through the Perspex and riddled his body, which protected Freddie from the blast. As the navigator recoiled and fell out of the astrodome, he flung out a despairing hand and, in his death agony, inadvertently grasped and pulled the ripcord of Freddie's parachute. It immediately opened and spread across the cockpit, soaking up the blood spurting from his wounds.

There was no time to reflect on the unforgiving brutality of war; both inner engines were on fire. Freddie tried feathering them and activated the extinguishers, but they both failed. Wilf yelled, 'Get out!' as he struggled to keep the aircraft steady, so Freddie bundled up his parachute with the wireless operator, Jack Speers, and they both headed for the forward escape hatch as the aircraft continued to be battered by flak. The fuel tanks in the wings had now been breached, and there was an inferno towards the rear of the aircraft. Both gunners must be dead. Speers saw the navigator's lifeless body, then hit the pilot's knee hard, the usual drill as you evacuated, to alert him to follow. 'There was no response,' Speers recalled. 'The front of the cockpit had been blown away. He could not have survived.' Freddie Cole was now sitting on the edge of the hatch, wrestling with his unfurled parachute. Speers made sure the harness was clipped on and then gave Freddie a mighty shove in the back, out of the falling plane. Speers then followed close behind.

As the silk billowed and held him, Cole saw the blazing Lancaster he had just left fly into the side of a mountain and explode. 'That was a truly horrendous sight. I knew some of my mates were still on board. As I floated down I was hit hard by the realisation that they were dead. But there wasn't time for tears. They came later. For now I had to think about my own survival.' There were no further parachutes. Pilot Wilf de Marco, the navigator and the two gunners hadn't made it. The three survivors were captured and would spend only a few weeks as prisoners of war.

Adolf Hitler hadn't been at the redoubt. He eventually shot himself in his Berlin bunker on 30 April.

Still, the Allied press made much of the raid. 'Berchtesgaden Flattened' trumpeted the headline in the *Globe and Mail* of 26 April: 'The last spot over which the swastika will fly.' Photo reconnaissance the following day had revealed heavy damage to huts in the camps occupied by Czech forced labourers, and even more alarmingly in a settlement for evacuated children – though this last report was excised from later official documents.

Bormann's and Göring's villas had been destroyed and the SS barracks had sustained heavy damage, but not so the Berghof, which was burnt down anyway soon afterwards by the retreating SS.

On their flight home, Don MacIntosh's Lancaster flew over the ruins of Munich and Stuttgart – 'peaceful and shattered beneath us' – all their fears gone: 'On our return to Bardney, there was no particular elation at the bombing of Hitler's house. We listened to the radio over the next few days, as the last pockets of the German army surrendered one after another. We wondered when Victory in Europe would be declared, so we could organise our parties.'

The Berchtesgaden raid was the last major offensive operation of the war for most of its participants, and returning safely home had deep significance. Mid-upper gunner Ken Johnson reckoned that 'this raid was perhaps the only time I experienced any sense of fear and relief. We were on the way back and I suddenly felt myself shaking, sweat running down my brow. I'd never felt this way before and I think it was a reaction to the fact that it was almost certainly our last op. It seemed I'd *survived*. That realisation really did hit me. Our only disappointment was to find that Mr Hitler hadn't been home!'[29]

Ken Johnson was one of a number of veterans the author interviewed for this book who sadly passed away before publication. Ken died in January 2020.

\* \* \*

Four days after the Berchtesgaden raid, his last bombing operation of the war, Ken Trent was summoned to Buckingham Palace for the official presentation of his DFC by King George VI. Various officials fussed around advising on protocol – 'Don't press the King's hand too hard when he offers it' ... 'Please address him as "Your Majesty"' – and Ken was allowed just two guests: his father, and, in place of his recently deceased mother, her best friend.

'Suddenly, without any fanfare, the King was there, and we all craned our necks to see him. He was dressed in full uniform with all his medals on show; he had quite a few more than me! Before I knew it, my name was called: "Flight Lieutenant Ken Trent, DFC".

'*Just do it*, I thought, and marched, with all the vim I could muster, up to the King. I imagined Mum watching over my shoulder as I came to a smart stop, and shot up the best salute I had ever made. My DFC was handed to the King, who hooked it carefully onto the clip on my uniform.

'"Congratulations," he said. "And thank you for your outstanding efforts."

'I was very aware of the silver cross flashing on my uniform, and as the proceedings came to an end I stood up, feeling a little self-conscious, but of course very proud. As I looked around at the opulent surroundings, the gold, the paintings, the velvet and the plush carpet, I realised that I didn't belong in such a setting. I would far rather be having a piss-up with the boys in the Mess; I was far more comfortable in my scruffy battledress milking a cow on the farm, or taking off into the darkness at the controls of my Lancaster.'

# CHAPTER FIFTEEN

# 'THE BEST RAID OF THE WAR!'

Lancaster navigator Cy Grant had been a prisoner of war in Stalag Luft III, deep in Silesia, 120 miles south of Berlin, for over eighteen months. On their secretly constructed radios, the prisoners had been following the course of the war with mounting excitement during the second half of 1944, plotting the advance of the Allies from the west, and the Russians from the east.

'Prisoners of war were unabashed optimists! We were always prepared to wager that the war would be over within the next six months. Even if we had to keep moving the date forward, six months was long enough to maintain reasonable hope. By January 1945, the chances of being liberated did seem very good indeed. Our secret maps, smuggled in with food parcels, indicated that both the American and Russian armies were closing fast. There were bets as to which of them would get to us first, but it was chiefly to the east that we looked for our salvation – the Russians were sweeping all before them in a colossal drive now. The first signs of this, and of the proximity of the war front, came with the first bedraggled columns of the retreating German army passing our camp; followed by German civilian refugees. A tiny trickle at first, but within a few days their numbers had swollen to a long, never-ending pilgrimage of misery and suffering. Ox-drawn carts and creaking wagons laden with the entire effects of families, the old and the very young plodding their weary souls over the frozen ground in a weary procession.

To us prisoners, though, this misery was the prelude to our own liberation. The Russians could not get to us fast enough!'[1]

Then, on the night of Saturday 27 January, at 9.30 p.m., the bombshell struck.

'No, we were not blown to bits, but our dreams were; our cherished dreams which had kept us going for so long. The Germans informed us that we were to be ready to be evacuated in thirty minutes. Panic! Thirty *minutes*! We were to be moved westwards, away from the advancing Russians. Dejection, like a grim vulture, hovered over the camp. Fear crept into our hearts. We were without large reserves of food. There had been very heavy snowfalls all month, and the landscape was a sea of glistening white. The Germans would be hostile in the towns as well as the villages. And we might well be caught between the two armies advancing from the east and the west.'

Thousands of prisoners of war and their guards set out through the deep, unforgiving snow, away from the Russians, now only 28 miles away. The distant clamour of heavy artillery followed them.

'The weather was below freezing. We wondered if we were strong enough to survive a rigorous trek. As a group, our hut of twelve men had taken the decision to stick together and pool our resources. We'd built a sledge out of odd bits of wood to hold our bare necessities. We took turns in pulling it, three shifts of four men, each for a period of twenty minutes, so none of us had to carry a rucksack. The first day was a nightmare. We got so tired that it would have been a relief simply to collapse on the snow and go to sleep. We stopped only twice, just long enough to eat something, because to stand still for more than five minutes would have been to invite disaster. The cold was intense and the risk of frostbite was great. It was better to keep moving on frozen feet all day long.'

They made 12 miles that first day, with no casualties, and spent the night in a huge, dark barn. Cy would never forget the stampede as the prisoners vied with each other to grab the best places to sleep among the straw and cattle.

Day after day, they marched further into Germany, their

destination – and their fate – unknown. They received their first German rations five days after setting out – one-fifth of a loaf of black bread.

'We awoke the next day to find that a miracle had happened overnight. A great thaw was in progress, induced by torrential rain. It was rapidly transforming everything into a sea of slush and mud. It was impossible to move, and we spent a miserable day hanging around in the slush, wet underfoot, mud and straw sticking to our soaking boots and making them even heavier. The knowledge that we'd have to abandon our sledges and carry our packs on our backs didn't help.'

Hunger was beginning to take its toll as the going became more treacherous: 'There were stragglers, and men collapsed onto the banks of sludge which had built up alongside the river of mud through which we waded ankle-deep. Many would have been left behind had it not been for the strenuous work of our untiring Medical Officer, who, equipped with an ox-cart, rescued the fallen and tended the sick.'

At last they arrived at the small town of Spremberg, 50 miles north-east of Dresden. Cy's group was given a few dry biscuits thinly spread with margarine, then locked in a filthy, damp barn for the night. The next morning they were marched, exhausted, to the railway station and loaded into cattle trucks, packed so tightly they had to take turns to sit down. It was 4.30 p.m. and they had walked 70 miles in treacherous weather in seven days. It had felt like a lifetime.

The train set off after a wait of five hours, heading north-west through desolate countryside. The prisoners used the toilet bucket in the corner as sparingly as possible, though many now had dysentery. After a day's travelling, they arrived at the huge POW camp of Luckenwalde, south of Potsdam.

They were to spend the next months there with 25,000 other Allied inmates. Another phase of waiting, and hoping against hope, lay ahead of them.

\* \* \*

Lancaster pilot Jim Penny's camp was evacuated on 7 April 1945. He had been a prisoner of war for just over sixteen months after being shot down during the Battle of Berlin in November 1943. In snaking columns, tens of thousands of prisoners were marched out of the camp at Fallingbostel in northern Germany, 60 miles south of Hanover.

Food was scanty and, to make matters worse, Jim was suffering from severe diarrhoea. In his weakened state, he had to let go of some of his treasured possessions, accumulated while in the camp: a pocket chess set, a Canadian blanket, and two books – an anthology of epics and Frederick Bodmer's *The Loom of Language*. 'I hated like hell ditching those books. I'd already left behind *Mathematics for the Million*, which with the two others had been sent by my brother Tommy.'[2]

Two days into the march, Jim was able to buy an egg from a guard in exchange for three cigarettes. In his diary, he recorded, 'first food that has stayed down since we left. First egg since 23 November 1943. Oh boy, it tasted really lush. Feel better tonight.'

The following day, the column rested, and Jim, feeling slightly better, bartered with the Germans for a tin of meat – a week's ration. He ate the lot in one sitting and began to feel more optimistic, though the same couldn't be said for many of his fellow POWs. They'd only been on the road for 30 miles, but months of short rations in the camp were already beginning to take their toll. The Germans' contribution to their wellbeing amounted to some gnarled and rotten potatoes. They covered many miles over the following days. There was nothing to be done other than putting one foot in front of the other, biting your lip against blisters and cramp in your sides. But Jim was suffering again, this time from gingivitis.

On 17 April they crossed the River Elbe at Hohnstorf, heading north-east. It was a low point for the POWs. They were moving away from the advancing British and American troops, deeper into Germany. Were they to be used as hostages? Some even thought they could be marching towards their own executions, a final act of bitter vengeance by the collapsing Nazi regime. Huge columns of prisoners and refugees now crammed the roads; it was a Biblical exodus. A large section of Panzer and Tiger tanks passed them, moving west, retreating from the Russian advance. The next day, heading north towards the Baltic coast, they arrived at Gresse, a village high on a hill, dominated by the squat steeple of its brick church. By now, many of the prisoners thought the Germans had neither instructions nor plans. The future looked bleak.

The next day, however, their spirits lifted when Red Cross food parcels arrived. After little to eat in the preceding days, they fell on the boxes ravenously. All too soon, though, they were back on the road. It was the thirteenth day of the march, but the noise of battle was close by. Could they dare hope their ordeal might soon be over?

At 11 a.m. on 19 April, they were stood down for a brief rest, and eagerly attacked their new supplies. In the distance, they could see a flight of RAF Typhoons, circling like hawks. Recognising them as British, some of the prisoners started to wave and cheer, presuming the Typhoons had been attacking formations of retreating German troops. It was marvellous to see them battering the enemy into submission. Here was the symbol of hope that signified the end really was in sight. Suddenly, the Typhoons seemed to change direction, wheeling towards the column of POWs. Was this a typical RAF low-level flypast, a 'beat-up'? The sort of antic most of the prisoners had performed themselves in their early days of flying?

As the aircraft roared in, the men noticed puffs of smoke from under the wings, then, to their abject horror, realised that the rockets slung there had been fired, were in flight, and heading at great speed straight for the column. Caught out in the open, one of the airmen reacted instinctively: 'They were firing at us! We flung ourselves to the ground. Men were trying to bury themselves in the ground, hiding behind anything they could. We tried to get off the lane and into the fields, to use any hump that could give cover.'[3]

For some there was nowhere to hide. As the rockets hit, bodies were flung into the air like rag dolls. For those lucky to survive the onslaught, the memories were vivid:

'I saw sparks coming out of the machine guns. I shouted, "Oh my God," and dived for the deck, scattering my belongings in all directions. I saw the earth being kicked up by machine-gun bullets just in front of my nose, and the next moment I felt as though my head had blown off; there was a shattering explosion and a tremendous concussion. When I opened my eyes there was nothing but grey and I thought, *Well, that's that! Pity, it's been a good life.* I thought I'd died. But suddenly I found that I was running again and as I burst out of the smoke, I realised it was the smoke of a rocket that had landed just in front of me. More bullets came after me. Time and again the earth kicked up just in front of me.'[4]

'It was the greatest tragedy of the whole war. They just came out of the blue and opened up on us with cannons and rockets, and, with no cover, many of my comrades were blown to pieces. As the survivors fanned out into the fields on either side of the lane, the planes came in, once, twice, three times more. I was crouched in a furrow in a ploughed field and fifty yards away I saw one brave guy stand up and wave his blue RAF greatcoat to try and show them who we were. They just cut him down. In just a few seconds dozens were dead and as many again severely wounded. Some had been in captivity for four or five years, men we knew better than our own brothers.'

Human remains lay everywhere. A torso was lodged in the branches of a tree. A head lay on the ground. With the planes gone, there was an uncanny silence, broken only by crying and moaning.

'It was strange but there wasn't a lot of loud screaming. I passed several dead and wounded. Some people were wandering aimlessly, others were bending over injured friends. I saw a pair of legs with nothing attached to them – just lying in the field. Complete with trousers. I remember one chap whose stomach had been ripped out. It was a scene of total carnage – by far the worst sight I had seen through the whole war. The Medical Officer was doing what he could but it was a hopeless task. Nobody was talking much. We were all very silent and with our own thoughts. People were angry.'[5]

Jim Penny had realised what horror was about to unfold and had taken cover.

'I hurtled into the wood by the road and dropped behind a tree. All I could hear was the noise of the explosions as the shells blasted around us. When it was over, there was silence for a moment, only to be broken by screams and shouts. As I stood up the sight which greeted me was horrendous. The dead and dying lay everywhere. We had all gone through so much, survived warfare in the skies, then life as POWs, and it was such a terrible tragedy that so many died at the hands of friendly forces. I went round to help the wounded. I put a tourniquet on what remained of one man's leg but couldn't stop him bleeding to death.'

Twenty-nine men were killed and another fifty wounded in the attack.[6] Jim's friend Paddy Ross was shot in the back and the leg, so while the remainder of the column moved on, Jim continued to tend the wounded, accompanying the doctor to the hospital in the nearby town of Boizenburg.

He was recovering slowly from his gingivitis, but when they weighed him at the hospital, he was down to just 6 stone (38kg), from his former weight of 10 stone (63.5kg). 'I saw the German doctor today who gave me some stuff to treat my mouth,' Jim wrote in his diary. 'Our treatment here is really good. The food is excellent, but – just my bloody luck! – I have bread and Red Cross supplies for the first time in days, and I can't chew anything! Our guns are getting closer again. All these chaps here, some so badly wounded, and I've got this footling mouth infection, making me such a bloody nuisance, when I should be helping more.'

As more men injured in the Gresse tragedy died from their wounds over the following days, the battle raged in the vicinity of the hospital and their guards and German medics began melting away. Jim was terrified by the screams and explosions of shells. 'If we don't get bumped off here, we may possibly get home soon. I daren't hope too much.'

In the early hours of 1 May, Jim was awakened by 'a General in a red beret'.

'"You've been liberated, son," he said.

'"About time, too," I replied, and promptly went back into a sound sleep.'

Later that morning, he wandered outside to see a line of British tanks, their crews relaxing on the grass, brewing up tea. Jim's captivity was finally over.

* * *

Cy Grant's life at the massive POW camp at Luckenwalde in southern Germany had been no picnic either.

'The barracks were squalid and dirty, with broken windows and damp walls. There were no stoves, no water, and the filthy palliasses [mattresses] on the three-tiered bunks were overrun with bedbugs. Within half an hour, we were filthier than we'd ever been before. We began to itch before even crawling into our bunks.

'Life there was beastly. There was little to eat – our daily ration was one-fifth of a loaf, an ounce of margarine, six potatoes and a bowl of soup. The soup was made of wormy peas and horsemeat, but we just scooped out as many of the maggots as possible and wolfed the rest down.'

At night, the bitter cold, the thin scratchy blankets and the relentless bedbugs conspired to make sleep a near-impossibility.

'The guards were jittery and unpredictable; sometimes they wanted to keep in our good books, but at others they were resentful of the way things were going for the Reich.' In the coming weeks, as Germany collapsed and the end neared, the guards became more despondent, even contrite. Early on 21 April, a German fighter flew over the camp and strafed it. 'We baled out of our beds in great panic and huddled on the floor.' The attack had a profound effect on the German guards, who simply abandoned the camp, and their prisoners.

At 10 a.m. the following day, the Russians finally arrived.

'Six tanks and twenty-nine motorised units full of soldiers crashed through the camp, literally tearing down the perimeter fence, amid our cheers and excitement. This was the day we'd been awaiting for so long. At last we were liberated. Soon, we thought, we'd be able to start living our lives again. Words cannot describe the scene! Our liberators were war-scarred fighting soldiers, a few women among them, flushed, wild-looking and armed to the teeth. We crowded around their tanks in joy and disbelief, taken aback by the magnitude of the moment.

'A new chapter had opened in our lives and the question uppermost in our minds was, *How soon will it be before we get back to Blighty?*'

But liberation didn't mean it was all over. Pockets of German resistance in the area had to be dealt with, and there was still a great shortage of food. Under Russian supervision, Cy and five of his hut companions went out in two lorries on a meat-foraging expedition later the same day. 'We were expecting to collect it from some butcher's stores, so you can imagine our surprise when we were deposited at a farm and told to fill the lorries with cows!' They crossed the fields in the gathering dusk, littered with the mangled corpses of the German dead.

'For the first time I came face to face with the stark horror of war. We had dropped bombs but never witnessed the consequences of our actions. We scurried over the bodies, lying there in the mud, eyes averted. We were in search of the cows. We had to keep alive!'

Their efforts to round up even one cow were primitive. A POW managed to fell one of the unfortunate beasts with a blow from a huge fencepost. He then cut its throat with a penknife. As the blood spurted across the ground, their Russian officer began screaming expletives in rage. 'Immediately we could see why he was furious; we now had to drag the dead animal to a lorry and haul it in. Only then did we cotton on to using a halter to capture a cow, and eventually to drive eleven of them into the lorries.'

Cy had the misfortune of travelling back among the panic-stricken creatures.

'I was splattered with a bountiful benediction – warm, moist and extremely revolting. By the time we arrived back at the camp, being cheered like conquering heroes, I was feeling utterly filthy and miserable. But not for long. The laughter and back-slapping which greeted us made our ordeal well worth it!'

Although now better sustained with prime German beef, it was still far from clear how or when Cy might get home.

*Loading a Lancaster at RAF Waterbeach*
*with supplies for Operation Manna*

For the Lancaster crews of RAF Waterbeach, a few miles north of Cambridge, the operation that started on Sunday 29 April 1945 was 'the best raid of the war',[7] and their feelings were shared by many others.

Operation Manna was the first occasion on which Lancasters would bring life and sustenance, rather than fear and death, to mainland Europe. The Netherlands had been suffering serious food shortages, further exacerbated by the terrible winter of 1944/45, since their Nazi occupiers had flooded some 500,000 acres of farmland as a defensive measure. Fuel shortages rendered the distribution of what little food existed almost impossible, especially to the western provinces, which had a population of some 3.5

million and contained the largest cities – Amsterdam, The Hague, Rotterdam and Utrecht.

City dwellers had no direct access to food, nor could they forage for firewood. Starvation first claimed the lives of the very old and the very young. During the long winter, remembered by the Dutch as the 'Hunger Winter', 20,000 perished and 800,000 suffered long-term effects of malnutrition. A young Dutch girl recorded, 'one day when my mum and my gran were out walking, they saw a man dressed like a real gentleman. Someone had spilt a little soup in a puddle of rain. My mum was shocked to see this elegant gentleman bend over to fish a few peas out of the water. That's how desperate people were for food.'[8]

People ate their pets, but only after they had eaten the last tulip bulbs, fried, roasted or raw. Taps ran dry. Some city folk ventured into the countryside in search of sustenance, making what came to be known as 'famine tours', and exchanging watches and necklaces for black bread and turnips. By April 1945, the situation for the survivors was more than desperate and pleas were made to the occupying German authorities to allow food drops to the beleaguered cities. They finally relented, but under the most exacting conditions. The Germans would surround the designated drop zones with heavy flak batteries to guard against any treachery on the part of the RAF, whose aircraft were to fly along prearranged corridors and deposit their loads only within designated areas. Any contravention of these strictures would result in the aircraft being fired on.[9]

Four large, specially designed panniers, known as 'blocks', weighing 1,254lb, were loaded into the Lancaster bomb bays. Each contained seventy sacks from the British Ministry of Food's reserve stocks of sugar, dried egg powder, margarine, salt, cheese, tinned meat, flour, dried milk, coffee, tea, cereals, high-vitamin chocolate, beans, peas, carrots and potatoes. The Lancasters would drop them without parachutes from very low level, typically 400–500ft, and at slow speed.

The BBC Home Service had broadcast announcements of the

'delivery' since 24 April. Not all the Dutch had access to secret radios, of course, but it was hoped that the news would spread by word of mouth. Within Bomber Command, the mercy mission wasn't greeted with universal enthusiasm.

At RAF Hemswell in Lincolnshire, news of Operation Manna was met with derisive laughter. Remarks such as 'Since when do we trust the bloody Hun?' and 'My God, who has gone crazy?' echoed around the briefing room. No one knew for certain how long the war would continue, and they certainly didn't want to perish in its final moments. There was real concern that the crews would be flying into a German trap – and that at 500ft they would be an unmissable target.[10] The less cynical saw the opportunity to save rather than take lives as something to celebrate. 'We were being told to drop food, not bombs. That was absolutely superb!'[11]

The first two Lancasters to carry out the trial sorties took off on the morning of 29 April. Each side had no reason yet to trust the other, and for the airmen, the Dutch population and the German gunners, the prelude was tense. Bob Upcott, flying the lead Lancaster, bit his lip as they approached the designated target areas. He knew exactly what the German 8.8cm flak 16 guns could do – and at this height, and this speed, they'd be sitting ducks.

'When we crossed the Dutch coast we could see all the anti-aircraft muzzles pointing at us. We were looking right down a number of barrels. We saw very few people on this first mission; evidently the Dutch didn't know we were coming, so they were not yet prepared to welcome us as they did later. We flew directly into the designated drop zone at Duindigt racecourse, near The Hague, the other Lancaster in echelon formation, slightly behind me, to port. None of the German anti-aircraft guns fired at us, but we later found that a 9mm round had made a small hole in the starboard side of the aircraft, near the tail.'[12]

Despite few people turning up to benefit from this first drop, it had been successful, and at 2 p.m. that same afternoon the other 242 Lancasters engaged in Operation Manna made their appearance. By now the word had spread like wildfire. People came out in their thousands, waving and cheering as the low-flying aircraft passed slowly over them.

'From 200ft above Rotterdam, the view brought tears to my eyes – laughter and tears,' one pilot remembered. 'The reception from the people below was overwhelming! They were standing on rooftops, on balconies, hanging out of the windows, in the streets and in the fields, all with their faces turned towards the sky, laughing, cheering and waving handkerchiefs, the Dutch flag and Union Jacks. Some had banners proclaiming their gratitude.'[13]

The Lancaster crews, waving back, could see messages painted on roofs: 'Thank you, RAF'.

Thomas Murray, the 27-year-old pilot who'd joined the RAF in 1937, first flying Manchesters, then Lancasters, then with the Special Operations Executive, had returned to active duty on Lancasters in March 1945. He approached the racecourse at Duindigt ready for his food drop. 'I could make out this chap standing outside the arena with his arms up. The preceding aircraft had a hang-up with its load and the supplies were dropped late. A bag of flour broke open and burst over this chap, making him all white, from head to toe – a very funny sight!'[14]

On the ground, the rapture of the starving increased. There was so much manna from heaven that there was no longer any need to fight for it, though unfettered excitement had its dangers, as seventeen-year-old Arie de Jong discovered.

'There are no words to describe the emotions experienced that afternoon. More than 200 Lancasters, flying exceptionally low, suddenly filled the western horizon. You could see the gunners waving in their turrets – a marvellous sight! One Lancaster roared over the town at 70ft – I saw the aircraft tacking between church spires and dropping its bags to the south. Everywhere we looked, bombers could be seen. No one stayed indoors and everybody dared to wave cloths and flags. What a feast! Everyone is excited and joyful! The war must be over soon now! Our first taste of the heavenly food came when a sack dropped by one of the Lancasters fell nearby. My friends and I rushed over and found a container full of yellow powder. We gorged ourselves on it without hesitation, but it turned out to be dried egg! We were soon spouting yellow clouds and throwing up!'

Arie and his teenage friends survived the ordeal, and once they'd found out how to cook the dried egg, 'you can't imagine how good they tasted after a diet of stinging nettles'.[15]

Another pilot looked down and reflected, 'These brave people, who so often had risked their own lives to save an airman and return him safely to England, were thanking us! I felt very humble.'[16]

The RAF dropped 6,684 tons of food during the course of 3,000 Operation Manna sorties. The American and Canadian forces added many more to this total.

*Former POWs clamber aboard a Lancaster*
*during Operation Exodus*

In the dying days of the war, the Lancaster had one further mission of mercy to fulfil. It wasn't the ideal passenger aircraft, but, stripped of as much equipment within the fuselage as possible, and carrying a crew of five, the planners knew that with the weight properly distributed it could carry twenty-four men with ease, if not comfort. But comfort was low on the list of priorities for liberated prisoners of war.

Operation Exodus, as aptly named as Operation Manna, began on 3 May 1945. It required just as careful preparation. The Air Ministry estimated that there were at least 250,000 Allied prisoners of war (excluding those from the Russian forces), and they all needed to be brought home.[17] The operation would be carried out at a time when millions of displaced people were on the move, Nazi fugitives among them. Airfields capable of accommodating Lancasters had to be found and reconnoitred in what had until recently been enemy territory.

Rear gunner James Flowers was on one of the early missions. 'We made a trip to Brussels to collect twenty British former POWs. The fact that the Lancasters didn't have any seats didn't matter a jot to them – they felt they were going home in style. To fly in a Lancaster was a dream come true for most of them. They were crammed into every part of the aircraft, with only a few inches to spare, but they still wanted to see everything. I spent all my time escorting them on visits to my rear turret. Most had never flown before, so it was a really exciting experience for them; and most had been POWs for years. I can still remember their excitement and their tears as they caught their first sight of England. And for me, it was a great contrast and a great joy to be able to use the Lancaster, a weapon of war and destruction, for a peaceful purpose, and to bring these poor men home to their families after so long.'[18]

Among those brought back was Australian Lancaster pilot Gordon Stooke, who had survived being shot down in the summer of 1943. His return flight home took him over Cologne.

'Its devastation beggared description. We could have easily been convinced that we were looking down on a huge, treeless cemetery. Grotesque tombstone-like bits of buildings were standing in rows which used to be streets. In the centre of this destruction, like a massive mausoleum, stood the apparently undamaged Cathedral.'

Looking at it, Gordon reflected on the dozens of cities razed during the war, and wondered, *Where was the sense of it all?*

They landed in Brussels to change aircraft, taken in British Army lorries to a transit depot.

'There were about forty of us, and a scruffier lot you would not have found in a day's march. A few wore dirt-encrusted remnants of RAF battledress, but most, including myself, were dressed in a bedraggled assortment of American Army and British Army uniforms, and civilian clothes. We hadn't washed for weeks, so even our best friends wouldn't want to know us. Even so, we were led into a hall at the depot and seated at long tables draped with freshly laundered and ironed white tablecloths. In came Mess orderlies, carrying trays laden with fresh white bread, pure butter, and real fruit jam.

'It's hard to describe the pandemonium which followed. Some started to gulp the fresh bread on its own, not even taking the time to spread it with butter. Those who included the butter and the jam experienced gastronomic ecstasy. Most of us had been living for years on strictly rationed portions of sour black bread with occasional, unsavoury, ersatz margarine. The fare in front of us tasted like cake – no – even *better* than cake. It was a simple meal by most standards, but one I will never forget, especially when the Mess orderlies topped it off with cups of real tea, real milk and real sugar. Their encouragement to "Get stuck in, lads!" brought tears to many eyes.'

The next day, Gordon flew back over the White Cliffs of Dover, home to a new life – though one that would be affected irrevocably by 'our service in Bomber Command and our experience as guests of the Third Reich'.[19]

Those first glimpses of the White Cliffs were deeply moving, and more than one returning airman found his heart close to bursting upon seeing them. 'It was a glorious sight, and one which at times I thought I would never see again. It was overwhelming. A week ago, we were all starving to death, just waiting for the end, and now, suddenly, we were crossing the English coast, and we were home again. I cried with sheer joy. No more rifle butts in the back, no more being herded around like cattle, and being treated like the lowest form of human life.'[20]

One former POW was allowed to take over the controls of the aircraft as they crossed the Channel. When Britain loomed out of the coastal cloud bank, he said, 'My eyes filled with tears, and there was a lump in my throat so large I felt I would choke. I gripped the stick and breathed through my open mouth. Beside me, the pilot was silent. I'm sure he knew my difficulty. The engines sang sweetly in my ears as I checked temps, pressures, fuels, revs and so on, before commencing a very shallow descent to the soil we had longed to tread for so long.'[21]

Ken Trent also took part in the evacuation.

'It was a strange feeling, flying over countries which up until now had represented danger and death to me. We all kept a good look-out, but as a matter of habit rather than the expectation of anybody attacking us. I could look down and enjoy the sights of towns, rivers, hills and cities in the afternoon sun, instead of sweating into my suit waiting for the first burst of flak or the command to *corkscrew left*.' As the English coast approached, 'as many chaps as possible would crowd into the cockpit and wherever else they could get a view, and peer out with eager eyes. I used to wonder what their thoughts were. I couldn't ask them. There was a lump in my own throat.'[22]

Lancaster pilot and former POW Jim Penny, still weak from the privations of the march and his brush with death at Gresse, was flown home from the British hospital at Lüneburg.

'I was very weak and now a stretcher case. I couldn't see anything out of the Dakota as I was flat on my back. In fact I was bloody annoyed as I'd wanted to come home in a Lancaster, the same way as I'd started my journey, eighteen months earlier.'

Operation Exodus ran for twenty-four days, during which 75,000 men were shipped home.

*Thomas Murray*

On 8 May 1945, Prime Minister Winston Churchill addressed the populace: 'My dear friends, this is your hour. This is not victory of a party or of any class. It's a victory of the great British nation as a whole.'

Thomas Murray, by then an Acting Wing Commander in charge of 138 Squadron, drily followed Churchill's announcement of VE Day with his own Tannoy broadcast to his men: 'The station is now shut down, and you may go into Mildenhall to celebrate. Before you go, I am going to tell you that I am going out to each aircraft to lock them. Each and every one of them. I am going to put the keys in the safe and the safe keys will be in my pocket, so don't try to get back to Australia – or anywhere else!'

His squadron would continue to fly Exodus missions for months to come, but the last Operation Manna runs also took place that same day. 'We actually made a drop on VE Day. We heard Winston Churchill's message on the aircraft radio and by the time we reached the Dutch coast it was clear the Dutch people were aware it was all over. British and American flags were being waved and we even saw

Germans standing on top of their gun batteries, waving. Truly an amazing sight.'[23]

Cy Grant and his fellow prisoners liberated by the Red Army were still wondering when, and if, they would ever get home. The Americans were close by. What was preventing their handover? Why were the Russians prevaricating? They had fired warning shots over their heads to dissuade them from trying to leave the camp.

'I made up my mind that I would leave at the first possible opportunity. Shortly after this came the news we had always prayed for: *Der Krieg ist fertig* – the WAR IS OVER!' The news was greeted with a mixture of overwhelming relief and deep frustration: 'A kind of hysteria prevailed. We were smiling but tense. I knew that nothing was going to stop me leaving now.'

A rumour spread that American lorries were waiting a short distance away. Cy managed to sneak out of the camp to check, and, to his surprise and relief, he discovered them nearby. Cy knew he could easily pass for a black American, and the Americans with the trucks agreed, so on the morning of VE Day he clambered aboard with hundreds of other prisoners. 'The driver started to make for the Elbe. We were quite delirious.'

Most of VE Day, however, would pass in harassment and aggravation for Cy. Bridge by bridge, the convoy was turned away at Russian guard-posts, all of whom refused to grant them the necessary permission to cross the river. 'Our feelings of dejection and frustration were overpowering. We were shattered – physically, mentally and emotionally. It was getting dark, and we knew a curfew would be in force by 6 p.m.' With just a few minutes to spare, they arrived at a temporary bridge manned by a single young Russian sentry.

'Our hearts were really thumping. This was our last chance. Would we be stopped again? Behind the sentry lay the pontoon bridge stretching across the Elbe. We could see movement on the other side as some American soldiers casually looked over in our direction. The sentry moved to one side, stood to attention and saluted. We drove straight past him and in a moment we were crossing to freedom. This was a dream, surely? Any moment now I'd awaken and be back in my louse-ridden sack at Luckenwalde. But it was no dream. My ordeal was indeed finally over. Five days later I was back in England. It was cold and wet, but nothing could have dampened my spirits – for ahead of me lay the exciting challenge of a brand-new life.'

\* \* \*

Despite the fact that sorties in support of Exodus would continue the following day, preparations for a 'Victory in Europe' celebration dance got under way at RAF Metheringham immediately after the Station Commander had announced the cessation of hostilities. They emptied the Repair and Inspection hangar and cleaned it, created a dance floor and festooned the rafters with WINDOW – suddenly put to happier use than it had been hitherto.

They spent the day making sandwiches, and to speed things up 'the butter was heated slightly then put on the bread with a brush similar to a shaving brush'.[24] Each Mess set up a bar, local breweries provided extra beer, and residents from the surrounding villages were sent invitations. Everyone danced the night away to the music of the station band. At midnight, several crews left the party to help load the Lancasters with blankets and sweets for the POWs waiting to be repatriated, as the ground crews prepared fifteen aircraft for an 8 a.m. take-off.

The underlying mood on VE Day was often surprisingly subdued. As Ted Watson celebrated with friends at a local pub, what struck him most was the end of the blackout: 'We enjoyed at least a little lighting in the streets once more. The King gave a speech over the radio at 9 p.m., and the Home Service presenter described the floodlights at Buckingham Palace and the two great searchlights over St Paul's Cathedral, creating an immense "V" for Victory image in the sky.'

But his joy was not unconfined.

'There were many families for whom it was a time of sad reflection and remembrance of loved ones lost. For others the uncertainty surrounding the fate of POWs remained; and nor was it the end of the war. In the Far East the Japanese remained undefeated, and, unwilling to contemplate surrender, determined to fight to the last man.'[25]

Perhaps inevitably, VE Day brought no closure for some, no inner peace. Elaine Shaw had lost her father, Stanley, when his Lancaster was shot down during the raid on the V-weapons development centre at Peenemünde two years earlier. She was now eleven.

'I remember VE Day very well. There was bunting in the street, a huge party and joyful celebrations. There were tables of food and everyone had a wonderful time. But not us. My mother said we had nothing to celebrate. She was right; we didn't. And despite all the food, and the joy, I didn't want to take part either – I remember standing at our gate, watching my friends enjoy the day, laughing, joking, celebrating victory and the end of that terrible war. They were with their parents, their fathers – and my father had gone. It didn't feel like much of a celebration to me. My mother called me in and we sat quietly in the house. We had nothing to celebrate.'[26]

Pilot Don MacIntosh marked VE Day at RAF Bardney, 10 miles east of Lincoln. A hangar was cleared for the party and WAAFs decorated it with homemade bunting while the electricians hung dim blue bulbs from the girders and the ground crews lit a pathway of flares on the road outside. The party was open to all.

'When I saw the women and children and elderly villagers in civilian clothes, I realised how isolated we'd been in the camp.' Among the villagers, Don recognised a woman who'd supplied him with eggs arrive with her two small boys. She was looking around, slightly dazed. When Don went up to greet her, she said, 'I just wanted to see what it was all about, if you don't mind. We've lived with it all for so long. It seems so strange now that it's all over. I brought the boys along so they can remember it when they grow up.'[27]

'I shouted some inanities back at her, above the noise of the airmen's band playing loudly and badly behind us. The whole thing was an anticlimax. Most of the bright sparks had made a beeline for

London, where all the action was, and the hangar was too big, and dwarfed us. I felt depressed, and I couldn't think of anything to say to the villagers. I went back to the Mess, to think and drink alone. I suppose I was a little sad that the war was over. I had enjoyed the war, with all the dangers and excitement. I suppose I'd become somewhat addicted to it. I wasn't too sure what the peace would hold for me. Would it provide as much stimulation?'

* * *

RAF High Command now decreed that the Lancasters and other transport aircraft could be put to further peacetime use. They would give the ground crews who had served so faithfully the opportunity of flying over mainland Europe to see the outcome of their endeavours. These trips quickly acquired the nickname 'Cook's Tours', after the long-established travel agency.

But seeing the reality of the damage caused by the bombing proved to be something of a mixed blessing. Ken Trent remembers a time he flew a group of Lancaster ground crew in the aircraft they had so lovingly cared for:

'We took off to fly over the Ruhr and other bombed areas to see just what they looked like – this time in relative safety, at low level, and in daylight. Instead of having to clench my hands over the steering column and grit my teeth flying into a storm of flak while dodging searchlights, I could drop down to two or three thousand feet and have a good look at what remained of our targets. Sure enough, I could clearly make out smashed sidings and railway yards, shattered factories and installations, and of course devastated homes, shops, churches and roads. It amazed me, as I banked to survey the sea of rubble which was once the heart of Cologne, that anyone could have survived there. We had certainly done as Bomber Harris had asked, and brought destruction on a huge scale to the Germans – which to my mind was no more than they deserved. But I remember looking down and thinking to myself, *However will they be able to make that right again?*'

In the midst of his own victory celebrations, Don MacIntosh also flew passengers on a 'Cook's Tour' in his Lancaster.

'The month of May in 1945 was idyllic, with blue skies and constant sunshine, as if the heavens were smiling on Victory; and we marvelled for a few days at the light shining again from lamps and windows at dusk. I celebrated continuously for two weeks, drinking beer at lunchtime, falling asleep in the afternoon, and making the rounds of the Lincoln pubs in the evening. Occasionally, we were called to dump incendiaries and now-unnecessary bombs in the North Sea. I also took half-a-dozen WAAFs from the motor pool on a "Cook's Tour" of the Ruhr. We flew over northern Germany, while the WAAFs took it in turns to crouch in the bomb-aiming compartment in the nose. I descended to 500ft over Essen, Bremen and Emden to give them a better view of the eerie spectacle. Not a single building had a roof and the cities were completely gutted. I couldn't see how any human beings could exist there, let alone fight a war. From the air, it looked impossible that life of any kind could be carried on in the ruins. What did they do for food, water and sanitation? How on earth did they keep going for so long? But although I found it difficult to believe how anyone could survive such obliteration, I didn't feel any sorrow for those on the ground. There'd been a war to fight, and we'd done what was necessary to defeat the scourge of the Nazis. We returned gratefully to our home base, RAF Bardney, glad to be away from the moon-landscape of devastation across the Channel.

'I enjoyed the war and what it gave me. It was a wonderful experience for a young man. I felt I'd done a good job, which was all that could be asked. And there's no doubt the Lancaster was part of my survival; it was an amazing aircraft to take to war.'[28]

But the peace would bring its own challenges and recriminations. The battles of the Lancaster, and those who had flown them, were far from finished.

# CHAPTER SIXTEEN

# LOOKING BACK

Air Chief Marshal Arthur Harris, the Commander-in-Chief of Bomber Command, wrote to Avro's managing director, Roy Dobson, after the war, thanking the 1.5 million people who contributed to the building of his Lancasters: 'I would say this to those who placed that shining sword in our hands: Without your genius and efforts we could not have prevailed, for I believe that the Lancaster was the greatest single factor in winning the war.'[1]

While Harris's claim could clearly be disputed, Ron Needle, the rear gunner whose aircraft had crashed in a freezing French forest in January 1945, took a similarly profound, but more personal, view; his Lancaster had saved his life. He was one of only two survivors, and the memory of his fellow crewmen never faded. They had been bound by their common sense of purpose – to protect their country from the darkest of threats and, if necessary, to sacrifice their lives in the process.

\* \* \*

*Ron and Sylvia Needle on their wedding day*

Ron and his fiancée Sylvia married on 24 November 1945. He wore his uniform; she was dressed in a stunning white dress and wore a veil topped with white flowers, offsetting her flowing dark hair. It was a joyful day, though not everything had gone entirely as planned.

'Unfortunately my first artificial leg wasn't ready, and I had to get married on crutches. I'd decided to wear my best RAF uniform and I was very pleased the photographer was able to take the photographs making it appear that I had two legs! During the reception I was a little disappointed at having to watch the dancing, without being able to join in with Sylvia. Nevertheless, it made me more determined than ever to overcome my difficulties. After all, I remembered how bravely the lads in the hospitals had coped with injuries far worse than mine.'[2]

After the marriage, the happy couple were lucky enough to find a flat to rent in the Birmingham suburb of Erdington. They hadn't a stick of furniture, nor money to buy any. Like many returning veterans, they would need to rely on charity to get them through the lean post-war years. 'The RAF Association gave me an interest-free loan to help with buying some basic furniture.'

Life for them began to return to something like normal, with a major change of gear in February 1946. 'At last I was able to collect my leg. I felt like a kid at Christmas with a new toy. Walking to a tram stop people weren't staring at me like they used to when I was using crutches. I was delighted. I was able to play cricket, football, and golf. I could dance, climb ladders, and drive a car.

'In the aftermath of war our lives moved on – I didn't really discuss much of the circumstances of my crash with Sylvia as there wasn't much to say. Once I had my false leg, it was the beginning of a new phase of my life. The war was forgotten and it was time to move on. The war was in the past. It was time to get on with the peace.'

Unfortunately, it wasn't that simple.

'There were nightmares where I could see the burning Lancaster, and my mate Jack Elson's bloodied legs hanging out of the mid-upper gunner's turret. The images of death were vivid and distressing, though with time they faded in intensity. But there was always a hole in my story, something not quite right, a final chapter to be told, and as the years trundled on, the memories started to rise again. As I got older, I began to yearn for some kind of reunion with my past – to look for some kind of closure. Over the years, the same deep longing kept returning. I desperately wanted to visit the graves of my fellow crew members.'

The opportunity finally came in 1982, when a friend mentioned a cheap weekend package deal to Paris. Ron and Sylvia gathered a small party of friends and relations and took the plunge. They weren't great travellers, but he would get the chance to see Paris, which, confined to his hospital train, he had missed thirty-seven years earlier. And, more importantly still, he'd have the chance to find the cemetery where his fallen comrades lay.

'When we started the journey, I was very tense, nervous and, for no apparent reason, very irritable. I was starting a new journey, a reunion with my past, with my dead friends, nearly forty years after parting from them. I kept all these thoughts buried and didn't want to show how much I was affected.'

On their first day in the French capital they skipped the organised tour of the city and set off instead for the RAF cemetery at Choloy, 180 miles to the east. It took many hours by taxi, train and bus, but with cheerful local help and rough '*Franglais*', they finally arrived at 3 p.m.

The minor frustrations of the day were forgotten as they made their way into the immaculately maintained plot. Of the 461 Second World War casualties buried there, twenty – all airmen – are still unidentified. After searching the record book, Ron took a short walk along the serried ranks of white headstones to his destination. Each of his friends had his name, age, crew position and the date of his death inscribed beneath the RAF service badge. Most also had a personal inscription which had been added later. Beneath the name of his pilot Jim Scott, he read: '*Too short your life my darling son, but peaceful be your rest.*'

'It was so terribly sad to see them again, but, in a strange way, quite wonderful too. I had to work hard to stop the tears from flowing. I understood now why I needed to make this journey; I was at last partially reconciled to what had happened. My eighteen-year-old daughter Maria stood by me, tears running down her cheeks. "Oh, Dad," she said. "I didn't realise they were so young!" I thought, *What a bloody waste* – and not just for our boys; I felt the same when I visited the German cemeteries later. All dead before they'd really begun to live. And my demons hadn't gone away. This journey of discovery into my past raised other questions I needed answers to. Closure still eluded me.'

Ron knew that Méligny-le-Grand was less than 25 miles to the west, but it is a remote village, and there was no time to go there on this trip. He would have to be patient. 'We eventually arrived back in Paris at midnight. I felt miserable and depressed. I should have realised how it would affect me. Now I knew I had to find the site of the crash, to thank those who had saved my life. I was determined to achieve this second goal.'

But it would be another four years before he could return. Family life, his work as an engineer, his involvement with BLESMA,[3] the charity for limbless service personnel, all took priority. There was no time to make that trip to Méligny. Or was he avoiding this confrontation with the past?

Soon after Ron's early retirement, brother-in-law Reg and his wife Ruby took matters into their own hands. They were keen travellers and had driven across Europe the previous year. 'Come on, Ron! Let's make arrangements to find this village where you crashed. We can all go in my car!'

In June 1986, they set off to finish the job.

* * *

Méligny-le-Grand is a tiny, isolated village, and, before the era of personal satellite navigation, was not easy to find. They got as far as Commercy with no difficulty, but then spent a day driving around in circles, quizzing locals, all to no avail. Ron again became upset and frustrated.

'I was angry at myself for having forgotten to bring my detailed French Michelin map of the region. I knew we must be close and I thought our luck was in when we passed a police van at the side of the dual carriageway. We stopped, and I made my way over to the two gendarmes. I showed them Reg's map, and said "Méligny-le-Grand", but I pronounced the name so badly that they didn't understand. I became very downhearted!'

Finally, despite the fact that no one spoke English and they had almost no French, Ron asked directions of a couple of ladies chatting over their garden hedge. 'When I mentioned Méligny-le-Grand, one of them pointed down the road. Off we went and, YES! There was a signpost to the village! Was it the right village? Would anyone still be alive who remembered the crash? Driving down the narrow road I began to feel very strange, almost apprehensive. Then, suddenly, we rounded a bend and the village and the church came into view. The church of St Evre, whose Angelus bells had rescued me forty-one years before.'

St Evre, dedicated to a local sixth-century bishop, and built in pale Lutetian limestone, was unchanged, its squat black tower pointing heavenwards in the centre of the tiny village, which nestled in gently rolling farmland and wooded hills. How calm and peaceful it seemed now, so very different to the day of his first 'visit'.

Like so many of his generation, Ron had always found it difficult to express emotion openly. Now he was trembling. They got out of the car and walked towards St Evre, passing an old lady outside a nearby house. There was something familiar about her, but she certainly gave no sign of recognition. After asking one or two people in the rue de Saint Aubin, the main street, they were introduced to Colette, who'd moved to Méligny after marrying her husband soon after the war. She knew nothing of the crash, but spoke enough English to allow them to communicate.

Colette listened to Ron's story and quickly sent her husband off on an errand. He returned with a grizzled and suntanned companion driving a tractor.

'This, is André Fromont,' Colette announced.

André Fromont! The man who had rescued Ron over four decades earlier. The man who had rung the Angelus bell that had guided him to safety!

'When I saw the look of recognition and relief on André's face, I realised what I had been searching for all these years. *This* is what had been missing from my story, *here* was the end of my journey. The sense of joy etched on André's face wiped away the dark past and replaced those images of the death of my friends and the destruction of my Lancaster. At last I had closure. We simply hugged and looked into each other's eyes and smiled; there was no need for any tears, nor words. The moment was between us alone. We had both been on a journey which had now ended. It's difficult to put into words how I felt. Suffice to say, he had saved my life and was a truly good man. I knew at that moment I had never met a truer friend.'

Ron was then introduced to the elderly woman he'd passed on the way to the church. Now he recognised her! Mariette Bouchot,[4] the deputy mayor's wife, who had given him a boiled egg, cut off his flying boot, and nursed him immediately after André had brought him, near death from exposure, to her house. There was more to come. Later, he and André were able to visit the crash site. There was little trace except a small clearing and some scattered metal, but Ron, his heart pounding, recognised it immediately. He wondered which tree he might have leant on, waiting for death, all those years ago. Their leaves rustled gently in the wind. It looked as if a storm was coming. They stood together in silence.

When they returned to André's house, his daughter Cathérine greeted them.

'Ron didn't speak French and Daddy didn't speak English, but you could see from their eyes that they understood each other. When they were at the site of the crash, an enormous squall came up, with a lot of heavy rain. They hadn't noticed. They were soaked to the skin, but I don't think either of them knew it. They were so glad to be reunited, so glad that they were both still alive to share this indescribable moment.'[5]

Back at his house, André vanished, then reappeared with the baking tins made from the aluminium skin of Ron's aircraft, and proudly showed them off, telling him about the other uses the wreckage had been put to. To Ron's delight, André presented him with one. A final reminder of the Lancaster he had flown to war.

'I try not to show my emotions, but this was one of the most moving aspects of my story. Our Lancaster was a war machine, an aircraft designed to deliver death and destruction. It'd been devised with the sole purpose of carrying men and bombs to drop them on the enemy, to destroy their buildings and kill their people. The last time I had seen this cake tin, it was part of the wreck-age – blackened, charred, smouldering, the metal it was made from shrouding the dead bodies of my friends. Now the wreckage had been transformed: cake tins, a water-trough, a wheelbarrow; symbols of life, pleasure and sustenance. Our magnificent Lancaster had come full circle.'

Cathérine watched the two friends interact. 'I could see that message in their eyes again; a huge "thank-you". Daddy had saved Ron's life, but Ron had helped save France, and we knew thousands had died to do so. I think both Daddy and Ron would always live under the shadow of that thought.'

Ron and Sylvia would make many return trips to Méligny over the next decade, and in 1990 he wasn't the only survivor of their crash to visit the site. The last time he had seen Harry Stunell, their wireless operator, was aboard their doomed Lancaster in January 1945. Like so many of the Bomber Command crews, they had simply lost contact in the post-war years. It was a time before email or social media and the only way of seeking out an old comrade was to put adverts in local newspapers and write endless letters. They thought they had better things to do, busy lives to lead. But, as the years unfolded, they yearned to find out what had become of their old crewmates. Veterans' groups and associations were established to help rekindle old friendships.

Eventually, Harry and Ron arranged to hook up.

'I was so excited waiting for him at Snow Hill station in Birmingham. For a moment I thought he had missed the train as I couldn't see him after all the other passengers had left. He hadn't recognised me and walked straight past! It was only when he retraced his steps that we came face to face. It was such an emotional meeting. I could hardly believe it was him. It seemed like just a few months earlier that he was a young man, with black hair. Now he was white-haired. We were old men, I suppose, but at last we were together again!'

The occasion of their visit in 1990 was the unveiling of a marker at their crash site and a memorial plaque in the church of St Evre to the companions they had lost. A service was held, which everyone in the village attended. As the ceremony drew to a close, Ron and Harry drew back the curtain draped across the plaque:

*To the glory of God and Remembrance*
*Of our Comrades, who gave their Lives*
*In the Fight for Liberty, Jan. 8th 1945.*
*F/O James Scott, F/O Kenneth Darke,*
*F/O Robert Dunlop, Sgt. Leslie Knapman,*
*Sgt. Jack Elson.*
*For Our Tomorrow They Gave Their Today.*

*To the People of Méligny-le-Grand*
*With their Help and Comfort we survived.*
*Our Grateful Thanks –*
*Sgt. Ron Needle, Sgt. Harry Stunell.*
*We Shall Never Forget.*

The church bells sounded the Angelus once more; the wheel of time had come full circle.

*Ron Needle and Harry Stunell in*
*Méligny-le-Grand in 1990*

Former prisoner of war and Lancaster navigator Cy Grant's post-war ambition was to practise law. He returned to Britain and qualified as a barrister at the Middle Temple. But, unable to find a chambers willing to accept him,[6] he changed tack and launched himself into a highly successful career as a singer and actor. Between 1957 and 1960, his was the first black face to appear regularly on BBC television, on the current affairs magazine programme *Tonight,* for which he regularly composed and performed a 'topical calypso' inspired by the day's news:

> *We bring you the news you ought to know*
> *With Tonight's Topical Calypso.*

The racial stereotype, innocently imposed, would make Cy a pioneer of black awareness in Britain – a household name. As he says in his memoir:

'Being a POW taught me to cope with disappointment and adversity; but my experience in conflict led me to the conclusion that warfare was indefensible and barbaric even when it appeared that it could be justified. Peace will never be achieved by a morality which justifies the manufacture and trade of arms. Hiroshima could never be justified on whatever grounds. How could the "civilised" West ever explain it away? How could it live with the memory of the Holocaust? Who possesses the right to produce weapons of mass destruction?'[7]

Cy's family had been touched by war in many different ways. His daughter, Sami Moxon, remembers, 'When I was little, every time *The Great Escape* film came on TV, my dad always said that he had been in that camp: Stalag Luft III. But we never really questioned him about what he meant! He just didn't talk much about his war experience; it was only when he started to write his memoir that it began to come out. We were always far more aware of our mum's war history; she was a Holocaust survivor who had been in Theresienstadt concentration camp. She and her mother survived miraculously, but both her father and brother were killed.

'Although I know he must have been petrified when his Lancaster was hit and the panic of the parachute drop, my dad never mentioned that he was traumatised by his experience. He always considered himself to be very lucky. He spent much of his time campaigning for peace and equality; he was a proud pacifist. I think that's why he didn't seem to seek any glory or recognition for his RAF contribution. I also think that his awareness of my mother's huge suffering and loss in war made him feel that his experience was somewhat privileged.'[8]

* * *

Former Lancaster pilot Billy Strachan hoped to settle once more in Jamaica with his wife Joyce and their three young sons. The spirited youth was now a war hero held in high regard, but gaining promotion in the Civil Service under white colonial rule remained as difficult as ever.

He returned to Britain, where he became a senior Law Court clerk, and later head of equal opportunities with the Inner London Education Authority. After playing his part in the defeat of Nazism, he found himself immersed in a lifelong battle for equality. 'We passionately believed that the abolition of exploitation of man by man, of oppression and of human degradation, could be achieved.' He was not alone in hoping that the courage and sacrifice of his generation would create a legacy of peace and harmony, the end of nationalism and right-wing extremism, and a safer, kinder world. As did many of his compatriots who also returned, full of hope, to Britain.

The *Empire Windrush* had arrived at Tilbury docks in June 1948. Britain had once again reached out to her colonies for help rebuilding the country after the depredations of war. Roughly one third of her passengers were returning veterans. Baron Baker, a West Indian former RAF policeman who had stayed in Britain after the war, was there to greet them. 'Many of those on the *Windrush* were exservicemen, and there was an immediate understanding between us.

There was a greater feeling of togetherness among that generation than I have seen in any group I have come across.'

Yet, despite the passing of the British Nationality Act that same year, 'An Act to make provision for British Nationality and for citizenship of the United Kingdom and Colonies, extended to all members of the Dominions and Colonies',[9] there were dissident voices among politicians, journalists and the general public.

As the *Windrush* approached her destination, Sam King, a West Indian RAF engineer now returning to pursue a career in the 'Mother Country', was aware of 'great apprehension on the ship because we knew there was a national debate in Britain as to whether we would be allowed to dock'.[10]

It was far from misplaced. Not all their fellow passengers faced a warm reception, and some would suffer difficulty finding lodgings and work because of racial prejudice. But they didn't give in to adversity. Sam went on to help establish a scheme in south London enabling newcomers to buy their own houses, while Baron Baker used his RAF police experience to create a neighbourhood watch self-support group run by black veterans for the immigrant community in Notting Hill at the time of the infamous 1958 riots.

It was a long way from being the welcome they deserved from a nation that should have more vigorously applauded the Caribbean and African nationals who had abandoned the safety and comfort of their homes to help in its darkest hour.

\* \* \*

Since Winston Churchill had distanced himself from Arthur Harris after the Dresden firestorm, Bomber Command itself came under increasing criticism for the ferocity of its strategic bombing. The odium extended to the aircrews themselves and was reinforced by the 'Strategic Bombing Survey' report. Following a damage-assessment tour of Germany in 1945, it noted:

In the wake of these attacks there are great paths of destruction. In Germany, 3,600,000 dwelling units, approximately 20% of the total, were destroyed or heavily damaged. Survey estimates show some 300,000 civilians killed and 780,000 wounded. The number made homeless aggregates 7,500,000. The principal German cities have been largely reduced to hollow walls and piles of rubble. German industry is bruised and temporarily paralyzed. These are the scars across the face of the enemy, the preface to the victory that followed.[11]

The destruction caused by Bomber Command had been brutal and comprehensive, and, over time, the criticism by some members of the media and historians extended to the airmen themselves.

Former Lancaster pilot and prisoner of war Jim Penny remained in the RAF until 1971, then taught English in a number of regional schools. He was one of many to be hurt by the slights the men experienced.

'I am proud of my role in Bomber Command and what we all did; they were some of the best years of my life. We had a job to do and we did it to the best of our abilities. The criticism of Bomber Command has always annoyed me. It shows a complete lack of understanding about the reality of what we had to do for this nation's survival during the Second World War. When I was training to be a teacher in the early 1970s, a young man on the course said to me, "You used to be a bomber pilot, didn't you? Aren't you ashamed of yourself?" I asked him if he spoke German, and when he told me he didn't, I said, "You bloody well would do if we hadn't won the war!"'

This wasn't to be his only such experience.

'Another incident happened many years later when I was a teacher working with a colleague who'd been a Battle of Britain fighter pilot. We were both introduced to another teacher, and when he heard my friend had been a fighter pilot he was delighted; but when I was introduced as a bomber pilot his face changed, and he looked at me in disgust! I said, "I presume you don't approve of me, then?" He replied that he didn't approve of me at all! I tried to explain what we had done and why we had done it, [but] he wasn't interested; he had made up his mind and that was that. I was annoyed by his reaction and thought it was a great insult to everyone who'd served in Bomber Command, and especially to my crew, who'd given their lives for his freedom.'

Jim was twenty-two when the war ended, but its resonances will remain with him for ever. Talking with the author about those days, his voice falters as he remembers his crewmates, killed when their Lancaster was blasted out of the sky over Berlin.

'I still think of my crew every day. I can still see their faces now as they looked as young men. I can see them and hear them exactly as they sounded in 1943. It has been with me all these years and it still hurts me to think of their loss. Unless you have lived the experience yourself, you can never understand how it feels to lose a crew like that, and how it hurts. It's a narrow dividing line between life and death. There's no rhyme or reason why I survived and they didn't; it was just a matter of luck. They were the best; we were a family and they trusted me as their skipper to get them through the war. They were my responsibility, and, seventy years on, I still feel as if I'd let them down. It still hurts today because I survived and they didn't. Their deaths hit me hard back then. They still do today.'[12]

Sadly, Jim Penny was another of the veterans who passed away before the publication of this book and his Lancaster experiences; he died in October 2019.

* * *

The conflict left mental as well as physical scars, and different men found different ways of coping with the peace. Navigator Reg Davey met former colleagues who had pushed the memories so far out of their minds that they couldn't even remember what squadrons they had served on. His own memories, however, remained fresh and clear.

'After we were demobilised, we didn't know how life was going to work as the peace settled upon us! There was a fear for the future, since war had taken up most of our young adult life. I wondered what I would do now; I worried about going back to a normal life. It was very hard to settle and I had a wife and a baby. Responsibilities.

'In the Air Force *I* was the one being looked after. I suppose we thought the world owed us a living after what we'd done; but, as far as the world was concerned, it didn't owe us a thing! Your workmates and neighbours knew you'd been in Bomber Command but it was no big deal for them, no one was interested. Everyone was trying to pick up their own pieces and it was every man for himself; look after Number One. I would hear criticism about the bombing of the cities, especially Dresden, and it would really get me down. When I look back on those days now I think of them as very thrilling, and I'm very grateful I was allowed to take part, grateful I survived, grateful to have been in the company of some very brave people. We went through it all so that we can all be free today.'[13]

Lancaster flight engineer Ted Watson also found civilian life challenging. 'I started to have real difficulty sleeping as my subconscious began to replay some of my ops in a disjointed and irregular pattern. Nightmares of burning aircraft, fighters, searchlights, flak and the faces of men I had known all haunted my dreams.'

But with time, the nightmares faded. 'Today, I try to forget about the deaths and loss of friends. I try again to concentrate on the good times – that camaraderie, and living life to the full with close companions. We served our country together, and we did our bit. Looking back now, I can say I enjoyed the war. It was dangerously exciting. We were young, we were idealistic, and we were doing something to protect our country from the scourge of the Nazis. I take pride in my small contribution to winning the war while flying Lancasters!'[14]

Ted Watson is another of the Bomber Command veterans the author interviewed who sadly died before publication, passing away peacefully in February 2020.

Pilot Don MacIntosh would agree with Ted. Ever pragmatic, ever optimistic and ever forward-looking, he went on to become a civil airline pilot – a job he stayed in for thirty years.

'I enjoyed my war, it was a wonderful experience. There were times of fear and loss, but, for the most part, it was the best time of my life. I just shrugged off the subsequent criticism of Bomber Command, of what we had done. People seemed to forget that it was a total war, and we faced the very real possibility of extinction. There was a war to be fought until the very end, and that's what we did.'

Don married three times, and eventually worked, with his third wife, as a personal assistant to Miles Copeland, manager of rock band The Police. He died in January 2019, aged ninety-six. His funeral was held at Crieff Parish Church in Scotland. Don's daughter Allyson had asked the current IX(B) Squadron[15] Association to assist in its organisation; she wanted her father's service to be fully recognised. Air Vice Marshal Ross Paterson, the most senior RAF officer in Scotland, attended, as did many of the current generation of aircrew and ground crew, and hundreds of local schoolchildren.

The RAF Lossiemouth Station Warrant Officer and eight technicians from IX(B) Squadron – now flying modern Typhoon, fighter aircraft – formed a guard of honour as Don's coffin, dressed in the Union Flag and topped with his service medals, entered the church. The Order of Service was emblazoned with a picture of his beloved Lancaster bomber, and a section of his personal memoir about the attack on the *Tirpitz* battleship was read as part of the eulogy. The congregation sang some of his favourite hymns, including, perhaps most aptly, 'I Vow to Thee, My Country'.

As the service drew to a close, Sergeant Ruth Sidney, Trumpeter of the Band of the Royal Air Force Regiment, played 'The Last Post', and then, after two minutes' silence, 'Reveille' was sounded. Before his coffin began its final journey, the honour party removed the Union Flag, folded it into the traditional tight triangle, and presented it to Allyson for safekeeping. As Don left the church, an RAF Typhoon jet roared overhead in tribute, to mark the passing of one of their own.

Don MacIntosh's duty was done.

\* \* \*

The war never truly went away, even for those who managed to adjust. On the whole, survivors had to fend for themselves. Wireless operator Reg Payne had survived so much – countless sorties over Germany amid the heaviest of flak, and baling out of his burning Lancaster after a training mission had gone wrong. He married his beloved Ena in October 1945, had a family, taught engineering, and lived a contented life. He found great therapeutic consolation in painting, his favourite subject being his beloved Lancaster.

But it was far from easy.

'My memories of that most violent and devastating war had to be buried deep in my subconscious in the years afterwards if I was to survive the transition to peace and make a future. It was this focus on the necessity of the moment which helped me keep the dark memories of the Battle of Berlin locked away, but I couldn't escape the nightmares that relived the horrors of those missions. I would wake up, soaked in sweat, convinced that our aircraft was on fire and I was trapped at my wireless operator's table. At other times it would be Don Moore's face that I would see, his haunted stare as he looked at Death before turning away in search of a parachute.

'I never told Ena about these dreams as she lay sleeping quietly beside me. The armchair moralists who blame the young men of Bomber Command for carrying out the decisions of our political masters have no idea of the burden which we have carried down the years to give them the freedom to blame us. Only those who have faced violent death can understand.'[16]

\* \* \*

One of Reg's treasured paintings, a Lancaster flying over Lincoln Cathedral, hangs in pride of place in the hall of rear gunner James Flowers' bungalow. He lives in Cleethorpes, north-east Lincolnshire, just a few hundred yards from the coast, with his wartime love, Eunice. The bungalow's garden is a riot of flowers and shrubs – Eunice's pride and joy before her increasing frailty prevented her from tending to them.

They are both in their nineties, their experiences during the Second World War long behind them. As James chats to the author, their granddaughter pops by to check on them, as she does every day. The sun streams through the windows, bathing the room in warm yellow light. It is a picture of domestic contentment, of lives well-lived. James sits in the living room, in one of a matching pair of reclining chairs, surrounded by framed family photographs. Eunice sits in the other, watching a television placed just a foot away from her. She is wearing headphones and listening on full volume; age has taken its toll and she is almost totally deaf and blind. But she still enjoys the entertainment; especially game shows and the nature documentaries. As James Flowers remembers his years at war, Eunice is oblivious to our discussion, watching a bear feeding her cubs in some Canadian forest.

'I wouldn't want them to go through what I went through,' James says, pointing to the pictures of his children and grandchildren. 'But I wouldn't have missed it for the world! Those were some of the best days of my life.'[17] It took many years to adjust to civilian life after demobilisation in 1947. 'I missed my crew, I missed the camaraderie and I missed the life. It was such a good life, but it's like a different world now. If you weren't there, you could never understand.'

For a long time after 1945, James didn't talk about the war. No one wanted to. Everyone just needed to move on. He certainly didn't talk to Eunice about what he'd seen. What he'd done. He looks fondly at his wife and gently takes her hand. 'Even though she is ninety-five, she is still the same beauty I married in 1944. Although she can barely see or hear, we still sit together every day in our chairs only a few inches apart, holding hands. She is still by my side, the same as she was next to me seventy-five years ago during the war. We are lucky we are still together after all this time. She was my rock during the fighting and I have no doubt she was a major reason for my survival. She was always there to provide comfort, and an escape from the brutality of war.'

There are still aspects of those battles over Germany which rankle, however.

'I was very disappointed by the criticism of Bomber Command after the war. I felt very bitter towards Churchill and the way he simply cast us aside – everything we'd done and endured was forgotten or decried. Churchill was a true politician: he took all the credit for winning the war and accepted no responsibility for the reality of what had to be done. But we were in a fight to the death. The Nazis had swept through Europe right to our doorstep, and the nation's survival was teetering on the brink. *We* were the ones taking the war into the heart of Germany, *we* were sacrificing our lives. For much of the war, *we* were the only ones who could take the fight against the enemy to their home ground. Bomber Command was the bulwark against Nazi Germany, and it's a shame that some people don't appreciate that.'

That antipathy to Bomber Command is borne out by the story of the memorials to its principal leader during the Second World War, and to the Command itself. Arthur Harris was decorated and promoted after the war, becoming Marshal of the RAF in January 1946, but he resigned in September of that year.

Members of Bomber Command were eligible for the standard wartime medals of the 'Aircrew Europe Star' and the 'France and Germany Star', but they were denied their own, specific 'Bomber Command' campaign medal because of the enduring controversy. Harris refused a peerage at the time in protest, and thus was the only Commander-in-Chief not to be so elevated. He died in 1984, but it would be another eight years before his RAF service was acknowledged with a statue outside the west end of the RAF Church of St Clement Danes in London. It was vandalised with red paint on a number of occasions after it was unveiled.

James Flowers acknowledges that, with the inauguration of the Bomber Command Memorial in Green Park, some measure of recognition has at long last been achieved, though the cost of its construction and upkeep is not covered by the state. The money was raised by public donations after an appeal for £5.6 million.

The neo-classical memorial is built of Portland stone and designed by Liam O'Connor. It houses a bronze statue by Philip

Jackson which portrays a seven-man bomber crew in battledress, some gazing skywards. Its inner roof is of aluminium recovered from a Halifax of 426 Squadron, which crashed in Belgium in May 1944. The stately memorial is inscribed with a quotation from Pericles: 'Freedom is the sure possession of those alone who have the courage to defend it.' It was unveiled by Queen Elizabeth II in the year of her Diamond Jubilee on 28 June 2012 – sixty-seven years after the end of the war. It, too, has been the subject of vandalism, daubed with white paint, as recently as January 2019.

In February 2013, veterans could belatedly apply for the 'Bomber Command Clasp' to be affixed on the ribbon of their 1939–1945 Star; the military campaign medal awarded to all who served during the Second World War. There would be no individual campaign medal.

Though James appreciates the memorial in Green Park, however late in the day it appeared, there are still regrets. 'All my fellow crewmates are gone. I am the only one left alive, and I'm just so sad that the rest of my friends are no longer here to see the monument.'

*Stan Shaw pictured shortly before he was killed*
*on operations in 1943*

Elaine Shaw, now Mrs Elaine Towlson, is still haunted by the memory of the dad she lost when she was a little girl of nine. Stanley Shaw, thirty-one years old and the 'father' of his crew, lost his life during the raid on the V-weapons site at Peenemünde on the night of 17–18 August 1943. His body was never officially identified or buried, and he has no known grave.

Sitting in her neat house in Leicester, she is surrounded by photographs of her father and books about the Lancaster bombers he flew. Alongside them are other photographs – of her children and grandchildren, people Stan Shaw didn't live to know. A picture of a Lancaster hangs in pride of place above the black iron stove in the fireplace. The giant aircraft sits on a deserted airfield on a misty morning. Ghostly figures look up at it, perhaps contemplating what the day might bring. It is an image that harks back to a time most have forgotten. But not Elaine. Her eyes are moist as she recalls those days.[18]

'I treasured the photos and letters I got from my father and his crew, and they were all stored in my little orange desk, which I'd kept even though I'd grown out of it. They were my link to the past. But my mother remarried in 1947 and when we moved house the desk got thrown on a bonfire while everything was being cleared out.

'I was devastated – all those mementos, those last links to my father and his friends, all gone. In the years after the war, the memories of my father didn't fade one bit. My mother died in 1996 and she was still talking about my dad on her deathbed. She knew she was finally going to be reunited with him. He was her first love, and she never got over his death.'

Elaine wipes away a tear.

'I had such nice times together with Dad and his crewmates. They were only boys, except for Dad, and they used to bring me and my little sister sweeties. Poor Pam. She was only eighteen months old when Dad left us. She didn't really know him at all.

'But I remember him. I'll never forget him. I wish I could go back in time just to see him once more. He'll never change, never get old.

He'll always be my dad, just as I saw him by that bus stop when we said goodbye for the last time in 1943.'

In 2014, in her eighty-first year, Elaine Towlson finally had a chance to find some sort of ending to her father's story. The official graves of the crew, if they indeed exist, are still unlocated, but a section of Lancaster fuselage was discovered marooned in the shallows of Lake Kölpiensee, only a few hundred yards from Peenemünde, and there was every indication that it was Stanley Shaw's aircraft – Lancaster DV-202. As part of a BBC documentary about the iconic bomber, Elaine was invited to visit the site with veteran broadcaster and Lancaster enthusiast John Sergeant.[19] At first she was reluctant to go, unsure if she wanted her memories to be rekindled so fiercely. But her son Russell persuaded her that she would always regret not taking the opportunity, and suggested that they should go together.

It was a bleak day, thin sunlight filtering through the clouds, when Elaine, Russell and John Sergeant approached the little wooden jetty on the shore of Lake Kölpiensee. The factory towers of Peenemünde loomed behind the bare trees on the flatlands, and water birds fussed in the reeds lining the water's edge. It seemed a truly desolate spot. A rowing boat was tied to the jetty, awaiting them. Elaine tensed as she saw a familiar shape towards the other side of the lake – what remained of Lancaster DV-202. The three of them climbed into the boat, and Sergeant rowed them gently across the still, grey waters. Russell put his arm round his mother as she fought back the tears. Sunbeams pierced the clouds 'like search-lights', Elaine thought.

At last they arrived beside the fuselage and tied up. Elaine looked at the small plaque that had been fixed to the metal by the local villagers, bearing the names of her father's crew. 'They've never found the graves where the Germans buried them; this is the closest I'll get to Dad.' Now the tears were flowing fast, but Elaine fought them down to make her last tribute, and say goodbye – not just to her father, but to the whole crew, dearly remembered friends, and, in her mind's eye, still the young men she remembered so well. There was a moment of silence as she placed her hand on the cold metal of the dead Lancaster. Despite herself, she was crying again. Russell pulled her close, lacing his fingers through hers. 'He'll be watching,' he said, 'and he'll know.'

Russell knew that the aircraft had never *officially* been confirmed as DV-202. What *mattered* was that his mum was able, finally, to bid farewell. Elaine looked at her son. 'I'll never do anything like this again. It's something that happens only once in a lifetime. And I've waited so very long.'

She'd brought seven red roses with her. One by one, she cast them into the body of the Lancaster, calling out the names of the men who had died alongside her father.

*Reg Harding, the skipper.*
*Tom Weston, flight engineer.*
*Les Prendergast, navigator.*
*Mac McDermott, bomb aimer.*
*Billy Quance, wireless operator.*
*Peter Pynisky, mid-upper gunner.*

She held one rose back, reluctant to let it go. Finally, she kissed it and threw it into the wreckage.

*'And . . . Dad.'*

Elaine held on to the fuselage for a few moments longer, alone with her thoughts. But the day was darkening and it was time to go. They rowed away slowly and in silence. Although peace had been declared on a sunny day in May 1945, for so many who mourned, so many who bore deep physical and mental scars, the war hadn't ended at all. But perhaps for Elaine, it had, finally, on a desolate stretch of water in northern Germany, during a cold, grey day in 2014.

Elaine had found closure, but she still thinks of her father often. 'Especially on days like Remembrance Sunday, when it all comes flooding back. I have a quiet moment, shed a few tears, and then I carry on. Whenever I watch a documentary about Bomber Command, I always look at the faces of the men intently, in case my dad is in the background somewhere. He never is. Today, you'd have videos or recordings of your loved ones. I have nothing other than some fading photographs and yellowing letters. I don't think any of us really got over it – my mum, my grandparents – we were all totally shattered by his death. War touches people personally; but I look back with pride on Dad and his Lancaster mates. Dad was just one of 55,573 who died. But he was my *one*.'

\* \* \*

It was a time for sober reflection. Of the 125,000 men who served in Bomber Command, 55,573[20] lost their lives; 32,890 Britons, 9,856 Canadians, 4,029 Australians and 1,668 from New Zealand. Poland lost 1,000 men, and volunteers from as far afield as India and the Caribbean 500. Life expectancy for a crewman on active service could be as little as two weeks compared with six for a soldier in the trenches in the First World War.

Avro and other manufacturers produced 7,373 Lancasters, and for a while they were to live on in such improved and adapted versions as the Lincoln, and the passenger airliners York and Lancastrian. Tragedies would be linked with both passenger versions. A prototype aircraft crashed on take-off at Woodford on 23 August 1947 – among the dead was Lancaster designer Roy Chadwick. He was fifty-four years old. Avro CEO Roy Dobson lost his son, Jack, when a British Overseas Airways Corporation Lancastrian crashed into the sea en route to Australia on 24 March 1946. A later incarnation, the Shackleton, flew with RAF Coastal Command in the late 1940s and early 1950s, and went on to be part of the RAF's Airborne Early Warning system, finally going out of service in 1990.[21]

During the war, Lancasters flew 156,308 sorties, dropping 608,613 tons of bombs, consuming 228 million gallons of fuel. But by 1945 the writing was on the wall: the day of the jet engine had already dawned. The glory days of the Lancaster were over.

Seventeen Lancasters survive around the world, but only two are airworthy. One is in Canada, at the Canadian Warplane Heritage Museum in Hamilton, Ontario; the other is part of the Royal Air Force Battle of Britain Memorial Flight based at RAF Coningsby in Lincolnshire. Their Lancaster was built by Vickers-Armstrongs Ltd at its Broughton factory near Chester just after the war ended in 1945 and was destined to be part of the 'Tiger Force' for strategic bombing in the Far East. But at the end of the war with Japan, she wasn't needed. She was retained in RAF service eventually ending up on the BBMF, where their mission statement is to *'maintain the priceless artefacts of our national heritage in airworthy condition in order to commemorate those who have fallen in the service of this country, to promote the modern day Air Force and to inspire the future generations'*.

The Lancaster continues to capture the imagination, eighty years after its birth. The Battle of Britain Memorial Flight's 75-year-old veteran Lancaster is fully restored and will hopefully be operational for many years to come.

Flight Lieutenant Tim Dunlop, a former BBMF Lancaster pilot and 'Bomber Leader', knows more than most just how important the aircraft was, both during the war and as a survivor today. It is fitting that this book's final words about this remarkable aircraft are left to him:

'The Avro Lancaster is without doubt an aviation icon; revered, romanticised, loved. Will her modern-day counterparts achieve such status in seventy-five years' time? I doubt it.

'I had the immense privilege of flying the RAF's Lancaster for ten years and every time we climbed aboard the Lanc, as a sign of respect for everything she stands for, the crew would touch the Bomber Command brass plaque on the left of the main crew door inscribed with the words "To remember the many". And it is "The Many" we honour every time we take her airborne.

'Designed around the bomb bay below our feet, inside the fuselage she is an ergonomic nightmare; cramped conditions and sharp protruding metalwork. Flying her in peacetime was pure joy, but I only ever had a camera shooting at me. It is difficult to imagine what it must have been like heading into battle night after night, surrounded by flak and terror, particularly when seeing your comrades go down in flames.

'Compared to modern-day aircraft, she was more difficult to handle, punishing any mistakes made, but that was part of her charm; when you flew her well, she rewarded your efforts. On those occasions it was as if we were guided by the spirits of those we represented. I have had the pleasure of flying many of the RAF's modern aircraft, and a few of the historic ones too. It is the honour of flying the venerable Lancaster which has touched me most deeply. With her formidable bombload and daring crews, she took the fight to the very heart of Nazi Germany for a great part of the Second World War. To me she is more than just an aircraft; she is a symbol of British freedom; a monument to all those who gave their lives during the war, and those who have fallen since.

'Without the incredible Lancaster, and bravery of "The Many" in Bomber Command who flew her, the freedom we enjoy today would not exist.'

# AFTERWORD

The deep roar of engines marked the beginning of the Lancaster rear gunner's final journey. Staff and residents of his retirement home looked on with a mixture of surprise and delight as three military veterans, members of the Royal British Legion Riders Branch, gripped their throttles and revved their huge motorbikes.[1]

It was an incongruous sight. The coffin lay ready in the hearse, neatly shrouded in the RAF Ensign – light blue material emblazoned with the Union Flag, and a red, white and blue RAF roundel. Another RAF Ensign and Union Flag fluttered on the rear pannier of each machine, and large poppies were mounted next to their skull-and-crossbones motif. The bikers' leather jackets were adorned with their own campaign medal ribbons and the insignia of their former units: Royal Air Force, Royal Military Police and Royal Corps of Transport. In years gone by they might have been rivals; today they were united in an increasingly common escort duty. This was the funeral procession of a wartime hero, deserving of every honour that could be bestowed, and his passing had to be properly marked.

The assembled crowd bowed their heads as, lights blazing, they led the hearse and family vehicles through the neatly manicured grounds, past flower beds filled with purple petunias. A Royal Navy veteran in a Land Rover, also adorned with poppies, RAF Ensign and Union Flag, took up his station as rear gunner to the cortège. The bikers roared ahead to stop any traffic and ensure a last, peaceful, uninterrupted sortie for the Bomber Command sergeant. The few lunchtime commuters stopped and stared, perhaps wondering who it was that warranted such a send-off.

Around 130 mourners stood in silence as the procession reached the crematorium. Some were in uniform or sporting the berets of their former units. Around a third had never known the veteran. It mattered not; the word had gone out via social media that one of their own had died and was worthy of their presence. To the strains of Nat King Cole's 'Unforgettable', the coffin was carried into the chapel. The fluttering Standards of the Royal British Legion and the Royal Air Force Association were lowered in respect.

As the service progressed, one of the leather-clad veterans came forward to the lectern.

'*When you go home, tell them of us and say: For your tomorrow, we gave our today.*'

As the words of the poignant epitaph from the Second World War Battle of Kohima faded, a recorded bell began to toll – the bell of St Evre church in the French village of Méligny-le-Grand, sounding the Angelus call to prayer.

The bell tolled for Sergeant Ron Needle, just as it had rung when guiding the badly injured Lancaster rear gunner to safety one freezing dawn in January 1945.

'It was a wonderful tribute to my father,' Ron's daughter, Sue Efthimiou, remembers. 'The Méligny church bell, the motorbikes, the flags, the uniforms. Total strangers who had never even met my dad gathered next to his closest family; it was so moving. I wept so much that day, tears of sadness, but tears of joy too, seeing such an incredible send-off. Jean-Pierre Fromont, the son of André who had rescued Dad in 1945, had driven all the way from Méligny with his family to be with us. I thought, *Dad, you'd be very happy with all of this!*'[2]

Ron's death had not been unexpected. When the author spoke to him in late 2018, he said, 'I have had a wonderful life, I am the luckiest man alive to have experienced so much and to have such a fabulous family. I did my bit during the war and afterwards, so I can die happy. I have seen death close up and when my own time comes I will be ready. Death holds no fear for me.'[3]

'In his final year, it was clear to me that my dad had decided it was time to go,' Sue says. 'And once he understood that the end was approaching, he was resolute in meeting it, determined to speed up the process.'

Diagnosed with a terminal illness and confined to hospital, Ron showed the same courage and resolve he had needed while trying to escape his burning Lancaster during the war. He simply stopped eating and drinking. He was moved to a specialist unit to be looked after by a dedicated nursing team providing end-of-life care, where his loving family could be with him. As would be expected of that wartime generation, he bore his suffering with dignity, sought no special treatment, thanking every doctor and nurse for the smallest assistance.

'He was as strong as an ox,' Sue says. 'He survived three weeks and I didn't hear a single word of complaint.'

Ron's room in the hospice was neat and simple; a few green plants and a beautiful flowering orchid brightened the space where his family would gather around the single bed. A picture of his 106 Squadron badge, a seated red lion, forepaws holding a banner, was pinned to the wall in pride of place. Their wartime motto, '*Pro Libertate*' – 'For Freedom' – never more apt.

In his closing days Ron was in obvious pain and found it difficult to speak, but there was still no sense of self-pity or complaint. His family look back on the last few hours with 'joy and affection'. 'Dad was propped up in the bed and we were gathered around listening to Johnny Cash's gospel album, *Hymns*,' Sue says. One song, 'Lead Me Gently Home', particularly resonated.

A short time later, Ron leant forward and whispered one word: 'Whisky.' A syringe was charged with his favoured tipple and a few drops placed on his lips – his final opportunity to toast his missing crewmates. He smiled, winked at his beloved family, lay back and held both thumbs in the air. Then he closed his eyes, his breathing quietened, and he slipped away.

Sergeant Ron Needle was finally reunited with the friends he had lost when their Lancaster bomber had crashed in a remote French forest in January 1945.

Their duty at war was complete; they could all rest in peace together.

# ENDNOTES

## Foreword

1 This account comes from a number of interviews with Ron Needle by John Nichol.

2 Wartime Bomber Command aircrew rarely used the term 'missions'; only the terms 'operations' or 'ops' were used.

3 RAF Museum archive, Hendon, https://www.rafmuseum.org.uk/ documents/collections/74-A-12- Avro-Lancaster-R5868.pdf

4 Details from the RAF Museum website, https://www.rafmuseum. org.uk

5 Quoted in Max Arthur, *Dambusters: A Landmark Oral History* (Virgin Books, 2008).

6 Figures vary for the number of Lancasters completing over 100 operations, depending on the definition of 'combat' operations. This is the RAF Museum figure, others suggest thirty-five Lancasters may have achieved this feat.

7 By the nature of war, exact statistics are difficult to establish. Much of this information is taken from what is regarded as one of the best sources: Martin Middlebrook and Chris Everitt, *The Bomber Command War Diaries: An Operational Reference Book, 1939–1945* (Viking, 1985).

8 Figures vary for the exact number of casualties depending on source.

## Chapter 1

1 See Richard Bailey, *In the Middle of Nowhere: The History of RAF Metheringham* (Tucann Books, 1999).

2 Bombers were positioned at individual 'dispersal points' around the main runway. This made it impossible for an enemy fighter or bomber to destroy several aircraft at once.

3 Ron Needle, *Saved by the Bell* (Tail End Publications, 2006), and interview with John Nichol.

4 Miles Tripp, *The Eighth Passenger*; see also John Nichol and Tony Rennell, *Tail-End Charlies: The Last Battles of the Bomber War 1944–45* (Penguin, 2004).

5 Mel Rolfe, *To Hell and Back: True Life Experiences of Bomber Command at War* (Grub Street Publishing, 2003). Also Ron Needle and André Fromont's recollections of Harry's story. Some of Harry's recollections have been edited for clarity and brevity.

6 Ken Darke's private family papers, kindly supplied by Stephen Darke.

7 Information from Lincolnshire Aviation Heritage Centre, East Kirkby.

8 Quoted in Mel Rolfe, *To Hell and Back*, op. cit.

9 A glancing blow – accounts of this incident differ somewhat.

10 Quoted in Mel Rolfe, *To Hell and Back*, op. cit.

11 Ibid.

12 Modern military parlance would not use the terms 'machine guns' or 'bullets'. They are used throughout the text because the veterans themselves used these terms.

## Chapter 2

1 Ron Needle, *Saved by the Bell*, op. cit., and interview with John Nichol.

2 Maurice Garlick, *The Mystery of Uncle Joe* (personal memoir). Kindly supplied by his widow Beryl. Parts of Maurice's memoir have been edited for brevity and clarity.

3 Ted Watson, quoted in Kenneth Ballantyne, *Through the Gate* (Laundry Cottage Books, 2018), and interview with John Nichol.

4 By contrast, three months later, a formation of Wellington bombers, aiming for German naval shipping at Wilhelmshaven, didn't in the event attack at all, because they had orders not to 'if there was any danger of hitting the shore' – thereby endangering civilians. Max Hastings, *Bomber Command* (Zenith Press, 2013; first published 1979).

5 Gladys Cox, quoted in the *Sunday Express*, 23 August 2009.

6 'A Personal Account' by Sir Edward Heath, printed in *The Independent*, 3 September 1999.

7 George VI spoke to the nation later the same day, manfully controlling his stutter.

8 Elaine Towlson (née Shaw), interview with John Nichol.

9 It was largely the Heinkel 111s that flew with unsynchronised engines: a ploy either to confuse Allied attempts to locate them, or simply to strike fear in their victims. The noise is by all accounts very unsettling.

10 Maurice Garlick, *The Mystery of Uncle Joe*, op. cit. (Note that Garlick's recollections are approximate.)

11 Ken Trent (with Chris Stone), *Bomb Doors Open: From East End boy to Lancaster Bomber Pilot with 617 'Dambuster' Squadron* (Seeker Publishing, 2016). Some of Ken's recollections have been edited for brevity.

12 Don MacIntosh, *Bomber Pilot: A Veteran's First-Hand Account of Surviving World War Two as a RAF Bomber Pilot* (Browsebooks, 2006), and interview with John Nichol.

13 Anderson shelters were designed in 1938 and distributed free of charge to families whose income was lower than £5 a week. More affluent households had to pay a small charge for them. Over 3.5 million were installed during the war and they were surprisingly effective. They comprised a tall hoop of corrugated steel half-buried in the ground and could accommodate up to six people.

## Chapter 3

1 Thomas Murray (with Mark Hillier), *Suitcases, Vultures and Spies: From Bomber Command to Special Ops: The Story of Wing Commander Thomas Murray DSO DFC* (Yellowman, 2014). Edited for clarity and brevity.

2 Pip Beck, *Keeping Watch: A WAAF in Bomber Command* (Goodall Publications Ltd, 2004).

3 For further technical information, see especially Peter Jacobs, *The Lancaster Story* (Orion, 1998), and Robert Owen, 'The Lancaster', *Everyone's War*, Issue 22, pp. 13–19 (The Second World

War Experience Centre, 2002).
Another Lancaster prototype, the
Mark II, was powered by Bristol
Hercules VI engines, owing to a
temporary shortage of Merlins.
The Merlin engine was, however,
the standard one for the vast
majority of Lancasters. There was
little variation in overall design
during the Lancaster's working
life: one prototype had an extra
gun turret on the underside of
the fuselage, but this was quickly
dropped for reasons of weight and
impracticability: there was little
enough room to move about in a
Lancaster as it was.

4  Pip Beck, *Keeping Watch*, op. cit.
5  Spitfire production costs are difficult
   to quantify; figures vary from
   £5,000 to £12,000.
6  For more on production, see Clive
   Rowley, 'Building Lancasters', in
   *Royal Air Force Memorial Flight
   Club Journal* (Autumn 2017), pp.
   55–60; Rowley, 'Avro Lancaster
   75th', *Official Yearbook 2016*, pp.
   43–6; and Tony Pay, 'The Lancaster
   and the Merlin: Two Icons of the
   Second World War', in *Britain at
   War* (October 2008), pp. 61–6.
7  Ted Watson, interview with John
   Nichol.
8  Clive Rowley, 'Building Lancasters',
   op. cit.
9  Ibid.
10 *Pathé Gazette* – undated, but soon
   after the Augsburg Raid, which took
   place in mid-April 1942. Television
   was not current in 1942. News was
   disseminated by newspapers and the
   radio. Visual news was available via
   newsreels shown in cinemas, usually
   alongside the feature films.
11 Nettleton's VC citation, quoted in
   Peter Jacobs, *The Lancaster Story*,
   op. cit.

## Chapter 4

1  Henry Probert, *Bomber Harris: His
   Life and Times* (Greenhill, 2006).
2  Harris and his first wife divorced
   in 1935. They'd had three children.
   Harris got married again in 1938, to
   Therese Hearne, twenty-six years
   his junior. Their daughter Jacqueline
   was born in 1939.
3  The Smuts Report, 17 August 1917,
   RAF Museum.
4  This is the official figure, though
   other estimates put the final death
   toll much higher.
5  They came not only from white
   South Africa, but also, among
   others, Australia, Canada, the
   Caribbean, India, New Zealand and
   the two Rhodesias.
6  See Chapter 3.
7  Jack Currie, *The Augsburg Raid:
   The story of one of the most
   dramatic and dangerous raids ever
   mounted by RAF Bomber Command* (Goodall Publications, 1987).
8  The wholesale bombing of cities
   and towns with the specific purpose
   of targeting civilian populations as
   well as military and industrial ones.
   Harris was an enthusiastic exponent
   of strategic bombing throughout the
   war, and though he didn't introduce
   it on his own initiative, it became a
   tactic that he clung to with stubborn
   determination against mounting
   opposition in the latter years of the
   war.
9  Henry Probert, *Bomber Harris*, op.
   cit.
10 Some sources erroneously give
   the codename as 'MARLIN',
   since Arthur Harris's Senior Air
   Staff Officer and later Deputy
   Commander-in-Chief, Robert
   Saundby, was a keen naturalist,
   lepidopterist and fly-fisherman, and
   tended to name operations after
   game fish.

11 Quoted in Martin Bowman, *Last of the Lancasters* (Pen & Sword, 2014). Accounts of the Augsburg raid appear in many sources and there are multiple individual memories and discrepancies in each.

12 Quoted in James Holland, *Dam Busters: The Race to Smash the Dams 1943* (Corgi, 2013).

13 Brian Hallows, quoted in Steve Snelling, 'Audacious Raid Which Rivalled the Dambusters', *EDP Weekend*, 21 April 2012.

14 Some sources give 'Eric'. Ernest Edward Rodley is the name given in Spink's record of sales of his decorations and attendant military documentation (www.spink.com/lot/18002000511). In *The Augsburg Raid* (op. cit.), Jack Currie gives 'Edward Ernest'.

15 Martin Bowman, in *Last of the Lancasters* (op. cit.), gives 2,134 gallons as the maximum load.

16 Bf = *Bayerische Flugzeugwerke*. The official designation of this fighter, introduced in 1937 and in use throughout the war, was Bf109, but it came to be known more familiarly as the Me109, after its principal designer, Willy Messerschmitt. For some coverage of the attack from the German point of view, see Andrew Thomas, 'The Nettleton Room', *Britain at War*, September 2014, pp. 79–84.

17 James Holland, *Dam Busters*, op. cit.

18 Some reports say it was a machine-gun mounting.

19 Despite incredible efforts at evading the Germans, each member of Crum's crew was eventually captured.

20 There is some discrepancy between accounts of this action. Currie's and Jacobs' are followed here.

21 Interview on 19 April 1942, Imperial War Museum Sound Archive, 2148/G/B.

22 Richard Overy, *Bomber Command, 1939–1945: Reaping the Whirlwind* (Bookmart Ltd, 2000).

23 Jack Currie, *The Augsburg Raid*, op. cit. See also: Andrew Thomas, 'The Nettleton Room', op. cit.

24 As described by Rodley.

25 Richard Overy, *Bomber Command, 1939–1945*, op. cit.

26 Steve Snelling, 'Audacious Raid Which Rivalled the Dambusters', op. cit.

27 Pip Beck, *Keeping Watch*, op. cit.

28 Martin Bowman, *Last of the Lancasters*, op. cit.

29 Information from 97 Squadron Association archive.

30 Quoted in Steve Snelling, 'Audacious Raid Which Rivalled the Dambusters', op. cit.

31 Quoted in Allyn Vannoy, 'Deep Strike on Augsburg', Warfare History Network, https://warfarehistorynetwork.com/2016/09/13/deep-strike-on-augsburg/

32 Arthur Harris, quoted in www.militarian.com/threads/augsburg-raid-april-17-1942.5696/

33 Göring chose a typical Jewish surname to use in his boast.

## Chapter 5

1 Ken Darke's family papers.

2 Elaine Towlson (née Shaw), interview with John Nichol. The Hemlock Stone is a 200-million-year-old isolated outcrop of New Red Sandstone, reminiscent of a Tony Cragg sculpture. It is 28ft high and a local tourist attraction on Stapleford Hill, near where the Shaws lived.

3 A form of cowpox.

4 Elaine Towlson (née Shaw), private papers – elsewhere also quoted.

Stan's original letters have been edited for brevity.

5 James Flowers, *A Tail End Charlie's Story* (self-published, 2000), and interview with John Nichol.

6 Ken Johnson's personal memoir and interview with John Nichol.

7 *ETA: A Bomber Command Navigator Shot Down and on the Run* (Fighting High Publishing, 2016).

8 *Britain at War* magazine, May 2017, pp. 63–88.

9 Ibid.

10 Tom Dailey, 'The Thousand-bomber Raids', BBC Southern Counties Radio, https://www.bbc.co.uk/history/ww2peopleswar/stories/73/a4616273.shtml

11 See John Grehan, 'Behind the Offensive', *Britain at War*, October 2008, pp. 17–22; and Tim Bryan, *The Great Western at War* (Patrick Stephens, 1995).

12 See also Richard Overy, *Bomber Command, 1939–1945*, op. cit.; Peter Jacobs, *The Lancaster Story*, op. cit.; and Ken Delve, 'Lancaster, the Operational Story', *FlyPast* magazine, Special Edition, October 1998.

13 Don MacIntosh, *Bomber Pilot*, op. cit., and interview with John Nichol.

14 Ken Trent, *Bomb Doors Open*, op. cit.

15 Ralf Blank, 'Die Nacht vom 16. auf den 17. Mai 1943 – "Operation Züchtigung": Die Zerstörung der Möhne-Talsperre', *Landschaftsverband Westfalen-Lippe*, May 2006.

16 Jim Insull quoted in Max Lambert, *Night After Night: New Zealanders in Bomber Command* (HarperCollins New Zealand, 2005).

17 Maurice Flower quoted in James Taylor and Martin Davidson, *Bomber Crew: Survivors of Bomber Command Tell Their Own Story* (Hodder & Stoughton, 2005). Both this, and the previous testimony, have been edited for brevity.

18 Rob Pierson, 'Battle Stations: Lancaster Bomber – Target Germany', *War History* documentary.

19 'Operation Gomorrah Created "Germany's Nagasaki"', BBC News, 1 August 2018.

20 Elfriede Sindel, *Maserblut* (2001; original translation for this book).

21 Quoted in Max Hastings, *Bomber Command*, op. cit.

22 Ibid.

23 Thomas Murray, *Suitcases, Vultures and Spies*, op. cit.

24 Jonathan Falconer, *Bomber Command Handbook 1939–1945* (The History Press, 1998).

## Chapter 6

1 Gordon Stooke, *Flak and Barbed Wire* (Australian Military History Publications, 1997). Parts of his testimony have been edited for brevity.

2 These are Gordon's own terms for the various appointments of the briefing officers.

3 Quoted in Ken Wright, 'If Ya Gotta Go, Ya Gotta Go: Answering Nature's Call at 26,000 Feet', http://www.vintagewings.ca/VintageNews/Stories/tabid/116/articleType/ArticleView/articleId/400/When-ya-gotta-go.aspx (unattributed)

## Chapter 7

1 Martin Middlebrook, *The Peenemünde Raid: 17–18 August 1943* (Pen & Sword, 2006; first published 1982).

2 Ibid.

3 Shaw family papers. Some of the letters have been edited for brevity.

4 There is no date on the letter. HMS *Ceylon* was completed in July 1943 and sailed to join the Eastern Fleet in September.

5 Elaine Towlson (née Shaw), interview with John Nichol.

6 From Nichol and Rennell, *Tail-End Charlies*, op. cit.

7 Letter from RAF Air Gunner J. A. Clough to his parents. From the International Bomber Command Centre Digital Archive. Ref: NWrightJ150410-01

8 Letter from RAF Flight Engineer Ian Wynne to his wife. From the International Bomber Command Centre Digital Archive. Ref: EWynnIAWynnK421228-02. The letter has been edited to ensure it is easier to read in this context.

9 Quoted in Max Hastings, *Bomber Command*, op. cit.

10 Air Commodore J. H. Searby, *Peenemünde* (IX(B) Squadron archive).

11 Middlebrook, *The Peenemünde Raid*, op. cit.

12 George Whitehead, quoted in Middlebrook, *The Peenemünde Raid*, op. cit.

13 Ibid.

14 Ibid.

15 Quoted in John Grehan, 'Buying Time', *Britain at War*, June 2011.

16 Walter Dornberger, *V-2* (Viking, 1954).

17 Charles Cawthorne, quoted in Martin Bowman, *Last of the Lancasters*, op. cit.

18 Pilot Officer F. J. Wilkin, quoted in Middlebrook, *The Peenemünde Raid*, op. cit. Edited for brevity.

19 Friedrich-Karl Müller, quoted in Middlebrook, *The Peenemünde Raid*, op. cit. Edited for brevity.

20 Ibid.

21 Ibid.

22 Peter Spoden, interviewed for *What the Dambusters Did Next*, Channel 4 TV.

## Chapter 8

1 Don MacIntosh, *Bomber Pilot*, op. cit., and interview with John Nichol.

2 The name given to the female branch of the Royal Navy.

3 Richard Overy, *Bomber Command, 1939–1945*, op. cit.

4 James A. Penny, *The Lucky Penny* (FastPrint, 2013), and interview with John Nichol.

5 Mary Ellis, interview with John Nichol and elements of various obituaries.

6 Leo McKinstry, *Lancaster: The Second World War's Greatest Bomber* (John Murray, 2009).

7 Clive Rowley, 'Building Lancasters', op. cit., and 'Avro Lancaster 75th', op. cit.

8 Leo McKinstry, *Lancaster*, op. cit.

9 Ibid.

10 Tony Pay, 'The Lancaster and the Merlin: Two Icons of the Second World War', *Britain at War*, October 2008.

11 See Mark Connelly, *Reaching for the Stars* (I. B. Tauris, 2000).

12 Ken Trent, *Bomb Doors Open*, op. cit.

13 Reg Payne, quoted in Kenneth Ballantyne, *First Wave: The Story of Warrant Officer Reg Payne, Royal Air Force Wireless Operator with 50 Squadron During World War Two* (Laundry Cottage Books, 2013), and interview with John Nichol.

14 Thomas Murray, *Suitcases, Vultures and Spies*, op. cit.

15 'Guinea Pigs' was the term used for men who underwent the plastic surgery for disfiguring burns pioneered by Sir Archibald McIndoe.

See also Sunnie Mann, *Holding On* (Bloomsbury, 1990).

16 Bill Kiley, interview with John Nichol.

17 No first name is given in Penny's account.

18 Reg Davey, interview with John Nichol.

19 James A. Penny, *The Lucky Penny*, op. cit.

20 Leo McKinstry, *Lancaster*, op. cit.

21 Reg Payne, quoted in Kenneth Ballantyne, *First Wave*, op. cit.

22 Les Bartlett, quoted in Peter Jacobs, *Bomb Aimer Over Berlin: The Wartime Memoirs of Les Bartlett DFM* (Pen & Sword, 2007). Some quotes have been edited for brevity.

23 A signalling lamp used by Air Traffic Control.

24 Peter Jacobs, *The Lancaster Story*, op. cit.

25 Professor Freeman Dyson is a theoretical physicist and mathematician, born in 1923. At nineteen years of age, he was seconded from his mathematics degree course at Cambridge to work for the Operation Research Section, Bomber Command, where his job was to develop analytical methods for calculating the ideal density for bomber formations. He advocated removing two gun turrets from the Lancaster in order to increase its speed and manoeuvrability, a proposal rejected by Arthur Harris. The quotation here is from 'A Failure of Intelligence', *MIT Technology Review Magazine*, October 2006.

26 Peter Jacobs, *Bomb Aimer Over Berlin*, op. cit.

27 Joseph Goebbels, *Tagebücher* (Piper, 2008; translation here for this book).

## Chapter 9

1 Quoted in Nichol and Rennell, *Tail-End Charlies*, op. cit.

2 Ibid.

3 Don MacIntosh, *Bomber Pilot*, op. cit., and interview with John Nichol.

4 Nichol and Rennell, *Tail-End Charlies*, op. cit.

5 Taken from the *Bomber Command Newsletter*, April 2003.

6 Richard Bailey, *In the Middle of Nowhere*, op. cit.

7 Peter Scoley, personal memoir. Edited for brevity.

8 John Grehan, 'Behind the Offensive', op. cit.

9 Maurice Garlick, *The Mystery of Uncle Joe*, op. cit.

10 Navy, Army and Air Force Institutes, created by the British government on 9 December 1920 to run recreational establishments needed by the British Armed Forces.

11 Richard Bailey, *In the Middle of Nowhere*, op. cit.; Appendix 80 to Operations Record Book, June 1944: 'Report on Station Entertainment'.

12 The account of Jackson's exploits is constructed from a number of different sources: John Grehan, 'On a Wing and a Prayer', *Britain at War*, July 2007; Peter Jacobs, *The Lancaster Story*, op. cit.; and Norman Jackson obituary, *Daily Telegraph*, 26 March 1994, https://stmargarets.london/archives/2010/03/norman_jackson_vc_a_local_hero.html

There are some discrepancies in the various accounts, so every effort has been made to achieve the best balance.

13 Letter printed in the *Daily Mirror*, 19 July 2017.

14 Jackson was promoted after returning from captivity.

15 Richard Overy, *Bomber Command, 1939–1945*, op. cit.

16 Pip Beck, *Keeping Watch*, op. cit.

17 Ken Trent, *Bomb Doors Open*, op. cit.

18 Sid Pope, Imperial War Museum

Sound Archive 9667. See also Leo McKinstry, *Lancaster*, op. cit.

19 Jean Barclay, *The Brave Die Never* (1993), a posthumously printed record of her impressions kept while serving as an Intelligence Officer at Waddington and Bardney, 1942–1945. Supplied by the IX(B) Squadron Association. Edited for brevity.

20 This account is constructed from a number of different sources: Alexander Nicoll, 'WAAF on a Mission', *Britain at War*, April 2008; Bill Cummings, 'The Only WAAF to go on a Wartime Bombing Raid', *Flightlines* (Canadian Warplane Heritage Museum magazine), March/April 2018; and Doris Roberts in the *Rhondda Leader*, 31 August 1995.

21 The Women's Land Army employed women volunteers as agricultural workers to replace men who had gone into the services during both world wars.

22 Don MacIntosh, *Bomber Pilot*, op. cit., and interview with John Nichol.

23 James Flowers, *A Tail End Charlie's Story*, op. cit., and interview with John Nichol.

24 Auxiliary Territorial Service, the women's branch of the British Army in the Second World War.

25 Kenneth Ballantyne, *First Wave*, op. cit., and interview with John Nichol.


**Chapter 10**

1 Peter Devitt, 'Pilots of the Caribbean' exhibition, RAF Museum, and correspondence with John Nichol.

2 Cy Grant, *A Member of the RAF of Indeterminate Race: World War Two Experiences of a Former RAF Navigator and POW* (Woodfield, 2006) and *Blackness and the Dreaming Soul* (Shoving Leopard, 2007). Cy's books are used to tell his story by kind permission of the Grant family. Some sections of his memoirs have been edited for brevity.

3 Ibid.

4 Peter Devitt, 'Pilots of the Caribbean' exhibition, RAF Museum, and correspondence with John Nichol.

5 David Horsley, 'Billy Strachan: RAF Officer, Communist, Civil Rights Campaigner, Legal Administrator, and, Above All, Caribbean Man', *Caribbean Labour Solidarity*, London, 2019. There are some discrepancies in the various accounts of Billy Strachan's story.

6 blackpresence.co.uk/black-british-soldiers-the-forgotten-fighters/

7 At that time, such expressions were not necessarily or consciously meant to be derogatory or racist. A Bomber Command distress call of 'Darky' would be broadcast if a pilot discovered he was lost.

8 Peter Frost, 'As Britain Marks 100 Years of the RAF ...', *The Morning Star*, 30 March 2018.

9 Peter Devitt is the source for this background material and quotes unless stated.

10 blackpresence.co.uk/black-british-soldiers-the-forgotten-fighters/ (edited)

11 David Horsley, 'Billy Strachan: RAF Officer ...', op. cit.

12 Peter Devitt, 'Pilots of the Caribbean' exhibition, RAF Museum, and correspondence with John Nichol.

13 Ibid.


**Chapter 11**

1 Ils Mar Garthaus, *The Way We Lived in Germany During World*

*War II: A Personal Account* (Arale Books, 1977). Edited for brevity.

2 Navigator Harold Nash, quoted in Richard Overy, *Bomber Command, 1939–1945*, op. cit.

3 Patrick Bishop, *Bomber Boys: Fighting Back 1940–1945* (Harper Press, 2007); and Martin Kitchen, *A World in Flames: A Short History of the Second World War in Europe and Asia, 1939–1945* (Longmans, 1990).

4 Figures for the damage differ in varying sources.

5 Abridged from 'Review of the Work of Int 1', quoted in Max Hastings, *Bomber Command*, op. cit.

6 Martin Middlebrook, *The Nuremberg Raid: 30/31 March 1944* (Penguin, 1986).

7 Reg Davey, interview with John Nichol.

8 Harris to Portal, January 1943, quoted in Mark Wells, *Courage and Air Warfare* (Frank Cass, 1995).

9 Miles Tripp, *The Eighth Passenger* (Wordsworth Military Library, December 2002).

10 Campbell Muirhead, *Diary of a Bomb Aimer: Flying with 12 Squadron in World War II* (Ditto Publishing, 2002).

11 Tony Iverson, interview with John Nichol.

12 Ken Johnson, interview with John Nichol, and Ken Johnson's personal memoir, *et seq*.

13 Dennis Wiltshire, *Per Ardua, Pro Patria: Autobiographical observations of a World War Two Airman* (Woodfield, 2000), and interview with John Nichol.

14 Dennis does not give his crew's surnames.

15 Maurice Garlick, *The Mystery of Uncle Joe*, op. cit. Edited for clarity.

16 Royal Canadian Air Force.

17 Jack Currie, *Battle Under the Moon: The RAF Raid on Mailly-le-Camp* (Crecy Publishing, 1995).

18 Night-fighter units.

19 Jack Currie, *Battle Under the Moon*, op. cit.

20 See 'Heavy RAF losses in attack on Wehrmacht barracks', *World War II Today*, October 2018.

21 Jack Currie, *Battle Under the Moon*, op. cit.

22 Maurice Garlick, *The Mystery of Uncle Joe*, op. cit. There are several discrepancies between Garlick's own account and that of Jack Currie (*Battle Under the Moon*, op. cit.), published eighteen years earlier – both in the account of the raid and particularly in that of Garlick's evasion.

23 Martin Bowman, *German Night Fighters vs Bomber Command* (Pen & Sword, 2016).

## Chapter 12

1 Maurice's account is put together using his own memoir, *The Mystery of Uncle Joe*, op cit., and also Jack Currie, *Battle Under the Moon*, op. cit. There are some inconsistencies in the separate accounts; both have been edited for brevity.

2 Maurice's diary is unclear about how long he was on the ground.

3 Cy Grant, *A Member of the RAF of Indeterminate Race*, op. cit. Edited for brevity.

4 'Stalag' is a version of 'Stammlager', itself short for 'Kriegsgefangenen-Mannschaftsstammlager', or prisoner-of-war camp. 'Luft' was the designation for air force camps. Stalag Luft III was the scene of the Wooden Horse escape in October 1943 and the Great Escape in March 1944.

5 National newspaper controlled by the National Socialist Party.

6  Cy does not offer any explanation for how this might have occurred.

7  Nickname for prisoners of war, from the German for POWs: 'Kriegsgefangener'.

8  James A. Penny, *The Lucky Penny*, op. cit., and interview with John Nichol.

9  RAF Bomber Command Operations Manual.

10 Tom Tate, interview with John Nichol, 2003. Account first told in Nichol and Rennell, *Tail-End Charlies*, op. cit.

11 Abbreviated version of Tom's account initially told in Nichol and Rennell, *Tail-End Charlies*, op. cit.

12 In Jack Currie, *Battle Under the Moon*, op. cit., his name is given as Joseph Lebrun.


**Chapter 13**

1  Nichol and Rennell, *Tail-End Charlies*, op. cit.

2  Richard Overy, *Bomber Command, 1939–1945*, op. cit.

3  Percy Reboul and John Heathfield, *Barnet at War* (Alan Sutton, 1995), quoted in Stephen Darlow, *Sledgehammers for Tintacks* (Grub Street, 2002), child survivor (unattributed) testimony.

4  Basil Collier, *The Battle of the V-Weapons* (Elmfield Press, 1976).

5  Quoted in Philip Ziegler, *London at War, 1939–1945* (Sinclair-Stevenson, 1995).

6  Jack E. Thompson, *Bomber Crew* (Trafford, 2006). Edited for clarity.

7  Henry Samuel and Alastair Good, *Daily Telegraph*, 6 June 2014.

8  Ibid.

9  Antony Beevor, *D-Day: The Battle for Normandy* (Penguin, 2009).

10 Henry Samuel and Alastair Good, *Daily Telegraph*, 6 June 2014.

11 Maurice Garlick, *The Mystery of Uncle Joe*, op. cit.

12 Ken Trent, *Bomb Doors Open*, op. cit.

13 Ron Needle, *Saved by the Bell*, op. cit., and interview with John Nichol.

14 Middlebrook and Everitt, *The Bomber Command War Diaries*, op. cit.

15 William Lovejoy, *Better Born Lucky Than Rich* (Merlin, 1986). First told in Nichol and Rennell, *Tail-End Charlies*, op. cit.

16 Ibid.

17 Richard Bailey, *In the Middle of Nowhere*, op. cit.

18 Ibid.

19 Ken Trent, *Bomb Doors Open*, op. cit. Ken's words have been edited for brevity.

20 Kenneth Ballantyne, *Through the Gate*, op. cit., and Ted Watson, interview with John Nichol.

21 http://ww2today.com/25-november-1944-168-dead-as-woolworths-obliterated-in-v2-rocket-attack (edited version)

22 George Bernard Shaw's *Everybody's Political What's What* was published in 1944, when Shaw was eighty-eight, and sold 85,000 copies, but it's a late and not well-considered part of his political writing, going over much of the same ground as in earlier works reflecting his Fabian-socialist and socio-scientific views; and in part eccentric and controversial.

In it, Shaw blames the Allies' 'abuse' of their 1918 victory for Hitler's rise to power, and further expresses the hope that, after defeat, Hitler should escape retribution, 'to enjoy a comfortable retirement in Ireland or some other neutral country'.

After Hitler's suicide, Shaw expressed approval of Irish *Taoiseach* Éamon de Valera's note of condolence sent to the

German Embassy in Dublin, as well as disapproving of the Nuremberg Trials as 'an act of self-righteousness'.

But in 1944 Shaw was still considered a highly intellectual and admired critical force. Like most others who bought the book, Ken's reading of it probably wouldn't signify his approval of it in its entirety.

23 Darke family papers.

## Chapter 14

1 Ron Needle, *Saved by the Bell*, op. cit., and interview with John Nichol.

2 Liqueur made from mirabelles, small green plums grown in Lorraine, not unlike a greengage.

3 Letters from Cathérine Amiot (André Fromont's daughter) to John Nichol, and André Fromont's own memoir, translated and edited for brevity.

4 Stunell's account is constructed from Ron's account of Harry's story, Mel Rolfe, *To Hell and Back*, op. cit., Cathérine Amiot's recollections told to her by her father, and André Fromont's own written account.

5 There are a number of inconsistencies between Cathérine's account and André's, and also with Harry Stunell's – resolved here as far as reasonably possible.

6 Cargo ships built in great numbers by the USA during the war – 2,710 were completed, of which four survive today.

7 This and the letter that follows are from the Darke family's private papers. Edited for clarity and brevity.

8 There is some inconsistency in dates; the family must actually have received the news a day later.

9 Freddie Hulance, interview with John Nichol, 2003. Story taken from Nichol and Rennell, *Tail-End Charlies*, op. cit.

10 Peter Twinn, in Nichol and Rennell, *Tail-End Charlies*, op. cit.

11 Nichol and Rennell, *Tail-End Charlies*, op. cit.

12 Ibid.

13 Ibid.

14 Ibid.

15 Quoted in Henry Probert, *Bomber Harris*, op. cit.

16 Nichol and Rennell, *Tail-End Charlies*, op. cit.

17 Ken Trent, *Bomb Doors Open*, op. cit.

18 Götz Bergander, *Dresden im Luftkrieg* (Böhlau Verlag, 1977).

19 James Flowers, *A Tail End Charlie's Story*, op. cit., and interview with John Nichol.

20 Peter Jacobs, *The Lancaster Story*, op. cit.

21 Kenneth Ballantyne, *Through the Gate*, op. cit., and interview with John Nichol.

22 'Merlin 224 engines. – The throttle quadrant is fitted with a gate at + 9 lb./sq.in. boost; the fully forward position gives + 14 lb./sq. in. at ground level only, for take-off at moderate loads. The boost control cut-out gives + 18 lb./sq. for maximum take-off and combat.' 'Lancaster I, III, & X, Pilot's and Flight Engineer's Notes', Air Ministry, May 1944.

23 There is no explanation in Ted's memoirs as to why he had seemingly flown extra ops.

24 Ken Trent, *Bomb Doors Open*, op. cit.

25 F. H. Hinsley, *British Intelligence in the Second World War, Vol. III, Part 2* (HMSO, 1984).

26 Flying Officer John Noel, *Papers*, RAF Museum, Hendon, Archive X002-5699.

27 Don MacIntosh, *Bomber Pilot*, op. cit., and interview with John Nichol.

28 Freddie Cole, interview with John Nichol. Account first told in Nichol and Rennell, *Tail-End Charlies*, op. cit.

29 Ken Johnson, interview with John Nichol.

**Chapter 15**

1 Cy Grant, *A Member of the RAF of Indeterminate Race*, op. cit. Edited for brevity.

2 James A. Penny, *The Lucky Penny*, op. cit., and interview with John Nichol. Bodmer's *The Loom of Language*, a history and study of etymology by a Swiss philologist, was first published in 1944 and edited by the English academic and statistician Lancelot Hogben. *Mathematics for the Million*, a popular science book by Hogben himself, was published in 1936.

3 Batch Batchelder, interview with John Nichol. Account originally told in John Nichol and Tony Rennell, *The Last Escape: The Untold Story of Allied Prisoners of War in Europe, 1944–45* (Penguin, 2002). Paraphrased here.

4 A collection of individual memories from the event, ibid.

5 Ibid.

6 Figures differ between individual personal accounts.

7 Adam Sutch, 'Manna from Heaven', RAF Museum blog, 17 April 2016, https://www.rafmuseum.org.uk/blog/operation-manna-29th-april-to-8th-may-1945/

8 Maaike Steenhoek, 'Manna from Heaven', www.elinorflorence.com/blog/operation-manna

9 Clive Rowley, 'The Flying Grocers', *Royal Air Force Memorial Flight Club Annual Yearbook 2015*, pp. 41–4.

10 Alexander Nicolls, 'Operation Manna – Rescue from the Air', *Britain at War*, May 2009, pp. 17–22.

11 Testimony of former bomb aimer Frank Tolley, quoted in Adam Sutch, 'Manna from Heaven', op. cit.

12 Quoted in Clive Rowley, 'The Flying Grocers', op. cit. Edited for brevity.

13 RAF pilot Vic Tenger, quoted in Clive Rowley, 'The Flying Grocers', op. cit.

14 Thomas Murray, *Suitcases, Vultures and Spies*, op. cit., *et seq.*

15 Quoted in Clive Rowley, 'The Flying Grocers', op. cit.

16 RAF pilot Robert Wannop, quoted in Clive Rowley, 'The Flying Grocers', op. cit.

17 The total figure includes all the Allied POWs – air force, navy and army. Those from other countries experienced differing routes home.

18 James Flowers, *A Tail End Charlie's Story*, op. cit., and interview with John Nichol.

19 Gordon Stooke, *Flak and Barbed Wire*, op. cit.

20 Nichol and Rennell, *The Last Escape*, op. cit.

21 Ibid.

22 Ken Trent, *Bomb Doors Open*, op. cit.

23 Bob Pierson, *Everyone's War*, Autumn/Winter 2010, p. 31.

24 Richard Bailey, *In the Middle of Nowhere*, op. cit.

25 Kenneth Ballantyne, *Through the Gate*, op. cit. The BBC Home Service (1939–1967) was the forerunner of BBC Radio 4.

26 Elaine Towlson (née Shaw), interview with John Nichol.

27 Don MacIntosh, *Bomber Pilot*, op. cit., and interview with John Nichol.

28 Ibid.

## Chapter 16

1 Clive Rowley, 'Building Lancasters', op. cit.
2 Ron Needle, *Saved by the Bell*, op. cit., and interview with John Nichol.
3 British Limbless Ex-Servicemen's Association – now called 'Blesma, The Limbless Veterans'.
4 The Bouchot family still lives in Méligny-le-Grand.
5 Cathérine Amiot, letter to John Nichol.
6 This is all Cy says about this issue.
7 Cy Grant, *A Member of the RAF of Indeterminate Race*, op. cit.
8 Sami Moxon, interview and correspondence with John Nichol.
9 British Nationality Act 1948, legislation.gov.uk
10 Peter Devitt, RAF Museum website.
11 'United States Strategic Bombing Strategy, Summary Report', 30 September 1945.
12 James Penny, interview with John Nichol.
13 Reg Davey, interview with John Nichol.
14 Kenneth Ballantyne, *Through the Gate*, op. cit., and interview with John Nichol.
15 This is the correct designation of the squadron number; '9' has been used in the rest of the text as that is how Don wrote it in his memoirs.
16 Reg Payne, interview with John Nichol.
17 James Flowers, interview with John Nichol.
18 Elaine Towlson (née Shaw), interview with John Nichol.
19 Elaine's journey features in *Lancaster: Britain's Flying Past*, BBC TV, original transmission July 2014, and Warren Manger, 'Lancaster in the Lake', *Daily Mirror*, 16 July 2014.
20 Some sources give slightly different figures. Additionally, 8,403 were wounded, 9,838 taken as prisoners of war.
21 Richard Overy, *Bomber Command, 1939–1945*, op. cit.


## Afterword

1 Rob Thomas (ex-RAF), interview with John Nichol. The other riders were Steve Gambon (ex-RCT), Alan and Katrina Woodland (ex-RMP) – all members of the Birmingham branch of Royal British Legion Riders. The Land Rover was driven by Derek Jones (ex-RN).
2 Sue Efthimiou, interview with John Nichol.
3 Ron Needle, interview with John Nichol, September 2018.

# BIBLIOGRAPHY

Bailey, Richard, *In the Middle of Nowhere*, Tucann Books, 1999

Ballantyne, Kenneth, *Through the Gate*, Laundry Cottage Books, 2018

Ballantyne, Kenneth, *First Wave*, Laundry Cottage Books, 2013

Barclay Jean, *The Brave Die Never*, Dramrite Printers, 1993

Bartlett, Les & Jacobs, Peter, *Bomb Aimer Over Berlin*, Pen & Sword, 2007

Beck, Pip, *Keeping Watch*, Goodall, 1989

Bergander, Götz, *Dresden im Luftkrieg*, Böhlau Verlag, 1977

Bishop, Patrick, *Bomber Boys: Fighting Back 1940–1945*, Harper Press, 2007

Bowman, Martin, *Last of the Lancasters*, Pen & Sword, 2014

Bowman, Martin, *Voices in Flight*, Pen & Sword, 2015

Bowman, Martin, *Bomber Command, Reflections of War*, Pen & Sword, 2013

Carruthers, Percy, *Of Ploughs, Planes and Palliasses*, Woodfield, 1992

Clark, R. Wallace, *British Aircraft Armament Vol. 2: Guns and Gunsights*, Patrick Stephens, 1994

Collier, Basil, *The Battle of the V-Weapons*, Elmfield Press, 1976

Connelly, Mark, *Reaching for the Stars*, I. B. Tauris, 2000

Cooper, Alan, *Bombers Over Berlin*, William Kimber, 1989

Currie, Jack, *Battle Under the Moon*, Crecy Publishing, 1995

Currie, Jack, *The Augsburg Raid*, Goodall, 1987

Darlow, Steve, *Lancaster Down: The Extraordinary Tale of Seven Young Bomber Aircrew at War*, Grub Street, 2000

Darlow, Steve, *Last of the Kriegies*, Fighting High Ltd, 2017

Darlow, Steve, *Sledgehammers for Tintacks*, Grub Street, 2002

Delve, Ken & Jacobs, Peter, *The Six Year Offensive: Bomber Command in WWII*, Arms & Armour, 1992

Eriksson, Patrick, *Alarmstart*, Amberley, 2017

Falconer, Jonathan, *RAF Bomber Command: Operations Manual*, Haynes, 2018

Falconer, Jonathan, *Bomber Command Handbook*, Sutton, 1998

Farmer, Sarah, *Martyred Village*, University of California Press, 1999

Flowers, James, *A Tail End Charlie's Story*, Private memoir

Garlick, Maurice & Strong, Ian, *The Mystery of Uncle Joe*, Private memoir

Garthaus, Ils Mar, *The Way We Lived in Germany During World War II*, Arale Books, 1977

Goebbels, Joseph, *Tagebücher*, Piper Verlag, 2008

Grant, Cy, *A Member of the RAF of Indeterminate Race*, Woodfield, 2006

Grant, Cy, *Blackness and the Dreaming Soul*, Shoving Leopard, 2006

Hastings, Max, *Bomber Command*, Pan, 1999

Holland, James, *Dam Busters: The Race to Smash the Dams 1943*, Corgi, 2013

Jacobs, Peter, *The Lancaster Story*, Cassell, 2002

Kitchen, Martin, *A World in Flames*, Longmans, 1990

Lambert, Max, *Night After Night: New Zealanders in Bomber Command*, HarperCollins, 2005

MacIntosh, Don, *Bomber Pilot*, Browsebooks, 2006

McKinstry, Leo, *Lancaster: The Second World War's Greatest Bomber*, John Murray, 2009

Middlebrook, Martin, *The Peenemünde Raid*, Cassell, 1982

Middlebrook, Martin, *The Nuremberg Raid: 30/31 March 1944*, Penguin, 1986

Middlebrook, Martin & Everitt, Chris, *The Bomber Command War Diaries: An Operational Reference Book 1939–1945*, Viking, 1985

Murray, Thomas & Hillier, Mark, *Suitcases, Vultures and Spies*, Yellowman, 2013

Needle, Ron, *Saved by the Bell*, Tail End Publications, 2006

Nichol, John, *After the Flood: What the Dambusters Did Next*, William Collins, 2015

Nichol, John, *The Red Line: The Gripping Story of the RAF's Bloodiest Raid on Hitler's Germany*, Collins, 2013

Nichol, John & Rennell, Tony, *The Last Escape: The Untold Story of Allied Prisoners of War in Germany 1944–45*, Viking, 2002

Nichol, John & Rennell, Tony, *Tail-End Charlies: The Last Battles of the Bomber War 1944–45*, Viking, 2004

Nichol, John & Rennell, Tony, *Home Run*, Penguin, 2008

Overy, Richard, *Bomber Command 1939–45*, HarperCollins, 1997

Penny, James, *The Lucky Penny*, FastPrint, 2013

Potter, Steve, *Seven Short Lives: Pro Libertate*, Tucann Books, 2013

Probert, Henry, *Bomber Harris: His Life and Times*, Greenhill, 2006

Reboul, Percy & Heathfield, John, *Barnet at War*, Alan Sutton, 1995

Rolfe, Mel, *To Hell and Back: True Life Experiences of Bomber Command at War*, Grub Street, 2003

Smith, Peter, *Avro Lancaster: Britain's Greatest Wartime Bomber*, Ian Allan, 2008

Smith, Richard, *Jamaican Volunteers in the First World War*, Manchester UP, 2004

Stooke, Gordon, *Flak and Barbed Wire*, Australian Military History Publications, 1997

Taylor, James & Davidson, Martin, *Bomber Crew: Survivors of Bomber Command Tell Their Own Story*, Hodder, 2005

Thompson, Jack, *Bomber Crew*, Trafford Publishing, 2006

Thorburn, Gordon, *Bombers First and Last*, Robson, 2006

Thorburn, Gordon, *Luck of a Lancaster: 107 operations, 244 crew, 103 Killed in Action*, Pen & Sword, 2013

Trent, Ken & Stone, Chris, *Bomb Doors Open*, Seeker, 2016

Wiltshire, Dennis, *Per Ardua, Pro Patria*, Woodfield, 2000

# PICTURE CREDITS

p. 174 Reg Payne

p. 202 IX (B) Sqn Association Archive

pp. 209, 343 James Flowers

p. 216 © Pete Jacobs

p. 228 ©London Metropolitan Archive

p. 234 Strachan Family

p. 248 Ken Johnson

p. 253 Dennis Wiltshire

p. 273 Beryl Garlick

p. 282 Tom Tate

p. 297 Steve Thompson

pp. 307, 351 © Chris Stone

p. 330 Darke Family

p. 339 Freddie Hulance

## Plate section

1, 12, 17 © Claire Hartley

2, 13, 16 ©John Nichol

3 © Rob Long

4, 10, 19, 20 © Lincolnshire Aviation Heritage Centre/Silksheen
    Photography

5 © Kenneth Ballantyne

6, 15 © Andy Saunders Collection

7, 8, 14 © Pete Jacobs

9 Allyson MacIntosh

11 © Chris Stone

18 Towlson Family

Tornado image © Ian Black

# INDEX

(Page numbers in *italic* refer to photograph captions)

A. V. Roe & Company, *see* Avro
Addison, Joe, 237
Aeroplane and Armament
    Experimental Establishment, 53
Agreement of Mutual Assistance, 31
Air Defence Cadet Corps (ADCC),
    39
Air Force (Constitution) Act (1917),
    227
Air Ministry, 60, 162, 213, 215, 223,
    230, 235, 333
Air Staff Intelligence, 242
Air Training Corps (ATC), 45
Air Transport Auxiliary (ATA),
    158, 202
Aircrew Europe Star, 401
Allied Expeditionary Force, 243
Angelus bells, 324, 326–7, 388, 391,
    410
anti-Semitism, 243, 339
Atencio, Xavier, 163
ATS, 216, 217
Augsburg raid, 62, 65–79, 80, 82,
    89
Auxiliary Fire Service (AFS), 36
Avro, 48, 52, 52, 58, 87, 383, 406,
    407
    Chadderton factory, 57, 158, 160
    financial difficulties post-WWI,
        48
    first factory of, 158
    founding of, 47
    Harris's post-war letter to, 383

HQ, 57
'sweethearts', 160
'two Roys' of, *see* Chadwick,
    Roy; Dobson, Roy
Woodford factory, 93, 158, 347,
    406
Yeadon factory, 58, 161, 162, 163

Baker, Baron, 393, 394
Ball, Fred, 217–18, 220–2
Ball, Lucille, 344
Ball, Peter, 201
Barbarossa, Operation, 60
Barclay, Jean, 199–202, 202
Bardney, RAF, 186, 380, 382
Barnetby le Wold, RAF, 99
Barr & Stroud GJ3, 341–2
Barry, Joseph, 160
Bartlett, Les, 177, 216
Bate, G. J. L., 168–9
Battle of El Alamein, Second, 100
Battle of Berlin, 37–8, 172–83,
    242–3, 281, 299, 363, 399
Battle of Britain, xi, xii, 4, 35, 44,
    101, 189, 227, 243, 395, 406–7
Battle of France, 227
Battle of Kohima, 410
Battle of Peenemünde, 119, 122–3,
    128, 132, 133–4, 136–7, 140,
    144, 146, 147–9, 211, 223, 225,
    380, 403–4
Battle of the Atlantic, 62–3
Battle of the Bulge, 314

BBC, 71, 277, 370, 379, 392, 404
Beck, Pip, 51, *51*, 54, 55, 79
Beckett, Joe, 68–9
Beetham, Michael, 218–20, 222
Berchtesgaden raid, 353–8, 359
Bergander, Götz, 340
Berghof (Mountain Court), 353–8
Berlin, 1940 RAF bombing of, 37–8
Binbrook, RAF, 107
Blair, Tommy, 137
Blériot, Louis, 30
Blitz, 35, 36–7, 60, 91, 242
Bodmer, Frederick, 363
Boltrop, Mrs (headteacher), 149
Bomber Command, 1, 2, 4–6, 45,
    62–4, 82, 121, 124, 129, 132,
    183, 260
  'Berlin' ops, *see* Battle of Berlin;
    Berlin raids
  campaign medal withheld from,
    401
  casualty rates, 92, 148, 155, 328,
    331, 394–5, 406
  Churchill distances from, 337–8,
    394, 401
  Clasp, 402
  class and schooling irrelevant in,
    16
  crew casualties/fatalities of, 5–6,
    8
  D-Day ops, *see main entry*
  first black pilot in, *see* Strachan,
    William
  formation of, 47
  global expansion of, 226–33
  golden rule, 15
  Green Park Memorial, 401–2
  Harris appointed Commander-in-
    Chief of, 59, 60
  HQ, 89, 242
  Jackson's remarkable feat in,
    194–6
  Lancasters first delivered to, 58
  land requisitioned for, 187–9
  last sortie of, 410
  love interests experienced across,
    205–11
  mandatory photographs, 19–20
  Master Bombers, 133–4, 137–8,
    143, 261
  Overlord impacts operations of,
    243, 294
  pilot wages, 160
  post-war contact with members
    of, 390
  PR, 81
  propaganda trailblazing for, 48
  rituals and mascots, 168, 217
  stations, *see RAF stations by
    name*
  strategic bombing, 104–6
  USAAF works with, 294
Bormann, Martin, 353, 358
Bottesford, RAF, 135
Bouchot, André, 324, 325, 389
Bouchot, Cathérine, 389–90
Bouchot, Mariette, 389
bouncing bomb, 161
Bourn, RAF, 165, 172
Boy Scouts, 43, 44
Brackenwood Farm, 198–9
British Expeditionary Force (BEF),
    35
British Nationality Act (1948), 394
British Ropes, 88
Broadbent, Col, 112–14, 116, 117
Brown, Harry Albert ('Sam'), 52–3,
    *52*
Browning machine gun, 14, 16, 54,
    66, 72, 87, 88, 112, 139, 175,
    342
Brunt, Sidney Percy, 130, 131
Bruntingthorpe, RAF, 97

Calais-to-Dover flight, first-ever, 30
Campbell, Bob, 175, 179
Canada, 84, 120, 152, 157, 161, 202,
    253, 304, 406
Canadian Warplane Heritage
    Museum, 406
Caribbean, xi, 84, 226–33, 235, 394,
    406
Cash, Johnny, 411
*Ceylon*, HMS, 125

Chadwick, Roy, 48, 52, 55–6, 58, 347, 406

Chamberlain, Neville, 32, 34, 354

Channel Islands, Germany annexes, 37

Chastise, Operation, 100–1

Cherwell, Lord, 104, 123

Cheshire, Leonard, 260, 262, 263

Chetwynd Barracks, 35

Chichester, Bishop of, 105

Chick, Maurice, 137

child evacuees, 39

*Chocks Away!* 197

Choloy, RAF, 386

Choltitz, Dietrich von, 305

'chop' girls, 136, 208

Church of St Clement Danes, RAF, 401

Churchill, Winston, 4, 37, 62, 80–1, 104, 123, 164, 195, 243, 335, 337–8, 377, 394, 400–1

Civil Service, 229, 292, 393

Clarke, William Robinson ('Robbie'), 226

Clewiston, 153, 154

Clough, J. A., 130–1

Clydebank Police, 39–41

Cobham, Alan, 30, 36

Cold War, 4

Cole, Freddie, 356, 357–8

Cole, Nat King, 410

Colette (Méligny resident), 388

Colnbrook, RAF, 212, 224

Commonwealth Air Training Scheme, 253–4

concentration camps, 282, 337, 352, 392–3

Coningsby, RAF, 406

Conklin, Norm, 116

Copeland, Miles, 398

Coventry, Germany bombs, 35, 60

Cowan, Arnold, 298–9

Coward, Noël, 135

Cranwell, RAF, 47, 233

Craven, Clarrie, 116–17

Crosby, Bing, 261

Crum, Bert, 67, 68, 69–70

D-Day, 149, 290–1, 292–322

*D-Donald*, 107, 114, 115, 116, 117, 118

Dakota, 306, 376

Dalby, Clarence ('Clarrie'), 309–11

Dambusters, 100–1, 161

Danny and Mac (Garlick's crewmates), 305, 306

Darke, Ken, 10, 13, 15–16, 21–2, 84, 98, 312, 314, 320, 322, 328, 330–2, 330, 391

Darke, Peter, 84, 330, 332

Darke, Sylvia, 322, 330, 332

Darley Moor, RAF, 130

Davey, Reg, 171, 243–4, 396–7

De Havilland, 30, 122

Deane, Laurence, 260–1, 262

Dédion, Jacques, 287–8

'dehousing', 104

Delacroix, Josef ('Uncle Joe'), 288, 289

Deverill, Ernest, 76, 77

Diderol, Dr (Resistance operative), 288–90

Distinguished Flying Cross (DFC), 63, 98, 169, 251, 311, 312, 351, 352, 359

Dobson, Roy, 48, 52, 58, 163, 383, 406

Dodson, Jack, 406

Donkin, Grp Capt., 321

Dornberger, Walter, 140, 142, 147

Dornier bomber, 36, 37

Dowty, Bert, 67, 69–70

Dragoon, Operation, 304

Duggan, Plt Off., 344–5, 346, 347

Dunholme Lodge, RAF, 119, 129, 212

Dunkirk, BEF evacuated from, 35

Dunlop, Bob, 10, 18, 328, 391

Dunlop, Tim, 407–8

Dyson, Freeman, 182

*E-Easy*, 299

East Kirkby, RAF, 319–20, 321, 344, 347

Eden, Anthony, 338

Edward VIII, 354

Efthimiou, Sue (née Needle), 410, 411

8th Army Air Force (US), 101, 165

Eisenhower, Dwight D., 243, 294

El Alamein, Second Battle of, 100

Elementary Flying Training School, 234

Elizabeth II, 402

Elizabeth, Queen, 58, 223

Ellis, Mary, 159

Elsham Wolds, RAF, 89

Elson, Jack, 10, 23, 25, 323, 328, 385, 391

Empire Windrush, 393–4

Entertainments National Service Association, 135

Erhardt, Peter, 147, 148–9

Évreux base, 67

Exodus, Operation, 373, 374, 376

F-Freddy, 356

Fathers, Dickie, 179

Feltwell, RAF, 171

FIDO, 176, 316

First World War, 4, 12, 27, 28–9, 30, 32, 38, 48, 60, 83, 132, 156, 189, 226, 246, 292, 406, 408
    South West Africa Campaign, 59

Flak and Barbed Wire (Stooke), 448

Flowers, Eunice (née Oakley), 209–11, 340–1, 343, 343, 399–400

Flowers, James, 87, 88, 209–11, 209, 340–3, 343, 344, 374, 399–400, 401, 402

Fog Investigation and Dispersal Operation (FIDO), 176, 316

Foot, Michael, 105

Ford Motor Company, 161, 162, 277

44 Squadron, 61–4, 67–75, 81, 82, 124, 129, 145, 146, 148
    first Lancasters delivered to, 54
    much-decorated, 58

402 Squadron, 202

426 Squadron, 402

430 Squadron, A-Flight, 122

460 Squadron, 107, 110

Foy, Carson John ('Jack'), 247–51

France and Germany Star, 401

The Free Press, 224

Freeman, Sir Wilfrid, 161

French Resistance, 260, 268, 288–91, 304–5

Freya radar, 67, 128

Fromont, André, 324–5, 332, 388

Fuller, J. F. C. ('Boney'), 105

G-George, 302, 303

Garland, Judy, 344

Garlick, Maurice, 28–9, 30, 36–7 45, 189, 259–60, 263–5, 267–73, 273, 287–90, 292, 303, 304–7

Garthaus, Ils Mar, 241–2

Garwell, John ('Ginger'), 71, 72–4, 77

GEE, 50, 62, 70, 90, 92, 236

Geoff (rear gunner), 95

George (bomb aimer), 95

George V, 226

George VI, 34, 58, 61, 223, 330, 351, 359

Germany:
    blitzkriegs, 35–7, 60, 91, 242
    'Flensburg' device, 173
    Gestapo, 447
    reconstruction of, 337–8
    submarine warfare, see U-boat

Giroux, M., 327

Goebbels, Joseph, 110, 183, 283, 353

Gomorrah, Operation, 101, 104

Goodrich, Ena, 216, 399

Göring, Hermann, 5, 82, 91, 353, 358

Grant, Cy, 227–9, 228, 234, 235–40, 274–80, 281, 360–2, 367–9, 378–9, 392

The Great Escape, 392

Great War, see First World War

Gresse tragedy, 364, 366–7, 376

Ground Electronic Equipment (GEE), see GEE

ground-mapping, 101, 128, 141

ground war, 185–225

Grundy, Lilian, 57

Guderian, Heinz, 34
Gulf War (1991), 2

H-Harry, 70
Hallows, Brian, 75, 77, 79, 80
Halton, RAF, 46–7
Handley Page, 47
Harding, Reg, 120, 405
Harris, Sir Arthur, 5, 62–3, 65,
    80–1, 148, 158, 164, 172, 183,
    242, 244, 311–13, 333, 383
  aloofness but caring nature of,
    132–4
  becomes Bomber Command
    C-in-C, 59, 60
  birth of, 59
  'Bomber' sobriquet of, 381–2
  Churchill distances from, 337–8,
    394
  frontline strength plan of, 93
  as Marshal of RAF, 401
  'Most Secret Operation Order
    Number 143' produced
    under, 61
  Nuremberg attack ordered by, 243
  strategic bombing advocated by,
    104–6
  work ethic of, 89–91
Hart, Liddell, 105
Havelock, Betty, 82
Hawker Siddeley, 48
Hawkins, Nigel, 96
Heintz, André, 300
Hendon, RAF, 3–4, 6–7, 306
Higgins, Frank, 194
Himmler, Heinrich, 353
Hitler, Adolf, 38, 60, 81, 84, 243,
    282, 305, 338, 353, 354, 358
Hitler Youth, 284
Hoffmeister, Käthe, 103
Holocaust, 339, 392–3
Home Guard, 34
Hooker, Stanley, 161
Hornsey, Denis, 132
H2S, 101, 102, 128, 141
Hulance, Freddie, 333–4, 336–7,
    339, 339

Hunger Winter, 370
Hurricane, Operation, 313
Hydra, Operation, 124, 128, 148

Ian (airman), 'last letter' from, 131
Ivy (Ken Johnson's cousin), 246
IX(B) Squadron, 398

J-Jig, 298
Jackson, Alma, 192–3
Jackson, Ian, 193
Jackson, Norman, 192, 192, 193–6
Jackson, Philip, 401
Jake (Canadian officer), 201–2
Jamaica Fruit Shipping Company,
    229
Jean (Ron Needle's friend), 332
Joan (Fred's girlfriend), 217, 222
Jock (mid-upper gunner), 95,
    166
Johnson and Barnes Ltd, 34, 224
Johnson, Ken, 87–9, 246–53, 248,
    358–9
Johnson, Norman, 193, 196
Jong, Arie de, 372–3

Kelly, Gene, 344
Kiley, Bill, 168, 186–7
King, Sam, 229, 394
Knapman, Les, 10, 328, 391

La Belle Maison, 288
Lancaster bomber, 12, 17, 71, 333,
    369, 373
  as aviation icon, 407
  Battle of Britain Memorial Flight
    of, 406, 407
  birth of, 45, 46–58, 52–3, 59
  B1, 54
  Canadian, 161–2
  Castle Bromwich factory, 163
  'Cook's Tours', 382
  DV-202, 129, 140, 404–6
  early-production (B1), 54
  'eighth passenger' of, 12
  Eslan toilet aboard, 13, 111, 166,
    204, 309

Lancaster bomber – *continued*
  extra-curricular activity in,
    160–1
  female pilots, 158
  first delivered, 30, 54–5, 58, 61–2,
    65
  first independent outing of, 62, 64
  first significant venture of, 58
  forerunner to, *see* Manchester
    bomber
  44 Squadron, *see main entry*
  'gardening' exercises, 61
  George (autopilot), 114
  George VI inspects, 61
  ground crew, 135, 189, 259
  increased production of, 93–4,
    93, 158
  Jackson puts out fire on, 194–6
  Kölpiensee finding of, 404–6
  last-surviving, 4, 5, 406, 406–8,
    407
  maiden flight of, 54
  mandatory photos taken aboard,
    19–20
  Marks, 129, 161, 348
  names of, *see by name*
  P4 compass, 78
  prototypes, 53–4
  on 'Secret List', 62
  specifications of, 14, 19, 53–4,
    56–7, 62, 65, 110, 111–12,
    348, 406
  'Tail-end Charlies', 10, 87, 168,
    260
  test flights, 52–3, 52, 348
  total number produced, 406
  'two Roys' of, *see* Chadwick,
    Roy; Dobson, Roy
  U-boat raid by, 62
  'Vic' formation, 64, 72, 74, 75
Land and Requisition Directorate,
  187
Langille, Alton, 237–8
'last letters', 130–2, 136, 193, 196
Learoyd, Roderick, 63–4
Leclerc, Cecile, 300
Leuchars, RAF, 122

*The Life and Death of Colonel
  Blimp*, 197
Lloyd, Harold ('Taffy'), 263
London Fire Service (LFS), 36
Lossiemouth, RAF, 398
Low, Bill, 292–5
Luckenwalde, 362, 367, 379
Ludford Magna, RAF, 316
Luftwaffe, 11, 31, 35–6, 60, 67, 82,
  109, 243, 263, 281, 301

McDermott, Len, 120
McDermott, Mac, 405
MacIntosh, Allyson, xiii, 398
MacIntosh, Don, 39–45, 94–6, 96,
  151–3, 156, 157, 186, 205–9,
  354–6, 358, 380–2, 397–8
Mackintosh, Sq. Cdr, 50
MAN factory raid, *see* Augsburg
  raid
Manna, Operation, 369, 369, 371–3,
  374, 377
Marco, Wilf de, 356, 357–8
Margin, Operation, 63, 79 (*see also*
  Augsburg raid)
Marin-Catherine, Colette, 300–1
Marius and Blanche (Resistance
  operatives), 288–90, 291, 304
Mary (Land Girl), 205–7
Matlock, RAF, 258–9
Maxwell, Peter ('Maxie'), 259–60,
  263–5, 268
Méligny-le-Grand, 1, 2, 325, 332,
  386–8, 390, 391, 391, 410
mental health, 244, 258–9, 396–7
Metheringham, RAF, 9, 17, 23, 187,
  190–2, 196, 197, 292, 312, 315,
  320
Mifflin, Fred, 193, 196
Miller, Glenn, 261, 262
Ministry of Aircraft Production, 52
Ministry of Information, 80
missing in action, 79, 130, 150, 159,
  176, 184, 185–6, 211, 213–15,
  224, 331, 411
Mitchell, Kay, 58
Molly (widow), 207–9

Monica, 173, 193
Monk, Gerry, 345–6
Moore, Don, 219–22, 399
Mosquito, 18, 122–3, 128, 148, 260, 313, 355
Moxon, Sami (née Grant), 392
Müller, Friedrich-Karl, 144–5
Murray, Charles, 46–7
Murray, Thomas, 46–51, 57, 105, 168, 372, 377, 377
    first Lancaster test flight of, 54
    secret missions undertaken by, 105
Mussolini, Benito, 82, 126
Mycock, Tommy, 76

NAAFI, 191, 192
National Aviation Day, 30
Needle, Edward, 27, 83, 329
Needle, Ellen, 28, 329
Needle, Maria, 386
Needle, Ron, 1–3, 3, 8, 37, 312–15, 315–17, 320, 322, 332, 383, 384, 390, 391
    airship experience of, 27–8
    birth of, 27
    in civvy street, 16, 32
    crash landing and rescue of, 23–6, 323–5, 327–8, 331, 388–91, 412
    death of, 410–12
    French vacations of, 385–91, 391
    joins RAF, 10–11, 28, 83–4
    Lancaster sobriquet assigned to, 10
    leg amputation of, 326, 329–30, 384
    marriage of, 384–5, 384
    as rear gunner, 1, 3, 6–7, 10, 13–18, 21–6, 45, 96–8, 383, 410
Needle, Sylvia (née Valente), 84, 97, 98, 314–15, 322, 324, 329, 330, 332, 384–5, 384, 390
Nettleton, Betty (née Havelock), 82
Nettleton, John, 58, 61–3, 67–73, 77–8, 78, 80–2
Newman-Newgas, Rags, 130

Nichol, John, 8
'nickelling' sorties, 48
97 Squadron, 62, 63–4, 67–77, 79–81, 165
Nuttall, Jim, 107–8, 108, 109

O-Orange, 249
Oakley, Eunice, see Flowers, Eunice
OBOE, 92, 101
O'Connor, Liam, 401
103 Squadron, 89
106 Squadron, 187, 189, 193, 411
Oslo Report, 123–4
Overlord, Operation, 243, 294, 296, 304
Owen, Geoff, 206, 208

P-Peter, 76
Pape, Sophie, 159–60
Paterson, Ross, 398
Pathé Gazette, 58
Pathfinder Force (PFF), 18–19, 79, 92, 115, 128, 133–4, 137, 141–3, 172, 174–6, 256, 302
Payne, Ena (née Goodrich), 399
Payne, Reg, 166–7, 174, 174, 177, 178, 183–4, 216–22, 399
Pearl Harbor, 60, 84
Penman, David ('Jock'), 75–7, 77
Penny, James ('Jim'), 155, 156–8, 159, 164–77, 178–84, 281–2, 363–6, 376, 395–6
Penny, Laurie, 171
Perranporth, RAF, 50
Peter (bomb aimer), 95
Phoney War, 34
Plärrer festival, 65, 73
Portal, Sir Charles, 60, 81, 244–5
Postman Joe (Resistance member), 304
powered flight, first-ever, 30
Poynter, Edward, 264
Pratt and Whitney engine, 153–4
Prendergast, Les, 405
Price, Iris, 203–5
Purves, Bob, 203–4, 205
Pynisky, Peter, 405

*Q-Queenie*, 219–21, 264
Quance, Billy, 405

racism, 156–7, 231, 233, 234–5
RAF College, Cranwell, 47
RAF Museum, Hendon, 3–4, 6–7
Ratcliffe, Tom, 197
Red Army, 100, 351, 378
Red Cross, 214, 215, 280, 338, 364, 366
Rhodes, Cecil, 55
Rhodes, Dusty, 70–1
Riccomini, Ricky, 310–11
Roberts, Doris, 203–5
Robinson, William Leefe, 29
Rodley, Ernest ('Rod'), 64, 72, 74–5, 77
Roe, Alliott Verdon, 47
Rollins, Tony, 318–19
Rolls-Royce, 48, 50–1, 53, 161–2
Roosevelt, Franklin D. ('FDR'), 149, 243
Ross, Paddy, 366
Royal Air Force (RAF), 148, 409
    Air Tasking Orders, 122
    Airborne Early Warning system, 406
    Association, 410
    Battle of Britain Memorial Flight, 406, 407
    Bomber Command, *see main entry*
    casualty rates, 6, 79, 213–14, 215, 223, 331
    Committee of Adjustment, 184, 185–7, 201, 212, 224
    creation of, 46
    Dramatic Society, 315
    entertainment, 135, 197–8, 261, 262, 315
    female pilots, 158–60
    first WWII engagement of, 33
    Flying Control, 54, 108
    Group HQ, 109
    Harris becomes Marshal of, 401
    High Command, 252, 299, 333
    Induction Centre, 83, 88

LMF, 244–6, 252, 258–9, 261
    Operational Training Units, 88, 90, 91, 92, 93, 193, 228
    Operations Record Book, 191, 315
    people of colour serve in, 227–33, 234–40
    pilot training, 152–8, 165, 233
    radio transmissions, 262
    reception centres, 83, 88, 151, 152, 228
    secretarial branch, 46
    squadrons increase of, 34
    Transport Command, 235
    Watch Office, 54
Royal Air Force Volunteer Reserve, 35
Royal British Legion, 409, 410
Royal Canadian Air Force (RCAF), 261
Royal Corps of Transport (RCT), 409
Royal Flying Corps (RFC), 46, 59, 226
Royal Marines (RM), 46
Royal Military Police (RMP), 409
Royal Naval Air Service (RNAS), 46
Royal Navy (RN), 46, 60, 409
Royal Warwickshire Regiment, 27

*S-Sugar*, 4, 5
St John's Wood, RAF, 83, 151–2, 228
Sandford, Nick, 70
Savory, Gerald, 315
Scampton, RAF, 203
*Schräge Musik*, 146, 173, 342
Schrijver, Elka, 338
Scoley, George, 188
Scoley, Peter, 188, 190–1
Scott, Jimmy, 10, 16, 17–18, 19, 20–3, 98, 328, 391
Searby, John, 133–4, 137–44, 147
Second World War:
    Allied Atlantic convoys, 62
    blitzkriegs, *see under* Germany

Bomber Command, *see main entry*
bombing statistics for, 5
Britain enters, 32–3, 37
Christmas 1941, 30, 54, 55
Christmas 1943, 216–7, 223
Christmas 1944, 315, 319–20
Eastern Front, 60, 90, 243, 260
first significant military action of, 31–2
forced labour camps, 128, 141
Lancaster's profound effect on, 54
largest conventional weapon dropped during, 5
Pearl Harbor attack, 60, 84
phantom planes, *see* V1 flying bomb
'Secret List', 62
submarine warfare, *see* U-boat warfare
Tiger Force, 407
VE Day, 377–80
War Cabinet, 60, 89
warplanes, *see by name*
segregation, 156–7
Sergeant, John, 404
Sharman, Arthur, 356–7
Shaw, Alex, 90–1
Shaw, Elaine, *see* Towlson, Elaine
Shaw, Elsie (née Stendall), 33, 34, 35, 85, 86–7, 120, 127, 129, 132, 150, 211–15, 223–5, 403
Shaw, G. B., 330
Shaw, Pamela, 86, 129, 150, 212
Shaw, Stanley, 33, 34, 35, 36, 45, 85, 88, 119, 122, 127–8, 127, 136, 140, 145–6, 148, 224
death of, 223–5, 402, 403–6
joins RAF, 85
letters home from, 86, 87, 120–1, 124–6, 129–30, 132–3
missing in action, 150, 211–15, 222–3
Shaw, Victor, 34, 124–6, 222–3
Sherwood, John, 63, 74–6, 80
Sidney, Ruth, 398
Simpson, Wallis, 354

Sinclair, Sir Archibald, 164
Sindel, Elfriede, 103
61 Squadron, 246
617 Squadron, 100, 246, 260, 339, 348, 350, 354
Skarratt, Michael C., 187
Skellingthorpe, RAF, 177, 216, 342
Smith, Joyce, 232
Smuts, Jan, 60
Sparks, Neville, 261, 262
Special Operations Executive (SOE), 105, 168, 372
Speer, Albert, 353
Speers, Jack, 357
Spitfire fighter, 36, 53, 55, 219, 234
Stalag Luft III, 360, 392
Stalag Luft VI, 282
Stalin, Joseph, 243
Stammlager IVB, 448
Stendall, Elsie, *see* Shaw, Elsie
Stooke, Gordon, 107–8, 108, 109, 110–19, 113, 374–6
Strachan, Joyce (née Smith), 232, 393
Strachan, William ('Billy'), 229–33, 234, 234, 393
'Strategic Bombing Survey' report, 394–5
Stunell, Harry, 10, 11, 15–16, 20–1, 23–4, 98, 312, 314, 320, 322, 326–8, 331, 332, 390, 391
Swinyard, Frank, 177–8

T-Tommy, 67, 68
Tate, Tom, 282, 283–6
Tehran Conference, 243
Telecommunications Research Establishment (TRE), 92, 101
Territorial Army (TA), 36
Third Reich, 5, 18, 82, 183, 282, 287, 335, 355, 367, 375
Thompson, Jack ('Tommy'), 296, 297, 299, 301–4
Thorn, Bill, 52
Thunderclap, Operation, 333
Tiger Division, 364

Tiger Moth biplane, 232, 234
Toft, Maurice, 193, 194
*Tonight*, 392
Tornado, 2, 4
Torpex, 348
Towlson, Elaine (née Shaw), 34, 35, 85, 86–7, 119–21, 126–7, 127, 129, 132, 149–50, 211–15, 223–4, 225, 380, 403–6
Towlson, Russell, 404–5
Treblinka, 337
trench warfare, 12
Trent, Ken, 37–8, 39, 45, 98–9, 197–9, 307, 308–11, 312, 315–17, 320–1, 339, 348–53, 351, 354–6, 359, 376, 381
12 Squadron, 296, 302
Twinn, Peter, 334–5

U-boat, 62, 73, 79, 81, 101, 158, 162, 228, 348–9, 386
United Nations (UN), 353
United States Army Air Forces (USAAF), 163, 271, 287, 294
Up-Park Camp, 229
Upcott, Bob, 371–2

*V-Victor*, 68
Valente, Sylvia, *see* Needle, Sylvia
*Vicious Virgin*, 203–4
Vickers-Armstrong Ltd, 407
Victoria Cross (VC), 29, 58, 63, 78, 80, 192, 196
*Völkischer Beobachter*, 282
Vollans, Jim, 203, 205

*W-William*, 138
WAAF, 15, 16, 51, 79, 82, 90, 94, 118, 134, 136, 152, 164, 177,

183–4, 191, 197, 199, 203–8, 217, 315, 347, 380, 382
Waddington, RAF, 50, 51, 54, 61, 61, 64, 65, 66, 78, 82, 199
Wadsworth, Noel, 309–11
Wallis, Barnes, 100, 348
Wallis, Geoff, 278
Walt Disney Company, 163
*The War in the Air* (Wells), 60
Waterbeach, RAF, 369, 369
Watkins, Harry, 247, 249–51
Watson, Ted, 30–1, 32, 33, 43–5, 44, 318, 319–22, 344–7, 379, 397
Waugh, Evelyn, 295
Weather Office, 190
Wellington, 47, 91, 159, 231, 232
Wells, H. G., 60
Weston, Tom, 405
Whittle, Frank, 161
Wickenby, RAF, 296, 298, 302, 304
Wilhelm II, 28
Wilhelmshaven, RAF reconnaissance over, 33
Wilson, Jock, 197
Wiltshire, Dennis, 253–9, 253
WINDOW, 101–2, 104, 128, 145, 179, 379
Winter, Bill, 15
Women's Auxiliary Air Force (WAAF), *see* WAAF
Women's Land Army, 205, 209, 210, 211, 299
Woodbridge, RAF, 319
Woodhall Spa, RAF, 62, 64, 65, 66, 75, 77
*Wright Flyer*, 30
Wright, Orville and Wilbur, 30

Zeppelin raids, 28–9, 189, 265

*Read on for an extract from*
*John Nichol's previous book*

# SPITFIRE

# SPITFIRE

What is it about the Spitfire? Why do people stop and gaze in awe at her sleek lines? Why do eyes turn skywards when the distinctive growl of her engine is heard? Why, over eighty years after she first flew, is the Spitfire regarded as the very symbol of Britishness; tenacity, courage, dedication, faithfulness? Why is this *particular* aircraft loved so much?

To be honest, I hadn't thought about these questions until I had a chance meeting with an elderly Second World War Spitfire pilot. My background in the Royal Air Force had been on more modern aircraft – the Tornado Ground Attack and Air Defence jets. My post-RAF writing career had concentrated on the aircraft of Bomber Command during the Second World War; the iconic Lancasters and Halifaxes, and the staggering bravery of the men who flew them. The Spitfire had never been on my radar. This all changed during a visit to the Imperial War Museum at RAF Duxford, where my eyes were opened to the legendary status of an aircraft which had first flown in March 1936.

\* \* \*

Children and adults alike were experiencing the awe of the mighty warplanes close up. The mammoth B52 bomber, the menacing outline of the Stealth bomber, the hedgehog of machine guns covering the B17 Flying Fortress, the power of an F15 fighter and that great British warplane, the Vulcan bomber. The visitors to RAF Duxford were gripped by the aviation giants, eager to absorb as much detail in the limited time they had available.

As I stood on the airfield, away from the public areas on grass that had once seen scores of Spitfires take to the skies during the Second World War, I watched in amazement as an astonishing phenomenon unfolded. For a moment, the cough and splutter of an engine had gone unnoticed. Like the preliminary chords of an orchestra, people carried on their conversations. Then the stammer turned into a roar as soothing as anything philharmonic. Chatter stopped, cameras pointed away from the domineering warplanes – even the iconic Concorde – and towards the sound humming from the runway. People began to pour out of the exhibition halls and move, some even running, struggling to release cameras from their bags, towards the barriers at the edge of the airfield. They had recognised the distinctive notes of a Merlin engine; a few heads nodded in recognition, enthusiasts squinted trying to identify the variant and parents pointed and whispered to children: *Spitfire*.

The hum turned to the glorious crescendo of the Merlin engine at full power as the fighter streaked down the grass runway mere yards away from the admiring crowd. In seconds, its curved, leaf-like wings were outlined above as the wheels tucked neatly into its lean belly. As the fighter disappeared into the Cambridgeshire sky, the visitors turned back to the other displays with broad grins, happy that they had seen a legend, no, *the* legend, take to the air. Some had frowned at a slight deviation in the Spitfire's usual elegance. A second canopy sat behind the first, for this was one of the few two-seat versions which carried passengers. What they couldn't know, the reason I was there, the reason this book came about, was that a ninety-year-old veteran, who had not flown a Spitfire for nearly seventy years, sat in the rear cockpit, grinning like a schoolboy.

\* \* \*

After a frantic last few months fighting the Germans in Italy, Brian Bird had eventually landed after his final operational flight and jumped down from his trusty Spitfire on 28 June 1945. It was a sad moment, turning his back on the finest aircraft he had ever flown; the years passed and memories of his beloved fighter seemed to fade.

Then one day in August 2014, the phone was brought to him at his British Legion veterans' home in East Sussex. Brian was recovering from a hip operation and was on enforced bed rest.

The caller was a television producer I was working with on an aviation documentary. When she told me she'd found a Spitfire veteran we might be able to take airborne again I was delighted. Initially, Brian was doubtful about the reality of taking his beloved aircraft into the skies again. He was ninety, relied on a wheelchair and walking frame, was on a cocktail of drugs and fitted with a catheter – how could he possibly fly again? But his wartime spirit shone through and a few days later the GP had passed him fit to fly once again. The no-nonsense matron from his care home, understandably concerned about the risks involved and the number of disclaimers that had to be signed, took it on herself to supervise the whole trip. So it was she who had the honour of wheeling Brian across the hallowed Duxford airfield to stare again at the fighter he had loved so much.

Scrambling out of his wheelchair, he grabbed his walking frame and slowly, painfully, made his way around his beloved Spitfire. The joy, and perhaps a little sadness, on Brian's face was clear to see, and those of us gathered around were more than aware of the significance of this reunion. We stood back and allowed them both some time together.

While ageing marked Brian's face, the Spitfire's perfect lines remained smooth, polished and unchanged since their last meeting in 1945. He recorded his memories of the day in a letter he later sent to me; they are a testament to both him and the Spitfire. 'The sight of a Spitfire gracefully sitting there – no one will ever experience the degree of thrill I felt at that moment; it boosted my resolve to overcome my disabilities and get airborne.'

He marvelled at the sleek, elemental beauty of the machine, which perhaps more than any other had secured enduring freedom. He was twenty again, smitten by her curves and allure; one of just a handful of Second World War Spitfires still flying today.

Brian was among some of the few surviving Spitfire pilots to have fought in the war, flying during the conflict's closing weeks, hitting the Germans on the ground as they retreated from Italy. He had flown a Mark IX; in his opinion, the greatest of all Spitfire models. The Mark IX had evolved from the original Spitfire Mark I that, at the outbreak of war, had seen off raiders over the North Sea, helped protect troops over Dunkirk then established itself as a national icon by fighting alongside the sturdy Hurricane to keep the Luftwaffe at bay during the Battle of Britain. But the aircraft was constantly improved, getting stronger, faster and more deadly as the war progressed. It evolved, grew and adapted during the war; the final version of the near-23,000 Spitfires, and its naval counterpart the Seafire, built would be the Mark 47.

By the time Brian was flying a Spitfire, it had long evolved from its legendary status as a fighter in the skies during the Battle of Britain, and he was tasked to use it to strike targets on the ground, increasing the danger to pilots, bringing them well within reach of the Germans' anti-aircraft guns and small-arms fire. This fact had been made brutally clear to him in the briefing before his first operational flight in April 1945. Hence his nerves as he waited for the pre-dawn take-off, the Spitfire's engine ticking over.

'I can still remember the collywobbles I had at the end of the runway at 5 a.m., and I tell my family this – sometimes, if you get nervous, just switch off; ignore the fears and you will become lethal. And that is exactly what happened when I got to the end of the runway, I turned the fear off and I became lethal.'

On the Duxford airfield Brian was surrounded by former and current RAF fliers, including myself, who had experienced similar dangers in later conflicts. Air Marshal Cliff Spink had volunteered to take Brian flying again. Cliff had been my Station Commander at RAF Coningsby and had commanded part of the Tornado Air Defence force during the first Gulf War in 1991 when I'd been shot down over Iraq. He had also amassed huge experience on countless aircraft – Spitfires, Hurricanes, Mustangs, Hunters, Lightnings, Phantoms and Tornados, to name but a few. A legendary aviator himself, he was keen to ask a Second World War pilot what it had really been like to fly the Spitfire in action.

'Did you take any hits?' he asked.

'Oh yes, one or two during strafing runs,' Bird replied, shrugging his shoulders as if seeing bullet holes appearing in your aircraft was as common as ice on the car windscreen. 'But generally only in the wings,' he added, almost apologetically. Having taken a 'few hits' myself when I was shot down, I couldn't help laughing at his nonchalance. And, in a further nod towards just how much times had changed, he added, 'When you came down with holes in your wings, you just went off to breakfast and by the time you came back the mechanics had mended them and you were airborne again.' Sticky tape and filler; with such meagre items battles had been fought for our nation's survival.

It was time for the next part of Brian's adventure as Cliff asked him, 'How would you like to fly a Spitfire again?' His smile of unbridled delight said it all. 'I'd love to! Absolutely love to. Yes, yes, I'm game, I have not lived this long not to have another go!' Despite his ailments Brian was already trying to clamber back on the wing as Matron carefully moved to restrain his enthusiasm.

Getting Brian, who could not stand unaided, into the cockpit was something of a battle itself, but six of us managed to lift, carry and push him up some hastily found steps, and lower him over the side of the fuselage and down into the cockpit where he was securely strapped in. Although Matron wisely wondered how he might get out in an emergency, Brian wasn't about to wait for the answer.

As the remarkable song of the Merlin engine, with its hum and throb that spoke of power, endurance and consistency, filled the cockpit, Brian instinctively checked left and right, above and behind. He was back in April 1945, on that early morning in northern Italy, a line of Spitfires assembled in front of him, propellers blurring amid the collective sound of their Merlins' dominant roar.

'I had two 250lb bombs under me and guns full of ammunition. At the age of nineteen I was flushed with nerves as I sat at the end of the runway awaiting instruction to take off.'

It was Brian's first operation against an enemy who had developed a canny skill in using anti-aircraft fire to bring down ground-attacking Spitfires. He looked down the dusty runway and up to the brightening sky. He was struck by the sudden anxiety of going into the unknown, where the law was kill or be killed. His grip tightened on the stick. *Bloody collywobbles*. He opened the throttle and he felt his nerves dwindle as the aircraft gracefully lifted into the air. His instructor's words came back to him: 'become absolutely lethal'.

'Immediately I was airborne those nerves had evaporated, never to return. Thus it was no surprise to me at Duxford that, once the Spit was in the air, I felt no nervous emotion at all.'

He felt a bump as Cliff let the Spitfire rise from the grass runway and into the friendly skies above Cambridgeshire. Seventy years on, the fighter was still as doughty and reliable as it had been during the war. For twenty glorious minutes the present became the past as Brian swooped and roared around the airfield. The aching bones, the painful hips, the failing body were all forgotten. He had waited for this moment since 1945. Sergeant Brian Bird, Spitfire pilot, was back.

For those of us on the ground it was a magical experience; we had managed to give something back, a tiny reminder of a glorious past, to a man who had given so much to his country. As time went on, we began to search the skies in readiness for Brian and Cliff to appear. Matron, who had gone to enjoy a well-earned cup of tea, returned and asked, 'Where's Brian now?' As the words left her lips, we all ducked as the Spitfire roared over our heads at around fifty feet, waggling its wings in salute. I pointed to the sky at the retreating shape of a Spitfire: 'He's up there!'

As the Spitfire taxied back towards us, Brian pushed back the hood and undid his harness, just as he had done during his wartime sorties. His enthusiasm was contagious. 'It's a dream come true! It brought back so many memories. It was great, terrific. Really terrific! Everything came back to me!'

'Do you think you could take her up on your own?' I asked. There was no hesitation as Brian replied: 'Yes, yes.'

His hands hovered over the throttle as he glanced towards

Matron, who gently shook her head. There were a few more chuckles.

The Spitfire had acted like an elixir on Brian, as if the short flight had restored something from his youth, not quite a spring in his step, but certainly a revitalisation of the spirits. The freedom and delight of flying a Spitfire had never left him, and to step back into the aircraft in his nineties was a tonic he thought he'd never take again. I could see a mental and physical change in his demeanour; it had been a privilege to see how one of the last of those who had flown the Spitfire in its fierce wartime role could now revel in the pleasure it gave in peace.

Sadly, it was to be Brian's final flight, as he died just a few months afterwards. In his last letter to me he wrote: 'After a gap of seventy years since my last operational sortie in a Spitfire, the opportunity to sit in a Spit cockpit and to get airborne was an unimaginable thrill and made me wish for a return to my youth!'

In a way, though, he truly had recaptured a sense of his youth on that last flight.

So here was the very essence, the magic of this aircraft; the Spitfire was more than an aeroplane; it was an aircraft like no other, it was an icon loved, worshipped by all those – apart from her enemies – whose lives she touched.

I was determined to find out more about her and subsequently discovered many hundreds of books that already recount the technical development and wartime record of the Spitfire. This is not one of those books. I wanted more; I wanted to hear that 'human' story of the Spitfire, the story of the men – and women – who flew, serviced and built her. People like Brian Bird – why was he so desperate to have one last glimpse, one final flight in his beloved Spitfire, before he died? I wanted to understand the personal story of the Spitfire and why those connected with her seemed to fall in love with this iconic lady of the skies . . .

# TORNADO

## In the Eye of the Storm

We were doing around 620 miles-per-hour, 200 feet
above the desert, in total darkness. Everything was
running on rails as we approached the target.
Perfectly calm; no anti-aircraft fire.
Then all hell broke loose.

I remember the missile being fired at us.
My exact words were *'MISSILE LAUNCH!'*
I broke left and shouted, *'Chaff!'*

All I could see was a flame, like a very large firework,
coming towards me, then there was a huge white flash.
I remember an enormous wind and then I was unconscious.
My last thoughts were that I was going to die.